CRITIQUE
AND
ANTI-CRITIQUE

Essays on
Dependence and Reformism

The direction of our scientific exertions, particularly in economics, is conditioned by the society in which we live, and most directly by the political climate (which, in turn, is related to all other changes in society). . . . The cue to the continual reorientation of our work has normally come from the sphere of politics. Responding to that cue, students turn to research on issues that have attained political importance. . . . So it has always been. The major recastings of economic thought. . . were all responses to changing political conditions and opportunities.

Gunnar Myrdal
Asian Drama

The philosophers have only interpreted the world in various ways; the point, however, is to change it.

Karl Marx
Theses on Feuerbach

Man makes his own history, but not as he pleases.

Karl Marx

CRITIQUE
AND
ANTI-CRITIQUE

Essays on
Dependence and Reformism

Andre Gunder Frank

PRAEGER SPECIAL STUDIES • PRAEGER SCIENTIFIC

New York • Philadelphia • Eastbourne, UK
Toronto • Hong Kong • Tokyo • Sydney

Library of Congress Cataloging in Publication Data

Frank, Andre Gunder, 1929–
    Critique and anti-critique.

    Bibliography: p.
    Includes index.
    1. Developing countries—Economic conditions—
Addresses, essays, lectures.   2. Dependency—Addresses,
essays, lectures.   3. Economic development—Addresses,
essays, lectures.   4. Social sciences—Addresses,
essays, lectures.   I. Title.
HC59.7.F6865   1983   330.9172'4   83-13683
ISBN 0-03-063737-6
ISBN 0-03-063738-4 (pbk.)

Published in 1984 by Praeger Publishers
CBS Educational and Professional Publishing,
a Division of CBS Inc.
521 Fifth Avenue, New York, NY 10175 USA

456789 052 9876545321

Printed in the United States of America
on acid-free paper

Contents

ANTI-CRITIQUE

APPENDIX

Preface

These essays represent both a continuation and a modification of those collected in my *Latin America: Underdevelopment or Revolution*, written between 1962 and 1968 "to contribute to the Revolution . . . out of the author's attempt, like millions of others, to assimilate the Latin American Revolution and the inspiration it finds in the Cuban Revolution" (as the first paragraph of its preface explained). At that time, before the death of Che Guevara, the Revolution still appeared to be advancing in Latin America; and, accompanying it, this writer was still on the offensive.

The present collection of essays was written (or sometimes spoken and then transcribed) since 1968, first while the author was living and working in Chile before the military coup on September 11, 1973, and in Europe after that. Therefore, these essays reflect the compexity of the advance and retreat of popular and/or military reformism in Latin America—particularly in the Peru of Velasco Alvarado, the Bolivia of Torres, military and Peronist Argentina, and especially the Chile of Frei's Christian Democracy and Allende's Popular Unity governments —combined with the upsurge of antireformist and counterrevolutionary reaction. Thus, the essays were written (or spoken) increasingly from the defensive, in an attempt to defend a hopefully still revolutionary position against reformism and the necessarily reactionary and successful reaction it generates. Indeed, this symbiotic relation between reformism and reaction is a theme and thesis of several of the essays. Thus, like the previous collection of earlier essays, this one was —to quote from our epigraph taken from Gunnar Myrdal—"conditioned . . . most directly by the political climate (which, in turn, is related to all other changes in society) . . . responding to changing political conditions and opportunities." While maintaining our stance—as per the first epigraph taken from Marx—that the point in interpreting the world is to change it, we also responded to political conditions and opportunities that changed from the offensive to the defensive.

As the title of the book suggests, the criterion of selection is that these essays are critical, indeed often polemical, perhaps all the more so in being on the defensive. As the table of contents suggests, the essays range in subject matter from the "science" of social science, via political science, anthropology and sociology, history and economics, to politics, pure and simple. Having earlier "had to learn that social science must be political science" (as I emphasized in the preface to my first book, *Capitalism and Underdevelopment in Latin America*, p. xviii), I now argue that social and political science is politics, and sometimes very dirty politics, however subtly ideological or scientific sounding. Moreover, in battle with reaction and reformism, the best defense of a revolutionary position may be offensive (in more than one and significantly related sense of the word) and in ideological battle, polemical.

In Chapters 7 to 10 and 12 these political issues are partially hidden below the surface of the social scientific arguments about social structure and change in India (Chapters 7 and 8), the structure and development of the international economic system and the role of the Third World within it (Chapters 9 and 10), and the history of capitalist development in Mexico (Chapter 12). Nonetheless, no matter how much some of them may wish to deny it, much of the argument in these chapters between my scientific opponents and myself is essentially about political issues.

Like my aforementioned earlier books, these essays were written from a perspective of the dependence of Chile, Latin America, and the underdeveloped "Third World" generally within the world capitalist system. But as I stressed in these books and in my *Lumpenbourgeoisie: Lumpendevelopment*, "external" dependence is indissolubly linked with the "internal" class structure in these peripheral—but also in the central—countries. These real world circumstances also condition the social scientific study of the "dependent" world and, indeed, of the world as a whole. They give rise to our disputes with the reactionaries—for example, Rostow and Friedman (in Chapters 13 and 14)—who deny the existence of dependence and class structure outright, and the reformists—for example, Sathyamurthy, Moore, Dalton, Myrdal, and others (in Chapters 3, 4, 6, 11, and others)—who argue, if they recognize it at all, that the structure of dependence and class can be suitably modified through gradual and partial reforms. Our argument there is that in the Third World, and therefore in the world as a whole, only revolutionary class—including ideological—struggle can eliminate the causes and consequences of underdevelopment.

This argument became increasingly defensive (of long-term revolutionary positions) as the counteroffensive of reformism and reaction mounted. Chapter 24 lists over 100 critiques, most of them counteroffensive, of the present author's writings (and person) alone. As explained in that chapter, which also represents my most organized response and "anti-critique," this critique is a political reflection of the defeat of progressive reformism and revolution and the rise of reactionary reformism and outright reaction. The debate becomes most acrimonious with the spokesman of the Communist parties, whose critiques are extensively quoted in Chapter 24, for whom "it is not Gunder Frank, but what he represents that is at the center of the debate. He represents, basically, the existence of a widely promoted ultra-left thinking in international politics. . . . It is not a matter, therefore, of a little 'detail,' it is a matter of no less than the kind of revolution, the problem of alliances. . . ." "The kind of revolution" the Communists in Latin America, or "Latinocommunists," were proposing was—in the words of one of the just quoted Communists—"the key alliance of the proletariat and the peasantry in a front with the petit bourgeoisie, the middle classes and the progressive sectors of the national bourgeoisie" (Chapter 24, p. 257). The problem with this kind of alliance—under the military stewardship of Velasco and Torres or the civilian one of Peron and Allende—is that they all failed disastrously and led the proletariat and peasantry down to resounding and cruel defeat at the hands of reaction. Chapters 15 to 17, written in and about Chile before September 11, 1973 (and other similar critiques of the Popular Unity Government, all of which were lost in the coup because they had remained unpublished in quest of our own "alliance" with the C.P.) argued before the fact—against the position of the Communist Party— that their reformism had to and would lead to reaction; and Chapter 18 further examines "the lessons of Chile" after the fact.

But what are the lessons? For the Communist Party of Chile (and that of the Soviet Union which broadcast the former's declaration piece by piece every day for a week) it is that the revolutionary "ultra" left was and is a "Trojan Horse" of Imperialism and the CIA—the same Party's theoretical journal called the present author "the cat's paw of the CIA" (Chapter 24, p. 257)—while Communist Party policy was "basically correct" (First Report to his Central Committee by its general secretary, Luis Corvalan) except that the Party itself, and its allies, made too many "left deviationist" errors (and, with respect to the military, a few right ones). Similarly, the "self-criticism" of the Brazilian Communist Party after the 1964 coup was also that they had been too progressive. More significantly, the lesson from Chile explicitly drawn by Enrico Berlinguer, the principal leader of the "Eurocommunist" parties, was that even a majority alliance for progressive reformism is not enough and that a "historic compromise" with the Christian Democratic forces of reaction in support of antipopular "austerity" measures is called for. The Latin American Communist parties had invented and practiced Latino/Eurocommunism at home long before it became popular on the other side of the Atlantic. But they are not to be outdone by their Latino/European imitators in Southern Europe; and, having already *led* their peoples down to defeat in Latin America, the Latinocommunist parties made (if possible)—or pleaded for (if not yet possible)—alliances with the most outright reactionary governments and policies of a Videla in Argentina, Morales Bermudes in Peru, and a "military-Frei solution" (while Frei was still alive) in Chile. In support of their own policy, these Communist Parties and their ideological spokesmen have of course also been redoubling their efforts to eliminate all remaining obstacles by revolutionary (and even centrist/reformist parties and to disqualify their political and ideological spokesmen. As a result, further severe and ever more vitriolic attacks on the present writer are also the order of the day. What remains to be seen, in the meantime, is whether the Eurocommunist followers, and the people who still follow them in turn, will also suffer the same fate as their Latinocommunist predecessors and their cruelly suffering people. The most right-wing of Eurocommunist leaders, Santiago Carrillo in Spain, who has been pursuing a policy most akin to that of the contemporary Latinocommunists, published a book on *"Eurocommunism" and the State*, which attracted worldwide attention, including that of his former fellow party member, Fernando Claudin, who in his own book on Eurocommunism and Socialism offered a supposedly left Eurocommunist alternative. Therefore, we have decided to include here (as Chapter 19) a critique of our friend Claudin's book, written in 1977, which seriously questions the feasibility and advisability of a Eurocommunism of the left—and for the left—especially if we remember the historic lessons left by the erstwhile reformist (and now not even that) parties of Latinocommunism.

Chapters 20 to 23 are very recent critical essays on rather different lines. Chapter 20 on Kampuchea, Vietnam, and China was written in 1980 from a still more defensive perspective, after the invasions and other developments of 1979 and the years immediately preceding in these countries obliged me and many others to undertake an agonizing reappraisal of our revolutionary theses and perspectives.

Chapter 21 was written and revised in the spring and autumn (and the Stockman quote added after it became available in December) of 1981 during President Reagan's first year in office. The rise and decline of Keynesianism and its replacement by monetarism was explained and the failure of the latter and particularly of the voodoo "supply-side" branch of Reaganomics was foretold. The answer to the question "after Reaganomics and Thatcherism, what?" posed in the title was the prediction of greater attention to "social policy" at home and heightened foreign adventurism abroad as tactics to divert attention away from economic failure and the advent of the proposal to remedy the latter through "industrial (planning) policy." At this writing (in August 1983) these predictions have already been or are now being borne out by events. The dismal failure of Thatcherism and Reaganomics to deliver the promised economic fruits have sadly led Thatcher and Reagan to embark on war in the Falklands/Malvinas and on gun boat diplomacy and heightened belligerence in Central America and on anti-minority crusades at home. Industrial policy has already been inscribed on the electoral banner of each of the Democratic party contenders for the nomination, and President Reagan himself has appointed a federal commission to study the matter. 1984 is rapidly approaching in more ways than one.

Chapter 22 on "Global Transformation" is a critique of the two major political economic policy responses in the Third World (and in the socialist countries) to the present world economic crisis. One is helter-skelter integration in the emerging international division of labor as per the "newly industrializing countries" (NICs) model of the East Asian "Gang of Four" (South Korea, Taiwan, Hong Kong, and Singapore), Brazil, Mexico, and so forth, which has led to the dramatic debt crises of the latter and is not replicable on a whole Third World scale. The other option is the attempt to "de-link" (stop the world, I want to get off) and to socialize the economy. The recent experience of Angola, Mozambique, Zimbabwe, Ethiopia, Nicaragua, and other progressive Third World countries as well as the accelerated re-integration in the world market and remarketization and privatization of the domestic economy in the socialist countries and most especially in China suggests that this latter policy alternative also is no very realistic option today. Chapter 23 on "Policy Ad Hockery" suggests that economic policy in the industrial capitalist and socialist countries today is also practically bankrupt: right-wing reliance on the market, left-wing socialist planning, and, in between, Keynesian policy have all failed in the national arenas where they have been promoted and are individually and in combination all the more helpless in the international arena in a world economy that resembles a roller coaster out of control. Much of my other critical writing on the world economic crisis of the 1970s and 1980s does not appear here, because it was already included in my collection of essays *Reflections on the World Economic Crisis* published in 1981 or forms part of my longer expository and analytical books *Crisis in the World Economy* and *Crisis in the Third World* (1980 and 1981).

Finally, a paper commemorating the hundredth anniversary of the death of Marx has been included to complement the "anti-critique" section. It reviews the analyses and predictions/hopes of Marx and

Marxists with regard to development in the industrialized West, socialist East, and Third World South and concludes that historical materialist analysis is on better footing still today than the often voluntarist political policies that are in contradiction with materialist analysis and hard reality. Nonetheless, this last essay, written in 1983, represents a considerable modification in the author's thinking and hopes from those at the beginning of the book, which were written or spoken in 1968 and 1969—at the time of the Paris May 68 and other movements that proclaimed "imagination into power" ("l'imagination au pouvoir"). The author's skepticism, therefore, has grown with the years between the writing—or speaking—of the first chapters at the end of the 1960s and that of the last chapters at the beginning of the 1980s.

The Appendix (Chapter 26) presents the history and outline of a Reader on Underdevelopment in Asia, Africa, and Latin America in which I (with my coeditor and friend Said A. Shah) tried to piece together a "theory" of dependence as the cause of underdevelopment. This work, which was completed in 1969 but never found anyone willing and able to publish it, was my greatest effort to criticize received theory and to offer a theoretically coherent, empirically valid, pedagogically useful, and politically progressive alternative. The circumstance that this, my most constructively critical effort, was stillborn for lack of a publisher to bring it to the light of day occasions the publication now of at least the outlines of that project in this book devoted to critique and anti-critique.

For the acceptance and efficient preparation of the present book (including finally at least the introduction to the ill-fated Reader) for its publication in English many years (to which the three dates at the end of this preface bear testimony) after its initial conception by the author and its subsequent publication in Spanish in 1978, I am most thankful to my Praeger editor Lynda Sharp, my Macmillan editor Steve Kennedy, and my copyeditor and printing supervisor Eric King.

Like my earlier book of essays mentioned at the beginning of this preface, I dedicate this new collection of essays to my wife Marta Fuentes, who has borne with me all these years in various countries and has helped me with much insight gained from being triply dominated, oppressed, and exploited (by me first among others) through being a Latin American woman in a dependent country and then abroad, in a class society and sexist culture, and has done the most—as an "anti-" intellectual nonsocial scientist—to help me see through the emperor's and his court jesters' robes to their naked political color, and who was the first to show me the Latinocommunist parentage of Eurocommunism. My education, let alone reform or revolution, in the dialectical symbiosis between imperialist dependence and social class on the one hand and sexist and racist caste on the other hand—and their expression through my own activity and behavior—is still continuing at her hands and is not yet reflected here; perhaps next time, if she succeeds. . . .

A.G.F.
Frankfurt, December 21, 1977
Norwich, September 21, 1980
Amsterdam, August 16, 1983

Photo by Miguel Frank.

ON
SOCIAL SCIENCE

1

What Is the Scientific Value of the Study of the Development of Underdevelopment? None!

"What, in your judgment, is the scientific value of the study of the development of underdevelopment?" None. While the capitalist system, which generates underdevelopment and avails itself of exploitation and alienation for development, subsists—and even while the class struggle in the establishment of socialism subsists—science can only have an instrumental political and ideological value, and no value in and of itself. On the contrary, capitalism and the bourgeois ideology have long been employing both social and natural science as purely reactionary tools in defense of their interests. This is the case, for example, with the concepts and even the very terms "development and underdevelopment" that are used in the class struggle on the ideological level, to make it appear that entire peoples develop through their own efforts thanks to national capitalism, while other entire countries remain underdeveloped because of supposedly inherent conditions—the lack of capital and inadequate intelligence and institutions or cultures—that is to say, because of traditionalism. This focus or, better yet, this deviation from the problem, hides the real cause of underdevelopment and the necessary remedy in order to maintain underdevelopment and the exploitation that the aforementioned cause determines.

Problemas del Desarrollo, Revista Latinoamericana de Economia, Año 1, Num. 1, Octubre-diciembre 1969, Mexico, translated from the Spanish original.

It is therefore necessary to reformulate the question and to ask two things that are slightly different: (1) What is the value of the scientific study of development and underdevelopment and (2) how can or should one study development and underdevelopment scientifically? The answer to the first question is, then, in my judgment, that scientific study has a political and ideological value: ideological, because it permits us to unmask orthodox but antiscientific study and to prove that imperialism and national capitalism are the fundamental causes of underdevelopment; political, because the scientific study of social and natural reality is a necessary, although not sufficient, tool to change it.

How then must one study development and underdevelopment scientifically in order to fulfill the requirements imposed by those same processes as an ideological and political responsibility for all honest progressive researchers? In the very first place, one has to follow the fundamental rule of all science (something that orthodoxy does not do)—that is, to focus on the study of the whole social system, which is really causal or determining, and to analyze it. For development and underdevelopment, the causal determinant is without a doubt the world capitalist system, since it was capitalist development throughout the last five centuries that promoted economic development in some parts of the world at the cost of simultaneously generating, as an integral part of the same process, the development of underdevelopment in Asia, Africa, Latin America, and some other areas.

One would have to study, in addition, how the colonial, semi-colonial, or neocolonial structure of the capitalist system in its entirety and its development has formed and transformed the economic and class structure in the colonies and in the cities themselves at each stage of the aforementioned development. In the case of countries that are underdeveloped today, through this scientific procedure—global, historical, structural, and therefore dialectic—one would see how colonial relationships formed the class structure and how this determined the interests and the policies of the ruling sector of the colonial bourgeoisie. And it would be proved why, given its dependence and its political and economic interests, these (neo) colonial bourgeoisies of necessity had to, and still have to, impose on their people repressive economic systems that generate and deepen underdevelopment, while their senior partners in the imperialist centers are interested in sponsoring development, albeit in a very unequal way.

Finally, the scientific study of the structure and colonial class dynamic of capitalist development and underdevelopment can and should offer the people knowledge and tools—that is, political weapons —for their fight to liberate themselves from the imperialist and capitalist system and to permit the establishment of socialism, which offers the only road to escape from increasingly profound under-development. It is clear that part of this scientific study of the nature of the battlefield and its methods should not be published if it provides weapons to the enemy. Rather, it will have to be done within the bosom of the liberation movements that will utilize it for the benefit of the people.

2

Science and Underdevelopment in the Third World

I will confine myself to some of the relations between liberal social science and liberal politics with respect to what has been called the third world, i.e., the underdeveloping countries.

To begin with a clarification: The third world does not exist! I say this because I have been asked to talk about it. I think when the term the third world was first used one thought of the first world as the capitalist one, the second as the socialist one and the third world was then an expression used to denote the rest, above all the underdeveloped countries. The very term reflects a political position and a supposedly scientific approach. In the first place, this means that the under-developed countries are not part of either the first or the second world. More specifically, use of this terminology contends that the under-developed world is not part of the capitalist world. This is manifestly contrary to fact, and any theorization that begins by placing the under-developed countries outside of the capitalist system is, I suggest, bound to fail; since asking the wrong question leads to a totally wrong answer.

More recently the term the third world has been accepted by others also. Nowadays it often is taken to mean underdeveloped

Lars Dencik (Ed.), *Scientific Research and Politics* (based on an international symposium held in Lund, Sweden, 1968), Lund, Studentlitteratur 1969.

countries whether capitalist or socialist. This new meaning of the term is scientifically still more inappropriate, because it emphasizes even more the supposed distinction between the underdeveloped countries in the capitalist world and in addition to that confuses the difference between countries like China, Cuba, Vietnam and Korea (I am referring to the Democratic Republic of Vietnam and the Democratic Republic of Korea) on one hand, and the capitalist underdeveloped countries on the other. The difference is scientifically speaking that the former are—to use the new phraseology of the UN—developing countries whereas the other countries are getting more and more underdeveloped each year. This confusion in terminology leads to considerable confusion in analysing the status of the so-called third world.

As has been pointed out by Mr. Poulantzas among others, liberal social science has followed two lines, one of them more abstract and the other more empirical.

The abstract one might be illustrated by neo-classical economic theory, structure functionalism in sociology and anthropology. These abstractions of liberal social science as Lévi-Strauss himself has emphasized, are not derived from any concrete reality but are instead abstract constructions. Similarly the competitive market model, functionalism, etc., all the self-regulating equilibrium models, are based ultimately on the idea of harmony and consensus and on the absence of any real conflicts.

The more empirical branch of social science has all the outward traces of real social units, ranging from the individual, the family, the tribe, the village, the region, the community, the country, the nation-state, to the first, the second, and the third world. But one thing it never deals with is the really determinant social system which, if we look at reality and analyse its structures and historial development, will—I suggest—turn out to be the force behind the transformation of the village, the tribe, etc. If you go to the books by Radcliffe-Brown and Evans-Pritchard or other of the British functionalists, you get the impression that imperialism never existed in Africa and that they here studied some pristine societies untouched by human hands. Manifestly this is not the case. The entire contemporary social structure of all African societies, but not jut African, has been in the most intimate and total way formed and transformed by the development and spread of mercantile, industrial, and financial capitalism over the past four or five centuries. This social system in its evolution is not at all studied by any of the combinations of abstract and empirical liberal social science, whose very formulations do not admit the study of evolution, and of course still less the study of revolution. In fact, people like Durkheim, and of course the fathers of neo-classic economy, Jevons, Menger, and also Wiksell, who fashioned much of our contemporary social science, clearly understood they were only fashioning tools of analysis to replace evolutionism, and of course most particularly Marxist evolutionism. Instead of studying social reality, and particularly the dominant factors—I think that is what we scientists ought to do—liberal social science in studying development takes all sorts of isolated characteristics, which rather reflect the liberal conception of North America and Europe. These liberals then go on to say that these isolated characteristics, the free market, free enterprise and freedom of speech and free elctions, Roosevelt's four supposed freedoms, are the characteristics of "development" of the developed countries, and that underdeveloped countries, which according to these scientists are in an entirely different category, have quite different characteristics, such as traditional, archaic, feudal, retrograde, etc. The program of development will then be to substitute the modernization of developed countries for the traditionalism of "developing" countries. One step towards this goal will be to give the nations in the so-called third world foreign aid. Since their institutions are no good we have to offer them ours; since their culture is really barbaric we have to offer them the American way of life. Thus development is visualized as a kind of diffusion from the world capitalist metropolis to these national metropolises like São Paulo or Bombay or New Delhi, etc. and from these into their hinterlands and this diffusion supposedly calls for its grateful acceptance by these poor slaves. Sometimes these poor people don't really appreciate our "help" because they are either fanatic nationalists or stick to odd ideas of their own, worshipping the cow instead of the dollar, just to take one example. When we meet with this sort of resistance, what we have to do is of course to re-educate them, to make them ready to welcome us with open arms. I think that the consequences of this development program are clearly to be seen by everybody: None of the innovations brought to the "third world", be it sailing vessels, railroads, IBM machines, or Coca Cola, has in any way led to the development of these countries and to the betterment of the majority of its people's lives. Isn't it after all rather remarkable that these states should still be in the second "pre-take-off-stage" (I am using Rostovian terminology) after in some cases more than 400 years of civilizing activity on the part of the West?

After all these centuries, they have not taken off yet. Should it not be evident to everybody that this kind of policy will lead them nowhere? What has happened is that the majority of people today are better off than 100 years ago in Western Europe and in North America, whereas their position is worse in Asia, Africa and Latin America. I am considering both their standards of living in a purely economic sense and their cultural standard.

I shall bring some evidence to support my statements. According to the UN-FAO reports, food production per capita has gone down from 1934-38 till now in Latin America 8 percent, in Asia and Africa about 3 percent. This should perhaps be compared with the results in those parts of the world which are known for their failures in agriculture, the Soviet Union and Eastern Europe, where food production per capita during the same period increased 45 percent.

Let me now talk a little about the uses and abuses of this sort of social science. As Prof. Gunnar Myrdal has recently pointed out in the introduction to his *Asian Drama* changes in scientific research orientation are not due to autonomous re-orientation on the part of the investigators, but to mighty political changes. Let me quote Charles Wagley, an anthropologist writing in *Social Science Research on Latin America*, published in 1964, who observes that in the United States for the last three decades:

> Latin America has also been neglected by our scholars who must provide the basic data for academic and public consumption. As much as Africa, Latin America has been in many ways a "dark continent". This situation is now changing. There is a new public interest in Latin America stimulated by a realization of its importance to our own national interests. The National Defence Education Act supports the study of Spanish and Portuguese and of Latin American society.... Private foundations supported research on the study of Latin America. . . . [etc.]

The same can be said for the sudden take-off of African studies in the US. Although it is true that they coincide with the supposed decolonisation of Africa in the sixties, they respond rather less to any supposed independence of Africa than to increasing dependence of Africa on the US, and to the transfer of the white man's burden from one side of the Atlantic to the other.

Project Camelot has been mentioned in this Symposium before. As you may recall, that project was a brain child of the Pentagon and financed by that institution. Its goal was to go and get Chileans and Americans to inquire into certain facets of their society in order to be able to predict adequately when there might be insurrection in Chile. This project blew up in the face of vivid opposition, particularly on the side of liberals who claimed that their chances were now all ruined since they would no longer be welcomed by people who might suspect them of being spies. I am sorry to have to say this, but I think that all North American and nearly all Western European social science is one huge

Camelot project. In evidence, let me now quote from the horse's mouth, as it were. I am going to read from a document entitled "Report of the Panel on Defence Social and Behavioural Sciences", issued by the Defence Science Board, National Academy of Sciences of the US, 1967:

> In recent years the Department of Defence has been confronted with many problems which require support from the behavioural and social sciences. . . . The Armed Forces are no longer engaged solely in warfare. Their missions now include pacification, assistance, "a battle of ideas", etc. All of these missions require an understanding of the urban and rural populations with which our military personnel come in contact—in the new "peacefare" activities or in combat. For many countries throughout the world, we need more knowledge about their beliefs, values, and motivations; their political, religious, and economic organizations; and the impact of various changes and innovations on their sociocultural patterns . . . [Innovating in] conventional social science methodology . . . is one of the happy cases in which there is substantial overlap in the interests of both DoD [the Department of Defence] and the academic community producing the research . . . [We] believe that DoD [Department of Defence] has been singularly successful in enlisting the interest and services of an eminent group of behavioural scientists in the most of the areas relevant to it. . . . On the other hand, the DoD [Department of Defence] could probably make improvements by assuming more responsibility for stating its needs in terms which are meaningful to the investigator rather than the military. To ask people to do research in "counter-insurgency", "guerilla warfare", etc. not only produces a less than enthusiastic reaction but also provides no basic insight into the ways in which they might contribute. . . . The behavioural science community must be made to accept responsibility for recruiting of DoD [Department of Defence] research managers. . . . The following items are elements that merit consideration as factors in research strategy for military agencies.

Then comes something called *"Priority Ordered Research Undertakings"*. I pick out those which I consider most significant.

> 1. . . . Methods, theories and training in the social and behavioural sciences in foreign countries. . . .
> 2. . . . Programs that train foreign social scientists. . . .
> 3. . . . Social science research to be conducted by independent indigenous scientists. . . .
> 4. . . . Social science tasks to be conducted by major U.S. graduate studies centers in foreign areas. . . .
> 7. . . . Studies based in the U.S. that exploit data collected by

overseas investigators, supported by non-defence agencies. The development of data, resources and analytical methods should be pressed so that data collected for special purposes can be utilized for many additional purposes. . . .

8. . . . Collaborate with other programs in the U.S. and abroad that will provide continuing access of Department of Defence personnel to the academic and intellectual resources of the free world. . . .

I suggest in a word that this social science really is part and parcel of the imperialist system and inseparable from other aspects of that imperialist system.

One other observation. The U.S. does not just *say* the things that are reflected in the documents I just read but they actually do things. These is a very clear, very conscious, very highly organized American campaign, now world-wide, to co-opt social scientists and others, intellectuals of all sorts, for these American global, imperialist purposes. This is not limited to the famous "brain drain." The object is to use intellectuals also in their own country, sponsoring research projects which are suitable for American purposes, and most particularly neutralizing any possible political and scientific role that progressive intellectuals might play in their respective countries. That is why the Americans are now acting in a very clever way. They do not care so much any more about supporting reactionaries. They go for any left-wing guy they can find in India and Africa and Latin America. They invite him to congresses; they give him a year at the University of Chicago; they give him a Ford Foundation grant; they give him the "Red Carpet Treatment." I don't know how many of these guys they buy, but I venture to say, unfortunately quite a few. They don't limit this Red Carpet Treatment to the capitalist underdeveloped countries. They give it also to some people in the socialist countries, apparently with very considerable success.

The question now arises, what is to be done?

One of the things to be done was announced in Havanna in January 1968 by nearly 500 intellectuals from 67 countries. 150 were from France. Over half were from Western Europe. These intellectuals unanimously agreed to something they called "The Appeal of Havanna" to the intellectuals of the world, from which I would also like to quote a part:

Imperialism seeks by the varied techniques of indoctrination to ensure social conformity and political passivity. At the same time a systematic effort is made to mobilize technicians, men of science and intellectuals generally in the service of capitalistic and neo-colonial interests and purposes. Thus talents and skills which should and could contribute to the task of progress and liberation become instead instruments for the commercialisation of values, the degradation of culture and the maintenance of the capitalist economic and social order. It is the fundamental interest and the imperative duty of intellectuals to resist this aggression and to take up without delay the challenge thus posed to them. What is required of them is support for the struggles of national liberation, social emancipation and cultural de-colonisation for all the people in Asia, Africa and Latin America and for the struggle against imperialism waged in its very center by an ever greater number of black and white citizens of the United States, and to enter the political struggle against conservative, retrograde and racist forces to demistify the latters' ideologies and to attack the structure upon which these rest and the interests they serve. . . .

The document ends thus: "This commitment must begin with an unqualified rejection of the policy of cultural subjection of the United States, and this implies the refusal of all invitations, scholarships, employment and participation in programs of cultural work and research where their acceptance could entail collaboration with this policy."

What does this mean? For people in the developed capitalist countries it means a commitment, and it means to the extent possible breaking with the establishment in their scientific, and of course, political world; it means ceasing to be schizophrenic in the sense of having one's progressive sort of politics here at the coffeehouse, whereupon one goes back to one's laboratory to pursue the same research that we have just been discussing. Instead one should become a *partisan*, no longer of a liberal science but of a science of liberation, which of course also involves the liberation of science itself.

Two North Americans have recently suggested some of the implications of this kind of commitment for what they call radicals in the professions. I shall quote from them as well:

1. The movement must be seen as a utility which helps us define what to do and without which our work loses political relevance. . . . If our personal aspirations of professional work preclude our doing things that are safe or respectable then we are kidding ourselves about our politics.
2. High status and respect or rewards in the professional establishment are foreclosed. We must expect job instability, the likelihood of getting fired periodically, the danger of increasing difficulty in finding jobs.
3. A radical cannot see his loyalty as being to the profession or the institution in which he works. Our loyalty is to our political comrades

and to the political aims for which we are organizing. . . . Obviously this presents a moral difficulty, as others will assume that we have other traditional loyalties, [meaning liberal ones]. . . . We are not intellectuals above it all who say the truth to whomever will listen or asks: we are *partisans.* . . .

4. Radicals cannot accept without reservation the code of ethics and responsibility of their professions. Ethics are not abstract ideals. They are sanctifications of certain types of social relations, purposes and loyalties. Conventional ethics entrap us into the support of things which we do not support politically and into loyalties which conflict with our own values in politics.

I should like to associate myself with this statement and to suggest that this is not only our political and moral responsibility but also our scientific responsibility. It is true that I cannot in a few words demonstrate that this kind of political commitment translated into scientific activity will produce better science, more scientific science in all respects than the commitment, latent or manifest, to the liberal ideology as translated into our scientific research and teaching. But as far as liberalism goes, at least in its work on underdevelopment, I think virtually any other commitment is likely to produce more scientifically acceptable results.

What then, Mr Dedijer asks me, do I propose to be done? In the developed capitalist countries, first of all I would say those who are really responsible and committed, shall realize that like charity, revolution and the science of liberation begins at home. This means to stop trying to do the job for the people elsewhere and to start working at home. I would say this presents intellectuals and particularly social scientists with three main tasks: 1) one is to analyse the shoddiness of the emperor's scientific clothes, to display imperialism in its ideological nakedness, and to denounce those colleagues who continue to enjoy the physical comforts that their pseudo-scientific suit affords them. That I think is one of the tasks. 2) Another task is clearly to develop theory and engage in analysis that is required and requested by the movement of liberation at home. So far the movement has available only received theory, which has not proved to be entirely adequate. There is a great deal of scientific work to be done in developing theory and doing analysis of one's own society that could be used in the liberation movement. 3) Thirdly, related to the second, I would say that the intellectual should do specific research tasks, assigned to him by his political comrades in the same sense in which if he were a gunsmith and found himself on the barricades, he would use his gunsmith's knowledge to repair and construct guns. But this means passing from being a revolutionary *intellectual* to becoming an intellectual *revolutionary.*

Evidently this also leaves considerable tasks for the social scientists and other intellectuals in the underdeveloped countries themselves. I think it is quite clear that the task of developing scientific theory and analysis, adequate to their own needs, falls to them and that there is absolutely no hope that this will ever be forthcoming from the developed capitalist countries. This goes also for the socialist countries. At least so far there is not a great deal of such science forthcoming from the Soviet Union. It has been remarkably poor in offering the under-developed countries any kind of social science of liberation.

As social scientists we are likely to accept the suggestion that one's world view, and that I think would include one's scientific world view, is necessarily, if not determined at least influenced by the structure of the society in which one lives. In that case, I suggest that the perspective necessary for a science of liberation among the colonized in the world is likely to be available only among the colonized themselves. They would have to stop importing models and try to take into account the structure and development of the world-wide imperialist system that has in fact formed and still forms the class structure in their respective countries. They also must analyze, just as scientists in the developed part of the world, their respective societies at the service of their liberation movements. Of course they must also do very specific dirty work, not in any derogatory sense, but simply hard research needed by the forces of liberation. It is perhaps true as some claim that Che Guevara had been inadequately informed about the reality in which he was working. All the more reason then that the social scientist in Latin America—and the same goes for Africa and Asia, and everywhere—who is really commit-ted to science and any kind of humane society should put himself at the service of the liberation movement and engage in the research neces-sary to make this liberation movement prosper. In order to achieve this, the social scientist would have to—and Frantz Fanon also wrote about this—follow the example of Che Guevara who was asked once by a writer what this person as a writer might do for the revolution. Che Guevara answered "I used to be a doctor."

* * *

Gertrude Stein has written a poem: "A rose is a rose is a rose" and Mr Dedijer seems to have been telling us "science is science is science" and also that "politics are politics are politics" as if there were no difference between one science and another or between political systems. But if indeed all sciences were the same and if all political systems were the same I venture to say we would not be having this conference because there would not be any scientific interest in the comparison nor any political interest in debating the subject. Moreover as I wish to suggest in these remarks, Mr Dedijer himself belies his own words and shows that his science and his politics—and I am not referring of course to him personally—are of a very particular nature. Mr Dedijer said for instance at the very beginning of his remarks that the growth of science is both good and necessary, irrespective of its use (which according to him can be discussed later). He also said that science and technology promise to reduce the necessity for labour and increase the opportunities for creative work. He also said—and here I think there begins already to be some internal contradiction in his own remarks—that there is a very small amount of investment in science in the underdeveloped countries (less than 0.3% GNP compared to 3.5% in the US) and he attributes this small degree if I understood him correctly to the decisions of politicians. He did not tell us what politicians but I think that becomes apparent from some further remarks that he made. Mr Dedijer quite rightly pointed out that the use of science is for "the national goals of the US", and there are in fact a great many documents from the US, one of which I quote in my own introduction, to the effect that science there is used for national goals where we understand "national" of course to stand not for the whole nation but for certain interests in the American nation. But if it is the case that science is used for "national" goals of the US then this would seem to call into question the first two remarks of Mr Dedijer namely, (1) that the growth of science is good and necessary irrespective of the use to which it is put ("national interests") and, (2) that science and technology promise to reduce labour and increase the opportunity for creative work. It has not come to my attention at least that the goal of the US government and the American bourgeoisie is to reduce the amount of labour or to increase the capacity for creative work in the world as a whole. Mr Dedijer, I think, supplies some further evidence in support of this statement when he says that in the US there is so much science and technology as to place the independence of all other countries in danger. I think he is rather understating the case as mon général De Gaulle has made eminently clear. The danger is more manifest than latent perhaps. But this again seems to call into question the desirability of the growth of science, (any science), and the ability of technology and science to contribute to a kind of ideal society. Evidently the lack of independence of these other countries—and I am thinking perhaps particularly of the under-developed countries but by no means exclusively of them—this lack of independence on their part and particularly the increase of the dependence of these countries which is caused by the use of science and technology in the hands of those who monopolize it and thereby increase their power and domination, has not, I think, in the past and does not promise in the future to increase the part of the Gross National Product of these countries that can be devoted to science and technological research. Nor will there be an increase in the ability of free people for truly creative work and the construction of a humane society. The evidence, it seems to me, is rather all to the contrary.

Mr Dedijer called for a sort of a meta-science, a science of the scientific study of production and the use of science and he suggested, if I recall correctly, that there is freedom of work in the social sciences in the West but not in China and, I think, by extension, in some other countries and that this is a great advantage that these "Western" countries—another euphemism—have over those unnamed countries. Well, if that freedom of work in the social sciences and of a social science of science is the freedom to produce the kind of scientific analysis, which, with all due respect, I have tried to summarize from Mr Dedijer's remarks, I will call into question how valuable that freedom is if it only leads to logical inconsistency and empirical invalidity. Finally, Mr Dedijer said that in China social science is limited to the Central Committee. I find this an empirically rather dubious remark after two years of cultural revolution in China. But even if indeed social science in China were only in the hands of the Central Committee, which it is not, I think the Central Committee of the Party in China could without great shame compare its social science with the social science that has been evidenced here and which I have been criticizing. To conclude: "Social science" in the capitalist world is not just any odd science, but a very particular kind of science, and it corresponds to a very particular kind of politics substantially different, e.g. from the social science either of the Central Committee in China or of those who have made the cultural revolution there.

Stevan Dedijer:
To me it seems to be an undercurrent of anti-scientism in this debate. I have been accused of being too optimistic about science and the good it leads to. The first point I made in my paper was that science and technology are with us and that they are going to build a better world. Today we live in a much better world than the world of a hundred years ago as is evident from every kind of statistics. If you do not believe that kind of evidence then I do not see what kind of evidence you would accept. It is a fact that many people today lead a better life than people did a century ago.

(*Aant Elzinga* from the audience: Many *more* people lead a worse life!

Stevan Dedijer: That can be debated.)

Andre Gunder Frank:
". . . nearly all of our major problems today have grown up under British rule and as the direct result of British policy. The princes, the

ethnic problems, vested interests, native and foreign, the lack of industry, and the neglect of agriculture, the extreme backwardness in the social services and above all the tragic poverty of the people—." I quote this not to compete in citatology but in order to produce some empirical evidence for the benefit of those who set great store by it without, however, producing any themselves. The quotation is from Nehru. The outcome of all the things described by Nehru must be that India underdeveloped under capitalism. I do not however suggest that these things are correct just because Mr Nehru has said them. Whether they are correct or not is something that can be decided by the facts only.

What has shocked me greatly is the allegation that I would judge the merits of a shashlik according to who invented it. Of course I do not. The evidence is all that counts. "The proof of the pudding is in the eating." My hope is that the program I have outlined will lead to liberation but whether it will do so, or not, history alone can tell. I consider it to be my duty to point my shashlik in a certain direction.

Although I have been mainly studying Latin America in recent years, I shall nevertheless try to discuss India since that topic has been brought up, and to marshal the evidence in the Indian case. Before doing that just a short remark. It has been said that India is not at all developing with the same speed as China is, but that such a comparison would in no way prove that communism is superior to capitalism. Since we have only one instance we could not possibly draw any conclusions from it. One must look further into the evidence. I think unbiased observers would agree with me that statistical records show a relatively high rate of growth in socialist countries, whereas underdeveloped countries with a capitalist system do not show that same growth. This goes not only for India and China but also for South Vietnam versus North Vietnam, South Korea versus North Korea. This does not prove my point but it does adduce a little bit more empirical evidence. I never said that these countries would have developed had it not been for capitalism. What I said was that due to capitalism they underdeveloped. I think India is a very clear case where capitalism has led to underdevelopment. Even when the Moguls conquered India they did not destroy the high civilisation they found in India or alter the social structure of the country. All they did was to substitute themselves for previous collectors of tributes. Quite different was the coming of capitalism. I invite you to read if you are interested in this problem the book by Mukherjee *The rise and fall of the East Indian Company* to find what the East Indian Company did. The essential thing about that company was that it changed the entire social system in India.

It so happens that the steam engine and other inventions were put into use in the second half of the eighteenth century. It is worthwhile mentioning that during this same period the East Indian Company sucked more capital out of India than the value of the total steam-driven industrial stock in England in the year 1800. In the first decades of the nineteenth century India still exported much more textiles to GB than GB exported to India. At that time India had a textile industry which was technically relatively advanced and produced much better textiles than the British industry did. But after the Napoleonic wars and the elimination of French competition England consolidated her position in many parts of the world and particularly in India. By introducing the doctrine of free trade England managed to eliminate all barriers to the importation of textiles to India while she maintained her own barrier to the importation of foreign products. In this manner Britain intentionally destroyed Indian industry. The outcome of all this was that many people in India were driven back to agriculture and became dependent on the land. Because of changes that were introduced at the same time into the Indian agricultural system, that also was destroyed. In all these ways the underdevelopment of India was accelerated because of the inherent structure of the capitalist system.

So far I have only been talking about India. I shall not trouble you with a similar description of what happened in China but merely refer to a paper presented by Mr Owen Lattimore at the Stockholm conference on economic history in 1960 in which he describes the impact of capitalism on China 1800–1950. There you will get the same picture. But from 1950 onwards all statistics tend to prove that China has developed much faster than India. Take one example. In 1950 steel production was actually higher in India than in China. Today the Chinese output is about 8 times as great as the corresponding output in India. In one word: I have tried to bring some empirical evidence to bear on my shashlik idea, which not everybody here speaking of ideological shashliks has managed to do.

My main point in this context is that instead of analysing these historical and structural relationships, liberal social science reflects isolated characteristics of the developed capitalist countries. Development is attributed to the availability of capital, the production of technology, and their organization according to such tenants of liberalism as private enterprise, a free market, entrepreneurship, social mobility, parliamentary democracy, etc, in short of economic, social, and political liberalism. Underdevelopment is attributed to the absence of these in societies that are said to be still traditional. The resulting development or "modernization" policy that liberal scientists recommend to the people of the underdeveloped countries is simply to shed the traditional characteristics and to adopt the modern ones—while remaining firmly within the capitalist system that generates these so-called traditional societies. The same distinction between relatively modern and relatively traditional society is repeated for the under-developed countries themselves, which are viewed as "dual" societies or economies, one part relatively advanced because of its contact with Europe or North America and the other part archaic, feudal, or otherwise retrograde for lack of adequate contact with the world capitalism and its own national metropolis. Development is attributed to the generous diffusion of capital, technology and liberal institutions from the European and North American metropolis to the various national ones and from these on.

In fact one to four centuries of precisely this sort of diffusion of slavery, serfdom, colonialism, liberalism, and now modernization from the capitalist metropolis to equally capitalist colonies has under-developed Asia, Africa and Latin America through the diffusion even to their most isolated outpost of the very world and national capitalist colonial and class structure that causes poverty and that liberalism still seeks to sustain.

Friedrich List rightly said that England's most important export product was the free trade doctrine or Manchester Liberalism, which was not born in Cottonpolis by accident. The same is no less true today for the American social scientific way of life, which is a global Camelot project that has its own essential role in the imperialist exploitation, oppression, and underdevelopment of the majority of mankind. As the source and justification for imperialist policy it contributes to a development policy that furthers the development of the imperialist monopolies and their bourgeois junior partners abroad while further developing underdevelopment for the poor majority, and as an ideology it co-opts potential revolutionary leadership and real scientific advance among Asians, Africans and Latin Americans into harmless refor-mongering and sterile scientism. The evidence is available in imperial-ist documents themselves, such as the revealing one of the Defense Science Board–National Academy of Sciences of the United States, from which I have already quoted.

What is required, therefore, as I see it is not liberalism even though it be reformed or reconstructed, but a science of liberation. For West European and North American scientists who are sufficiently conscious and committed to do so, this involves breaking with the establishment and to work for and in the political liberation movements. It is my conviction that this at the end will prove to be the only way out to make science a really liberating force to mankind and to liberate science itself.

3

On the Political Study of New Nations

Santiago, Chile, 24 v 73

Sathyamurthy's critique of political science is commendable, and so is his observation that its bourgeois practitioners are obsessed with policy. Should we understand this policy orientation to be "bad"? Surely, any political scientist who is not vitally concerned about political policy (or social scientist about social, that is, political, policy) is not worthy of the name. The question is, what policy? It is also quite correct that the policy in question is "of the developed countries . . . towards the [under]developing countries," and it is correct that it should be so. But Sathyamurthy's questions "whose policy?" and "in relation to whom?" and our answers to them must be further extended from the "countries" to the political *class* and interest of the practitioners (and of the practiced-upon): We are dealing with political scientists who act as representatives and in the interest of the bourgeoisie—both in the developed and in the underdeveloping countries—and against the people. Additionally, we should ask of policy not only whose it is, but what it is.

Current Anthropology, Chicago, Vol. 14, No. 5, December 1973, published by University of Chicago Press.

Simplifying, admittedly, we may answer this latter question by distinguishing two kinds. One is the development and propagation of what Sathyamurthy correctly called "a theory which assumes problems out of existence." In this kind of "political" theory, be it institutional, (later) functionalist, or (increasingly) behaviorist, the "political" motivations are "politically" processed through "political" institutions of the "political" nation—and imperialism, socioeconomic class and class struggle, political-economic interest and dirty politics are simply assumed out of existence. This is, as Apter (1968:7) points out, the kind of "general, systems-theory which requires one to know 'everything' before it is possible to know [and, we might add, to do] 'anything'," and in which Talcott Parsons reigns supreme. Or once did: "Parsonian analysis has begun to lose its impact," Apter adds (referring to sociology), while "Marxism . . . has emerged among younger intellectuals . . . to shape their research designs and formulations." Accordingly, he confesses, "I feel the responsibility to help create an intellectual space—small, not large—pitched somewhere between the great and powerful systems of a Marx or a Parsons. . . ." What in the world for? Apter answers in his own and his ideological soul-mates' way: "Marxism today represents such a highly generalized system that it 'precuts' all relevant experience for the observer. The result is a kind of theoretical 'over-kill' . . . one knows 'everything' of relevance by means of a small number of variables"—and, what is worse, one is likely to *act* politically on their basis. God forbid! Or if the Holy Ghost of Goliath Parsons has begun to lose its impact, then David feels a responsibility to replace him in his small way.

Sathyamurthy suggests that if political science departments have nothing better to offer than this, they should abandon the field. But why should they? From their point of view—and from that of the political-economic interests they serve—they are doing very well, thank you, and should keep up the good work, extending it (as they are, with foundation help) especially to the underdeveloping countries themselves: These political "scientists" are doing a big ideological job of spreading Parsonian know-nothingism and Apterian (or Lipsetian or whatever) know-littleism to combat Marxism, which threatens to shape increasingly not only political research but also political action, not only within the university but also outside of it. This more serious purpose of a policy designed to brake and break popular revolutionary policy and action does indeed dominate a large number of political scientists, as Sathyamurthy says; but it is by no means as limited to the subconscious as he suggests.

A second kind of political science, more practical than theoretical (though it also has the latter cover), is that designed for and largely produced or financed by the political or military repressive apparatus of imperialism for direct use against liberation struggles the world over, and especially in Southeast Asia. This is the kind of political science made infamous by such "applied research and development . . . in the fields of counterinsurgency and limited conflict" (as officially defined and defended in testimony before the U.S. House of Representatives Subcommittee on Defense Appropriations, quoted in Klare 1972:215) of the Defense Department contract Advanced Research Projects Agency's Project Agile in Vietnam and Thailand. This kind of political science, far from being subconscious, is also not at all averse to political policy and seeks to serve it according to the maxim that the only good "communist" is a dead one. This political science has in recent years been sufficiently exposed, even in the bourgeois "world" press, not to require further comment here.

Sathyamurthy suggests that anthropology could suitably step in and help improve political science. Again we should pose the questions, what anthropology and for whom? To begin with, anthropology itself has been far from immune to or innocent of the vices of political science. The "Social Responsibility Symposium" and subsequent discussion (CA 9:391–435; 11:72–79; 12:83–87) and the maxim of "ten anthropologists for every guerilla," whose implementation led to the "Thailand scandal" in the American Anthropological Association again save us the need for further comment. Further, the second kind of political scientist mentioned above would no doubt welcome the help of anthropologists and, indeed, has already received it (e.g., Thailand, Camelot, etc., not to mention those in the service of the internal-colonial "Indian" services); but is that kind of help what Sathyamurthy has in mind? Surely not. The first kind of political scientist, on the other hand, is likely to reject the best help of anthropology—as Apter does, as Sathyamurthy correctly points out— because consciously (not unconsciously) he understands that too much acquaintance with or concern for ethnographic reality and real ethnological analysis would undermine the very obscurantist ideological know-nothingist structure that he is intent on building and preserving.

Finally, there remains the very serious question of what anthropology we really have to offer those who seek—especially in the colonial and neocolonial countries themselves—to develop and practice a science of political liberation, as long as "political" anthropology remains splendidly isolated from the political economy of the peoples and their exploiters and as long as "economic" anthropology remains spiked on the horns of the false "theoretical issues" of "formalism" and "substantivism" as Dalton (1969, 1971) would have it.

REPLY BY SATHYAMURTHY

I find Frank's critique the most seminal of all. My own thinking during the last several years, and especially since writing this paper, has moved in the general direction indicated in it. In retrospect, my paper has touched only a very small part of the problem, much of which lies hidden underneath like a huge iceberg. An appraisal of the intellectual and ideological foundations of much of recent political science (e.g., Apter, Pye, Huntingdon) would have to include the close connection between professional social science and the policy preoccupations of the developed world (Hacker 1973), including the Soviet Union. These preoccupations mainly revolve round the maintenance of political order in the new nations as a prerequisite to the realisation of the global interests of the Big Powers (Klare 1972), with the aid of those leaders in the underdeveloped world who stand to gain most from it. Political analyses focusing on contradictions and conflicts within the new structures in post-colonial states have begun to appear with increasing frequency. This development is subsumed under the label of Marxist approaches in opposition to Parsonian "ideology." However, detailed analyses of conflicts and contradictions are still not very common, and some of the recent examples have made good use of anthropological results in developing path-breaking analysis (Alavi 1972a, b; 1973a, b; Balandier 1970a; Gough 1971). I fully recognise that in anthropology there is a dominant strain that can be encapsulated in the maxim "ten anthropologists per guerilla"; but even bourgeois anthropology, like the bourgeois press, can be sufficiently differentiated to eschew such a crude but powerful application of the "imperialist handmaiden" approach with a view to constructing an empirical basis for strong theories of change in the right direction. Frank's contribution has, in this sense, reached the heart of the matter.

REFERENCES CITED BY A.G. FRANK

Apter, David E. (1968) *Some conceptual approaches to the study of modernization.* Englewood-Cliffs, N.J.; Prentice-Hall.

Dalton, George (1969). Theoretical issues in economic anthropology. *Current Anthropology*, vol. 10, no. 1, pp. 63–99; and reply to Frank in Chapter 6.

Frank, Andre Gunder (1971). Discussion and criticism of George Dalton, "Theoretical Issues in Economic Anthropology." *Current Anthropology*, vol. 11, no. 1, February 1971.

Social Responsibilities Symposium, *Current Anthropology*, vol. 9, pp. 391–435.

4

On the Social Origins of Dictatorship and Democracy

Professor Barrington Moore
Russian Research Center
Harvard University
Cambridge, Mass. 02138

Dear Mr. Moore:

I should like to take the liberty of sending you a few thoughts arising out of your recently published book, *Social Origins of Dictatorship and Democracy.* Since I will write down only my critical thoughts and not the others, let me begin by congratulating you on the importance and high degree of scholarship of your work. Perhaps I would not even dare to write you if someone had not recently called me on the telephone and said that you had sent him to me. He never showed up, incidentally.

The book leaves me with the impression that you are in serious trouble. You begin, apparently many years ago, with a commitment to democracy, with the idea that there is a difference between democracy and dictatorship, and with the desire to account for why some places ended up being democratic and others not. Accordingly, you start with a

---

Personal letter, Montreal 1967.

major distinction between democracy and dictatorship and only a minor distinction within dictatorship between the fascist and communist varieties. You then spend many years carefully examining the evidence. Your trouble arises when the evidence and your honest scholarship increasingly begin to show that the really significant distinction is not between capitalist or bourgeois democracy on the one hand and fascism and communism on the other hand, but rather between capitalist democracy and dictatorship on the one hand and communism or rather socialism on the other hand. You seem to be increasingly persuaded by this evidence. At the same time, perhaps, the world is undergoing certain changes which, given your commitment and your honesty, cannot fail to influence you: the United States, particularly in its war against Vietnam, is blurring some of the distinctions between capitalist dictatorship and capitalist democracy. Your trouble, then, has two sources or takes two forms. One is that by the end of the book you have not yet been able to quite liberate yourself from the ideological position and commitment that normally leads to the support shall we say, of India rather than China. If you were less of a scholar or a gentleman you could have failed to see or once seen could have swept under the rug the accumulating evidence which crashes with your initial ideological position. But you can't do that, and so you are in trouble. The second source of your trouble is the framework within which you initially began your analysis. Since that informs your whole selection and organization of the data, and still appears in your title (I do not know whether your title is written at the beginning or at the end of your work), and you are also unable to liberate yourself from this intellectual as distinct from ideological straightjacket and cannot deal with your evidence as this evidence and your own increasing enlightenment bid you to do—until the next book you write. Having begun with the major dichotomy between capitalist democracy and capitalist or socialist dictatorship you are unable to shake it in your organization of the evidence, notwithstanding that your own evidence and increasingly both your intellectual and ideological position bid you to change the dichotomy to capitalist democracy or dictatorship on the one hand versus socialism on the other hand. Had you not begun with that intellectual and ideological commitment, you would not have landed into this trouble. But then you probably would also have lacked the motivation and drive to write the book, and the world would not have the advantage of what it teaches us.

These troubles manifest themselves most acutely in your book in your inability to deal, I am sure you will agree, to your own or your readers' satisfaction with the problem posed by India. On the one hand you classify it under democratic and on the other hand you are obliged to say that this democracy is a sham, that Indian society does not work, and that totalitarianism in almost certainly the next order of business. I quite agree with you that it is much more likely to be a move to the right than to the left. I am writing just a few days after the fall of the West Bengal Government, but I have for some time thought and said that India is moving in the direction of an Indonesian, Brazil, Ghana type of military coup, with the political decimation of the left and I can only vainly hope for the avoidance of its physical elimination on the Indonesian scale.

Your trouble with India is not accidental. It responds to and flows out of the intellectual and ideological positions, summarized above, that led you to start off with the democracy dictatorship dichotomy in the first place. If you were dealing with Latin America, to which you make some brief references, or any other underdeveloped region, you would, I suspect, run into the same trouble. The reason is, I suggest, because there is another source of your trouble. That is that you, like so many others, select the boundaries of the determinate social system at the boundaries of what is today the nation's state. You recognize, of course, that there are outside influences. But you do not systematically take account of them as the manifestations of a more inclusive social system or structure. In your case, of course, this is related to the fact that you seek to find the determinate factors in the social origins and particularly lord and peasant relations within the society prior to the political upheaval that led to the contemporary social political forms. Nonetheless, it is not in principle, and I hope not in practice, impossible to inquire into this aspect of the social structure as part of and in part determined by the social structure (in the wider sense of the term) of a more inclusive system, particularly in as much as, I suggest, in fact there has been such a single system in operation, the mercantilist now capitalist worldwide system.

Let me illustrate by reference to an important problem that arises out of your work, on which the experience of Latin America about which I know a little bit more can perhaps throw some light. You seek the origins of German and Japanese fascism in a certain kind of lord–peasant relationship which permits a later coalition between land-owners, merchants, and industrialists. On page 438 you suggest, rightly I think, that Poland, Hungary, Romania, Spain, Greece, and perhaps much of Latin America experienced some not too dissimilar circumstances. Then why did these places not end up where Germany and Japan did, not so much simply in political terms as in terms of economic development and industrialization? Why was there not in these places a landlord–merchant industrialist coalition, a marriage of rye and iron, that channeled surplus into industrialization? The reason, in one word, is that these were economic colonies. In these countries, either this class coalition does not come into being to any substantial degree, or it comes into being but does not lead to industrialization as it did in Germany and Japan. In these countries the class structure was either created, as in Latin America, or restructured in the historical course of their economic (sometimes yes and sometimes no political) colonization. Their participation in the wider social system, of which today's capitalist democracies were also a part, was significantly different from those of Germany and Japan. Japan, of course, was totally isolated and not part of the system at all. Germany was not part of the system as a colony. Accordingly, in these two countries there were not set up, as there were in the others a vested interest by these classes in the creation, the expansion, the consolidation, and the maintainance of an export economy on the Latin American model, with all that implies. Therefore, the marriage of rye and iron was able to produce an industrial offspring in Germany and Japan but not in Latin America and these other places.

Additional confirmatory evidence for your thesis and for mine, where they overlap, comes from the experience of the Latin American countries during the 1930s and 1940s. In 1929 begins the depression. In 1930 there are revolutions in Brazil, Argentina, Chile, etc. and soon thereafter the consolidation of the revolution in Mexico. In all these cases, and I am most familiar with the one in Brazil, there comes into being just the kind of marriage between rye and iron that you speak of. The agricultural interests are not displaced from power. But the industrial interests and some regional interests that previously did not share in policy making are now admitted to a seat in the government and to policy formation in concert with the traditional interest. And they begin a national industrialization drive. This lasts until about the Korean War. As you pointed out somewhere, this marriage bond has to be maintained by the shotgun of a strong government, which in Latin America are those of Vergas, Peron and Cardenas. But not even such strong governments would be able to maintain the coalition and most particularly the industrialization policy if the economic and political pressures to tear it apart were strong enough. They were strong enough to prevent this from coming into being before 1930 and they were again strong enough to break it up after the Second World War. These pressures were attenuated only during and by the depression and the world war which rendered the traditional export policies impossible or unprofitable. After 1930 in Brazil the government continued the price support policies on coffee which shifted income toward the coffee growers and exporters, despite the fact that the external market had disappeared. Since the lack of foreign exchange and the devaluation-caused increase in import prices severely restricted imports, and since expansion of exports was no longer sensible, and since the coffee people still had money thanks to price support, they started to put money into industry. The policies favored by industrial interests did not at this time conflict with the interests of the agriculturists. A Germany, Japan type situation arose. But in an economic colony this situation only arose while the metropolis was in trouble. And it only lasted while the metropolis was in trouble. And it was not long enough and did not go deep enough to permit Brazilian or Argentine industrialization on the German–Japanese model. After the war the whole process was reversed.

So this experience, it seems to me, supports your suggestion, but it also highlights the limitations of your suggestions. As you may recall, Dobb argues that German, Japanese, and Italian fascism are the results of johnny-come-lately capitalist development in an imperialist system in which the early birds have already taken up most of the slack. The resultant problems lead to, in Dobb's analysis, the fascism of the 1930s which is externally expansionist and internally repressionist. You do not mention this interpretation and seem to dismiss it by concentrating on strictly domestic issues. But the two interpretations are not mutually incompatible, and both kinds of factors, I would argue, were at work. If these "external" factors had not been at work in the case of Germany and Japan, and if these factors had not been different in Germany and Japan than they were in Latin American and the other countries you named, we would be left with no explanation for the differences in subsequent outcome. At the same time, as my above "analysis" suggests, such "external" factors seem to go a long way toward explaining the difference between Germany or Japan and Latin America or Southern Eastern Europe.

But these considerations also add additional evidence in support of the contention that the real dichotomy is not capitalist democracy versus capitalist or communist dictatorship but rather capitalism on the one hand, be it "democratic" or "dictatorial", and socialism on the other hand. You yourself find some kind of hybrid dictatorship/democracy in Latin America. Now we come, perhaps, to an initial and continuing difference between us. I find the whole question about democracy really terribly uninteresting. I find the question of economic and social development and within that the kind of democracy that some of the socialist countries aspire to much more interesting, and I submit that it is historically much more important. I get the impression from reading your book that you are coming around to this position as well. But, as I suggested above, you seem not to have liberated yourself from your starting point by the time you finished writing your book. I trust that you will have done so before you begin your next book and that you will then ask more suitably phrased questions which will cause you less trouble when you confront your evidence.

Let me say one more thing and take issue with you on a political matter. On page 438 you rightly say that "The notion that a violent popular revolution is somehow necessary in order to sweep away feudal obstacles to industrialization is pure nonsense, as the course of German and Japanese history demonstrates." I quite agree, but only if and when you are really dealing with such so-called feudal obstacles in a society in which the groups with economic and political power can find industrialization in their own interest and therefore institute it from above without any revolution from below. This is, precisely because they are economic colonies, decidedly not the case in Asia, Africa, and Latin America today, and that includes most particularly India. Therefore, what you say on page 505, "Industrialism, as it continues to spread, may in some distant future still these voices forever and make revolutionary radicalism as anachronistic as cuneiform writing" is not consistent with the evidence. The trouble is that industrialism does not continue to spread. Furthermore the kind of industrialism that was sufficient to develop the now developed countries is no longer sufficient to develop the now underdeveloped countries. The technological and military development of the United States has changed all that. Therefore, I submit, revolutionary radicalism is not anachronistic and will not become so thanks to industrialism. Rather, it is the other way around at least in Asia, Africa, and Latin America, where revolutionary radicalism, and revolution, is necessary before industrialism can even begin to spread.

After all that I take the further liberty of sending you a little article of mine on the received wisdom in the sociology of development. Though I proceed differently from you, I think you will find that my critique of pseudo science herein is at least not inconsistent with your own critique of some of these same people's work.

Sincerely yours,

Andre Gunder Frank

5

Anthropology = Ideology; Applied Anthropology = Politics*[1]

Anthropology: Plus ça change, plus ça reste le même.

(French saying)

Applied Anthropology: Changes must be introduced to keep things
as they are.

(The Leopard)

Maurice Freedman's essay is presented to us by Sol Tax as 'a
remarkable cooperative achievement; its breadth and high quality
make it worthy of the fullest attention: and its significance for
anthropology also requires critical discussion.' Yes and no, with certain
reservations! The essay exhibits breadth—and shallowness. Its occasional high quality insights are swamped and negated by a morass of
confused irrelevancies. The construction of the argument falls on
sophistry of false disjunctions and identities. Its significance lies in the
real problems—the function and future of anthropology and anthropological ideology—which in the essay are conspicuous by their absence
or avoidance. It is remarkable indeed that international cooperation

First published in *Race & Class*, London, XVII, 1, 1975.

*This paper is a comment on Maurice Freedman's 'Social and Cultural Anthropol-
ogy', written for the IXth International Congress of Anthropological and Ethnological
Sciences, Chicago, September 1973, at the invitation of its President, Sol Tax.

leads to such embarrassing results. That is why the essay requires critical discussion.

The whole of the 'co-ordinates' and 'opposite attractions' of the first two main chapters (A and B), which reappear in later ones as well, rest on, or more precisely fall with, a series of false disjunctions and a few false identities to boot.

The oppositions between description and theory, science and art, comparison and particularism, structure and history, and evolutionism and functionalism rest on an un- indeed anti-scientific sophistry that is the author's figleaf for the total misunderstanding and mystification of evolution and history. 'We may well wonder whether . . . the category of history has any great relevance to anthropology,' Freedman writes (p. 27). No wonder he wonders, if history is what Freedman claims. We may rescue him from his doubt and say that it certainly has no relevance at all, if history is no more than 'given to the particular, the descriptive, and the humanistic . . . when its opposite is structure' (pp. 27-9), if 'not all historical writing (*pace* some theorists) is diachronic and concerned with change' while much of it 'is a synchrony set back in time' (p. 97). It would be difficult to select a set of terms more erroneously opposite of concrete history and real historical writing, whose very essence is the diachronical interaction between the structure of change and the change of structure, which determine the descriptive particular, and which takes place throughout time, past, present and future in combined and uneven development.

It is only Freedman's total theoretical obfuscation and ideological negation of history and evolution that permit him to counterpose history to structure and the latter to evolution(ism) and function(alism) (pp. 27-31), or to pose such absurd disjunctions as 'in the long view [of the evolutionist vision], there is beautiful order; in the short, a recalcitrant variety' (p. 88), while identifying contemporary evolutionism and functionalism (that is seeking to attach some of the merited prestige of the former to the also merited growing disrepute of the latter) through 'indications of their common heritage' (p. 30), as though common origins could not lead to a diverse and even opposing present and future, as they have through all natural evolution and social history. Thus Freedman falls prey to and perpetuates the anti-scientific ideology of a 'Radcliffe-Brown, the arch-priest of anthropological structural-functionalism' (p. 30), who persuaded generations that history is irrelevant to his reactionary pseudo-structure, and pseudo-function, and that of 'the "structure" of structuralism, a doctrine [sic!] which, ramifying in the kingdom of knowledge, has a branch in anthropology to which the name of Lévi-Strauss is attached' (p. 28) 'in such a manner that time becomes irrelevant because neutral' (p. 30); because, in fact as Lévi-Strauss himself emphasizes but Freedman and others like to forget, that structuralism only deals with the structure of models and never of concrete—that is, historical—reality. No wonder that time is irrelevant and that Freedman wonders if history is relevant if by act of ideological definition 'history' is vacated of all real content and reality is left out of account! And that from someone who himself dares to tell us what it is all about, when he warns: 'Above all, there is a danger in those reduced and impoverished schemes of research which, for example, operate with simple notions of social class and class exploitation or, as in some forms of neo-Marxism, with equally rudimentary concepts of power and dominance' (p. 155). We may be thankful, indeed, to Mr Freedman and his colleagues for this warning, and the 'impoverished schemes' such as the co-ordinates of opposite attractions, and 'rudimentary concepts' such as that of 'history' marshalled to back up this warning.

Moreover, Mr Freedman's 'Co-ordinates of study in time and space' also disregard, and thereby falsify, history in another important regard. In questioning and disregarding the relevance of history they disregard the intimate relation between the history of the world and the history of anthropology itself. They disregard that, 'much of classical sociology arose within the context of a debate—first with eighteenth-century thought, the Enlightenment, and later with its true heir in the nineteenth century, Karl Marx',[2] and that 'it has been said that anthropology developed entirely independently of Marxism. More correctly, 20th-century anthropology developed entirely in reaction to Marxism'.[3] Mr Freedman and Co. and the anthropology they review further disregard—i.e., regard as 'irrelevant'—not only history, but also materialism. They regard it to be 'irrelevant' that their sociology and anthropology began as and continued to be an *ideological* response to historical materialism.

It may therefore be appropriate to review this ideological function of anthropology. Freedman himself offers us some insights and cues for such a review, which his own ideological position or limitations apparently inhibit him from pursuing to the reader's advantage:

> All anthropological theory changes with the world in which it is practised, but the response of applied anthropology in particular is more noticeable. . . . There is one point upon which nearly all anthropologists are agreed: applied anthropology is more like politics than engineering. It does not rest upon a secure and precise theory . . . (p. 111).

Agreed. But the political nature of applied anthropology is not so much a function of the insecurity or imprecision of its base, as it is a function of anthropology's application and function itself. And the anthropological theory on which it rests, all the more so but not exclusively in view of its insecurity and imprecision, is more ideology than science. But this extension of his argument, Freedman will not make (or perhaps even accompany). Nor does he, despite devoting a section to applied anthropology, apply his insight to say whose or what politics is so applied by or through anthropology. Moreover, the time and space coordinates of Mr Freedman do not show how or why anthropology changes—or remains the same—in the world in which it is practised:

> It is often said, and with some justice, that anthropologists working in colonial societies in the old days were blind to the total political and social environment within which they conducted their studies of small communities or of tribes. In independent states they are not likely to make the bias . . . [which] is now being corrected (p. 113).

> Changed political circumstances have reduced the Japanese interest in Korea, Manchuria, Mongolia, China (including Taiwan), and Micronesia, to the ethnography of which countries important contributions were once made. Since the Second World War a younger generation has begun to concern itself with other areas (South-East Asia, India, Africa, Latin America, and the Arctic region), but their number is tiny, and the greatest scholarly investment has been made in studies of Japan itself. . . . [Here] we have an example of how a lack of interest in the exotic hampers a national anthropology in the performance of its role in world scholarship. The politics of China's situation leaves the future of its anthropology in doubt (pp. 149-50).

Exotic interests in the performance of its role in world scholarship, indeed. Here we have an exotic example of how anthropological ideology inhibits perception and analysis of the ideology of anthropology and its political determinants and functions in the quite unexotic performance of its role in 'world scholarship'.

In this context we may therefore briefly propose a review in turn of the subjects of anthropological study, of anthropology as a subject of study, and of Mr Freedman's essay as a study of anthropology, emphasizing the ideological content, purpose and function of anthropology, theoretical and applied, classical and up to date.

Freedman himself lists and reviews the 'classical' subjects of a century of anthropological study: 1. kinship and marriage, 2. politics and government, 3. law in the context of social control, 4. economics, 5. religion and ritual, 6. visual art, 7. music, 8. literature, 9. technology. Items 5 to 8 might easily be recognized to be substantially ideology or vehicles for its expression under other names; while items 1 to 3 could be recognized as institutions, rules, and measures of what Freedman does not like to call 'power and dominance', which are importantly supported by and give expression to that ideology. Yet for Mr Freedman this elementary concept appears to be even less than rudimentary. The word appears only once (p. 113) in his 163 pages of text. Admittedly, therein Mr Freedman's review is true to much of the anthropological profession itself, for whom the denotation of its subject of study, let alone of anthropology itself, as ideology, is one of the greatest taboos (for instance, in the cumulative index of Volumes 1 to 10 of *Current Anthropology,* the world 'ideology' appears only four times— the same number as blood type groups, and Marcus Goldstein's review of 'Anthropological Research, Action, and Education in Modern Nations: With Special Reference to the USA'[4] with international CA treatment is not among them; even in such a critical review of anthropology as Robert Murphy's *The Dialectics of Social Life,*[5] the 'item' ideology does not appear in the quite detailed index at all). Yet most of the anthropologists concerned have been writing ideological prose (some without knowing it and others more literally aware), and doubly so; they have been writing *about* ideology in so far as they divorced these items from their 'irrelevant' historical and economic context; and they have been *writing ideology* in as much as they did so. Mr Freedman also writes true to this ideological tradition.

Anthropology's traditional old bias for antiquarianism and the exotic of the old days has been the subject of increasing recent analysis,[6] and Mr Freedman himself observes that it has left 'often unfortunate connotations' (p. 151) in Africa. But to call it a 'mistake' is a mistake; and to call the biased anthropologists 'blind' is an exaggeration. The author of *A Black Byzantium*, S.F. Nadel, for instance, saw clearly enough to write of:

> the application of anthropology to problems of colonial policy. . . . While certain anthropologists would remain aloof from these practical questions, others consider it their right and duty to 'apply' anthropology in practice. I count myself among the latter. . . . It has been said that modern anthropology is destined to be of great assistance to colonial governments in providing the knowledge of the social structure of native groups upon which a sound and harmonious Native Administration, as envisaged in Indirect Rule, should be built. Let me say that I for one firmly believe in the possibility of such cooperation between anthropologists and administrator. . . . At the end of the talk a number of West African students in the audience violently attacked me, all my fellow workers in the field, and indeed the whole of anthropology. They accused us of playing into the hands of reactionary administrators and of lending the sanctions of science to a policy meant to 'keep the African down'. . . . 'Pure,' value free anthropology is an illusion.[7]

So much for the 'blindness' of African Systems of Kinships and Marriage and African Political Systems, or for that matter the erstwhile exotic interests and important contributions of Japanese anthropology in the Japanese colonies before the Second World War deprived the Japanese simultaneously of their colonies and their exotic interests. Oh, these unfortunate connotations!

Beyond these, the 'mistake' of value free illusions has had other connotations that Mr Freedman and Co. perhaps regard as more fortunate. Beyond the direct application of anthropological theory through indirect rule of those exotic natives, there has been its indirect application to the direct rule of the imperialists. The same anthropology has lent the sanction of 'science' to the strengthening and the propagation of an ideology of imperialism, to justify the rule itself, both to the rulers and the ruled, as well as to third parties. The anthropological interest in those exotic natives lent scientific sanction to Kipling's literary tenet that the East is East and the West is West, and never the twain shall meet—except through the white man's burden. And the arch-priests of 'British' anthropology who so generously contributed to the assumption of this burden through the performance of their role in world scholarship were predominantly from the British Dominions themselves!

Now, as British structural-functionalism has become increasingly disfunctional, and as Marxism has re-emerged with sufficient vigour—especially in France—to merit a sound of alarm from Freedman, the name attached to anthropological structuralism in France, Lévi-Strauss, has been resurrected and trumpeted to the four winds. Its ideological function? Freedman himself suggests it: to make time, history, materialism, indeed all concrete reality, irrelevant. In the United States, which lacked substantial colonies other than internal ones, imperial policy was known as the 'open door'. Have exotic needlecase patterns of Boaz (oh, those Exotic Eskimos and Indians), Ruth Benedict's patterns of culture (even those of the themselves quite exotic Japanese of the chrysanthemum and sword), and the growing-up patterns of Margaret Mead (oh, those Samoans who can jump straight from the stone age to the nuclear age, and almost painlessly to boot) been playing any the less into the hands of reactionaries? Margaret Mead's attempt to apply her positivist anthropological cultural relativism in the American Anthropological Association itself to justify the application of the cultural relative formula 'one anthropologist vs. ten guerrillas' in exotic Indochina proved unacceptable to that august body during the Thailand scandal,[8] but the function of the theoretical patterns of Mead's cultural ideology, and that of her teachers and students, has proved much more culturally resistant both in the profession and among the public at large.

Enough. Lest, like Marvin Harris,[9] we be accused of beating a dead horse from those bad old days, whose 'mistakes' anthropologists are no longer likely to make, we may turn to modern up-to-date-ness, as Freedman calls it, or we may turn to the up-to-date-ness of the 'modernization' theory of acculturation and diffusion. For Mr Freedman, the exotic interests of those no doubt themselves exotic Japanese have shifted to domestic problems and—what a coincidence!—increasingly to those exotic areas of the world from which they must draw their raw materials and into which they are now pushing their investments and sales (the government-financed Institute of Developing Economies in Tokyo reflects the area specialization Freedman mentions). And among those still more exotic Chinese, Freedman sees anthropology to be conditioned by the political situation. So in these exotic oriental countries anthropology changes in accord with such quite worldly—one might say historical materialist—changes in the situation. But if 'all anthropology changes with the world in which it is practised', what does anthropology in the un-exotic western imperialist countries change with? Mr Freedman does not say. But some others do, for instance, the anthropologist Charles Wagley, writing under the sponsorship of the US Social Science Research Council:

> Latin America has also been neglected by our scholars who in the end must provide the basic data for academic and public consumption. As much as Africa, Latin America has been in many ways a 'dark continent'. The situation is now changing. There is new public interest in Latin America and Africa and Asia stimulated by a realization of its importance to our own national interests. The National Defense Education Act supports the study. . . . Private foundations have supported research.[10]

How exotic an interest of anthropology and social science in 'the performance of their role in world scholarship'! In the 'political situation' of neo-colonialism, as distinct from the colonialism of the old days, power is increasingly wielded through the 'modernizing', 'national' bourgeoisie of the 'new' countries. No wonder that Freedman observes and applauds that:

> the old bias in anthropology towards the study of the rural and powerless is now being corrected, and work is undertaken on elites and politicians as well as those they lead. Leadership and power in the Third World rest with social groups that are at once indigenous and in a number of cases alienated from those over which they preside. The models they adopt for economic development are sometimes borrowed wholesale from inappropriate contexts . . . (p. 113).

God forbid that we 'operate with simple notions of social class and class exploitation'. Now those once exotic natives, or at least the 'elites and politicians' which 'preside' over them, are adopting bourgeois models of 'modernization', including, no doubt, the impoverished schemes offered by Freedman and Co. And anthropologists are hurrying to study the process of 'diffusion', 'acculturation' and 'modernization' while it lasts. What makes Mr Freedman think that neo-colonial anthropology is not likely to make the 'mistakes' that colonial anthropology made?[11]

To what extent have anthropologists in the neo-colonial, mis-named third world freed themselves and anthropology from this heritage? The very self-appraisal of Warman et al and the programme of the Barbados symposium, which Freedman cites (pp. 115, 118) suggest, as other evidence in the 'field' confirms, that progress in this direction has been less than good, and that in 'new', that is neo-colonial, countries anthropology and anthropologists are not all as innocent as Freedman would like to make them out to be. The piper payer still calls the tune, and 'indigenous' neo-colonial anthropology still needs to be de-(neo)-colonialized.[12] And 'indigenous' applied anthropology remains the instrument of neo- and internal-colonial 'indigenous' 'community development' policy designed to 'integrate' those lost tribes and communities more efficiently into the class exploitation, the analysis of which—not to say struggle against—Freedman warns us of. Here too applied anthropology is political, but not because of its admittedly impoverished theoretical base.[13] Thus, the disjunction between the 'classical' anthropology of the old days and the 'new' one of up-to-date-ness which Mr Freedman makes (chapter 1 and elsewhere) is also about as spurious as his 'theoretical' disjunctions.

Finally, Freedman wishes to prophesy the future of anthropology; and, he adds, to prophesy is in some measure to dictate. Perhaps. But on what basis does he prophesy, to what end does he dictate?

> In a few years it [anthropology] may need to incorporate more grandiose schemes for remedying the world's ills and internationalizing its peoples. . . . That is to say, there is just perceptible the beginning of a trend to try to make of anthropology a healer of the large-scale ills that particularly strike the sensibilities of the young: war, racialism, environmental pollution, poverty, sexual inequality (pp. 117-8).

True to Freedman and Co.'s ideological form, the 'simple notions of social class and class exploitation or, as in some forms of neo-Marxism, [the] equally rudimentary concepts of power and dominance', not to mention imperialism and neo-colonialism, against which Mr Freedman warned us on page 115, are conspicuous by their absence in his list of 'large-scale ills' of the world two pages later. What is it that Mr Freedman wishes to dictate through his prophecy? Answer: that anthropology assume part of the ideological task of stilling or numbing the sensibilities of the young, and if it cannot achieve so much, that it at least ideologically re-direct their sensibilities from those dangerous rudimentary Marxist concepts and their contents to those he lists by offering grandiose schemes for internationalizing peoples! Good Luck!

But if 'all anthropology changes with the world in which it is practised' and if 'the politics of . . . [the] situation leaves the future of its anthropology in doubt' not only China, but, scientifically instead of ideologically speaking, in all the world, both prophecy and diction of the future will require less impoverished schemes and less rudimentary concepts than the crystal ball employed by Mr Freedman. We would have to inquire, instead, what the historical, if not the evolutionary, process is and what it holds in store for the world and its several parts. For that task, of course, Mr Freedman's rudimentary concept of history is more than impoverished. We would have to inquire into the historical process of capital accumulation in the world as a whole and in the various parts, exotic and not, that capitalist development has incorporated into that process. Then we might find, perhaps, that since the late 1960s the world has been in the throes of a crisis of accumulation analogous to that of 1873-95, which ushered in the classical imperialist colonialism that anthropologists then did so much to defend, and analogous to that of the 1930s which ushered in the era of neo-imperialist neo-colonialism, which anthropologists have been so intent to disguise, and which is likely to undergo profound structural changes in the wake of this capital and capitalist crisis. This crisis may engender a capitalist world economic depression and political crisis of which the 'dollar' or 'financial' crisis is only the incipient monetary reflection and of which Nixon's talks with Brezhnev and Mao are only the incipient international political manifestations of the new multipolarity cum re-enforcement of economic bloc politics, as in previous major depressions. We might find that the imperialist countries are destined by this economic crisis to pass through successive phases, from 1 to n, of attempts to raise again the rate of profit and real investment (which have fallen in all of them since 1966) by weakening union power or militancy, increasing unemployment and depressing the wage rate, first through social democratic 'openings to the left', and when these fail, through refurbished and neo-fascist remedies reminiscent of the 1930s, while at the same time pressing for sub-imperialist and militarist regimes and neo-fascist policies, economic blocs and 'Honduras-Salvador,' 'India-Pakistan' type wars in the neo-colonial world, whose super-exploitation is similarly destined to improve the falling rate of profit in the imperialist world.

In such a depression generated acceleration in the transformation of the international and national division of labour and the concomitant political struggle between neo-fascism/corporativism, neo-social democracy and new socialist revolution, what new ideological roles if any will the contending forces assign to anthropology and what political ones to applied anthropology? That is the question.

Of course, both neo-fascist and neo-social democratic forces, nationally and internationally, will wish to harness anthropology and anthropologists, along with others, to the tasks of ideologically mystifying the young and also themselves, just as in the old days. To this end, Mr Freedman and Co., in a remarkable show of international co-operation, have already shown us an early sample of the goods to be delivered.

But will anthropology be assigned, and will anthropologists assume specific new ideological functions in the imperialist and neo-colonial countries? What new analogues may we expect to the white man's burden of the old days and to the cultural relativism of more recent ones? What scientific sanctification and ideological justification for neo-fascist or social democratic corporativism in the imperialist and neo-colonialist countries? What domestic political application of anthropology to help replace defunct incomes policies and reduced welfare payments by new versions of CCC camps, *Eintopfgerichte, Kraft durch Freude* and other programmes for the young, ethnic, racial, foreign and domestic migrant, and ghetto dweller unemployed in a new holy 'war against poverty' in industrialized capitalist countries? What scientific sanctification for 'zero-growth' environmentalism to depress wages in the industrialized and to control industrialization in the underdeveloping countries. What new jingoist covers for international economic blocs and wars? What scientific sanction and ideological justification to extend capitalist development through the advance of 'green' revolution instead of 'red'? And what anthropological ideology and political application of anthropology may the revolutionary forces expect and deliver? Or will such a world political crisis render anthropology and anthropologists, not so much too much of a non-functional luxury, as too little of a functional utility to preserve?

REFERENCES

1. Written for the IXth International Congress of Anthropological and Ethnological Sciences, Chicago, September 1973, at the invitation of its President, Sol Tax.
2. Irving M. Zeitlin, *Ideology and the Development of Sociological Theory* (Englewood Cliffs, 1968), p. vii.

3. Marvin Harris, 'The Rise of Anthropological Theory,' *Current Anthropology* (Vol. 9, no. 5, December 1968), p. 520.

4. See *Current Anthropology* (Vol. 9, no. 4, October 1968).

5. Robert Murphy, *The Dialectics of Social Life: Alarms and Excusions in Anthropological Theory* (New York, 1971).

6. See Kathleen Gough Aberle, 'New Proposals for Anthropologists,' published in modified form as 'Anthropology: World Revolution and the Science of Man,' in Theodore Roszak (ed.) *The Dissenting Academy* (New York, 1967); and 'Anthropology: Child of Imperialism' *Monthly Review* (Vol. 19, no. 11, 12–27). Marvin Harris, *The Rise of Anthropological Theory* (New York, 1968). Dell Hymes, *Reinventing Anthropology* (New York, 1969–72).

7. Quoted and analysed by James Faris, 'Pax Britannica and the Sudan: S.F. Nadel in Theory and Practice', paper prepared for the conference on Anthropology and the Colonial Encounter, University of Hull, England, 1972, (mimeo).

8. Eric Wolf and J. Jorgensen, in *New York Review of Books*, Nov. 19, 1970.

9. Marvin Harris, 'The Rise of Anthropological Theory,' op.cit.

10. Charles Wagley (ed.), *Social Sciences Research in Latin America* (New York, 1964), Introduction.

11. For evidence that it continues to do so see, for instance, Bernard Magubane, 'Pluralism and Conflict Situation in Africa: a New Look,' *African Social Research* (Vol. 7, 1969) and 'A Critical Look at Indices used in the Study of Social Change in Colonial Africa,' *Current Anthropology* (Vol. 12, no. 4-5, 1971); and Andre Gunder Frank, 'The Sociology of Development and the Underdevelopment of Sociology,' *Catalyst* (No. 3, Summer 1967), reprinted in A.G. Frank, *Latin America: Underdevelopment or revolution* (New York, 1969), and elsewhere.

12. Rodolfo Stavenhagen, 'De-Colonialising Applied Anthropology,' *Human Organization* (Vol. 30, no. 4, 1971).

13. Ibid.

6

On Theoretical Issues
in Economic Anthropology

Santiago, Chile, 15 v 69

A medieval curse on both your houses (the substantivist one inhabited by Dalton plus eight of his commentators and the formalist one occupied by four of the latter [CA 10:63-102]) for continuing to debate how many angels can dance on the head of a pin or—to seem more advanced—on the moon. It is of less than credit to these protagonists who claim to study man, *anthropos,* and his home, *oikos,* to contest a race between astronauts and cosmonauts to a planet where no one lives, no matter who wins. No more credit is due the eight commentators who do not express a clear preference for either of the above celestial houses, but also do not dedicate their commentary to the construction of a theoretical house consummate with man's terrestial habitat.

If, as Dalton claims, economic anthropologists are increasingly concerned with socioeconomic change and its promotion, then they must—and he should let them—come down to earth and study its homely reality. Yet only four of the 24 comments evoked by Dalton even refer to this reality and the real issues it poses, and some of these refer

Current Anthropology, Chicago, Vol. 11, No. 1, February 1970, published by the University of Chicago Press.

only in passing from one of Dalton's nonissues to another. These lines, which did not reach the editor in time for inclusion among the comments on Dalton's article, remain in their original formulation, except for the addition of a few phrases placed in parentheses. Nevertheless, they serve equally as 'discussion and criticism' of Dalton's article and of all the comments, with the exception of those by Blacking, Frankenberg, Riegelhaupt, and especially Kowalewski, who made some effort at earthly realism in their discussion of the theoretical issues posed by the reality of *anthropos's oikos*.

The intensified disputes stimulated, as Dalton says, by Polanyi and others' publication of *Trade and Market in the Early Empires* in 1957, were perhaps justified in 1959. In that year I took the initiative (which I have lamented ever since) to organize such a discussion which was reported in *Current Anthropology* (1:149–50). But if that and the ensuing discussion were justified at all, it was so only to bring home two obvious facts, both recognized by Dalton, Polanyi's disciple, himself. These facts were (CA 10:79, 65) that

> Polanyi's theoretical categories are addressed principally, but not exclusively, to the organization of primitive and archaic [early] economies under static conditions... and that he did not analyse... change, growth and development...

and that among his opponents reliance was on

> the leading ideas of elementary economics (Samuelson 1967: Chaps. 1–3) as a guide to analysing all economies.

Samuelson himself aptly demonstrates the uses to which this application of 'the leading ideas of elementary economics' to 'all economies' are put. He asks (1958: 754–58):

> Why worry especially about the problems of underdeveloped countries? We can list a number of reasons, all vital. (1) Widening differentials. ... Many authorities believe that living standards in India, Indonesia, and certain other underdeveloped countries have actually deteriorated. ... (2) Ideological struggle. In the modern ideological war between the free and communist worlds. ... (3) Great expectations. ... (4) Desired markets. ... (5) Need to avert slump by economic imperialism? ... we never have to buy prosperity by throwing goods abroad. (6) Exploitation of colonial peoples? ... the evidence tells against this notion. ... (7) Plain altruism. ... The key to development rests in the four fundamental factors: population, natural resources, capital formation and technology.

For this professor at the Massachusetts Institute of Technology, who authored the most widely used introductory economics text of the capitalist world, who writes a column in the American business magazine *Newsweek*, and who was offered (but refused) the chairmanship of the President's Council of Economic Advisers, neither economic nor social structure, not to mention political structure, offers a key. He does think, however (p. 771), that

> the increasing political self-consciousness of such [underdeveloped] countries, plus the eagerness of the communist ideology to help them 'skip the capitalistic stage of development,' reinforces our own self-interest in finding new sources of mutually advantageous trade—not, mind you, new objects for imperialistic make work programs.

To continue today this sterile debate between the methods of the irrelevant on the one side and of the self-interested on the other, and to add to it as Dalton (and most of his commentators) do, only confirms Gough's contention (CA 9:406) that

> much of [post-war American writing in applied anthropology and in economic and political anthropology concerned with development] springs from erroneous or doubtful assumptions and theories that are being increasingly challenged by social scientists in the new nations themselves.

Gough goes on to list seven such assumptions, and has been sharply criticized by some of her commentators for doing so. Dalton recognizes 'relatively few theoretical insights and conceptual categories with which to analyse socio-economic change' and names only the contributions of Myrdal, Hagen, Smelser, and Adelman and Morris. But in doing so Dalton (and his co-debatants, since only one of the four 'formalists' writes from the U.S.) further confirm Gough's claim (p. 406) that

> a large number of studies, indeed a whole literature, on Western imperialism . . . tend in America to be either ignored or reviewed cursorily and then dismissed. They rarely appear in standard anthropological bibliographies.

Gough listed 15 examples. One might also add the following contributors to 'theoretical issues in economic anthropology,' many of whom are from the 'new' nations: Amin (1965, 1966, 1967), Dike (1957), Davidson (1961, 1964), Suret-Canale (1961*a, b,* 1964), Afana (1966), Rodinson (1966), and Issawi (1961), all on Africa; Dutt (1955), Thorner and

Thorner (1962), Thorner (1964), Mukherjee (1955), Sen (1962), and Singh (1964), on India; and Furtado (1965), Gibson (1964), Guerra y Sanchez (1964), Bagú (1949), and Prado Junior (1961, 1962) on Latin America.

Most of these authors (only some of whose works are listed here) are historians and economists. Their contributions are perhaps off limits to Dalton and his 'economic anthropologists.' If so, however, the limitations of Dalton and his followers and—as I shall maintain below—their total misstatement of the real theoretical issues in economic anthropology are all the more indefensible inasmuch as the past decade has happily seen a host of anthropologists and sociologists make major contributions to clarifying the real issues. One might mention only Wertheim (1959, 1964), Geertz (1966), Kosambi (1956), and Desai (1959a, b) for Asia; Verhagen (1964), Barnett and Njama (1966), Ziegler (1964), Laroui (1967), Abdel-Malek (1968), and Diop (1964) for Africa; or Wolf (1959), Stavenhagen (1965, 1968, 1969), González Casanova (1965a, b), Cardoso and Faletto (1967), Cardoso (1968), Quijano (1967, 1968), and Marroquin (1957) for Latin America. Yet none of these contributions seems to have made any impact on Dalton and his co-debatants (with the honorable exception of Kowalewski), for they go unnamed or—what is worse—if named, like Geertz and Wolf, unappreciated. That this is not a simple omission to conserve space is clear, since Dalton fails to appreciate even the contribution of his own study of 'growth without development' in Liberia (Clower, Dalton, *et al.* 1966) to the real-life issues on this planet.

These real contemporary issues for economic anthropologists are the ones to which Gough and the authors cited here and by her have drawn attention, even if they have not yet exhaustively analysed them. The central fact is that the worldwide historical expansion of mercantile, industrial, and monopoly capitalism brought all humanity on this particular globe into a *single* social system. This system has always functioned, and still functions, so as to generate socioeconomic development for the few while simultaneously causing degenerative change without development for the many. This occurs irrespective of whether the 'many' previously enjoyed civilizations, as in the early empires of China, India, Ghana, the Aztecs, the Incas, etc., or 'primitive' cultures in parts of the same continents. In all cases the majority of these peoples has been converted into peasants, proletarians, lumpenproletarians or lumpen-bourgeois in the name of 'the white man's burden.' This process involved more than the destruction or restructuring of their economies, although not even that is recognized on either side of the debate. It also involved the destruction or drastic restructuring of their politics, cultures, and psyches. Therefore, this system, which was worldwide until some peoples began to escape from it through socialist revolution, is less aptly denoted by Samuelson's term 'world market' or Polanyi's term 'early empire' than by the term used by the adversely affected people themselves: 'imperialism.'

Rather than face the real theoretical issues raised by the existence of imperialism and the problems of war, starvation, racism, alienation, and genocide which attend its continuance, these scholastics in general and Dalton in particular raise a whole series of false issues. Thus Dalton asserts that the matter of the size of the economy to be studied is a 'semantic' difficulty. On the contrary, as Gough has demonstrated in her CA article, and as the reactions of Beals (CA 9:407–8) and others of her critics make clear, the problem is empirical, theoretical, and ideological. It is empirical because the size of the determining and therefore most relevant social system—imperialism—is lamentably very large and quite objectively determined. The problem is theoretical in that—as Gough stresses (but at least 20 of Dalton's commentators fail to see)— we need a theoretical framework that is adequate for encompassing the size and complexity of the system, and therefore suitable for guiding our enquiry into how any particular peasant or other communities fit into the larger system and how it can liberate itself from that system. The problem is also, finally, ideological, in that these critics of Gough and practitioners of celestial economic anthropology, be they pious or liberal, steadfastly refuse to face the reality of the existence of the imperialist system because their ideological and political interests prevent them from doing so.

Dalton speaks of thousands of economies (and most of the debatants on *both* sides agree), whereas in fact he is confronted by only thousands of parts of a single economy. Dalton would have us compare the similarities and differences between these 'thousands' of economies, and particularly the differences between primitive and peasant economies and between both of them and 'our own.' Yet the real issue for economic anthropologists is to follow the lead of the above-cited authors by analysing the connecting ties between 'our' economy and 'theirs' and by enquiring into the consequences of these ties for their cherished primitive and peasant peoples. Dalton cites the anthropologist Eric Wolf on *Peasants* in general, but has he read Wolf's analyses of particular peasant societies? Wolf writes (1959: 176, 195, 199, 211, 213–14):

> The Indian before the Spanish conquest had been a cultivator, a seed-planter. . . . The Spanish colonist, however, labored for different ends. He wanted to convert wealth and labor into saleable goods—into gold and silver, hides and wool, wheat and sugar-cane.

... The motor of this capitalism was mining. ... All claims to Utopia—economic, religious, or political—rested ultimately upon the management and control of but one resource: the indigenous population of the colony. The conquerors wanted Indian labor, the crown Indian subjects, the friars Indian souls. ... Between 1519 and 1650, six-sevenths of the population of Middle America was wiped out: only a seventh remained to turn the wheels of paradise ... the Conquest not only destroyed people physically; it also rent asunder the accustomed fabric of their lives and the pattern of motives that animated that life. ... The growth of capitalism in New Spain did not produce a greater measure of liberty and freedom for the laborer; instead it sharpened exploitation and increased bondage. ... Stripped of their elite and urban components, the Indians were relegated to the countryside. Thus the Indians suffered not only exploitation and biological collapse but also deculturation—cultural loss—and in the course of such ill use lost also the feeling of belonging to a social order which made such poor use of its human resources. They became strangers in it, divided from its purposes and agents by an abyss of distrust. The new society could command their labor, but it could not command their loyalty. Nor has this gulf been healed in the course of time.

Instead, the spread of the worldwide capitalist system has created and re-created this gulf again the world over. It seems incredible then, that Dalton should approvingly cite Deane (1953: 115–16) to the effect that

the market place seems remote, on the face of it, from the problems of the African village where most individuals spend the greater part of their lives in satisfying their own or their families' needs and desires, where money and trade play a subordinate role in motivatting productive activity

in reference to, of all places, Rhodesia (and it is strange that Frankenberg, writing from Zambia, should fail to rebuff him).

Yet Woddis (1962: 22), quoting *The Times Educational Supplement* (March 6, 1959, p. 388), says in contrast,

a recent traveller in Northern Rhodesia says: "I went into many villages in Northern Rhodesia hundreds of miles away from the Copper Belt where only old men and women were living. All the able-bodied men ... were off to the mine. ..." Thus food production has been left mainly in the hands of women, children and elderly men. ...

The *Keiskammahoek Rural Survey* (cited in Woddis 1962:26) reports further:

> The people of this district are seen to be dependent upon the earnings of emigrants for their very existence, and it is poverty which forces them out to work. But this very exodus is itself a potent cause of the perpetuation of the poverty at home, for the absence of so many in the prime of life inhibits economic progress and certainly accounts in no small measure for the low agricultural productivity of the district. In many cases land is not ploughed for the simple reason that there is no one to do the ploughing. . . .

Woddis (1962:25) also says:

> They cannot produce enough food to support themselves, and so have to purchase considerable quantities which are imported into the district. This is paid for, says the survey, 'principally by the export of the large number of workers.' In fact, so dependent are the villagers on the earnings of the emigrant workers that it would be more accurate, says the survey, to say that the economy of the district rests 'firstly upon the fact that it is a reservoir of labour for the mines and industries of the Union, and secondly upon the subsistence farming of those that stay behind.'

In the meantime Portugal earns foreign exchange by exporting over half a million migrant laborers a year on a contract basis from Mozambique to South Africa.

Unabashed, Dalton goes still further. He would have us distinguish the local economy from that 'outside,' instead of relating the two in order to find out how the 'local' and the 'outside' parts determine each other. Dalton alleges that peasant communities have markedly little economic, cultural, or technical integration into the world around them and that conventional economics is relevant only to the commercialized sector of the economy, which he suggests is small. But this is simply the 'dual' economy or society thesis that Boeke (1942, 1946, 1953) invented to defend Dutch colonialism in Indonesia, a thesis which others the world over have since used as a figleaf to hide internal colonialism and its intimate connection with external colonialism or imperialism.

Dalton cites Geertz as an exception to those anthropologists who work on small 'economies,' but has he read him? Writing about the birthplace of the dual-society thesis, Geertz observes (1966: 60, 62, 142, 143, 82):

> Peasant agriculture became a functioning element in the Indies' export economy rather than merely its backstop; peasant agricul-

ture was developed, at least in part, into a business proposition rather than becoming frozen into a kind of outdoor relief. . . . The Dutch economy which was situated in the Indies ('tropical Holland,' as it was sometimes called), and, cheek by jowl, the autonomous Indonesian economy . . . interacted continuously in ways which fundamentally shaped their separate courses. They steadily diverged, largely as a result of this interaction, to the point where the structural contrasts became overwhelming. What Boeke regarded as an intrinsic and permanent characteristic of Indonesian (or 'Eastern') economic life, 'a primarily spiritual phenomenon,' was really an historically created condition; it grew not from the immutable essence of the Eastern soul as it encountered the incarnate spirit of Western dynamism, but from the in no way predestined shape of colonial policy as it impressed itself upon the traditional pattern of Indonesian agriculture. . . . The difference in 'economic mentality' between Dutch and Javanese which Boeke took to be the cause of the dualism was in fact in great part its result. . . . The Javanese did not become impoverished because they were 'static'; they became 'static' because they were impoverished. . . . Similar practices connected with other crops did not isolate the disequilibrating forces of commercial capitalism from village life; they introduced them, following the path the Company and Culture system had blazed, into the very heart of it. . . . The real tragedy of colonial history in Java after 1830 is not that the peasant suffered. . . . The tragedy is that he suffered for nothing. . . . But what makes this development tragic rather than decadent is that around 1830 the Javanese (and thus, the Indonesian) economy could have made the transition to modernism, never a painless experience, with more ease than it could today.

Halfway around the world, the Instituto Nacional Indigenista (National Indian Institute) of Mexico—staffed primarily by anthropologists—observes (1962:33–34, 27, 60, translation mine):[1]

The Indians, in reality, rarely live isolated from the *mestizo* or national population; there exists a symbiosis between the two groups which we must take into account. Between the *mestizos* who live in the nucleus city of the region and the Indians who live in the

---

[1]"Los indigenas, en realidad, rara vez viven aislados de la población mestiza o nacional; entre ambos grupos de población existe una simbiosis que es indispensable tomar en cuenta. Entre los mestizos, residentes en la ciudad núcleo de la región, y los indigenas, habitantes de hinterland campesino, hay, en verdad, una interdependencia económica y social más estrecha de lo que a primera vista pudiera aparecer. . . . La población mestiza, en efecto, radica casi siempre en una ciudad, centro de una región

agricultural hinterland there is in reality a closer economic and social interdependence than appears at first glance.... The *mestizo* population in fact almost always lives in a city which is the center of an intercultural region, which acts as a metropolis of an Indian zone, and which maintains an intimate connection with the under-developed communities which link the center with the satellite communities. [Our study found] the Indian or folk community was an interdependent part of a whole which functioned as a unit, so that the measures taken in one part inevitably had repercussions in the others and, in consequence, on the whole. It was not possible to consider the community separately; it was necessary to take account of the totality of the intercultural system of which it was a part.... That the large Indian mass should remain in its ancestral status of subordination, with a strongly stabilized folk culture, was not only desired but even coercively imposed by the city.... [It is in] Ciudad de las Casas ... that one sees with greatest emphasis the dominion which the *ladinos* exercise over economic and political resources and over property in general.

Recently, recurring scandalous reports in the capitalist world press, as well as in specialized journals such as *Indian Voices* (January, 1966) testify to the fact that the world's most 'isolated' and primitive Indians, those in the Amazon Basin of Brazil, many of whom 'civilization' has long since obliged to retreat into further 'isolation,' are by no means exempt from the same forces and consequences of world and national capitalism. In short, they are being deliberately exterminated.

Notwithstanding this and endless other evidence from all around the globe that Boeke's and all other dual society theses are empirically fallacious and theoretically indefensible, not to mention politically reactionary, commentators Cohen and van Emst (CA 10:82–83) expli-

---

intercultural, que actúa como metrópoli de una zona indígena y mantiene, con las comunidades subdesarrolladas, una íntima conexión que liga el centro con las comunidades satélites. [Nuestro estudio mostró] la comunidad indígena o folk era parte independiente de un todo que funcionaba como una unidad, en tal forma que las acciones ejercidas sobre una parte repercutían inevitablemente sobre las restantes y, en consecuencia, sobre el conjunto. No era posible considerar a la comunidad separadamente: había que tomar en cuenta en su totalidad, al sistema intercultural del cual formaba parte.... La permanencia de la gran masa india en su situación de ancestral subordinación, con el goce de una cultura folk fuertemente estabilizada, no sólo fue deseada por la ciudad, sino aún impuesta en forma coercitiva.... [Es en] Ciudad de Las Casas ... donde se ve con mayor énfasis el dominio que ejercen los ladinos sobre los medios económicos, políticos y de la propiedad en general."

citly refer to the thesis to give it their support. Grigor'ev (CA 10:85) goes so far as to invoke '*Marxist*' theory to write from *Leningrad*,—God is benevolent; he has spared both of the last named from noting as we must—that

> the theoretical issues posed by Dalton are acceptable from my point of view. . . . Dalton's delineation of the main features of primitive economy seems to me accurate. . . . Dalton's refinement of theoretical issues and definitions will be very helpful in the future concrete study of primitive economies.

On the contrary, it is not in Dalton's 'refinement,' but rather in the development of capitalism and imperialism that we must seek the cause and explanation for 'growth without development,' to use Dalton's felicitous terminology. By the thousands of local 'economies' in Mexico, Indonesia, or Liberia, the externally stimulated growth of the primary goods export sector condemns the majority of the people (whether they work directly in it or not) to a colonial and class structure that not only impedes development but generates underdevelopment. Yet all this hastens the development of those outside the underdeveloped world, and of a few intermediary junior partners inside. The im*plantation* of Firestone Rubber in Liberia, the colonization of the interior by the coast, and the resulting growth without development that Dalton studied is one classic case. But its significance for the real theoretical issues in economic anthropology everywhere in Asia, Africa, and Latin America seems to have escaped Dalton and other scientists who seem bent on studying a planet where the 'thousands of economies' have few, if any, economic, cultural, and technological links with 'our' world economy.

Dalton wants us to distinguish degenerative change, growth without development, and socioeconomic development among his thousands of economies. But it will never be possible to analyse the nature and causes of their differences if we do not first place each 'economy' in the context of the forces that have done so much to shape them all. For that reason, among others, the structure and development of the whole system becomes the first theoretical issue in economic anthropology and all social science. Although the professional division of labor may well assign the study of small social units to anthropologists—and Dalton correctly observes that these are what they *do* study—it does not exempt them from the scientific responsibility of studying these units in the context of the social whole that determines their most important characteristics. Dalton is also correct when, speaking for himself and others, he states that 'knowledge of our own economic system . . . should figure explicitly and importantly in economic anthropology.' Contrary to his claim, however, that knowledge is certainly not obtained by reading the first three or any other chapters of Samuelson.

We must commend Dalton for posing the important questions,

> What is the nature of the initial incursion which starts the processes
> of socio-economic change, and to what extent does the character of
> the initial incursion shape the sequential changes that follow?

and,

> empirically, how do small groups—the tribe, the village—become
> part of a regional or national economy?

But to find the answers Dalton and his colleagues (instead of pursuing their sterile polemics) will have to follow the lead of the anthropologists and sociologists cited above. Further, to the extent that

> among those anthropologists who write in English there is only an
> occasional borrowing of Marxist concepts (such as economic
> surplus)

as Dalton correctly points out, they would do well to make more extensive—and intensive—use of these. Indeed, even this small loan is quite misused. Following Marx, it is necessary for economic anthropologists to *really* study the surplus value expropriated from peasant and primitive peoples. Following Baran (1957), it is also necessary for them to understand how a portion of this surplus is sucked out of primitive and peasant communities by 'our' economy, and how the remaining surplus is misused as a result of the economic, social, political, and cultural structure that our economy has imposed on them in order to exploit them. Through such studies Dalton and his colleagues would discover the cause and significance of the growth without development he found in Liberia, as well as its long-run, fundamental similarities with (rather than differences from) the degenerative change that he laments. They would also have to conclude that substantial socioeconomic development is not possible for the vast bulk of humanity in underdeveloped regions so long as they live under 'our' economic system and employ the concepts of economic anthropology so far used by Dalton (and all but a couple of his commentators, irrespective of the spacious—or specious—polemic among them).

REPLY

by GEORGE DALTON

Evanston, Ill, U.S.A. 8 viii 69

Frank hates social science that does not serve to justify revolution. His comment is not on economic anthropology. It is bombastic denunciation of almost everyone who does not share his revolutionary rage. There is no point in responding further to writing so full of anger and ideology.

REFERENCES CITED

Abdel-Malek, Anouar. 1968. *Egypt: Military Society,* New York: Random House.

Afana, Osende. 1966. *L'économie de l'Ouest-Africain.* Paris: Maspero.

Amin, Samir. 1965. *Trois experiences africaines de développement.* Paris: Presses Universitaires de France.

————. 1966. *L'économie du Maghreb.* 2 vols. Paris: Editions Minuit.

————. 1967. *Le développement due capitalisme en Côte d'Ivoire.* Paris: Editions Minuit.

Bagu, Sergio. 1949. *Economia de la sociedad colonial: Ensayo de la historia comparada de América Latina.* Buenos Aires: El Ateneo.

Baran, Paul. 1957. *The political economy of growth.* New York: Monthly Review Press; London: Calder.

Barnett, Donald L., and Karari Njama. 1966. *Mau Mau from within.* New York: Monthly Review Press; London: McGibbon and Kee.

Boeke, J.H. 1942. *The structure of the Netherlands Indian economy.* New York: Institute of Pacific Relations.

————. 1946. *The evolution of the Netherlands Indies economy.* New York: Institute of Pacific Relations.

————. 1953. *Economics and economic policy of dual societies.* New York: Institute of Pacific Relations.

Cardoso, Fernando Henrique. 1968. *Cuestiones de sociologia del desarrollo en América Latina.* Santiago: Editorial Universitario.

Cardoso, Fernando Henrique, and Enzo Faletto. 1967. *Dependencia y desarrollo en América Latina.* (United Nations Latin American Institute of Economic and Social Planning, mimeographed.) Paris: Maspero. In press.

Clower, R., G. Dalton, M. Harwitz, and A.A. Walters. 1966. *Growth without development: An economic survey of Liberia.* Evanston: Northwestern University Press.

Davidson, Basil. 1961. *The African slave trade.* Boston: Atlantic, Little Brown.

———. 1964. *Which way Africa?* Harmondsworth: Penguin Books.

Deane, Phyllis, 1953. *Colonial social accounting,* Cambridge: Cambridge University Press.

Desai, A.R. 1959*a*. *Social background of Indian nationalism.* Bombay: Popular Book Depot.

———. Editor. 1959*b*. *Rural sociology in India.* Bombay: The Indian Society of Agricultural Economics.

Dike, K.O. 1957. *Trade and politics in the Niger delta 1830-1885.* Oxford: Oxford University Press.

Diop, M. 1964. *Classes et idéologies de classes au Sénégal.* La Habana.

Dutt, R. Palme. 1955. *India today.* Bombay: Asian Peoples Publishing House.

Furtado, Celso. 1965. *The economic growth of Brazil.* Berkeley: University of California Press.

Geertz, Clifford. 1966. *Agricultural involution: The process of ecological change in Indonesia.* Berkeley: University of California Press.

Gibson, Charles. 1964. *The Aztecs under Spanish rule: A history of the Indians of the Valley of Mexico 1519–1810.* Stanford: Stanford University Press.

Gonzalez Casanova, Pablo. 1965*a*. *Internal colonialism and national development.* Studies in Comparative International Development 1 (4).

———. 1965*b*. *La democracia en México.* Mexico: Era.

Guerra y Sanchez, Ramiro. 1964. *Sugar and society in the Caribbean.* New Haven: Yale University Press.

Instituto Nacional Indigenista. 1962. *Los centros coordinadores indigenistas.* Mexico: Instituto Nacional Indigenista.

Issawi, Charles. 1961. Egypt since 1800: A study in lop-sided development. *The Journal of Economic History* 21 (1).

Kosambi, D.D. 1956. *An introduction to the study of Indian history.* Bombay: Popular Book Depot.

Laroui, Abdallah. 1967. *L'idéologie arabe contemporaine.* Paris: Maspero.

Marroquin, Alejandro. 1957. *La ciudad mercado (Tlaxiaco).* Mexico: Universidad Nacional Autónoma de México.

Mukherjee, Ramkrishna. 1955. *The rise and fall of the East India Company.* Berlin: VEB Deutscher Verlag der Wissenschaften.

Prado Junior, Caio. 1961. *Formação do Brasil contemporaneo (Colonia).* São Paulo: Editõra Brasiliense. (To be published in English by University of California Press.)

————. 1962. *Historia económica do Brasil.* São Paulo: Editora Brasiliense.

Quijano, Anibal. 1967. 'Contemporary peasant movements,' in *Elites in Latin America.* Edited by S.M. Lipset and A. Solari. New York: Oxford University Press.

————. 1968. 'Tendencies in Peruvian development and class structure,' in *Latin America: Reform or revolution?* Edited by J. Petras and M. Zeitlin. Greenwich: Fawcett Publications.

Rodinson, Maxime. 1966. *Islam et capitalisme.* Paris: Editions due Seuil.

Samuelson, Paul A. 1958. 4th edition. *Economics: An introductory analysis.* New York: McGraw-Hill.

Sen, Bhowani. 1962. *Evolution of agrarian relations in India.* New Delhi: Peoples Publishing House.

Singh, V.B. 1964. *Indian economy yesterday and today.* New Delhi: Peoples Publishing House.

Stavenhagen, Rodolto. 1965. *Classes, colonialism, and acculturation: Essay on a system of inter-ethnic relations in Mesoamerica.* Studies in Comparative International Development 1 (6).

————. 1968. 'Seven fallacies about Latin America,' in *Latin America: Reform or revolution?* Edited by J. Petras and M. Zeitlin. Greenwich: Fawcett Publications.

———. 1969. *Essai comparatif sur les classes sociales rurals et la stratification dans quelques pays sous-dévelloppés.* Paris: Editions Antropos.

Suret-Canale, Jean. 1961*a. Afrique noire occidentale et centrale: Géographie, civilisation, histoire.* Paris: Edition Sociales.

———. 1961*b. Histoire de l'Afrique occidentale.* Paris. Présence Africaine.

———. 1964. *Afrique noire occidentale et centrale: L'Ere coloniale (1900–1945).* Paris: Editions Sociales.

Thorner, Daniel. 1964. *Prospects for Indian agriculture.* Bombay: Asia Publishing House.

Thorner, Daniel and Alice Thorner. 1962. *Land and labour in India.* Bombay: Asia Publishing House.

Verhagen, Benoit. 1964. *Rébellion au Congo.* Bruxelles: CRISP.

Wertheim, W.F. 1959. 2nd revised edition. *Indonesian society in transition: A study of social change.* The Hague and Bandung: W. van Hoeve.

———. 1964. *East-West parallels.* The Hague: W. van Hoeve.

Woddis, Jack, 1962. *Africa. The roots of revolt.* New York: The Citadel Press.

Wolf, Eric. 1959. *Sons of the shaking earth.* Chicago: University of Chicago Press.

Ziegler, Jean. 1964. *Sociologie de la Nouvelle Afrique.* Paris: Editions Gallimards.

More on Issues in Economic Anthropology

by Andre Gunder Frank

Santiago, Chile. 20 II 70.

The scientific standards to which *Current Anthropology* has accustomed its readers hardly admit the personal likes, hates, or anger of any particular individual, whoever he may be, as suitable criteria of scientific inquiry or discourse. CA's international audience cannot, therefore, but expect that so world-renowned a scientific authority as Dalton, in his response (CA 11:70) to my comment on his paper, is also presenting his readers with the evidence that he has at his disposal and to which they are entitled. Is Dalton, then, asking the readers of CA to accept ad hominem arguments from his own ideology as sufficient circumstantial evidence that the empirical evidence I have presented cannot be refuted on scientific grounds?

by Dell Hymes

Philadelphia, Pa., U.S.A. 30 IV 70

The rage Dalton attributes to Frank (CA 11:70) may be real, and certainly would be justified, but it is beside the point. Dalton confesses himself unable to answer Frank's *arguments*.

7

On "Feudal" Modes, Models and Methods of Escaping Capitalist Reality

"The important point is that their incorrectness or otherwise [of questions and answers] can only be demonstrated by a much more intensive and rigorous application of the Marxist method to the concrete and historically specific experience of India itself. The incorrectness or otherwise of our ideas cannot be demonstrated simply by selective quotations lifted out of context from Marx and Lenin, when they are discussing a different set of historical conditions; or by vague charges that these ideas are against 'the spirit of Marxism.' We would welcome the sharpest criticism, for it helps to clarify ideas; but let that criticism be based on an application of the Marxist method to the concrete conditions under discussion . . . All we are arguing is that wage labour in Indian agriculture went with the accumulation of colonial super-profits by the bourgeoisie in Britain . . . it would show a very mechanistic understanding of the proposition 'wage labour and capital always go together,' if we completely ignored imperialism (i.e., its character as a world capitalist system) and hence ignored the specificity of the colonial situation. Above all we need to analyse the concrete developments in colonial history, rather than take over in an

Economic and Political Weekly (Bombay), Vol. VIII, No. 1, January 6, 1973.

abstract and schematic fashion, the propositions of the classical model."

An admirable model indeed, perhaps in part because Utsa Patnaik (September 30, 1972, pp A-149, A-150) has taken it over from Marx and Lenin. But the model is entirely belied by the method of UP (with apologies for use of initials). So that UP shall not have used my name entirely in vain, and since UP calls for the development of an ongoing debate with Paresh Chattopadhyay and Amiya Bagchi (p A-150), presumably among others, we may perhaps be permitted to make public here a personal letter I wrote to these two on May 29, 1972.

"Another curiosity: Of the critiques you [PC] make of Utsa Patnaik's article — which latter caught my attention because of its far out definition of 'capitalism' in agriculture — I find, unless I misread you, that you did not make the critique that struck me and a colleague of mine to whom I read part of the UP article as the most obvious: to say that extended reproduction and accumulation is a criterion of capitalism is one thing and to say that because the surplus is not invested in agriculture itself, or not in agriculture in the same geographical area, but is instead siphoned off for investment in industry, not to say industry in Great Britain, is another thing altogether. The fact that the British industrialised with the help of the drain — which was of course drained out of agriculture in India in large part — does not seem to me to be useable proof as UP seeks to do that Indian agriculture is feudal (or was)." PC's answer on July 3, 1972 (with further apologies for quoting private correspondence) was: "About U Patnaik's paper what you say is very true. My point was however somewhat different, I tried to show that what she thought to be the conditions of capitalism were really not so much *conditions* as *consequences* of capitalism, once the latter is established. This followed from my contention, that Lenin's definition of capitalism — on the basis of *productive relation* — is a complete definition, containing the necessary as well as the sufficient conditions of capitalism." (In this connection, incidentally, one may find particularly unsatisfactory UP's straw man method of setting PC up as someone who "appears to be" an Althusserian and then expressing "surprise" at his analyses and conclusions — as any of us might after reading his various concrete analyses of concrete conditions.) But our points *are* different, or at least point to a different aspect of UP's argument. However, although after UP's earlier presentation of her argument it seemed sufficient to make the point privately, now that in her reply UP has herself carried the argument (or carried herself) "to its logical extreme conclusion" (*sic!* p A-149), it seems necessary to make the obvious point publicly.

UP repeats her allusion to the Marxist model: "The criterion of accumulation and reinvestment must be specified as well" (p A-148). And her method? Her concrete analysis of concrete reality? What reality? What economic formation? Up answers concretely: "I submit that if we wish to retain 'capitalist production relation' as an analytical category, as it has been used so far in Marxist theory, a category which implies something about the laws of movement or dynamics of the economic formation concerned, then we cannot take wage-labour to be *sufficient* condition for identifying the capitalist FARM, under the specific historical conditions we have outlined" (p A-148 italics in the original, capitals supplied). So now UP has specified the economic formation with which she is concerned: the FARM! And not accidentally so: "Of course, if we are interested in using the term 'capitalist production relation' or 'capitalist farm' as ... a 'capitalist' enterprise ... (p A-148) we may as well, as UP evidently does not in the selection of her title but as appears from the whole context of her argument, make these terms — and the concrete economic formation to which they refer — equivalent also to the "mode of production." UP looks for the criterion of the mode of production on the individual farm! That is a point of view far more extreme (we may leave the question of logic in abeyance) than that which I had dared attribute to her in my letter to PC and AB in which I innocently supposed that the purview of UP extended as far as "agriculture itself, or ... agriculture in the same geographical area" in India. No wonder, if the UP method is to "extend" the criterion of extended reproduction, accumulation and re-investment of them each of the impoverished farms in India, that she is hard put to recognise the capitalist mode of production when she sees it. And she does *see* it: "We find that generalised commodity production was *imposed* from the outside in the process of imperialist exploitation itself: India was forced to enter the network of world capitalist exchange relations" (pp A-148-149). (Didn't we just say that capitalist relations are by definition *productive* relations, and indeed reproductive ones?) But UP cannot believe what she sees — and we cannot believe what she writes. All we are arguing is that "wage labour in Indian agriculture [including the UP farm — with apologies to the state that shares the initials, though its farms may be included as well] went with the *accumulation* of colonial super-profits by the bourgeoisie in Britain (as a result of the complex exploitative relationship ...)" and that there is madness (i.e., divorce from concrete reality) in the method of UP that seeks accumulation and reproduction only within the confines of the individual farm. "If this is the argument we would reject it emphatically. At worst such an argument would completely ignore imperialism, at best it would represent a highly unrigorous application of Marxist concepts to Indian conditions" (p A-149). Amen!*

---

*UP *rightly* also draws or points to some political conclusions: "The Andre Gunder Frank type of position. . . . Therefore all these countries are 'capitalist.' Therefore the only possible immediate programme of a revolutionary political party in each of these countries, must be a socialist revolution. . . . I am sure PC will not choose to draw the extreme conclusion which Gunder Frank has done . . . believe the fallacy in this chain of reasoning lies at its starting point." Well, what conclusions will UP choose to draw from her other extreme method? That socialist revolution will not become the programmatic order of the day until capitalism by her criterion reinvestment of surplus value produced by farm labourer on the same farm itself — has penetrated each and every one of her individual farms? If this is the argument we should reject it emphatically. The fallacy of this chain of reasoning lies at its starting point.

8

Reflections on Green, Red and White Revolutions in India

Like the (mis)appropriation of the word itself, the green "revolution" is, of course, counter-revolutionary in intent. Cleaver's* invitation, to ponder why the high-yielding Borlaug was awarded the Nobel Prize for peace, was followed by some of us the day the prize was announced. Like other recipients of this bourgeois designation — such as ex-Prime Minister of Canada Lester Pearson for his work in the Middle-East crisis, West German Chancellor Willy Brandt for his "eastern" policy, the United Nations International Labour Organisation for its "harmonisation" of conflicting labour-management-government interests around the world — this award represents the bourgeoisie's reward to Borlaug and his followers' contributions or least intention to contain revolution through 'peace'.

Economic and Political Weekly (Bombay), Vol. VIII, No. 3, January 20, 1973.

*These reflections were inspired by Harry M. Cleaver, Jr, "The Contradictions of Green Revolution" and other contributions on the same in *Monthly Review*, Volume 24, Number 2, June 1972. Page references in the text are thereto unless otherwise noted. The intent of these reflections, made in August 1972, was to relate certain tendencies in the green and red revolutions to the apparent present day tendencies in the process of capital accumulation. A Postscript, written in November 1972, presents some evidence that seems to portend a trend towards a white fascist (counter) revolution.

Economically, the green "revolution," far from being revolutionary, should be regarded rather as the extension or expansion of business as usual. Like the technological "revolution" and agri-business in the metropolis of the imperialist system, the green revolution in the third world today is the contemporary manifestation of the process of capitalist development that was begun long ago. For his time and place, Lenin analysed it in his "The Development of Capitalism in Russia."

The apparently confusing contradictions of this process, as they emerge for instance in India, should come as no surprise and need not remain a mystery. For the Russian case of his time, Lenin analysed them particularly in Chapter 2, entitled 'The Differentiation of the Peasantry', of his study of the development of capitalism in agriculture. For Mexico, the counter-reform of the past three decades (after the land reform of the Cardenas regime in the 1930s) has been analysed by Eckstein[1] and by Stavenhagen, Paz, *et al.*[2] Reminiscent of the development of "second serfdom" in Eastern Europe, as analysed by Marx and Engels long ago and more recently by Kula, the differentiating and contradictory manifestations of (especially export) market induced plantation and latifundo development in many parts of Latin America, Africa, and Asia, have been the subject of innumerable revealing analyses. In India, the contemporary differentiation of the peasantry according to the rule, that to him that hath shall be given, from him that hath not shall be taken the little that he hath (not), is reflected almost weekly in the pages of the *Economic and Political Weekly* and particularly in its special numbers and reviews of agriculture.

Technically more intensive use of labour in the production of, or with, high-yielding varieties (HYV) which is heralded by its defenders and mentioned by M S Fatemi in *Monthly Review* (p 114) in combination with other factors of profit maximisation, far from mitigating it economically, is an important cause of the displacement of labour from land and its ownership as well as the relative and often absolute decline in real income for the most adversely affected — thereby contributing politically to the intensification of the class struggle in the countryside.

The public recognition of these "ironies" of green revolution and of capitalist development by Wolf Ladejinsky (see excellent and important article in *Concerned Asian Scholars Bulletin),*[3] writing in US Imperialism's oracle, *Foreign Affairs* and elsewhere,[4] as well as similar analysis by Clifton H Warton, Jr,[5] only testify to the bourgeoisie's increasing political alarm at the "green" Frankenstein they have unleashed on Asian soil.

The political projections of the revolution from green to red, which Cleaver and Meeropol made through Wolf's[6] and Alavi's[7] analysis of the role of middle and middling poor peasants, may be extended to two further circumstances. These authors, as well as Landsberger[8] and Huizer[9] in their analysis of Latin America experiences, have observed that the political mobilisation of middle peasants frequently occurs after they have been adversely affected by economic circumstances and the more so upon the actual or threatened loss of earlier economic gains. The natural development of the green revolution may be expected to generate just such effects in economic and political terms. At one stage, it displaces poor and lower middle peasants to the advantage of richer ones: and, upon the eventual arrival of an ecological debacle or economic recession, the previously favoured richer middle peasants may be faced with economic ruination as well. It is known, and recent events in India and Ceylon have again confirmed, that such peasants — not unlike urban members of the petit bourgeoisie — not only become potentially mobilisable by reformist and revolutionary movements but failing adequate political works by the latter often fall easy prey also to populist, fascist, and repressive movements of and to the Right.

The potential ecological dangers of the green revolution — extension as it is of the capitalist industrial and technological revolution — may be more than speculatively potential, even in India; the *Far Eastern Economic Review* (Hong Kong, June 17, 1972 p 17) thought "the other state currently in the grip of food shortages is West Bengal . . . West Bengal's problems centre on intensive drought, apparently the result of over-enthusiastic green revolution irrigation schemes which interfered with water levels in the ground and upset ecological balances."

Fatemi quotes Paul Baran to remind us; "whether there will be meat in the kitchen is never decided in the kitchen. Nor is the fate of agriculture in capitalism ever decided in agriculture. Economic, social, and political processes unfold outside of agriculture and in particular the accumulation of capital and the evolution of the capitalist class . . . become with the onset of capitalism the prime movers of historical development." To understand the green revolution and to foresee its consequences, particularly in India, we must further extend our analysis to this process. Three aspects of capitalist development *and capital accumulation*, particularly, warrant more attention in this connection than they have received.

(A) It has been observed in India (but strangely it is not reflected in the discussion under comment) that the green revolution was put into high gear *to replace* the increase in American food shipments under PL 480 when President Johnson imposed more stringent conditions for delivery, not only to achieve more political leverage abroad, but also in view of economically declining surpluses at home. Now Cleaver observes that foodgrain supplies are growing again in the industrialised countries. It is normal that political demands for agricultural price support and protection increase in years of recession such as those of the recent past and present (and future?), and that these occasion reduced domestic import demand and generate increased domestic and export supplies. Moreover, in peripheral central economies, such as Canada and particularly Australia, the process of world and national capital accumulation at this stage may well increase the balance-of-payments pressure to increase the export of certain mineral and agricultural raw materials in order to pay for high-level technological industrial imports. Much the same is all the more so the case in the sub-imperialist underdeveloped countries, although their experts do not seem at present to be particularly competitive with the green revolution elsewhere; and a similar process may be discernible in some Socialist economies. What do these trends harbour for the prospects of the green revolution in these poorer countries?

(B) As Cleaver observes, barring the production for export, the green revolution can only proceed on the output side as long as there is sufficient, growing, effective demand in the internal market to absorb increases in supply. In his analysis of the development of capitalism in Russia, Lenin argues in answer to the Narodniks that the very same differentiation of the peasantry itself was contributing to the development of the internal market and effective demand in Russia, as it had in the capitalist development of Western Europe earlier. But, these same circumstances are not necessarily reproduced in India and other underdeveloped countries today, as they were not earlier in the past. Indeed, a major reason for their present underdevelopment is precisely that in these colonial countries the industrial revolution did not effect the displacement of labour from agriculture to industry as it did in the metropolitan ones. Nor has import substituting industrialisation achieved this greater displacement of the internal market since then. The accumulating evidence suggests that the green revolution in agriculture alone, or even in combination with sub-imperialist industrialisation (excepting perhaps in such special cases as Singapore and Hong Kong), will also fail to generate its own effective demand and internal market development. (For a projection of this demand limitation in India, see Ranjit Sau.) [10]

(C) Perhaps most important and least considered in deciding the political economic state of countries in green revolution, and particularly of India, is the complex relation between the development of the green revolution in agriculture and the process of capital accumulation in industry. It has been widely observed that the green revolution is far from being limited to the development and use of high-yielding varieties of seed, in fact involves a far-reaching technological development and capital investment programme. But radicals, and even planners, seem not to have translated this recognition into an analysis of its relation to the process of capital accumulation as a whole — though perhaps some industrialists may privately have inquired into the demand that the green revolution may generate for their particular industry. No doubt, this is the case for domestic and especially multi-national producers of inorganic fertiliser, such as the American petroleum companies at whose instance the Texas President Johnson made food deliveries during the 1967 famine in India contingent on her simultaneous acceptance of green revolution and American fertiliser plants. But to what extent can, and will, the green revolution provide a market for industrial imports required as agricultural implements, storage and transportation facilities, materials required to construct irrigation systems and tube wells, motors to pump the water, etc? Or, perhaps more accurately, to put the question the other way around, to what extent can and will the green revolution offer and generate effective demand for the supply that industry, foreign and national, wishes to supply in the process of capital accumulation? Fatemi correctly implies (p 113, point 4) that the problem of industrial development is traditionally considered to be one of capital shortage, which agricultural and green revolutionary supplies help to alleviate. But if, contrary to the traditional view, it is also correct as the present writer and others consider that in terms of effective demand for its use in countries such as India and Mexico, capital is in *excessive* effective supply, then we may also ask to what extent the green revolution and its effective demand is an effect rather than a cause of industrial capitalist development and of the efforts of the Governments of India, Mexico, etc, to promote such development through appropriate policies that are in the interests of the industrial bourgeoisie which they represent far more than even the landowners who provide votes for the Congress Party. What other explanation is there for the recent refusal of the Minister of Agriculture to reduce the Indian support price for wheat which supports the green revolution in the Punjab, on the grounds that this price reduction to the benefit of consumers is also opposed by various ministers in the cabinet who represent interests that would be adversely affected by such a policy? Of course, this problem raises further questions about the present stage of the process of capital accumulation in these countries. At a certain stage of the process in Britain, for instance, it became important for the bourgeoisie to reduce the cost of wage goods, and the corn laws were finally abolished. But here, again, the generation of a much greater reserve army of labour in the underdeveloped countries today makes policies such as eliminating a support price of consumer staples may be much less necessary. Although Britain has been able to develop its textile industry by forcing India to absorb a significant part of its output, further industrial development required that workers in the internal market receive sufficient purchasing power and effective demand to buy an important part of the products they produced. During this century as well, in the process of import substitution of consumer goods in Brazil, Argentina, Mexico, and some other under-developed countries, it is necessary through appropriate distribution policies to provide part of the market for textiles and other light industrial goods among the workers who produce them. Perhaps in India the textile industry can continue to grow by replacing handicrafts and rural cottage industries on the one hand and catering to the new demand generated by enrichment of those sectors of the rural popula-tion who benefit from the green revolution. In the major Latin American countries, including green revolution Mexico, this growth possibility is all but exhausted. Profitable investment must flow into more advanced industries whose products, however, cannot significantly be bought by their own workers. Increasingly, not only capital investment but also the "consumer" effective demand for these industries must be generated or provided by the State. The results are the State capital absorbing investments, military procurement demands, and such sub-imperialist postures analysed in *Monthly Review* by Marini, who elsewhere has also observed the implications of the present stage of capital accumulation in Brazil for its government's nuclear development policy. [11] In relation to the capital absorbing investments of the green revolution as well as for its own sake, it is not amiss to inquire to what extent the process of capital accumulation in India is approaching a stage analogous, or similar, to that of Brazil. Ultimately, it will be necessary to take this inquiry much farther to appreciate and understand the economic potential of the green revolution and for revolutionaries to direct its political projections into the red one. The evidence is accumulating on many political economic fronts such that in this respect the comparison with Brazil is not so far-fetched. Although necessary, the pursuit of this inquiry would go far beyond these brief reflections, so that, perhaps suitably, we may conclude with the following reflection from the *Far Eastern Economic Review* (March 11, 1972, p 5).

"A serious reappraisal of India's nuclear policy is in motion . . . there is every possibility that India may at last decide to go for the Bomb."

POSTSCRIPT
(November 1972)

Since writing these reflections in early August 1972, I have had the opportunity to consult three sources, which confirm and extend certain parts of the argument that was explicit and implicit in these reflections. These sources are, "The Challenge of Our Opportunities," an editorial in *Eastern Economist* Annual Number 1972, New Delhi, December 31, 1971, mouthpiece of big capital in India; "Growth for the Few" and "South Asian Portents," editorials in *Economic and Political Weekly*, Special Number, Bombay, August 1972, and "From Euphoria to Panic" by a correspondent in the same number of *EPW*; and several numbers of the *Far Eastern Economic Review*, Hong Kong on the current debate in India on the whys and wherefores of building the atomic bomb. Drawing on these sources, we may briefly refer back to the following parts of our argument: (A) Capital accumulation and excess capital; Demand creation through (B) High income markets, (C) Public and military demand, (D) Sub-imperialism, and (E) the Political implications and prospects, all of which are related to the "Brazilian Model." Having posed these questions, the very titles of our sources offer only the most sombre premonitions. . . .

(A) Capital in India far from being in insufficient supply as theoretical orthodoxy would have it, is in fact in excess supply, as evidenced, among other things, by excess installed capacity. The *Eastern Economist* assures us, "an idea of the under-utilisation of capacity in the steel sector can be had from the fact that although we have nearly nine million tons of ingot capacity . . . total output last year was of the order of 6.11 million tonnes ingots. The production last year was even lower than what had been achieved in the previous year. . . . The story of tool, alloy and special steel is similar . . . An idea of the under-utilisation of capacity in the machine-building industry can be had from the following table.

	1969	1970
Number of industries utilising less than 50% capacity	34	36
Number of industries utilising less than 50 to 75% capacity	16	13
Number of industries utilising over 75% capacity	7	12

The capacity utilisation has been less than 50 per cent, particularly in such industries as woodworking machinery, cement machinery, vehicular type diesel engines, road rollers, structurals, cranes, railway wagons, transmission towers, steel castings, and steel pipes. If note is taken of the fact that, in most of the engineering industries, the capacity is calculated on one or two shift basis and not on three shift basis, the seriousness of the problem of under-utilisation should be much more than suggested by the above table . . . the production now estimated in 1973-74 in most industries falls short of the Fourth Plan anticipation by varying degrees. Among the reasons, other than raw material shortages, which are responsible for the expected shortfall in the engineering sector because of under-utilisation . . . the more important are: (1) the fall in demand for some products. . . . there are however several other machine-building industries the products of which are not being picked up due to tardy progress in the setting up of various consumer industries . . . " (pp 1135, 1146, 1147).

No wonder that the *Economic and Political Weekly* can confirm: "The lack of resources argument in reference to the private sector gets a knock on the head also from the fact that there seems to be no dearth of funds flowing into non-manufacturing sectors like urban real estate, commodity speculation, and a whole range of not-so-essential services. . . . An altogether impressive number of industrial units thus appear to thrive on a regime of below-capacity output, high prices and high unit margins. . . . In fact, even as capacity utilisation has remained low and the rate of growth of industrial output has declined, established units had had by and large highly satisfactory profitability experiences without, however, being impelled to expand output or to launch on fresh investments. The high-price-low-offtake phenomenon of green revolution wheat has innumerable parallels in industry. . . . The growth of industrial output has declined for the third year in succession — from 7.1 per cent in 1969 to 4.8 per cent in 1970, and to just 2.9 per cent in 1971. . . . The climate in New Delhi has undergone a sudden and disconcerting change in just two weeks. The euphoria is no more. Anxiety bordering on panic is writ large . . . dread of another drought and even famine. . . . Talk of a major economic crisis broke out as soon as Parliament began its session on August 1" (pp 1453, 1469).

(B) Where can new or additional demand be derived from? One sector is the upper income consumers: "Most of the industrial activity in the country is really relevant to, income-wise, the top 10 or 15 per cent of the population, if even that." (*EPW* 1453). The *Eastern Economist* observes that inadequate profitability for long spells has hampered the growth of such industries as cotton textiles and paper and board and adds, "it was only when controls over their prices were removed and the market mechanism was allowed to function, that increased investments were attracted to these consumer industries leading to increased production. . . . There is no immediate prospect of an early recovery in the case of cotton textiles . . . that the man-made fibre industry in our country has made spectacular progress during the past two decades, there is no doubt" (pp 1172, 1177). That is, price increases and reduced sales are profitable; so is the higher income synthetic textile market while most of the cotton textile market is not. Among the latter, high priced fine textiles find an increasing market, while coarse textile production does not grow. The policy implications are obvious and are no doubt being urged on the government. The political implications may be hazarded below.

(C) "The long-awaited upsurge of public sector investment in industry . . . remains pie in the sky. . . . Private industry will perk up only when investment in the public sector picks up" (*EPW* 1453). The *Eastern Economist* proudly reviews: "We have, indeed, progressed a great deal on the road to self-reliance in defence production. . . . Self-sufficiency in small arms was achieved about five years ago. . . . Much more significant and laudable achievements, of course, have been registered in the manufacture of tanks and aircraft. . . . The first MIG-21 produced from the raw materials stage, thus, was made available by this complex this year. Arrangements for the manufacture of an improved version MIG-21, called MIG-21M, have been completed. . . . Bangalore division is now engaged in the development of an advance strike aircraft. . . . A new factory is likely to be set up for the manufacture of helicopters. . . . As regards our naval forces . . . concerted action has been taken to establish facilities for their manufacture within the country. . . . Started the assembly of anti-tank missiles. . . . [and last but not least the *EE* observes with satisfaction] The defence forces buy substantial quantities of a large number of products from the civilian sector also" (1164-1168). The development and manufacture of the atomic bomb in India is not mentioned in this review, but it is increasingly discussed elsewhere in India.

(D) A related economic, political and military policy — and potential source of demand — is sub-imperialism. The *Eastern Economist* again proudly observes: "In some industries the progress has been phenomenal. One such industry is the engineering industry [the very same that is working at about 50 per cent capacity according to the *EE*]. . . . This industry has developed so much confidence that it is thinking in terms of exporting its products to the extent of as much as Rs 250 crores by the end of 1973-74 and to as high a figure as Rs 1,000 crores by 1980-81. To achieve this target of exports, it feels confident that with adequate governmental assistance forthcoming, it will be able to raise its total output to nearly Rs 7,000 crores in the next 10 years. . . . Our entering into some joint ventures in the African countries which have unexploited deposits of these [non-ferrous] metals should also be helpful. . . . Our engineering industries can also profitably participate in the rehabilitation of the recently freed [*sic!*] Bangladesh economy. . . . The producer goods industries, therefore, can look forward to better times" (*EE* 1131, 1145, 1149). The *Economic and Political Weekly* looks at the same "South Asian Portents" from another but complementary angle: "Now that the main danger to India, Pakistan, 'has been cut to size' . . . the rulers of the two countries are, perhaps, beginning to feel the need to develop bonds with each other which could prove useful in confronting popular movements. . . . the most vivid — and clear — sign of how overriding the 'maintenance of power' interest is, was demonstrated by the instant and crushing response by all and sundry ruling groups when the Sirimavo Government in Ceylon was gravely threatened by a serious popular youth movement in April last year. . . . In South Asia the most likely ground for this type of upheaval is Bangladesh. . . but the ingredients are also very much there in Sri Lanka [Ceylon] and Pakistan and also in India and Nepal . . . such movements are likely to attract the unfavourable attention of the Government of India . . . " (*EPW* 1454). Which makes the alternative of fascism and white terror doubly threatening in each of these countries. Not incidentally, at the time of writing, Indian troops are *still* stationed in Bangladesh!

(E) What are the domestic political implications and prospects in the face of these facts of the present and foreseeable future crisis in the process of capital accumulation in India and the just reviewed existing and prospective pressures — and policies — to face the crisis? The *Eastern Economist* has an opinion: "The labour unions have succeeded in wresting increased wages from the [cotton] mills for the worker. The pressure of rising costs has steadily eaten into the meagre profits . . . The more serious cause of the setback to production and the consequent under-utilisation of HSL's [Hindustan Steel] capacity, however, is labour trouble. . . . It is indeed regrettable to note that instead of squarely facing the labour problem, the government till lately had been playing it down, presumably on political considerations. The labour indiscipline needs to be curbed with a heavy hand; a handful of trouble-makers, obviously, cannot be allowed to hold the country's economy to ransom. . . . the steel industry cannot be allowed to become an arena of political manoeuvres. . . . Ideological considerations should not be allowed to stand in the way of accomplishing this task . . . " (*EE* 1174, 1136, 1139, 1163). Whose ideological considerations? we may ask. Those of a handful, no doubt! The *Economic and Political Weekly* correspondent asks: "What next? . . . the next thing that might happen is that on the argument of checking the government deficit worthwhile social welfare expenditure might get severely slashed. . . . What stands out in the current panic and hectic activity in the government is that the populist slogans which have paid the ruling party such rich political dividend in the last three years are beginning to lose their relevance and effectiveness. It is beginning to dawn on even some of the Congress leaders that they have served their purpose and that to persist with them will not do. But where to go from this point . . . " (*EPW* 1470-1471). After the battle defeat of the red forces and the start of the white terror there, one bleak answer is: "One is not yet sure whether to call it pre-fascism, semi-fascism or neo-fascism" according to Sumanta Banerjee, writing (in *Frontier*, October 14, 1972, p 4) on "West Bengal: Premonitions".

NOTES

1. Eckstein, Solomon: *El Marco Macroeconomico del Problema Agrario* Mexicano, Mexico, Centro de Investigaciones Agrarias 1968.

2. Stavenhagen, Rodolfo, Fernando Paz S *et al: Neolatifundismo y Explotacion de Emiliano Zapata a Anderson Clayton and Co.* Mexico, Editorial Nuestro Tiempo 1968.

3. McCoy, Al: 'Land Reform as Counter-Revolution', *Bulletin of Concerned Asian Scholars,* Volume 3, Number 1, Winter-Spring 1971, pp 14-49.

4. Ladejinsky, Wolf: 'Ironies of India's Green Revolution', *Foreign Affairs,* July 1970. Also articles in *Economic and Political Weekly,* June 1969, September 1969 and other numbers.

5. Wharton Jr, Cliff: 'The Green Revolution: Cornucopia or Pandora's Box?' *Foreign Affairs,* April 1969.

6. Wolf, Eric: 'Peasant Wars of the Twentieth Century', New York, Harper and Row 1969.

7. Alavi Hamza: 'Peasants and Revolution' in *The Socialist Register 1965* London. The Merlin Press, New York, Monthly Review Press.

8. Landsberger, Henry A in H A Landsberger, editor 'Latin American Peasant Movements', Ithaca, Cornell University Press 1969. Also H A Landsberger and Cynthia N Hewitt, 'Ten Sources of Weakness and Cleavage in Latin American Peasant Movements', in R Stavenhagen, editor 'Agrarian Problems and Peasant Movements in Latin America', chapter 16.

9. Huizer, Gerrit: 'Emiliano Zapata and the Peasant Guerillas in the Mexican Revolution', in R Stavenhagen, editor, 'Agrarian Problems', *op cit,* chapter 11. Also 'Peasant Unrest in Latin America', Washington, OAS-CIDA 1967 mimeo, and

forthcoming book on the same topic to be published by Doubleday Anchor, New York, 1972/73.

10.   Sau, Ranjit K: 'Indian Economic Growth: Constraints and Prospects', *Economic and Political Weekly,* Annual Number, February 1972, pp 361-78; also 'Resource Allocation in Indian Agriculture', *Economic and Political Weekly,* September 25th, 1971.

11.   Marini, Ruy Mauro: 'Brazilian Subimperialism', *Monthly Review,* volume 23, Number 9, February 1972. Also see R M Marini and Olga Pellicer, 'Militarismo y Des-nuclearizacion, en America Latina', *Foro Internacinal* Mexico, July-September 1967.

12.   Barreto, Antonio: 'A Study of the Social and Economic Implications of the Large-Scale Introduction of High-Yielding Varieties of Foodgrain. A Selection of Readings', Geneva, United Nations Research Institute for Social Development, Report Number 71.6, UNRISD/72 C3; CE 72-3457, pp 173.

ON
ECONOMIC HISTORY

9

On Commercial Imbalances in the Third World

The following essay complements the important and excellent study by Paul Bairoch on "Geographical Structure and Trade Balance of European Foreign Trade from 1800 to 1970" in *The Journal of European Economic History* (Vol. 3, No. 3, Winter 1974). But there are two notable differences between the two studies: Mr. Bairoch's is much longer in range (170 years), broader in scope (exports, imports, and balance of trade), and more detailed in country and decennial breakdown of the data for Europe, whereas the present study concentrates on the trade balances between 1880 and 1928 and examines the participation of the now underdeveloped Third World in greater detail. The second notable difference between the two studies is that, for the period for which they overlap, they come to diametrically different conclusions about the role and importance of the Third World and its trade balances with Europe and North America—and this despite using essentially the same data on trade balances! We can here only inquire briefly why this may be.

Mr. Bairoch writes

> The observation of the relatively restricted role played, in general, by the Third World, leads one to wonder why there is a tendency to overestimate this role in so many theoretical analyses. (p. 568)

Journal of European Economic History (Rome), Vol. 5, No. 2, Fall 1976.

Between 1880 and 1910, the volume of Europe's imports from temperate overseas countries (North America, Oceania, South Africa, and the temperate zones of South America) was much greater than that of imports from tropical and semi-tropical countries: 22% of total imports for temperate countries and 15% for tropical countries. Thus, on the whole, the supplier role of the Third World in the 19th century was relatively limited. (p. 580)

The most significant conclusion to be drawn from an analysis of the geographical structure of European foreign trade would be the preponderance of inter-European trade and trade between developed regions. ... This has meant that trade with what is today called the Third World was relatively marginal, i.e., about 20% of Europe's foreign trade in the 19th century. (p. 592)

The following study on "Multilateral Merchandise Trade Imbalances and Uneven Economic Development"—written in 1970 and revised in 1973, long before Mr. Bairoch's came to our attention—comes to the opposite conclusion:

To summarize the discussion that follows, the secular excess of the underdeveloped countries' exports over imports has throughout this period made a fundamental contribution to the accumulation of capital, technological progress and economic development of the now developed countries; and the generation of this export surplus from the now underdeveloped countries has there developed the mode of production which underdeveloped Asia, Africa and Latin America. (p.1)

. . . the underdeveloped part of the world through its excess merchandise exports over merchandise imports really finances all the rest of the world both directly and indirectly. Specifically, the export surplus of the underdeveloped countries (1) supplied much of the excess merchandise consumption of Europe represented by the latter's merchandise export deficit or import surplus, (2) helped finance the export surplus of the United States and Dominions to Europe, (3) helped domestic investment and development in Europe, and/or (4) helped Europe finance its foreign investment in the United States and Dominions, whose development was thereby accelerated, while the underdeveloped countries also financed much of the "foreign" investment in themselves, which however accelerated their underdevelopment. (p. 18)

The diametrically different conclusions about the role and importance of the Third World in the capitalist development of the world as a whole—at least during this classical imperialist period of the end of the nineteenth and the beginning of the twentieth centuries—seem to turn on the different evaluation of the role and importance of its trade balances with Europe *and* with the temperate newly settled regions of the world (that is, the excess of merchandise exports from the Third World and of merchandise imports by *both* of the latter from the Third World), as well as the assignment to one or another category of the significant wheat- and meat-exporting temperate regions of Latin America. As to the latter, relatively minor, point, Mr. Bairoch's data naturally include them in Latin America; but in his evaluation (e.g., above-cited p. 580) he excludes them from the Third World, while the present essay exerts considerable statistical effort to include them where they belong!

With regard to the fact of Third World excess (i.e., unrequieted) merchandise exports and European—especially British—excess (i.e., unpaid-for in merchandise) imports, the two studies are in essential agreement. Thus, in his long section on trade balance (Section C), Mr. Bairoch notes Europe's

> ... trade deficit which for 1980 exceeded 20% of imports. After having slightly regressed, the deficit in European foreign trade in merchandise once again exceeded 20% in 1900, then fell below 16% in 1913. After the first World War, the disequilibrium of the European trade balance was aggravated and the deficit was at its maximum during the crisis of the 1930's. (p. 583)

> The second phase—from the 1880's to the eve of World War II— was characterized by a quasi-stagnation of the relative size of the deficit which fluctuated between 9–12% of imports in real terms, and in preadjustment terms 20% ... in absolute terms, this deficit reached $1000 million for the adjusted balance and $900 million for the gross balance in 1913 (for 1928, 2400 and 4000 million respectively). (p. 594)

Mr. Bairoch's Tables 11 and 13 on pp. 585 and 587, respectively, clearly show the emergence and level of Europe's excess merchandise imports over exports by decennial dates for this period of classical imperialism. Hardly a marginal contribution to Europe's consumption or investment, considering that these were real imports in excess of real exports! (The reasons for and calculations of the "adjustment" of balances for transport and other costs by Mr. Bairoch—also undertaken in the present study—are less clear, despite his statistical appendix; and the reasons for his statement on p. 584 that "Europe's adjusted trade balance ... was gradually replaced by a 12–13% import deficit [does he mean "trade deficit"?] around 1900" when his tables seem to show the contrary, is still less clear.)

Mr. Bairoch also writes, "As regards differences between the countries, the most worthy of note is the very different geographical structure of foreign trade of the United Kingdom" (p. 592), but he fails to note that and how this difference meant that the UK—who had an excess and ever-growing "deficit" of total merchandise imports exceeding exports for over a century from Waterloo to Versailles—also had a surplus of merchandise imports over merchandise exports with each of the other regions of the world, except the Third World, with which it had about an even balance because of the latter's absorption of British manufactures. Nor does Mr. Bairoch note, as the following study stresses, that and how the working of the global system of multilateral merchandise imbalances and Britain's most privileged position in it— most particularly with respect to India, but also relative to continental Europe—permitted Britain to continue its own accumulation of capital while investing in North America, Oceania, and South Africa. For in these regions of new European settlement Britain invested capital that it received from the now underdeveloped Third World, directly, as particularly from India, and indirectly through continental Europe's import surplus from the Third World and Britain's import surplus in turn from the continent. Moreover—as the following study also shows— Britain effected these transfers of capital and the regions of new settlement amortized their debts partly by relying on the very inter-regional imbalances in the global system of multilateral trade and settlements.

On the other hand, the argument of the following essay with regard to Europe is further strengthened by the detail of Mr. Bairoch's data for European trade balances by country, which permits us neatly to distinguish—as our essay's cruder classification unfortunately does not—that

> of the [European] countries which during the 19th century generally had a favorable [that is, in standard parlance, more exports than imports!] trade balance, all were countries exporting agricultural products. These were Austria-Hungary (at any rate, until 1890), Romania, Spain and Serbia. However, this is not a determining factor, since a number of other agricultural-exporting countries had severe deficits. These were Bulgaria, Denmark, Finland, Italy, Norway and Portugal. Portugal had the largest deficit with export earnings not covering even half its import expenses around 1910. This heavy deficit was covered mostly by transfer of wages of Portuguese labor working in Brazil! (pp. 586-7)

Not determinant, indeed! Not determinant or significant if, like Mr. Bairoch, one wishes to conclude that the importance of the Third

World was relatively "marginal" and has been "overestimated." But very determinant if one analyzes the date—the *same* data!—to look for the real role, significance, and importance of the agricultural and mineral raw materials-exporting countries of the now underdeveloped Third World (or of the then "central," now "eastern" European countries that thereby were underdeveloping and since have gone on to industrial development under socialism). For then it becomes clear that these underdeveloping countries of Europe, just like those of the Third World in Asia, Africa, and Latin America, suffered from an excess of (raw) merchandise exports relative to their (processed) merchandise imports—even at market prices, let alone when notionally calculated at values that would eliminate the decline in their terms of trade and the unequal exchange at even the most favorable of their terms of trade— and that the now developed countries of Europe, North America, and Oceania benefited importantly through their bilateral excess of merchandise imports from the underdeveloping countries and from the multilateral transfer of trade balances among major world regions. The balance of *payments* (as distinct from merchandise trade) deficit of underdeveloping countries is largely—as the following study suggests—the counterpart on financial and other "service" account of the Third World's excess of merchandise exports over merchandise (albeit not "service") imports and may help to explain the apparent paradox of Mr. Bairoch's "favorable" and "deficit" countries in Europe. Certainly Mr. Bairoch's observation of how Portugal covered its deficit with transfers from Brazil (as it has since from there, from Africa, and more recently from its workers in Western Europe) supports our argument in this particular case.

In short, the data and its analysis in the following essay, but also the data of Mr. Bairoch's own study, suggest that, far from being "marginal" and subject to "overestimate" in many theoretical analyses, the role of the Third World and the underdeveloped agricultural-exporting countries of Eastern and Southern Europe has, through their excess of merchandise exports over real imports and through the multilateral (im)balance of the world capitalist system of trade and payments, made a determinant contribution to European and North American development, which has been vastly underestimated by most theoretical analysis, including Mr. Bairoch's own.

10

On Some Questionable Questions about Marxist Theory and International Capital Flows

Al Szymanski's interesting questions about "Marxist Theory and International Capital Flows" [*URPE Review* 6(3), 1974] constitute a questionable combination of questions and data to draw questionable conclusions. Furthermore, Szymanski makes quite unwarranted inferences from theory and false attributions to some theorists whom he criticizes.

It is false—and it is false to claim that Marx so viewed it—that in the first two stages of capitalist development that Szymanski distinguishes before 1800 "technologically backward areas were merely used by the capitalist countries without actually *inter-acting* with them" (p. 22, his italics) or that so-called primitive accumulation left the colonized areas immune from disruptive forces without transforming their modes of production (pp. 20–21).

Though this was substantially the case in much of the Oriental trade before 1750 or so, which was quantitatively almost insignificant relative to the economic relations with Africa and the Americas, the Rape of Bengal after the Battle of Plassey in 1757 left its mode of production anything but immune from or to transformation. And certainly the slave trade in Africa as well as slave and colonial

URPE Review, New York, Summer 1976.

production in the Americas did not leave them immune in the three centuries before 1800. As Marx observed in his chapter on the genesis of the industrial capitalist, "in fact the veiled slavery of the wage-workers in Europe needed, for its pedestal, slavery pure and simple in the new world." As for the third period that Szymanski reviews—he leaves a bit unclear just when it began—it is not true, as he argues, that net "capital flowed from the advanced capitalist countries to industrialize the backward ones" (p. 25); nor is it true that "the assumption of a new flow of resources or capital away from the developed capitalist countries is integral to Lenin's argument," which was concerned with the imperialist placement of capital abroad and did not, like Szymanski suppose without measuring the misnamed "return" flow of earnings, let alone of resources, to be smaller, and still less argued that this would industrialize the "backward" ones. (For a discussion, see Hamza Alavi's classic article on "Imperialism, Old and New" in Socialist Register 1964 and elsewhere.) Indeed, Szymanski himself notes—albeit in a footnote (5, p. 39)—that "all these studies agree that at all times for which records have been kept that the direction of the net aggregate capital flow has been from the less developed to the more developed capitalist countries." For the nineteenth century generally and from about 1880 to 1928 particularly, the evidence gathered by Imlah, Saul, Hilgert, and others is overwhelming that the now underdeveloped countries were net merchandise exporters (the only way real capital can really be exported) and Europe, and especially Britain, was a net merchandise importer (as shown in A. G. Frank, "Merchandise Trade Imbalances and Uneven Economic Development," 1973 mimeo)—even at market prices and over and above the unequal exchange, noted by Marx, Emmanuel, Amin, and so forth, which these prices imply.

Turning to "an examination of the data" in Part II, it is more than questionable—and questionable Marxism—to select for examination a period (1952–1971) of "normal operation of the forces affecting capital flows, i.e. no major depressions, wars or other cataclysmic disturbances." Since when are war and depression not normal forces of capital accumulation that normally affect capital flows? Far from being "normal," as everyone except apparently Szymanski has learned since the onset of the 1970s stag/slumpflation, the normality of economic expansion is at best a questionable half-truth. Nor surprisingly, Szymanski's data show a turn-around in the last period (1969–1971) of his series, which jumbles up his "normal" extrapolation of "normal" trends and which he attributes to "special atypical conditions or perhaps political interference" (p. 37), when more than likely they are simply the reflection of a perfectly normal capitalist crisis of accumulation (since the mid-1960s), which itself, of course, has political repercussions such as those Szymanski observes. Investment and capital flow patterns are, of course, normally different—for Szymanski atypical—in periods of depression than in those of expansion. Investment in previously leading industries and areas declines relatively or even absolutely during depression and war, and investment in raw materials and underdeveloped countries experiences a relative or absolute increase. At the same time, the exploitation of and in at least some underdeveloped countries typically increases during periods of depression or crises of accumulation. Thus, however heuristically convenient because of the availability of data, Szymanski's choice of the period (1952–1971) for study is itself more than questionable. Even more so is his supposition (p. 29) that "it is of greatest contemporary interest for those concerned with the practical political consequences of capital flows." Might we not argue much more persuasively that, if we cannot or will not draw our conclusions from the entire history, or at least an entire cycle, of capital accumulation, that practical political consequences for the present period of crisis can, then, perhaps more suitably be derived from the examination of previous periods of crisis, which Szymanski excludes as not "normal"?

It is questionable, to say the least, to claim that "a fair test of the two versions of Marxist theory outlined above must exclude the raw materials sector from consideration, since classical Marxist theory was not meant to apply to it"—and that after quoting Lenin and Luxemburg on classical raw materials-exploiting imperialism and before observing that this sector still represents the bulk of imperialist investment in the underdeveloped countries! It is questionable to exclude "flows from indirect ownership, loans, rents, royalties, fees, services such as insurance, etc." (p. 29) in view of the quantitative and qualitative importance they play in the total flow and given the substantial data thereon also published by the same U.S. Department of Commerce whose data Szymanski uses. It is similarly questionable to suppose that "profits which do not appear on the books in one Third World country appear on the books in another" (p. 30) when it is known, and Szymanski himself recognizes on the previous page, that the multinationals take their profits where they wish, including in the Western European countries that he compares with the underdeveloped ones. It is certainly questionable that the U.S. Department of Commerce data "seem to close enough approximate Marxist categories" (p. 30) when they do not even approximate bourgeois ones satisfactorily. Thus, for instance, both U.S. Department of Commerce and IMF balance of payments data count as "inflows" into countries the foreign investments that are made there out of foreign-owned capital that was raised there and that does not flow across the border at all! This accounting convention, and still more the facts of "foreign" investment, namely that the large bulk of "foreign" investment in underdeveloped countries is made with locally provided capital and not with capital supplied by the foreign investor, renders more than questionable several of Szymanski's "tests," especially if Third World countries provide more "foreign"-owned capital than European countries do. For what real meaning has a "measure" of "profit" if it only covers declared profits on declared book value, when neither the former (as Szymanski notes) nor the latter (as we claim as well) really reflect the categories—bourgeois or Marxist—that we really want to measure?

Szymanski's questions are themselves questionable. Several of them, for example, I, II, III, IV, V, etc., are based on his own questionable attribution of a questionable premise to "neo-Marxists" and to his still more questionable derivation from this assumption of theses that he places in their mouths or pages: based on a single isolated quotation from Magdoff and Sweezy (p. 25) and some references to Baran and Frank about surplus and monopoly, respectively, Szymanski constructs his own "neo-Marxist theory" to the effect that the degree of monopoly —and only the degree of monopoly—determines the amount of investment and the direction of capital flows. It is hard to believe that any of the four writers mentioned, or anybody else except evidently Szymanski, could believe that investment and capital flows are a function only of monopoly, and that the organic composition of capital, wage rates, and so forth have nothing to do with it. Certainly none of the four ever said so on any page I have read, and Sweezy, for instance, wrote a whole book on the theory of capitalist development, which places due emphasis on the latter. From this questionable premise, which Szymanski attributes to his "neo-Marxist theory," he then questionably derives still more questionable theses and questions that would be questionable even if the premise were correct, which it is not. Thus, Szymanski and only Szymanski argues in Question III, p. 32, "the neo-Marxist theory on the other hand would seem to predict that a growing percentage of total investment should be in the advanced capitalist countries, because the monopoly barriers to investment are lower there." To construct his Question IV, p. 33, Szymanski repeats the same nonsensical argument, and for Question V, p. 34, he twists it a bit further to argue, perhaps correctly, that repatriated profits are greater from underdeveloped than from developed countries, but attributes this to capital's desire to preserve and not to undermine its monopoly position in the former.

Still more questionable is Szymanski's attempt to draw political consequences from the questionable relationships he sets up:

> In sum, the theories of which class(es) are the revolutionary agent(s) are integrally related to the theories of the direction and effect of

capital flow. . . . If our study finds that capital flows to the Third World, the proponents of the industrial working class are supported, if we find that the direction of capital flow is away from the Third World then proponents of peasantry and lumpenproletariat are supported. (p. 28).

Szymanski offers no rationale at all for this curious argument, except to say that it was "natural" for proponents of one or the other supposed views to see things each in their own way. I, for one, see nothing "natural" at all. Just as questionable is Szymanski's identification of a supposed "U.S. Marxist theory . . . led by the journal *Monthly Review* (with which both Baran and Frank have been associated), to focus their hopes on peasants and lumpen," to the exclusion of industrial workers in either developed or underdeveloped countries. On which page of *Monthly Review*, Baran, or Frank did Szymanski ever read this notion of his? Perhaps I read different pages of all of these, since before reading Szymanski's p. 28, I do not recall having encountered this notion before.

This unquestionable mix-up of questionable premises, questions, and theses, their supposed test with questionable measures and data for a questionably selected period, and the supposition that this questionable procedure permits political conclusions, are themselves more than questionable, and leave us with the question posed to Szymanski: What *were* you trying to do?

11

Even Heretics Remain Bound by Traditional Thought in Formulating Their Heresies

"Even the heretics remain bound by traditional thought in formulating their heresies. . . ." "Throughout this book I am making the generous assumption that the western approach is fairly adequate to western conditions." These statements are not mine but those of Gunnar Myrdal in the introduction to his book "Asian Drama" (Vol 1, pp. 17, 16n).

The evidence to be examined here shows that the first of these statements is entirely correct, particularly about Myrdal himself. In his heresy he also remains bound by traditional thought, as he says. As to his second statement about the generous assumption that the western approach is fairly adequate to western conditions, the same evidence shows it to be more than generous; it is erroneous. I shall not talk much about the western world *per se* but rather about the relations between the so-called third world and the so-called western world. Nonetheless I hope it will be seen from the discussion of these relations that Myrdal's assumption is indeed more than generous.

The very term "third world" implies traditional thought, because it is not simply a phrase. The very idea of a third world reflects the essence of traditional thought about the problems of Asia, Africa and

Economic and Political Weekly (Bombay), Vol. V, Nos. 29–31, July 1970.

Latin America, which is that these problems are caused by characteristics that are peculiar to these areas. In the first place, the term third world implies that there are two other worlds, a first one and a second one, which I understand generally to mean that the first one is capitalist and the second one socialist, while the third one is neither capitalist nor socialist. In the second place, the term third world implies that indeed there is something peculiar about the third world which makes it third or underdeveloped. If we examine the historical evidence we will see that in fact the so-called third world is an integral part of the so-called first world. That is, we will see that the underdeveloped countries are an integral part of the world capitalist system, and that is why they came to be underdeveloped.

But before examining this evidence it may be worthwhile to look briefly at the orthodox approaches to the problems of the underdeveloped countries and also at what Myrdal calls the heretic approaches, including his own.

The orthodox approaches to the study of underdevelopment are limited to the framework of the idea of a third world and focus primarily on a variety of supposed characteristics that the third world has, which are said to be different from those of the first world. One might summarise these supposed characteristics of the third world to be those of traditionalism and the characteristics of the first world to be those of modernism. Examined more closely, modernism turns out to mean liberalism, in the usual sense of that word. In the orthodoxy, the process of development is then regarded as the replacement of the traditional characteristics by the modern, that is to say, liberal characteristics.

The supposed traditional characteristics are variously defined. One of the stereotypes made up from these supposed characteristics is a cartoon in which the problems of the underdeveloped world are characterised by a Mexican who sits leaning against a wall doing nothing with his sombrero covering him; and the implication is that underdevelopment is simply caused by laziness.

ROSTOW'S STAGE MANAGEMENT

A supposedly more scientific but really only more sophisticated version of the same characterisation claims that the traditional characteristics are really traditional values, traditional technology, traditional social relations, traditional subsistence economy in which money is not important, and so forth. The cartoonist translates this more scientific sounding terminology into a picture characterisation of what is really the same thing without the pseudo-scientific clothing that self-styled scientists give it.

One of the most famous orthodox approaches which seemingly goes a step beyond the most orthodox approach is that of the "Stages of Economic Growth" by Walt Whitman Rostow, a book which he wrote while he was at MIT and before he went to Washington where he became the principal architect of the Vietnam policy, first for President Kennedy and later for President Johnson. The book's sub-title is "A Non-Communist Manifesto", but more accurately, it is an anti-communist manifesto.

Rostow remains quite within the orthodox approach but he suggests that in the interregnum before underdeveloped countries acquire the characteristics of developed countries there are several stages through which all societies must pass in the process of economic growth and economic development. Rostow's supposed contribution is the identification of those stages. The first stage is that of traditionalism; the second that of creation of pre-conditions for economic growth, when the traditional society is opened up by the progressive influence emitting from the developed countries, initially Great Britain and later all of Western Europe and North America. These influences come from abroad, destroy the fabric of traditional society and so permit the society to take-off from traditionalism into economic growth like an aeroplane, which is Rostow's third and most famous stage. The fourth and fifth stages, corresponding to the present ones of Western Europe and North America, are those of the drive to maturity and mass consumption. Thus, orthodoxy, including Rostow, suggests that all the underdeveloped countries have essentially the same characteristics of traditionalism and the developed countries the quite different ones of modernism.

GALBRAITH'S GAMBOLS

The supposed triumph of the heretics over orthodoxy is to distinguish between different varieties of traditional or underdeveloped societies. What makes them heretics is that they claim that different characterisations distinguish different underdeveloped regions or countries. For instance, J K Galbraith, former US Ambassador to India, distinguishes between three major types of underdevelopment: the Asian type in which he attributes underdevelopment to inadequate natural resources — too many people and too few natural resources; the African type, in which he attributes underdevelopment to inadequate human resources, which means that Africans are not yet sufficiently educated or cultured to be able to develop; and third, the Latin American type, in which he attributes underdevelopment not to a shortage of natural resources or human resources, which he says Latin America has, but to inadequacy of social, political and economic institutions. If we look closer to see what that supposed inadequacy is, we find again that the missing institutions are those of western capitalist liberalism. If only Latin America had these institutions then, Galbraith says, Latin America also could develop.

MYRDAL'S SACRED COWS

Myrdal's own heresies are just as traditional as those of Galbraith although they are slightly different. Myrdal says in the introduction to "Asian Drama": "Conditions that are peculiar to the South Asian countries are responsible for their underdevelopment" (p. 20). The difference between Myrdal and Galbraith is that Myrdal attributes underdevelopment not to the characteristics that Galbraith sets out but rather to other characteristics. In fact, after reading the three volumes of "Asian Drama" it will be seen that Myrdal attributes South Asian underdevelopment primarily to the characteristics that Galbraith finds in Latin America, namely that there is something wrong or inadequate with the social institutions and values of South Asia. What the 2,500 pages of "Asian Drama", which is the produce of ten years' work by Myrdal and his staff, really boil down to — and this is aptly summarized by Myrdal himself when he says that South Asian underdevelopment is due to conditions that are peculiar to South Asia — is a cartoon-like caricature of Indian underdevelopment explained in terms of the same old sacred cows.

But the really sacred cow here is traditional thought to which, to use Myrdal's words, he remains bound even in his heresy. What is sacred to the orthodox and heretics alike is the limitation in thought which refuses to acknowledge that the characteristics which are peculiar to these countries have a connection with the metropolis that makes these countries underdeveloped. This refusal to accept a connection is the really sacred cow in all this pseudo-science. I say pseudo-science with conviction, because the most elementary principle of science is to try to explain any kind of regularity, such as under-development in many countries, through controlled comparison. This really holy principle of social science is totally disregarded by all these pseudo-scientists who do not examine the *total* social system at all and only look at the characteristics they find convenient and disregard all the characteristics they find inconvenient in their explanation.

To summarise, what all of these people do is to view the so-called third world as being different from the first world, in that it supposedly has certain fundamental characteristics (on which they do not entirely agree) that supposedly cause underdevelopment. None of these people see any systematic relationship between the third world and the first world; still less do they see any connection between this systematic relationship and the underdevelopment of the so-called third world.

In all of the ten years that he devoted to the study of South Asia, ten years which he says obliged him to totally transform his own way of understanding its problems, Myrdal (and, of course, Galbraith and Rostow or any other of these so-called scientists) never looked at what the evidence shows to be the really determinant factors in the processes of development and underdevelopment. They do not care to see that these processes are really the opposite sides of the same coin.

THE SYSTEM ESCAPES THEM

These pseudo-scientists do not see a world capitalist system or rather, they see it when they talk about the "free world", but they deny its existence and importance when they engage in their so-called scientific work. This was not true of Adam Smith who in 1776 wrote his "Inquiry into the Nature and Causes of the Wealth of Nations." Adam Smith, the intellectual father of Rostow, Galbraith, Myrdal and all economists, writing "Of the Motives for Establishing New Colonies", said two centuries ago: "Columbus turned his view towards their minerals; and in the richness of the production . . . he had found full compensation. . . . In consequence of the representations of Columbus, the Council of Castille determined to take possession of countries of which the inhabitants were plainly incapable of defending themselves. The pious purpose of converting them to Christianity sanctified the injustice of the project. But the hope of finding treasures of gold there was the sole motive which prompted them to undertake it. . . . All the other enterprises of the Spaniards in the new world, subsequent to those of Columbus, seem to have been prompted by the same motive. It was their thirst for gold . . . that carried Cortez to Mexico, and Almagro and Pizarro to Chile and Peru. . . ."

In another chapter, Adam Smith continues: "The East Indies is another market for the produce of the silver mines of America, and a market which, from the time of the discovery of these mines, has been taking off a greater and greater quantity of silver. Since that time, the direct trade between America and the East Indies, which is carried on by means of the Acapulco ships, has been continually augmenting, and the indirect intercourse by way of Europe has been augmenting in a still greater proportion . . . In the East Indies, particularly in China and Indostan, the value of the precious metals, when the European first began to trade to those countries, was much higher than in Europe; and it still continues to be so . . . The silver of the new continent seems in this manner to be one of the principal commodities by which the commerce between the two extremities of the old one is carried out, and it is by means of it, in great measure, that those distant parts of the world are connected with one another" (Smith, pp 528–529, pp 204–207).

Adam Smith recognised that already in the 16th and 17th centuries and, of course, in the 18th, there existed and developed a single world-embracing mercantile-capitalist system which connected the "extremities" of India with the New World of America by way of the trade between both and Europe. I should like to briefly review the historical development of this world-embracing system focusing primarily on its Asian, African and Latin American parts.

It would perhaps be more politic to present the conclusions after the historical review. But it may help to guide the reader through the review if I present the conclusions at the beginning. Throughout this history we can see three major elements. One is a colonial or new neo-colonial relationship between the metropolis and its colonies or neo-colonies in Asia, Africa and Latin America. Second, this colonial relationship forms and transforms the whole domestic economic, political, social, cultural, even psychological structure of Asia, Africa and Latin America. And third, this new economic and class structure creates the economic and class interests of a bourgeoisie which is tied to the metropolis as a colonialised junior partner of the metropolis. The colonial relationship or structure as well as the economic and class structure at home give this dependent bourgeoisie a natural interest in pursuing policies in the colonial countries that do not generate economic development but rather generate ever more economic, social and cultural underdevelopment. From these three conclusions it becomes apparent that it is not possible to achieve economic development in Asia, Africa and Latin America without destroying both the (neo)-colonial dependence on the metropolis and the resulting internal economic and class structure. The experience of capitalism shows that this cannot be done through reform but requires a revolution which totally changes both the domestic and the international relationships.

We might begin by asking why North America is developed and South America is underdeveloped today. All of us have often heard two major kinds of explanations, which are in fact related to each other. One explanation is that progressive British capitalism exported or transplanted progressive capitalist institutions to North America, while backward feudal Spain and Portugal transplanted to Latin America backward feudal institutions that were unable to generate economic development. The other, but related, explanation which is associated with "The Protestant Ethic and the Spirit of Capitalism" of Max Weber is that the kinds of people who went to South America were different from those that went to North America. To South America went Catholics, caricatured by the lazy people described in the cartoon referred to earlier, while to North America went Protestants, people who were intent on working and had the capitalist spirit and all that.

The first explanation is historically almost totally false and the second is only half true. The first one is false because capitalism was born in Catholic Italy, Spain and Portugal and because, evidently, Protestant Britain did not transplant its progressive capitalist institutions to Jamaica or Barbados or Trinidad or to any of the Caribbean islands that are today just as underdeveloped as Latin America, and in fact it did not transplant these institutions to the South of the United States either, where a slave society grew up. Furthermore, though there is not enough space to go into this theme here, examination of the historical evidence shows that Spain did not transfer its institutions to Latin America either, but rather that institutions grew in Latin America in response to local needs.

The second explanation, that the people who went to the South of the continent were different from those that went to the North, is in part true. It is true to the extent that to North America went people who were escaping religious persecution and who became small farmers in New England, whereas to Latin America went people who as Adam Smith said, were in search of gold which, Columbus himself said, could do anything, even send souls to heaven. We must ask *why* the people who went to the North were different from those that went to the South.

Why did the Spaniards exploit gold and silver mines — really, of course, exploit the people who worked in the gold and silver mines — in Peru and Mexico? The reason is obvious: because there was gold and silver to be found there. Why did the Spaniards and the Portuguese not exploit gold and silver mines in the Caribbean, Brazil and Argentina? The reason is also obvious: not because they did not want to find mines, but because there were not any mines there. Why did the people who went to North America not exploit gold and silver mines there? Also not because they did not want to, but because there were none. Why did the Spaniards and the Portuguese, as well as the British and French, build sugar plantations in the Caribbean and in Brazil for production of sugar and its export to the metropolis? Why did the British create cotton plantations in the South of the United States? The reason is obvious. They did so because there were no gold or silver mines there, but a suitable climate for the production of these export crops. But since in these regions they lacked the necessary labour, they supplied that labour by bringing slaves from Africa to work on these plantations. Why did not the British or the French do this in New England and in New France, which is today called Quebec? The reason is also obvious. There were neither mines nor a suitable climate for the production of an export crop such as sugar or cotton.

Therefore, if we examine the historical evidence honestly, we must come to the conclusion that if Europeans went to New England in order to work, it is not because they wanted to, but because in New England they could not do anything else. There was nobody and nothing to exploit, whereas it was possible to build an exploitative colonial economy in the South of the United States, in the Caribbean and in most of Latin America, although for a long time it was not possible to do so in Argentina because the land there was not suitable for export production, until wool, meat and wheat could be profitably transported to Europe in the 19th century. So, we must come to the apparently paradoxical, but on reflection not really so surprising, conclusion that development occurred where there was poverty and underdevelopment occurred where there was wealth. That is to say, in the "rich" colonies, rich in silver or rich in climate and rich in native or imported but *exploited* labour, underdevelopment developed; and in the "poor" regions, where it was not then possible to exploit anybody, development developed.

Thus, we should not think that with the creation of an export economy in Latin America and also in the non-Latin Caribbean and the South of the United States, the colonial relationship so formed was only external. On the contrary, this capitalist colonial relationship totally forms the economic and class structure of the society there, and when the colonial relationship changes it transforms the economic and class structure. In fact, the new colonial relationship that the Spaniards imposed on the Aztecs and the Incas in Mexico and Peru immediately transformed the pre-existing economic and class structure. The Spaniards came and imposed a new commercial and productive bourgeoisie that lived on the production and export of silver and gold and some other things to the metropolis and the production of foodstuffs and other supplies that were necessary for this mining economy. Not only that, but the whole Indian chieftancy system was then incorporated, as the African one would be again in the 19th century, into this new and, as Adam Smith noted, worldwide social system to supply the metropolitan market with export commodities.

NEW METHODS OF CONQUEST

The Europeans were not the first imperial conquerors in pre-Spanish America or India and Africa. But this capitalist conquest was fundamentally different from previous ones. The Incas and the Aztecs themselves had been conquering people who had swept over the land and incorporated the peoples that previously lived there into the Inca and Aztec empires. At least part of Africa had been conquered by Arabs who had come out of the Near East. In India, the Moghuls had conquered a large part of the subcontinent. But between these earlier conquerors and the European ones there is an important difference, not because the Europeans were Catholic or Protestant, good people or bad people, but because this new conquest was the expansion of world capitalism, as observed by Adam Smith. The earlier conquerors — the Aztecs, the Incas, the Arabs and the Moghuls — simply eliminated the pre-existing rulers and substituted themselves to demand the payment of tribute by the population they had conquered. But people have to produce in order to be able to pay tribute over the years. So what did these earlier conquering people do? Did they transform the productive system? No, they left the pre-existing productive system standing and simply skimmed the cream off the top for their own consumption. And what they did not consume themselves, they returned to the population in the form of public works, etc. Is this what the Europeans did? No. The Europeans did something altogether different, not because they were Europeans and not even because they were capitalists as individuals. But because they were part of a growing, world-embracing mercantile and, later, industrial capitalist system, they had to — in many cases against their will — transform the entire mode of production, and thus the entire economic, social, political and cultural structure of these peoples. And they shipped a significant part of the economic surplus produced by these peoples overseas. This is what the Spaniards did in Latin America and the British in India, and this is what the Portuguese, the English and the North Americans, who derived much of their initial capital from the slave trade, did in Africa. Thus the resulting characteristics of underdevelopment were not peculiar to any of these areas.

The economic, social, political, cultural and even psychological structure which grew up in Mexico and Peru was not, to use Myrdal's term, peculiar to Mexico and Peru. This is shown by the fact that the Caribbean, Brazil and the South of the United States, to which a totally different population was brought from Europe and Africa and where a totally new society was formed on what was essentially a *tabula rasa,* also gave birth to a similar structure — at least as far as the generation of underdevelopment is concerned — as that which transformed the already existing societies of the Aztecs and Incas, and those of much of Asia and Africa.

The essentials of this social structure in all of these export economies was that a small metropolitan-orientated bourgeoisie exploited large masses of labour to produce and export usually only one major commodity — silver, gold, sugar, cotton, slaves — and to import manufactured goods from the metropolis. The distribution of income that resulted was highly unequal. Many people, slaves as well as those who were not formally slaves, worked for little or nothing, so that, unlike in North America or, to be more accurate, in New England, no internal market grew up and purchasing power was concentrated in the outward-orientated bourgeoisie, which bought goods abroad.

The structure and development of this world-wide mercantile capitalist and, later, also industrial capitalist system necessarily gave the bourgeoisie in the colonial countries an economic self-interest, which was and is totally different from the economic self-interest of the bourgeoisie in the metropolitan countries. In these economically and politically colonial countries the economic and political bourgeoisie, which concentrated all economic and political power and social prestige in its hands, necessarily had an economic interest in producing for export. Since it was a subordinate bourgeoisie, a large share of the surplus above consumption that was produced in its economy was remitted to the metropolis. This immediately initiated a capital flow from the poor colonial countries to the ever richer metropolis. And since there was no substantial internal market, because the distribution of income was too unequal, the colonial bourgeoisie did not have any interest in investing what remained in the creation of productive facilities for the internal market. On the contrary, their interest was to use whatever investments they did make to further expand the apparatus for export production. And it was to their interest also to import from abroad the capital goods they needed to make this export economy function and the luxury consumer goods they wanted for their own use. Thus, they did not have any economic interest in creating a domestic economy which would produce for the internal market, which would stimulate substantial development of manufacturing industry, and which would eventually witness the creation of a process of self-generating and self-sustaining economic development, as did the bourgeoisie in the metropolis, which did have a natural economic interest to do so.

So it is not that the bourgeoisie in Britain was smarter or more entrepreneurial than was its counterpart in the colonies, but simply that the structure and functioning of this world-wide system, that Adam Smith had already talked about, necessarily induced interests and possibilities among the metropolitan bourgeoisie that generated very different results from the quite different economic interests that the bourgeoisie in the colonial countries had. Of course, this was all the more true when economic and political control of the colonies was vested in a branch of the metropolitan bourgeoisie, which simply produced in the colonies and sent everything home, or when many people went to the colonies only to earn money and then came home to retire and live on the earnings they had taken out of the colonies. But though this was especially true of the metropolitan people who went to the colonies, the same thing naturally was substantially true also for the colonial bourgeoisie that was born, lived and died in the colonies and had its economic interests there as long as these interests also remained tied to the fundamental colonial relationship with the metropolis. Finally, to make this whole system function, the bourgeoisie in the colonies needed cheap labour, and cheap labour meant that it had to exploit the masses.

This colonial relationship created an internal structure within the colony, which in turn gave the ruling group in the colony an interest in pursuing policies which necessarily led to the underdevelopment rather than to the development of the colony, but which led to the development of the metropolis. Not only did this structure generate a capital flow from the poor to the rich, but additionally this whole colonial economic, political and social structure of an underdeveloped society prohibited it from producing enough, and especially enough of the right products, to be able to generate development. This restriction is much more important than the capital drain from the poor to the rich. And it is quite obvious, with all due respect to our learned colleagues, that underdevelopment is not a question of innate laziness or peculiar values. Quite the contrary. Evidently slaves worked a great deal more than their masters in the colonies or the metropolis and even today most people, including small children, in the underdeveloped world work a great deal more than in the developed ones, just in order to survive.

AFRICANS TREATED AS A COMMODITY

Where in the New World cheap labour was not "naturally" available, it had to be imported; and slaves were brought from Africa. This meant that Africa was converted into a single product export economy in the 17th and 18th centuries. That single product was people, rather than silver, cotton or sugar. For Africa this was not simply an external relationship. The many millions of Africans who were shipped overseas in two and a half centuries were not standing at the seashore waiting to jump into the ships any more than did the gold or silver or sugar or cotton elsewhere jump into the ships by themselves to cross the sea. Slaves also had to be made available for export, and this meant that like the gold trade, the silver trade, the sugar trade, the cotton trade, and all trade elsewhere, the slave trade also formed or rather transformed the whole economic, social and political structure of Africa in a manner fundamentally and essentially similar to what happened in the New World. An economic interest group grew up in the port cities of Africa which came to specialise in importing human beings from the interior regions and exporting them abroad. This produced, not only in the port cities but also in much of the interior of Africa, the total change in the African structure that was necessary for the continuous generation of this new export product. This generated a structure of underdevelopment in Africa essentially similar to the structure of underdevelopment that had been or was simultaneously created in the export colonies of the New World. In the 19th century, colonialism was to further transform and deepen this structure of underdevelopment in Africa.

Let us go on to Asia and specifically to India, which occupies about 2,000 of Myrdal's 2,500 pages. Adam Smith had already noted the connection between India and China on the one hand and Latin America on the other, which was created by the silver which was dug up in Mexico and Peru and which ended up being buried again in India after it was exchanged for the goods the Europeans at one time imported from there. Notwithstanding this observation by the intellectual father of all economists, including Myrdal and myself, Myrdal pays no attention to this fact at all. Instead, as we observed, this self-proclaimed heretic pays primary attention to the holy cows.

Let us look at what really happened in India. In the beginning the British came and only traded with the Indians. And since they had nothing the Indians wanted, they had to pay with the silver that came from America. But increasingly, and particularly after the 1757 Battle of Plassey in Bengal where the Indians were defeated in military combat, the British and the East India Company began to transform India, or at least the parts they had been able to penetrate, into an export economy. In the process they also began to transform the cultural structure of India. It is not true that India, Africa and Latin America still have the same culture that they had centuries ago. This so-called traditional culture instead of being the supposed cause of a supposedly traditional state of underdevelopment, is in fact largely the product of this process of colonial capitalist underdevelopment.

The British found pre-existing social institutions and zamindari landowners whom they used just as the Aztec, Inca and African institutions elsewhere were used by the conquerors. Outwardly some of these institutional forms remained the same (eg, zamindari survived) but their internal function was now transformed into something entirely different. The zamindars were converted into tribute collectors for the British in North India. In South India the British instituted the ryotwari system of smaller landholders, who nonetheless had to pay tribute. And in the very South, the British implanted plantation economies for the export of commodities to the metropolis. All of these, of course, generated the export of capital from India to the metropolis.

CAPITAL FOR BRITISH INDUSTRIAL REVOLUTION

It is no accident that the industrial revolution occurred in England after 1760, that is after the Battle of Plassey, which permitted the English to such a tremendous amount of capital out of India. Ernest Mandel has calculated that the amount of capital drained out of the East and West Indies between 1760 and 1800 was more than the value of the entire installed capacity of mechanically driven machinery in Western Europe in the year 1800. That is to say, not only the economic take-off of England, but even the fact that inventions such as the steam engine of Watt were put to use at this moment was related to the tremendous influx of capital from the now increasingly poor India and the West Indies.

The development of the worldwide capitalist system and of the colonial relations within it transformed not only the colonies but also the economic and class structure of the metropolis itself. And, consistently with the thesis that this system-wide structural change generated new class interests in the colonies, this transformation of the economic structure also created new class interests for the sector of the metropolitan bourgeoisie whose dominance was growing. The changing international capitalist colonial relations contributed to the ascendancy of the industrial interests in Great Britain, and these in turn increased their economic and political challenge against the colonial merchant monopoly interests of the East India Company and the West Indian planter class, until the industrialists dealt the British merchants and landowners the *coup de grace* with the abolition of the corn laws in 1847 and the full-scale institution of the free trade policy, demanded by these industrial interests.

But, as was pointed out earlier, more important than the drain of capital is what happens inside the colonial economy and society. In India, as an integral part of the same development, the British deindustrialised the country. In 1800 India still exported more and higher quality textiles to Britain than Britain did to India. By 1840 this was entirely reversed and the entire textile industry of India had been destroyed, not accidentally but intentionally by the British. This was done to accomplish two things. First, Britain sought to convert India into an exporter of primary commodities, including cotton, to Britain. Secondly, once the industrial revolution had taken place in Britain, the British instituted free trade for Britain but not for India which was obliged to import the new British textiles through a variety of tariff and other measures. Only after the British had killed the Indian textile industry, did they institute free trade also in India.

Then, in the middle of the 19th century, began what from the left to the right of the political spectrum is still today called imperialism, the classical imperialism of the late 19th century. During this stage of world capitalist development the foregoing tendencies and structures were very greatly reinforced in Asia, Africa and Latin America.

The metropolis began to build railways in the colonies. Thereby the metropolis very much increased its extraction of raw materials from those areas and also very much increased its export of manufactured goods to these countries. The industrialisation of Great Britain could not have taken place as it did without the external markets in these continents. But in order to provide this vast external market, the internal markets of the colonies, be they politically dependent colonies or politically sovereign neo-colonies like the Latin American countries, had to be eliminated. And that is what the free trade policy did.

It is important to note that during this period not only did the external colonialism of the world capitalist metropolis intensify its relationship with Buenos Aires, Calcutta or Lagos, but through an internal colonialism within these countries, Buenos Aires colonialised its interior, Calcutta colonialised its interior and so forth. This happened not only in the colonialised countries themselves but also in Europe, where for instance the North of Italy colonialised and grew at the expense of the South of Italy, England grew at the expense of Wales and Ireland, and Sweden grew at the expense of Norway and Finland. Many regions grew at the expense of other regions, and today the consequences are coming home to roost in the form of bombs when the Prince of Wales goes to Wales to be crowned, of political disturbances in the South of Italy and among southern migrants in Turin and Milan and, most important of all, in the form of Black Power in the American internal colony that was also created as a necessary and still continuing part of this process of capitalist development of the world, at the national, regional and local levels.

DEPRESSION CAUSED BOOM

The First World War, the Depression of the 1930s and then the Second World War weakened the colonial relationship between the metropolis and its colonies or neo-colonies. Because of the wars, the metropolis was unable to export manufactured commodities to Asia, Africa and Latin America, and in some cases it was unable to import raw materials as well. During the intervening Depression of the 1930s trade had diminished very substantially between the metropolis and its colonies or neo-colonies. The consequences were that the economic and class structure of the colonies changed to some degree and the policies of at least a sector of the colonial bourgeoisie also changed to support a sudden spurt of industrialisation in India, Brazil, Argentina, Mexico and in some parts of Africa. The result also was the development of the liberation movements which after the Second World War resulted in formal de-colonisation and sovereignty in most of Asia and Africa. Latin America, of course, had already become sovereign a hundred and fifty years earlier, and in part thanks to this sovereignty, some countries in this region had been able to create at least the minimum bases which afforded the local bourgeoisie the political and economic strength to take advantage of the Depression and to build up the beginnings of a national industry in Brazil, Argentina and Mexico. But in Central America and the Caribbean, where the local bourgeoisie was much weaker as a result of great colonialisation and foreign ownership of the major productive facilities, the bourgeoisie was not able to take advantage of the relative liberty that the Depression afforded to generate any national capitalist development.

Even where this development was possible, it was weak, because it was limited by the economic and class structure that the colonial relationship had created. Moreover, the opportunity was only temporary. Once the wars and reconstruction were over, especially after the Korean war, the metropolis recovered and with renewed force reincorporated all of Asia, Africa and Latin America into ever closer economic ties with the metropolis, excepting of course those parts of these three continents, like the Soviet Union and China, that had broken out of this worldwide system through socialist revolution. Again, the new ties were much stronger and more efficient than they had been in the period of classical imperialism before World War I, just like the latter had been stronger than those in the period of colonialism two centuries before.

The new ties of foreign investment by the multi-national corporations now integrate even the national industry that had been built up in underdeveloped countries like India and Brazil into the multi-national corporate system whose centre is in the United States. Now not only the export or comprador bourgeoisie, but even the so-called national industrial bourgeoisie in India, Latin America and to the extent to which it exists at all in Africa is transformed into a dependent colonial or neo-colonial bourgeoisie.

So now even the so-called national industrial bourgeoisies pursue policies that are in their economic self-interest but which, due to their dependence, necessarily result in the further development of under-development in Asia, Africa and Latin America. Therefore, as the data of the United Nations clearly show, the rates of growth of national income, of industrial output, and still more, of the dynamic capital goods industries in these countries began to decline after the Second World War and are still declining. Most important of all, even the structure of industry and the economy as a whole again generate further underdevelopment. No longer do Latin Americans build basic industry; no longer do they create any technology of their own as they did during the short lapse of the Depression and the War. Instead, they have now become entirely dependent on the metropolis and simply produce durable consumer goods for the high income market and some materials to support that industry and import the equipment and technology needed from the metropolis.

The consequences, for instance, are that when Rockefeller recently went to Latin America not only was he badly received by the people at large, but the government of the local bourgeoisie in Brazil put 2,000 people into "preventive detention" so they would not disturb the peace during Rockefeller's visit. This illustrates that not only is there now a greater degree of economic dependency, but the entire social and political structure of these "sovereign" states is tied to metropolitan needs and prevents economic and social development or political freedom for Asia, Africa and Latin America even within the bounds of international or national capitalism. That is why, for real development to occur in any of the underdeveloped countries, it is now absolutely necessary first to eliminate this capitalist structure. What Myrdal euphemistically calls "soft states" are merely those in which the big bourgeoisie is still effectively unchallenged in doing what it pleases — playing the imperialist tune. And since neither this local bourgeoisie nor that of the United States is going to give up its power voluntarily and without resort to still further violence, liberation from capitalism and underdevelopment is only possible through popular force of arms and socialist revolution.

REALISTIC SOCIAL SCIENCE THEORY

What does all this imply for us as students and social scientists who have all been brainwashed by conservative ideology and liberal reformism? We have to unlearn. In Myrdal's terms, we have to unbind ourselves — far more than Myrdal himself has been able to — from the traditional thought that all of us were taught and which is entirely inconsistent with both historical and present world reality, which — now that liberalism has made it inconvenient — is not even true to the 'traditional' thought of Adam Smith.

We must develop a social science theory that is capable of encompassing this reality of the nature and causes of the wealth — and poverty — of nations; and this theory must be historical, structural and dialectic. Most important of all, it must embrace the really determinant social system — world capitalism — whose historical development, complex structure and dialectic conflictive relations have created both the wealth of the few and the poverty of the vast majority of the world's people. This is something that all those who are to be honest, that is real, social scientists must do if we wish to assume our moral responsibility to the exploited and repressed people in the world, at home and abroad.

Not only must we realise that traditional thought is not and cannot be at the service of development for the majority of mankind but we must demonstrate how and why both traditional orthodoxy and liberal reformism, however heretic the latter may appear, in fact obfuscate historical and contemporary reality through a pseudo-scientific smokescreen that serves to maintain the *status quo* to the benefit of the few and at the cost of the many. Indeed, we must show how and why liberal heresies, so long as they appear to reform traditional thought while in fact remaining bound by it, support the *status quo* even more efficiently than the orthodox emperor's clothes that now reveal too much of the emperor's ideological nakedness. But beyond fighting this ideological and scientific battle against pseudo-scientific and traditional thought and forging a scientifically valid theory to replace it, we must — if we honestly wish to support economic and social development for the vast majority of mankind — dedicate this theory to serve the revolutionary action necessary to destroy the capitalist system which caused and still maintains and deepens underdevelopment in Asia, Africa and Latin America and to replace this system with one capable of serving humanity.

12

A Critical Review of the *History of Capitalism in Mexico: The Origins 1521–1763**

With all his valuable store of interesting facts—although they may be from secondary sources—and his intelligent use and presentation, the author, who has been a high level leader of the Mexican Communist Party, does not do honor to the title of the work, at least in this first of two planned volumes: this volume does not constitute a *history*, even less one of *capitalism*, in Mexico.

On the contrary, the author is determined to show through the most varied arguments of his own and through quotations from Marx that during the period in question capitalism did not yet exist in the world and much less so in Mexico. The author forewarns us of this on the third page of the introduction when he says:

> The first volume of this History of Capitalism in Mexico begins with the conquest. However, one thing is clear: *the means of capitalist production, insofar as it manifests in one or another sector, is found to be in a form that is potential, embrionic and suppressed by the dominant precapitalist relationships.* (p. 15)

Problemas del Desarrollo, Mexico, No. 17, Feb–April 1974, translated from the Spanish original.

*Enrique Semo *Historia del Capitalism en México: Los Origines, 1521–1763*. Ediciones ERA, Mexico, 1973, 281 pp.

After repeated variations on the same theme, the author ends up by saying in his last chapter:

> *However—let's leave it well established—the combination of tributary despotism, feudalism and simple mercantile relations give the system a dominant precapitalist character during the colonial period.* (p. 251)

After the brief introduction, in Chapter I the author reviews the productive forces in order to emphasize the low, although varied, development in general and, in particular, the difference between the lesser level of development in the indigenous as compared to the Spanish economy, even though the Spanish arrived almost without technological knowledge, especially in mining. In Chapter II the author analyses tributary despotism, which is an important but not adequately defined concept in the argumentation of the book. In this chapter he examines the attempt by the Spanish Crown, whose failure we feel is not sufficiently explained, to set up a sort of "dual society" by separating the Spanish from the indigenous economy and trying to protect or preserve the latter, and after its relative decomposition even to reconstitute it by means of regrouping and resettling the Indian population. At the same time he emphasizes or overemphasizes the difference and the competition between the Indian tribute destined for the king and that destined for private persons; and he mentions the difference between pre-Hispanic tribute and "that which was paid to the Crown. While the first was consumed directly by the ruling classes of Indian society, the Spanish Crown—colonial power—had to convert the greater portion of the products into merchandise in order to export the excess" (p. 88). And the tribute paid to individual Spaniards—we could ask—was not that converted into merchandise, more so if the Spaniards invested a major part of this tribute which in the beginning constituted the base of the accumulation? On the same page the author reminds us that

> The gradual imposition of tribute in money had a double effect: it obliged the commune member to work in the Spanish enterprises and it promoted the integration of the community into the market economy. In order to pay his tribute in money, the Indian had to go to the market as a seller of merchandise which could only be commodities or manual labor. (p. 87)

Moreover, the exploitation of Indian communities by Spanish cities "was fundamentally based on an unequal exchange" (p. 94).

In Chapter IV, "The Republic of the Spaniards (the structure)," the author argues that

> We can distinguish two phases of primitive accumulation . . . the second stage, we will call primitive industrial accumulation. . . . In this first phase of primitive accumulation commercial capital can continue to exist and grow perfectly without transforming the productive structure of the people in question. . . . In the XVI and XVII centuries in New Spain, manifestations of the first phase predominated: primitive accumulation flows into the formation of commercial and usury capital. These types of capital penetrate weakly and accommodate themselves to the interstices of the heterogeneous structure. It is only toward the second half of the XVII century when the buds of primitive industrial accumulation begin to manifest themselves vigorously. (pp. 168–69)

In that case we need to explain how and why—as the author shows in the following chapter—the later processes and the social institutions changed even more brusquely and frequently in the sixteenth century than those of tribute, and why the Spanish schema of a dual society was progressively condemned to failure by the demands of reality.

Chapter V, "The Republic of the Spaniards (work)," reviews various forms of extraeconomic compulsion of the Indian worker. On the one hand the author gives more importance to manifest slavery after its formal abolition in 1533 than other authors, on the other he argues aptly "that the legal forms of 'encomienda' and 'repartamiento' hide latent and generalized slavery of the indigenous population" more than feudal forms (p. 206). Chapter III, on the empire and international market, is summarized in its last phrase: "Through the colonial links, Spain transmitted to America its feudal institutions, embrionic capitalism and above all the peculiar cycle of its brief flourishing and its long decomposition" (p. 128).

In essence—as reflected by the repeated "however's" as well as the contradictory contorsions in reasoning—throughout the book the author fights with a ghost that obsesses him, and, what is more, a ghost that he seems to see and in whose existence he appears to believe, at least a little, in the intimacy of his being, although he knows it cannot really exist:

> Since the second half of the XIX century a stream of thinkers arose who have continued until our time and whose common feature is the identification of capitalism as commerce, exchange and money and who underestimate the importance of the productive forces and the relationships of production. To this stream belong the German

historical school, the liberal English positivists and other researchers (Buecher, Schmoller, Hamilton, Pirenne, Doptch et cetera). This
conception has been revived and presented as a new vision of the
economic history of Latin America. (p. 245, n. 10)

The author hardly explains the aforementioned "conception" and never
mentions anyone who has or could have presented it with respect to
Latin America or Mexico—claiming only that there is more than one
such author. A mutual persecution appears between this argument or
its authors and the ghost or his mysterious authors throughout all the
chapters and a good part of the pages and corners of the book that never
become reconciled yet do not dare to battle to the death. "The features
of embrionic and dependent capitalism" predominated in the great
silver mines which were the vital nerve of Mexican life and at the same
time, according to the author, its exception. Neither does he impose nor
are there any "characters" of feudalism—nor its confabulation and the
fight against tributary despotism, in the rearguard with feudalism and
mercantile relationships—in order to make up a mode of production
("character" according to the author on p. 251) that is predominantly
precapitalist, leaving a slight indefiniteness that does not reach the
supposed level of definition that the Trotskyists demand for "unequal
and combined development."*

The same conditions of struggle that his ghost imposes on him are
the very ones that hinder the author—a historian—from writing a
history. Since he finds himself so involved in the escape/persecution of
the ghost through all the structural fields and functional problems, the
author—and with him the reader—almost loses sight completely of *the
historical process* between 1521 and 1763, both in Mexico and throughout the world. This is so much the case that this last date seems totally
arbitrary, since he does not analyze any historical movement that would
culminate or change direction or quality in or near the date. Not that is
does not exist, for this is the date, for example, of the Peace of Paris that
closed a cycle of struggle for worldwide domination between the winner,
England, and the losers, the French and the Spanish; it is the beginning
of a long descending phase in the world economic cycle, which on the
economic plane brought with it the upsets that permitted and gave
impulse to the beginning of the industrial revolution. In the political/
economic area this economic decline would generate the independence

---

*In this respect see Manuel Moreno and George Novack. *Feudalism and Capital-
ism in the Colonization of America. An answer to Andre Gunder Frank*, Buenos Aires,
Ediciones Avanzadas, 1972.

of the United States, the French Revolution, as well as the change of Spanish policy toward the colonies known as economic liberalism within enlightened authoritarianism. This period also marks the beginning of the end of the golden cycle of Brazil, of the relative fall of prices of many products and the costs of inputs, including labor, and, therefore, of the increase in the price of silver, especially of the new cycle of silver production in Mexico. But these and other historical movements are not taken into consideration in the eagerness to establish methods and historical models. Thus, the 1521 date also is no more than that of the arrival of the Spanish in Aztec lands, apparently in a manner isolated from the history of either peoples. The processes and historical movements between both dates were entirely omitted. Thus, for example, the formation of the "hacienda"—which represented a new form to organize work and acquired importance after the epidemic of 1575 significantly diminished the availability of Indian labor and became dominant during the century while (and because) mining and overseas trade fell to a third of its 1600 level—is not discussed until the next volume because, according to the author, a social formation cannot be studied well until "it reaches its fullness in the XVIII and XIX centuries" (p. 259).

Therefore, the author prefers to concentrate on the analysis of structures, formations, and even the "dynamic of the system in movement" schematically outside of the historical process and to leave the relationship and the analysis of this last—or of parts of the latter— to other authors, such as Enrique Florescano and his colleagues, who have no Marxist pretensions. This is so much the case that only the last and brief chapter is dedicated explicitly to analyzing the dynamics of the system in movement (recently mentioned in quotation marks, because the chapter is named for this), and even with this title more than half (pp. 237–58) of the chapter again pursues/flees from the ghost (as we have seen in previous references) through "Marxist" and his own schematas, leaving very few pages for what one might call a Marxist analysis or for one of his own of the history (capitalist or not) of Mexico. With this, lamentably, Enrique Semo, despite his more than occasional contributions and correct points, has made himself the inheritor of the worst of "Marxist" historiography of Mexico such as that of a Manuel Lopez Gallo, in his schematic and misnamed, *Economy and Politics in the History of Mexico* (First edition, Ediciones Solidaridad, Mexico, 1965) or that of the ultraschematic Ramon Losada Aldana, whose book, *Dialectics of Underdevelopment* (Mexican and Venezuelan editions), Semo quotes as an authority, despite the reputation the book has gathered as the *"underdevelopment of dialectics."*

It is high time—in this critical juncture of the historical process of capitalist development—for contemporary Marxists to once more honor in practice the proper and fortunate dialectic between theory and history, encompassed in the practice of the classics of Marxism, leaving behind the schematic and without abandoning history—neither its analysis nor its practice—to the exclusive dominion of liberal reactionaries or progressive reformists. Let us hope that in his second volume comrade Enrique Semo dedicates his wealth of talents to successfully confronting this challenge of history.

ON
POLITICAL ECONOMY

13

Politics and Bias:
A Critical Review of Rostow
and Hirschman

Politics and the Stages of Growth by W W Rostow: Cambridge University Press, 1971; pp xiii+410; Cloth $9.50; paperback $3.95.

A Bias for Hope: Essays on Development and Latin America by Albert O Hirschman: Yale University Press, 1971; pp x+374; Cloth $12.50.

"The economic profession comes very close to having its own party system: one party extols, the other criticises the price system — in almost all the great theory and policy issues the lines are neatly drawn and the parties solidly arrayed against one another. The problem before us is notable in that it provides an exception to the rule. Both parties... appear to be in basic agreement... " (AOH 161)*. Hirschman's introduction to one of his essays applies not only to the price system but also to the two-party system and to the two books under review, with one exception — that the basic agreement, all superficial appearances

Economic and Political Weekly (Bombay), Vol VII, No. 38, September 16, 1972.

*Throughout, references to page numbers are in arabic numerals and to chapters in roman numerals. Where necessary, they are preceded by the initials of the author and/or first word of the title in reference.

notwithstanding, far from being exceptional is the rule. And it applies also to the hawk Rostow and the dove Hirschman.

It would be unfair to the author and scientifically incorrect to review and evaluate Walt Whitman Rostow and his work outside of the socio-political context in which he intentionally places himself. On the one hand, he sits in the White House basement as President Lyndon Johnson's 'Scherman Adams' or 'Kissinger' to construct US imperialism's escalation policy in Vietnam and especially to plan for bombing the North up to the China border (which he defended in scientific economic terms as aiding the capitalist underdeveloped countries' development efforts by obliging the socialist countries to divert resources from development to defence). On the other hand (of the *same* body), Rostow uses the university to develop and diffuse the outright reactionary ideology of "A Non-Communist Manifesto", as he modestly sub-titled his earlier "The Stages of Economic Growth". That book successfully became, through over 15 printings and as many translations, the single most influential ideological weapon in the defence of bi-partisan US imperialist interests in the "Third" world during the first United Nations (Economic) Development Decade announced by J F Kennedy, when Rostow was in charge of his policy planning at the State Department. No matter that the first "development" decade has been (excepting by Rostow) universally lamented as a disastrous failure or that the "scientific" quality of "stages" has been totally discredited at home and abroad.[1]

No matter, for Rostow is and perceives himself a successful ideologist and policy planner (witness that circumstances now oblige Nixon to execute the bombing of Hanoi and mining of Haiphong that Rostow had planned for Johnson). With his "Politics and the Stages of Growth" Rostow now proudly offers the frankly political sequel and companion piece to his earlier work. As he promised in the preface to his "Stages" a decade ago, and confirms in the preface to "Politics and the Stages of Growth", Rostow now proposes to replace Marx's solution of the "broader problem of relating economic to social and political forces" ("Stages" ix) by "reacting against his underlying view that politics was essentially a super-structure to economic life" and substituting "a view of politics as the effort to balance and reconcile problems of security, welfare, and the constitutional order, with the stages of growth ("Politics" x, 2). Irrespective of any scientific standards, Rostow returns to the ideological offensive: "If the 1970's is to be a Decade of Political Development . . . I would hope that this book might stimulate such convergence of reflection, stocktaking, and prescription in the decade ahead" ("Politics" 6).

FANTASTIC RELATIONS

The bulk of "Politics" is devoted to reviewing the familiar stages he invented a decade ago and filling them with still more fantastic "relations" between the "three key issues" of "security", "welfare" and "order" in the growth of "modernisation" in Britain, France, Germany, Russia, Japan, China, Turkey and Mexico. The traditional first stage (ii) is irrelevant to reality as ever. To achieve its transformation to post-Newtonian society, the most basic change was "the impulse to contrive"! The political preconditions for take-off (iii) are external intromission, according to Rostow who seeks to replace the Marxist thesis that change is generated primarily by internal contradictions. By contrast, in "the politics of the take-off and drive to technological maturity" (iv) which combines his earlier stages 3 and 4, the primary engine of change becomes internal rather than external. This, the longest chapter of nearly 100 pages, is totally devoid of any political economy of development or of any other scientific analysis which Rostow seeks to replace by ultra-schematic juggling of empty phrases about electoral "democracy" and "organised labour". Then follow Rostow's ideological whitewash of "not special" American development and "the search for quality elsewhere" (v and vi). There is no explanation of why "the Great Society surge of public effort . . . was not sufficient to match the scale of the problem". There is no relation, in Rostow's analysis of the quality of life in America, between the Negro vanguard, which he estimates at 2 per cent, and the "perhaps 20-25 per cent of Negro population — who have, as it were, fallen out of American society . . . ". As to Rostow's rendition of "Politics and Democracy in the Contemporary Developing World" (vii) it is hard to know whether to weep or laugh. The "relatively successful democracies" are in Mexico, Malaysia and South Korea! Other countries, with a few exceptions, lack the "broad majority agreement" and "loyalty to democratic values" that are the necessary "conditions for successful democracy". Rostow cannot (or does not want to) explain why. But whatever the reason, it has nothing to do with the politics of revolutionary romantics like Mao, Ho, Kim, Sukarno, Nasser, Nkrumah, Ben Bella, Castro who have done no more than engage in "external expansion". Rostow's support goes to Nkrumah's, Ben Bella's and Sukarno's successors because they "elevated the priority of growth and welfare" (279-281).

The last chapter, on war and peace in the world, on the other hand can leave no doubt. One can only weep at its lies about the past and the present and the future portends of imperialist policy that Rostow and his henchmen plan to fabricate out of their tissue of lies. The reader may feel that the word "lie" should have no place in a responsible, let alone scientific discussion. Perhaps, but only if the lies themselves are excluded, which Walt Whitman and his brother Eugene Rostow are far from prepared to do. The entire chapter is intended to perpetuate into the 1970's the Cold War and the Big Lie on which it was founded and which Rostow repeats as the cornerstone of his argument: that the cold war and American policy from containment to escalation was started by Stalin in his speech of February 9, 1946 and perpetuated by Soviet and Chinese external "expansionism". That Rostow and company know this to be a lie may be surmised from his own planning of aggression around the lie of the Tonkin gulf "incident" and his participation, according to his own record, in a hundred conversations between heads of state. Ordinary mortals only have the napalm, defoliants, and bombs or the authority of the "Pentagon Papers", to belie Rostow. On the other hand (of the same body), we may surely believe, and fear, Rostow when he predicts future policy for the US imperialist bourgeoisie: "Despite the rise of neo-isolationist voices in the United States, there is nothing in US interest or the balance of national opinion to suggest that America would not act promptly and with great strength in the face of an actual disruption in the balance of power in Europe or Asia — the pattern of convulsive reaction to be observed in 1917, 1940-41, 1947, 1950 and 1965. The march of the stages of growth in Asia will increase its relevance to American security in the generation ahead . . . Thus, the bedrock position of President Kennedy, Johnson and Nixon on Vietnam is that failure to hold there would forceably risk a larger war in a nuclear age" (260). Whoever does not believe Rostow on this score because he is drawn by the sweet tune of McGovern's electoral promises, should remember that Lyndon Johnson was elected as the "Peace Candidate".

GIANT STEP BACK

The Introduction, Chapter 1 and Appendix on the relations between other approaches and his own, synthesise the essence of Rostow's ideological approach and purpose: "The structure that informs this book may help move political science back towards unity. It offers a more general and dynamic framework . . . this book's insistence on the inescapable uniqueness of culture . . . its revival of the Platonic-

Freudian state within us . . . A book stands on its own feet. It is judged useful by others to the extent that it illuminates problems that interest them . . . These are my hopes. It is for others to decide" (334-6). Though the decision is easy — and negative — upon inspection of the text reviewed above, Rostow further facilitates it through the criteria of evaluation he himself provides in his own negative evaluation of political science in general and functionalism in particular. Rostow defines politics as the exercise of power in the first sentence of Chapter 1; and on page 17 goes on to observe that "the grand, unresolved problem of political science is how to relate politics in the narrower sense to the evolution of societies as a whole. The problem still not satisfactorily resolved is to link the political process to the domestic and external forces which generate the major problems. . . . " That is an interesting problem indeed. But does "politics" illuminate, let alone help to resolve it? No, not one least little bit. On the contrary, it does all it can to detract our attention therefrom. Rostow rightly (and except for the above quoted prediction of US foreign policy and the orientation of the book, which he says "is not exactly a New Left Tract", this is about the only thing that is right about the book) criticises functionalist political and social science for being fragmented, partial (equilibrium), unhistorical, static, conservative! Is his book a better, let alone a more general, dynamic move towards unity? Decidedly not. On the contrary, it represents a giant step backward even from functionalism and interest group theory to say nothing of Marxist political economy and the historical materialist analysis of world imperialism and national class structure and struggle, which this book is meant to replace. Instead, Rostow retains the proven defects of his stages, not the least of which is that they are static, quite unhistorical and indeed anti-historical in their denial of the single world historical process; then Rostow forcefeeds into his stages the most ideologically loaded indexes of the discredited concept of "modernisation" which he retains from the functionalists whom he criticises and from his MIT-CIA cronies, Daniel Lerner, Lucian Pye, Thiel de Sola Pool, *et al*, whom he lauds and thanks; and then Rostow has the gall to take Mao Tse-tung to task for not having "modernised" China according to the schedule Rostow's stages would demand! Scientifically speaking, there can be no doubt that "Politics" is a pitifully giant step backward even from "Stages".

But perhaps there is a saving grace, or as Hirschman would say, blessing in disguise. Ideologically speaking, Rostow is much clearer this time and tells us himself where his "Politics" begins and in what direction it heads; for lest we be misguided, he hastens to warn us: "first, I would underline that the use of the stages of growth as a framework does not imply an economic interpretation of politics" (24) and "second, this argument underlines the staying power and influence of culture . . . ideas have an authority of their own and a great independent reality" (24-25). Indeed, "what is at stake is a steady awareness that politics is ultimately shaped not by 'the masses' or 'elites' but by . . . unique personalities"! (8) Ergo, let us inquire into "the state within us"; let us return to Freud and Plato — and "to the old precept 'know thyself' " (333). "The romantic revolutionaries of the developing world are not the wave of the future . . . the case for abandoning gradualism and ameliorative change is weak . . . humane possibilities open if we can generate sufficient perspective balance, and modernisation. To contribute to that end is one purpose of this book." And whatever happened to politics as the exercise of power and the grand unresolved problem of political science?

REFORM-MONGERING

Apparently, Albert O Hirschman's "A Bias for Hope" is different in tone, style, scope and intent. Subtitled, "Essays on Development and Latin America", it collects together 16 articles written during two decades and introduces them with a new essay on "Political Economics and Possibilism". The remaining essays, as he tells us, "fell almost naturally into three distinct parts": "Elaborating the Strategy of Economic Development", on which Hirschman built his fame; "Addressing the Rich Countries; Critiques and Appeals", in which he displays his apparently naive appeal to men of goodwill (to use his own words, p 29); and "Addressing the Developing Countries: A Bias for Hope", in which Hirschman persists, against all evidence and scientific analysis, in his bias for reform mongering (again to use his own words), already observed in his earlier "Journeys toward Progress" and "Development Projects Observed".

In contrast to Rostow and the hawks of the professional establishment of American economics, Hirschman displays dovish sympathy for Latin American "radicalism" represented by Mariategui and Haya de la Torre in the 1930's, import substituting nationalism in the 1940's and 1950's (iii, iv), and the United Nations Economic Commission for Latin America (ECLA) since then (xii, xiii), in the Introduction and final chapter Hirschman is even sympathetic to his interpretation of Marxism. And in between he addresses the "rich" and their professional hawks with competent critiques of the Alliance for Progress (vii); of false friendship (abrazo) and other inter-American ties, in order to "increase the range of practical co-operation in problem-solving activities between the United States and Latin America" (173, vi); of foreign, and specially programme instead of project, aid (viii); of foreign investment, which he appeals to be replaced by "devestment" (x, xi); he challenges export price and other anti-cyclical stabilisation policies (v), supposed social and institutional obstacles to change, which he supposes to be non-existent, blessings in disguise, or to do "a quasi-vanishing act" through gradualism, possibilism and a bias for hope (xiv); and he calls to task conservatives and radicals alike for their own supposed "obstacles to perception of change" that is supposedly taking place cumulatively, albeit imperceptibly (xv). In short, in most of these chapters Hirschman is perceptibly reform mongering.

QUITE CLEAR

But Hirschman is also quite clear, scientifically and ideologically speaking, about where he begins and where he is leading us. "A Bias for Hope" is the elaboration, as he says, of his strategy of economic development, which Charles Lindblom (co-author of Chapter II who shares "converging views") has aptly dubbed as "muddling through". But the "passion for the possible" and the "bias for hope" of Hirschman is not limited to reformist development strategy; it also extends to "The Science of 'Muddling Through' ", as Lindblom entitled his article (in the *Public Administration Review*, 19, 1959, 79–88). Thus, Hirschman clarifies in his Introduction and concluding chapter that "in proceeding now from economic theories of politics to political economy (or political economics, or politics-cum-economics) proper, I shall stay away for the time being, from any semblance of a general theory [7] ... it seems quite unlikely that there exists somewhere a key which would bring into view the usually hidden political dimensions of economic relationships ... Each time, it seems to be a matter of specific *ad hoc* discovery [12] ... this ambiguous situation, incidentally, characterises also less crucial, more 'middle-range' casual relationship, [357] ... we must be suspicious of paradigms that pretend to give a clear-cut answer ... large scale social change typically occurs as a result of a unique constellation of highly disparate events ... that makes prediction exceedingly difficult and contributes to that peculiar open-endedness of history" (354–356).

ALTERNATION AND OSCILLATION

In both his development and scientific muddling through strategy, Hirschman abhors clear definitions and optimal or pessimal solutions, as well as the "excessive constraints and unescapable dilemmas" they pose, instead of "looking for optimal combination" (26). Thus, both suggested that we devote at least a portion of our time and efforts to understanding the possible usefulness of alternation and oscillation, as opposed to optimal combination" (26). Thus, both booms and busts, if they come in appropriate sizes and sequences, are useful for economic development (v) and presumably scientific development as well. Similarly, Hirschman argues, "the developing countries could need an appropriate alternation of contact and insulation, of openness to trade and capital of the developed countries, to be followed by a period of nationalism and withdrawnness" and to be followed presumably by a further period of "exploitative, retarding, stunting, and corrupting effects on the underdeveloped countries" through their contact with the imperialist metropolis (25).

Hirschman explains "what I shall call my 'possibilism': . . . this 'native' disregard of sociopolitical realities and of vested interests precisely rooted in my possibilism . . . these proposals are not presented as being so revolutionary or so utopian that they have no chance whatever to be adopted . . . I feel an obligation to make them in concrete institutional detail thereby deliberately creating the optical illusion that they could possibly be adopted tomorrow by men of goodwill" (28-29). Like Walt Whitman Rostow, perhaps? "The notion of 'blessing in disguise' is so congenial to my thinking that I pointed to one such 'inverted sequence' . . . Take the seemingly self-evident [to Rostow, for instance] notion that a consensus of basic values and political procedures is a precondition for the establishment of a viable democratic system . . . The causation has often run the other way — democracy has come into being as a result of an accidental, but prolonged stand-off between forces originally quite bent on crushing each other; and what basic consensus about political decision-making is later found to prevail in these cases can be shown to have been the consequence of democracy, rather than its cause" (30). Witness the "difference" from Rostow: perhaps the "Republic" of Korea is not yet a "relatively successful democracy" as Rostow claims, but perhaps also there is still hope because if the stand-off in the class struggle there is prolonged enough democracy might result as an accident!

Thus, "a third general foundation for possibilism is in the notion of unintended change consequences of human action and in its relation to change . . . unintended change is often likely to be more revolutionary than change brought about by the most revolutionary of change agents" (31, 37). Notion indeed!

CONNECTION WITH MARXISM

In the light of these meta-scientic (or classically meta-physical) notions of Hirschman, it may seem strange that he expresses a sympathy for Marx, whom he now calls "the master" and, even more so, that he now writes "I was not aware how close I was to this generalised Marxian model of interaction between economic and political forces when I wrote 'The Strategy of Economic Development' . . . Why did I fail to make the connection between one of my principal theses and Marxism?" (17).[2]

We may hazard a double answer. First, the connection did and does not in fact exist and Marxism had not sufficiently revived from its post 1920's slumber for Hirschman to perceive and be obliged to come to terms with in the 1950's. Thus, the long chapter (xiii) on "Ideologies of Economic Development in Latin America" was first published in 1961 and contains no reference to Marxism of any kind. Republished today, that influence is of course conspicuous by its absence. Secondly, therefore, writing the introductory and concluding chapters in 1970 of a book that is largely "addressing the developing countries" in Rostow's "Decade of Political Development", Hirschman must now try to accommodate his dove approach to a tendency that, he says "has recently characterised Latin American social and economic thought" (351).

Hirschman cannot, like the Rostowian hawk party, reject Marxism out of hand. Nor can he ignore it like he once did. So Hirschman proposes that the "Marxism scheme can be usefully varied . . . in applying it to slices of reality smaller than was intended by the master. In any event, this is what I have been doing" (18, 17). Why on earth, we may ask, is it "useful" to do that? Hirschman tells us quite unabashedly on the very same page: "A number of points can be made about such transpositions of the Marxian scheme to smaller-scale processes of economic-political development. In the first place the political and institutional changes that are needed in any one of these sequences are less likely to be revolutionary than those that interested Marx"! (18). Moreover, "it is useful in permitting him to get away from one feature of the Marxian system which is still very much on the — conscious or unconscious — mind of numerous contemporary writers: The obsessive search for the vanguard or spearhead of revolution" (22). In the same connection, we may recall the cogent observation that the dean of American sociology, Talcott Parsons, made in his centenary commemoration of the Communist Manifesto: "It is this analytical breakdown which is for present purposes the most distinctive feature of modern sociological analysis . . . It results in a modification of the Marxian view . . . The primary structural emphasis no longer falls on . . . the theory of exploitation but rather on the structure of occupational roles." For Rostow, of course, even role theory is too radical and must be replaced by "the Platonic-Freudian state within us". In this "age of the *action-arousing gloomy vision*" (emphasis in Hirschman's) he "would caution against the exclusive reliance on it that has recently characterised Latin American social and economic thought" whose "vision ties in directly with my dislike of paradigms laying down excessive constraints on the conservable moves of individuals and societies" (351). "But with the view of revolutions as overdetermined or unique events, it turns out to be a toss-up which form of large-scale change is more unlikely: so we may be on the lookout for whatever rare openings in either direction appear on the horizon . . . Incidentally, this interpretation of revolutions undermines the revolutionary's usual critique of the advocacy of reform"! (359). "These essays are pervaded by certain common feelings, beliefs, hopes and convictions, and by the desire to persuade and to proselytise which such emotions usually inspire" (27). Amen!

THE TWO PARTIES

In conclusion, Hirschman's reference to the two parties that apparently differ because one criticises while the other extols, which was quoted in our opening paragraph, and the whole discussion reviewed here may remind us of Marx's debate about the capitalist (or, as Hirschman and Rostow call it, the price), system with Proudhon in the "Misery of Philosophy" or about free trade with the bourgeois industrialists of his time. They all wished, in the words of a song that was popular in the United States not so long ago to accentuate the positive and eliminate the negative — not realising that the good and evil of the capitalist system, the two parties of the American economics and political establishment, as well as the "different" arguments and styles of Rostow and Hirschman are indissolubly linked and complementary. (We have had to make the same observation about the "analysis" of another liberal reform monger, Robert Heilbroner, who seeks to accentuate "Point Four, the Peace Corps and foreign aid generally" while trying to eliminate Rostow's "policy of defeating communism". (See "Mr. Heilbroner's Rhetoric and Reality" in A G Frank "Latin America", *op cit*, chapter 9.) They are no more than the "opposite" sides of the same capitalist economic coin or bourgeois political medal. The hawkish Rostow claims to resolve with one hand the grand problem of political science with grandiose "scientific" schemes while with the other he bombs Vietnam into a hell on earth only to (have us) conclude that "the case for abandoning gradualism and ameliorative change is weak". On the other side the dovish Hirschman muddles through smaller slices of reality to create the optimal illusion that the accidental unintended consequences of his naive appeals to the rich to divest themselves of their economic and political power "are less likely to be revolutionary than those that interested Marx" or the people who aspire, if not to heaven on earth at least to a humane society. Rostow assures us that "I do not believe peace in the world will be brought nearer by the unilateral weakening of American power and influence... President Johnson sought to translate this new environment into positive movements towards order and stable peace. And some progress was made... And President Nixon has pursued those efforts in continuity with his predecessors... There has been nothing automatic or explicit about this rule. It followed, simply, from the perceived danger of total war in a nuclear age" (WWR 350, 312, 308). But Hirschman's bias is to dislike the "excessive constraint" of being "constantly impaled on the horns of some fateful and unescapable dilemma" between Rostow's hell and a revolutionary earth. What hope does the bias of his muddled strategy offer? Hirschman answer: "After all, there *is*, at least temporarily, such a place as purgatory!" (352, emphasis and exclamation point *are* Hirschman's!)

NOTES

1. For the present writer's evaluation see the section on Rostow's "Stages" in my "Sociology of Development or Underdevelopment of Sociology" in *Catalyst* (Buffalo) No. 3, 1967, reprinted by Pluto Press, London 1971 and in A G Frank, "Latin America: Underdevelopment or Revolution", New York, Monthly Review Press 1970, Chapter 2, or J Cockcroft, A G Frank and D Johnson, "Dependence and Underdevelopment", New York, Doubleday Anchor, 1971, Chapter 12, as well as A G Frank, "Ode to Underdevelopment" in *Tricontinental*, No. 8, 1968.

2. In this connection, a personal *mea culpa*: While Hirschman then did not make the connection, the present writer made it explicitly in his review of Hirschman's book

in *Economic Development and Cultural Change* Vol 8, No 4, July 1960, pp 433–440. The reviewer was still taken in by the apparent difference between Hirschman's unorthodox possibilism and established obscurantism. Witness that in footnote 1 of Hirschman's present Chapter II (originally published in 1962) he writes: "Another line of related work is represented by Andre Gunder Frank's 'conflicting standards' organisation theory. It is . . . sufficiently similar to be of interest to anyone who wishes to explore further the areas of unorthodoxy described here. See A G Frank, 'Goal Ambiguity and Conflicting Standards: An Approach to the Study of Organisation', *Human Organisation* 17 (1959): 8-13".

14

The Theories of Milton Friedman on Chile: Equilibrium on the Point of a Bayonet

Andre Gunder Frank and Ted Wheelwright

This Lateline program (No 477) was broadcast on ABC Radio 2 on April 5, 1976. A. G. Frank was in the studios of Hessischer Rundfunk, Frankfurt, and Ted Wheelwright was in Sydney. The program was produced and presented by Mike Cosby.

I'd like to begin with a quotation from John Maynard Keynes: 'Practical men who believe themselves to be quite exempt from any intellectual influences are usually slaves of some defunct economist. Madmen in authority who hear voices in the air are distilling their frenzy from some academic scribbler from a few years back.' When that was written in 1936 the pace of life was slow enough to allow some of these economic doctrines to mature before they were applied. Today things move more quickly and for perhaps the first time in history an economist has been given a whole country to use as his laboratory — and the experiment has been a tragic disaster.

The country is Chile. The economist, Professor Milton Friedman of the University of Chicago, author of *Capitalism and Freedom* and *Studies in the Quantity Theory of Money* — a theory that gave rise to the term 'monetarism', a popular doctrine with conservative governments around the world, including those in Australia and New Zealand.

Australian Broadcasting Commission, *Political Economy of Development*, Sydney, 1977.

For almost twenty years Milton Friedman has been educating economists from the Catholic University of Chile and now, since the military coup d'état in 1973 these men, with Friedman still as their adviser, have been running the economy of Chile — with a little help from the military and the secret police.

One of Friedman's graduate students at the University of Chicago in the fifties was Andre Gunder Frank who was even then uneasy about the ideas that underlay the doctrines issuing from the Department of Economics at Chicago. When he graduated, Gunder Frank went to South America and was confronted with realities that seemed to him to contradict the theories with which he'd wrestled in Chicago.

Dr Frank, who has studied and taught economics and sociology at the University of Brazilia, the University of Chile and the National University of Mexico, is now becoming increasingly recognised for his theories on the nature and causes of underdevelopment. He is now a guest at the Max Planck Institut in West Germany where he's writing a history of capitalism.[1] Ted Wheelwright is Associate Professor of Economics at Sydney University.

Dr Frank, I would like to ask you about the situation in Chile, it has been described recently by Jonathan Kendal as the worst economic crisis in Chile's recent history. What exactly does this mean for the man in the street?

Frank: The man in the street experiences the crisis in one way and the junta and the bourgeoisie in another way. The man in the street has been suffering for a long time but is suffering increasingly now. For instance, in December the new official price of bread, which was one of the few fixed prices, and the new official minimum wage, were such that people had to work over six hours for one kilo of bread. There is increasing malnutrition. You get reports of 50% malnutrition in some cities, and much more in some zones. The children faint in school from weakness, and when they are fed from the school lunch program, they vomit because their stomachs are not used to food and reject it. Even now the junta has gone so far as to bar from the kindergartens, which are now more than anything else a lunch-breakfast program, children that are more or less normally nourished, and to accept only the under-nourished. In July last year the sale of bus tickets in Santiago alone was 12,000,000 a month less than normal, that is, 32% less than normal. That is to say, people walk to work because they can't afford to pay for bus tickets. In fact bread and bus tickets make up about 80% of the lowest public employee's wage. This is the level of the man in the street.

I might mention another individual case of how these policies work themselves out. A former student of mine, D. Perez, was killed last October with the intervention of helicopters and armoured cars and so on at a farmhouse, in a shoot-out lasting several hours. Two of his brothers had already disappeared, and have not been heard from in many months. They have been taken by the so-called DINA, the Chilean Gestapo (which incidentally is advised by a certain Helmut Raut who was a high Gestapo official in Germany and head of two concentration camps in France during the last world war). But getting back to this personal case, since that time his mother has been detained and his younger brother and sister, aged about eight, were killed in their home by the junta police. This is a policy of completely exterminating a whole family and this has been an institutionalised process of persecuting not only those who are opposed to the regime but of persecuting the whole family, including grandmothers, aunts, and little children, as a calculated policy of terror.

Wheelwright: Can I just butt in, Gunder, and say that the kinds of things you are talking about have as you know the support, believe it or not, of Eduardo Frei, the former Christian Democrat President of Chile; and according to the London *Guardian* (8/2/76) he has now published a book in which he describes the leaders as fascists, 'Totalitarian right wing nationalists marked by the maintenance of vast and costly repressive services, the domination of the economy by a few monopolies, subjugation of minds through propaganda and mass communications media and the destruction of the worker movement'. And in the same book he gives some overall figures which help to round out the theme. Unemployment is at least 18%, industrial output has gone down 20%, construction 15% and the rate of inflation, he reckons, was at least 340% last year. Now these statements are from the former President Frei of Chile, who was President before Salvador Allende.

> *If I can get back to the economic situation. In our newspapers here recently we had a letter to the editor about torture in Chile; the heading of it was 'Torture in Chile: The Economists are worse'. And it ended up by saying that the real sufferings of the vast majority of Chilean people result from the harsh and dogmatic measures being applied there by 'the University of Chicago school economists who have the military's ear'. Could we move on to talk now about this particular economic doctrine, which is being applied in Chile. What is this so-called Friedmanite doctrine?*

Frank: As far as Chile is concerned, it can, should and must be termed economic genocide; a calculated and massive policy of genocide through hunger and unemployment which is perhaps unknown in the recent or perhaps even distant history of the world in peacetime. The policy could be summarised by saying that it first started out with the so-called freedom of prices; secondly, freedom in the capital market, both of which produced a vast inflation. Thirdly, it destroyed the labour unions in order to thereby reduce wages. Wages were reduced through the destruction of the labour unions and also of course from the inflation which was the result of the first two policies. A further action was to sell, at give-away prices, the public enterprises that had been built up not only by Allende but before him, since 1940; to sell them off to so-called private enterprise; to return the land which had been expropriated in the land reforms during the terms of Frei and Allende to the former owners.

Really the policy was to export everything possible and impossible from the country at the expense of the population; to hand over the whole country, lock, stock and barrel to imperialism, particularly to American imperialism; and then to reduce the state sector in the sense of reducing state employment, and social security. Chile had the most advanced public health system in Latin America for many, many years. This has all been abolished, and the health system has been made private. A pay-as-you-go health system has been instituted, but since no one pays (they can't afford it), they die.

Wheelwright: That is all very familiar to us here. But what I would like to ask you at this stage — what people here in Australia are interested to hear, Gunder—is (a) why did Friedmanism develop in the USA, (b) how did it get sold to the people in Chile, and (c) why are so many other governments around the world really picking it up? You see our government here is influenced very much by this sort of thinking, by monetarism, and you have to relate this to what is going on here, so that there are three parts to this question. Why did Friedmanism develop when it did in the USA?; how did it get exported to Chile?; and why is it popular in countries like Australia with right wing governments?

Frank: When I was still a graduate student at the University of Chicago in the mid-fifties, a program of training Chilean economists from the Catholic University, that is to say, the most reactionary university in Chile, was begun. For many years students from that university came to the University of Chicago to study economics; and economists from the University of Chicago went to Chile to teach there, to advise and to reform the whole study program. This was all led, particularly, by Arnold Harberger. And they trained generations of economists in the Catholic University who have come to be known colloquially as the 'Los Chicago Boys', similar to the so-called 'Berkely Mafia' who took over the economic reigns in Indonesia after the Suharto coup. They have taken over the management of the Chilean economy after the Pinochet coup. And they have implanted the qualities that are associated with the economic theory of the University of Chicago, with Mr Friedman. So that is one way how it began in October 1973, one month after the September 11 Coup.

Ted Wheelwright, can you describe what Friedman economics is. What is the doctrine?

Wheelwright: It's an incredible reversion to the days of Adam Smith.

Frank: I would not want to blame poor Adam Smith for it. I doubt if he were alive today, he would subscribe to it.

Wheelwright: I know he would not subscribe to it, but how else would you describe a philosophy which goes back and puts the emphasis on individual freedom and the virtual abolition of government, the destruction of public sectors, welfare states, and all the other sorts of responses to the incredible injustices and the oppressions of the capitalist system? How else can one describe it, Gunder?

Frank: Well, I would describe it precisely as a policy of economic genocide preached by Friedman and others, who only select that part of Smith which is useful to them and reject, or forget about, and don't teach the other parts of Smith that don't fit in. You can hardly say that the state has been abolished when the budget of the military and the police have gone up multifold, when the number of soldiers have gone up multifold, when the state uses a repressive apparatus comparable to or greater than that of Nazi Germany.

Wheelwright: Yes, well that is the essential point, it is the destruction of one kind of state and the creation of another in its place, is it not?

Frank: That's right, but it is not a question of abolishing the state or the state's interference in the economy. Quite the opposite. It is a question of who the state works for.

Wheelwright: Yes, but it is, in the terms of most people's understanding, an abolition of the state's sector of the economy. The state-owned sector. This leads us to the point that Frei makes in his book, the de-nationalisation of the economic system. It seems to me that one of the ways in which the Chilean economy could have remained viable was to develop a form of state capitalism of some kind. It seems to me that this is now being destroyed. Frei gives the example of a couple of state-owned companies being sold out, one to Firestone and the other to Parson and Whitmore — American corporations.

Frank: What he says is that it is not only de-statisation, but de-nationalisation, in the literal sense of the term. As he says it's 'not that they are sold simply to private owners, but to the only ones who can buy them, namely foreign ones'.

Wheelwright: Yes. But he also said, and this is important too, that what is going on, and here I quote from him, 'is the concentration of economic power in fewer and fewer hands, that veritable empires are being built. People begin by setting up financial societies and end up by taking over banks and industries'. It is not only the question of the tremendous repression of the poeple both political, social and economic. It is a fact, it seems to me, that the economy is being handed over to American imperialists and at the same time there is this concentration of economic power, all in the name of Friedmanism — which is supposed to be based on freedom. It is a good example of the dialectics of freedom turning into its opposite, isn't it?

Frank: Well, that is why there has been increasing opposition even within the bourgeoisie in Chile, because they are also increasingly being squeezed out.

Wheelwright: I can see that Friedmanism goes back to the relationship of the University of Chicago with the banking people. There is a link between monetarism and the banking people, who don't like inflation because it is bad for actual debtors. There is something in that. There is something in the decline of capitalism which calls forth this backward looking movement. No doubt about that. But why people in Chile should find that this appeals to them is hard to understand.

Frank: People don't. A small part of the bourgeoisie . . .

Wheelwright: Right, but which part? Which part of the bourgeoisie and why?

Frank: The monopoly bourgeoisie and that which is associated with imperialism and particularly with American imperialism — as even Frei, who is a representative of the monopoly bourgeoisie, finally recognises. This policy plays into the hands of the monopoly bourgeoisie though Friedman and company claim, of course, that this is all very fine and neutral.

Wheelwright: Friedman's economics is not a neutral economics. It is an economics which is a class one and in the interest of a bourgeoisie;

which has the effect of redistributing income very much in their favour and concentrating economic power and selling out the underdeveloped countries to the imperialists. So let nobody think that it is in any sense a neutral, scientific kind of economics.

It has been suggested that Friedman's economics has failed in Chile. It seems to me that it in fact has succeeded. In your recent article for instance,[2] Gunder, you suggested that 25% of total income has been transferred from the lower and the middle income group to the upper 5% of income brackets. In other words, that a year ago the upper 5% of the income bracket received about 50% of the total income. So, in those terms, as you describe Friedmanism, it has been very successful.

Frank: Put it the other way around. At the time of Frei, wages and salaries amounted to about 50% of the national income. Allende raised that to over 60%, and the junta has depressed it to about 35%.

One of the complaints in the international sphere has been that the military dictatorship has never been able to solve the economic problems in Chile because they inherited the problems from Allende — so they maintain. Now one of those problems was a foreign debt of some $3.5 billion at a time when they only had $3 million in reserves. What is the situation now in terms of the foreign debt?

Frank: The question that you ask has several aspects. At the beginning, of course, they claimed that all their problems and all their policies were determined by what Allende had done. They went on to blame not only Allende but also Frei, in fact, all the governments since the 1938 Popular Front. More recently, they have stopped talking about the Allende period and the comparisons which they themselves make are with the year 1969 or 1970, before the Allende period. Because from a petty bourgeois point of view, and in many respects from a bourgeois point of view, the situation has become very much more unfavourable than it had been during the Allende period — so now they blame all their troubles on the world crisis. The fact, for instance, that the price of copper has gone down and the price of imports, oil and wheat and so forth, has gone up.

Mr Friedman comes and says 'No, you have to stop blaming Allende, you can not only blame the international situation, you have also to blame yourselves. You have to blame your own economic policies, which are based on my theories, but you do not carry them out as thoroughly as you should. You are not taking enough of my medicine'. The rate of inflation had been higher than the rate of the increase of the money supply, and even though they had reduced the increase in the money supply in the early months of 1975, the rate of inflation had increased again. And at that point Mr Friedman appeared personally on the scene and had interviews with Pinochet, interviews on television and radio and in the press and recommended his so-called 'shock treatment'. Friedman himself called it a shock treatment and brought this term into circulation.

His advice was then carried out: which was to reduce the money supply still further by reducing government expenditure. He proposed that expenditures be reduced by 25%. But since the 1975 budget already contemplated a 10% decline in state expenditure, what the junta decided to do was to reduce the budget from then on in escudos (the national currency) by 15% and the foreign exchange expenditure by 25%, thus drastically cutting imports. They anticipated inflation of 50% per year, but in fact the policy of reducing inflation by that method did not work. The inflation in 1975 was as Frei says — and his information is from the official cost of living index, from the official junta statistics — the rate was 340%. And in 1974, according to the same junta statistics, it had been 376%. Thus with the application of this policy the rate of inflation was reduced by only 0.8% per month, which is nothing.

Wheelwright: This is very important. You see the greatest thing that Friedman get publicity for in this country and others, is that he has the solution to inflation. What you are telling us is that with all that dreadful repression and ruination of the economy, it has only gone down a few per cent in twelve months. Is that your message?

Frank: That is right. But that is only a small part of the matter. Because the rate of inflation did not decline, real government expenditure declined much more than anticipated. The government spent a budgeted amount of escudos, but because the rate of inflation continued so high, the real worth of these escudos was less than anticipated. From the beginning of the implementation of the Carlos Plan — Carlos is the Friedmanite, super-economics minister — government expenditure actually declined between 30% and 40%.

The result has been, and Friedman knew that this would be the case, a choice between accelerated unemployment for a short time (according to Friedman, until the 'shock treatment' could shock the patient into a state in which he could then recuperate), or long-term unemployment. He says the same thing, incidentally, to the United States. The medicine for fighting inflation necessarily implies an increase in unemployment. He does not deny that.

Wheelwright: I get worried by these medical analogies. It seems to me that what he is doing is stopping the circulation of the blood by amputating all the limbs.

Frank: Right. Let me give you just a couple of indications. Unemployment in Frei's time was around 5% or 6% and rose to between 7% and 8% in the last year. Allende brought unemployment down to around 3% or 4%. The junta raised unemployment, and this is by official statistics (which as we know are always much understated), to 8% by August/September 1974, thus doubling it in one year. By January/March 1975, just before Friedman came, the unemployment rate had gone up to 12%, and by October 1975, five or six months after the application of the Friedman medicine, official unemployment had gone up to 17%. Similarly, industrial production had a capacity utilisation of only 50% in the textile industry. In particular plants you get utilisation of rates of 15%, 20%, 40%.

Wheelwright: Could I just interrupt you there, Gunder, and say that you have given us more than sufficient evidence to show that the policy is not working. I think people accept that, even the junta. But the question is why?

Frank: It is not working for the people, it is not working for that part of the bourgeoisie. But it is working for those people who, as Mr Frei said, benefit from this policy. Except that those who benefit are becoming a smaller and smaller number, and those who suffer from it are becoming a bigger and bigger proportion, not only of the people, but of the middle-classes and of the bourgeoisie itself. Even American capital finds that it has not been benefiting lately.

Wheelwright: But why has Friedmanism obviously failed? Is it anything to do with the Chilean economy? Would it fail wherever it is tried? And if so, why?

> *If I can interrupt. It seems to me that Friedman's policies are being attacked on two levels. Firstly, because it seems his policy can be implemented only with severe limitations on human rights; a sort of balancing the budget on the point of a bayonet. And secondly, because the policy failed as economic theory anyway. It seems to me that one thing that economic theory or economic policy depends on is accurate analysis of economic behaviour, of the way in which society is run. I wonder, Ted Wheelwright, if you talk about that kind of failure.*

Wheelwright: Well, there is one good point that is made actually by Frei and the articles surrounding this book, and that is that the Chilean economy, industrially speaking, has always been very heavily concentrated. There are one or two firms in each particular industrial sector.

Frank: As in all underdeveloped countries, and increasingly in the industrialised countries.

Wheelwright: Precisely. And if that is so, what happens when output is reduced is that costs go up, and being monopolists, or semi-monopolists, these firms are really interested in selling a smaller number of things to a smaller number of people and getting a higher profit. Instead of the other way round. In other words, I think the fundamental thing is that the basic institutions of both underdeveloped countries, and increasingly of advanced countries, are such that they do not fit with what Friedman thinks exists. He thinks in terms of smaller units competing with one another, but that went out with the Do-Do. I think this is the basis of it, Gunder. I know there obviously is something else to add. Would you agree with that?

Frank: Yes and no. I think we make a serious mistake any time that we use a sort of 'ignorance theory of history'. I don't think that anybody does things out of ignorance. Neither the junta nor the US Government nor Friedman. Friedman is not stupid, he knows what the world is like. It is true that he talks in terms of a competitive model in an increasingly monopolistic world, but he certainly knows, he must know, that what his policy does is to increase monopoly in the world. That is why he has political support from the extreme right. That is why he became economic adviser to Barry Goldwater. That is why in 1970/71 for a time, Nixon applied Friedmanesque policies in the USA. However, the results were similar to, though less drastic than those in Chile, and Nixon was obliged to abandon these policies and impose his so-called new economic policy in August 1971.

Wheelwright: I agree with that. The only thing is that if you read Friedman's books . . .

Frank: Capitalism and Freedom — but freedom for whom?

Wheelwright: Right, we know who it ends up being freedom for, but in his books he gives the impression that he is for freedom for the little fellow. At least that is what people reading these books get out of it. If you read these books in abstraction, you would not get the connotation that you and I are putting on it.

Frank: Well, the thing is, one should not look only at abstractions, but at the concretisation of these abstractions. The whole American and western so-called ideology is 'freedom', the 'free world'. But what does this mean? The United Nations General Assembly passes resolutions against Chile but at the same time the United Nations Agencies, the World Bank, the International Monetary Fund, the Inter-American Development Bank, have been supporting the junta to the hilt economically. Mr McNamara — ex-Director of Ford, ex-Secretary of Defence (that is to say Offence), President of the World Bank — says the World Bank operates only on economic criteria. What are these economic criteria? Well, he says they are such that because of inefficiency the World Bank made no loans to the Allende Government, but it has given a $100 million loan to the junta, and only two or three weeks ago made another loan of $30 million, despite the fact that a substantial number of members of the World Bank Board voted against this loan. Nevertheless, because the USA has such an overwhelming vote in the Bank, the loan went through.

At the same time the US Congress on an amendment from Kennedy now opposes the junta. The US also voted against the junta in the UN resolution, as I mentioned earlier on. But if you look at what the Executive does, you get the same thing that you got in Angola, Rhodesia and South Africa. The Congress says one thing, but what the Government does in fact is to support these right-wing regimes. And it has supported them to the tune, in the case of Chile, of $680 million loans from the US alone. The junta has received $2,000 million, that is to say in American terminology, $2 billion in loans in the twenty-seven or twenty-eight months of its existence: thus, more than $3 million a day, $100 million every month.

> *So what is going to happen now? We hear from the* New York Times, *for example, that the dictatorship now is obliged, and is in fact quite happy, to pay something like $750 million every year in debt service alone; that is, just paying the interest. Which is going to work out at something like 45% of the total export earnings in 1976. So what happens in that situation?*

Frank: Well, this is really a policy of economic genocide. The junta has drastically reduced the import of food, and it has drastically increased the export of what they call non-traditional commodities, that is, not just copper, but all kinds of industrial products, food products, and processed food products. They are denying their own people in order to export and earn foreign exchange. They go around and get these credits from the US and from the international agencies; now they are looking for them among the Arabs. What do they use these for? For one thing, of the $680 million loans from the US, $380 million, or 56%, is used to pay the copper companies that Allende had expropriated and for which the junta is now paying expropriation prices far above the book value of these companies. That is to say, this money is being used to pay limited American interests at the cost of a deliberate and calculated policy of economic genocide. This is going to continue and increase in 1976 unless there is a wholesale change in economic policy, and of course, this can only happen with a wholesale political change.

Wheelwright: So, what you are saying, Gunder, is that the Chilean people are being starved to pay the international bankers, the multinational corporations of the rich world, and Milton Friedman is the ideologue of that policy. That is it in a nutshell, isn't it?

Frank: That is it in a nutshell.

NOTES

1. André Gunder Frank's publications include: *Capitalism and Underdevelopment in Latin America: Historical Studies of Brazil and Chile* (Monthly Review Press, 1967), *Latin America: Underdevelopment or Revolution* (Monthly Review Press, 1969), *Sociology of Development and Underdevelopment of Sociology* (Pluto Press, 1971), *Lumpenbourgeoisie: Lumpendevelopment — Dependence, Class and Politics in Latin America* (Monthly Review Press, 1972).
2. This is a reference to Frank's 'Open Letter About Chile to Arnold Harberger and Milton Friedman', *Review of Radical Political Economics*, Vol. 7, No 2, Summer 1975. A second open letter, based in part upon material collected by Dr Frank in preparation for this radio program, has since been published. Both letters have been republished in a booklet, *Economic Genocide in Chile: Monetarist Theory versus Humanity* (Spokesman Books, 1976).

15

Critique of the Finance Minister's 1970 Report to the Congress of Chile

(written with Marta Fuentes)

It can be instructive to compare the Report on the State of the Public Treasury that Finance Minister Americo Zorrilla made to Congress on November 27 (1970) with the report given the day before by the secretary general of the Communist Party, Senator Luis Corvalan, to the full session of the Central Committee of the Communist Party, which participates in the government of Popular Unity (Unidad Popular, or U.P.) represented by the finance minister (who in turn is a member of the Central Committee of this same Party). Furthermore, this comparison can offer a basis for an indication—although brief and partial—of the political line and the corresponding measures that eminate from the Popular Unity's program and from the Communist Party itself, which do not appear yet to have been incorporated into the economic policy of the government of the U.P. as it was set forth by Finance Minister Americo Zorrilla.

Santiago, Chile, December 1970 Manuscript privately circulated but not then published in order not to offend the new popular government.

Luis Corvalan's speech is a political plan destined for the people. Americo Zorrilla's speech is an economic exposition directed at Congress. This difference between the speeches might seem at first glance to be natural and correct. However, the comrade minister's plan appears to be far less than adequate from a popular point of view, as expressed by his own comrade, Corvalan. The latter said that "One can already see that it is not a matter of just one more government, but of a popular and revolutionary government which the nation needs to firmly confront the solutions of its most primordial problems." Addressing himself especially to the working people, comrade Corvalan later added: "The fullfillment of this role demands in some cases a change of outlook and attitude to abandon nonpolitical, economicist, or narrow corporatist positions." Unfortunately, the tone and language of Minister Zorrilla's exposition and the major part of the economic policy he expounded do not seem to reflect the change of outlook and attitude that Corvalan considers necessary. This makes it extremely difficult to see that this government is not just one more government.

Although comrade Zorrilla's exposition was read by someone who came from the working class, it is precisely the apolitical and economicist tone and content which is inappropriate in a speech addressed to workers or to the general public. The ideology manifested in comrade Zorrilla's speech is by no means a popular—even less a worker—ideology, but rather a bourgeois and, in part, middle-class ideology.

Analyzing in the first chapter of his speech the current state of Chilean economy, Zorrilla begins: "The characteristics of the economy is the structure of the system which determines the factors. . . . " Underdevelopment, inflation, and the current economic standstill are repeatedly attributed by Zorrilla to the "system's structure" or to the "economic structure." He does not clarify that behind this economism and apparent apoliticism is basically the class structure, and he does not show how inflation has been a bourgeois weapon in its class struggle against the working class to seize the fruits of its labor. In his analysis of the Chilean economy, Zorrilla makes the distinction that this economy is a "monopolized economy," but he makes it seem that the monopoly lies more in the concentration of property than in its use by the bourgeoisie to exploit the people. In distinguishing, secondly, that the "Chilean economy is a dependent economy," Zorrilla does mention that the "interests of the big national bourgeoisie are identified with those of the imperialist monopolies" but he shows this identification to be only a "pillaging of our economy . . . and the drain of foreign exchange." Thus Zorrilla fails to identify dependence with this monopoly and exploitation, and he does not note how this dependence is also manifested in the bourgeois ideology which tries to hide exploitation and class struggle behind economicism and apoliticism. Thirdly, Zorrilla points out in his analysis of the present state of the Chilean economy "how the big monopolies take advantage of the State," but we will soon see that this close relationship between the state and the entrepreneurial bourgeoisie does not figure in Zorrilla's exposition of his economic plan for 1971.

Although he is finance minister—or by virtue of being a minister of a popular government—comrade Americo Zorrilla could leave behind economicism, apoliticism, and corporatism. He could distance himself from the group of finance ministers, and from those traditionally interested in their speeches, by giving speeches destined not only to awaken the customary public debates on financing the budget, but also capable of awakening—not to say encouraging—popular debate on the popular implementation of the Popular Unity's program. The comrade minister could aspire to transform the public treasury into a popular treasury and to make his statements not ex cathedra but ex-popular.

THE STATE: BY WHOM AND FOR WHOM?

Luis Corvalan pointed out in his report to the full Central Committee of the Chilean Communist Party that the "people have conquered the government which is a part of political power. It is necessary to secure this conquest and advance even more, to win total political power so that the entire apparatus of the State passes into the people's hands." He observes correctly farther on that the "political constitution, the laws, and the institutional organization respond above all to bourgeois interests . . . the bourgeoisie and the oligarchy still occupy strong political positions." Corvalan also adds that the "imperialist enterprises and the different groups of the oligarchy dream of seeing the popular government entertain itself with insubstantial measures. But this will only be a dream." As Corvalan explains, the policy of the Popular United Party,

> . . . however, would be a mere anti-inflationary attempt to redistribute income and promote economic recuperation and would scarcely have a reformist character if it did not go beyond this, if this were the entire economic policy of the popular government. Happily, it is not so. This policy is more ample . . . its true reach, its profound revolutionary sentiment are evident if one takes into account that in the days to come the greatest tasks will be broached,

such as the nationalization of copper and the banks, the state ownership of a group of monopolistic industries and of important groups in foreign trade, as well as a profound and accelerated transformation of the countryside.

Comrade Corvalan considers that such policy corresponds entirely to the interests of the workers and observes that "there is a cabinet composed of four workers and from which the personages of imperialism, big business, large landholdings, and elegant surnames are absent." Although this is so, and although the finance minister comes from the working class, it remains to be seen if the role that the finance minister assigns to the state in his speech truly corresponds entirely to the interests of the workers, or if many of the institutions and measures of the state still answer to bourgeois interests.

We have already observed that, referring to the past and the present state of the Chilean economy, Minister Zorrilla singles out the exploitation of the state by the big monopolies, pointing out that there exist "in this country large monopolies whose expansion and growth has been possible thanks to state credit and aid . . . whole branches of production have been initiated by the state sector and were then transferred to private monopolies." The finance minister also observes that the Chilean state has been "a mechanism for foreign penetration in regards to, among other things, its regulatory policy—the foreign exchange law—and that also some public and private enterprises which contract credit abroad" mock the norms supposedly established to protect national interest, that "various institutions from the public sector 'contract external debts,' which in great measure revert to the private sector through monopolistic groups," and "that there is an evasion in the transfer of surpluses among public companies."

Furthermore, the minister observes that the state has allowed "negative real rates of interest" although he does not mention other facts of public knowledge such as the state subsidy of the large private companies through credits from CORFO (the state industrial finance corporation), approximately half of which are never returned to the state.

The finance minister proposes to eliminate some of these abuses by which the great monopolies take advantage of the state (although he makes no allusion to the fact that the existence of these debts left unpaid beyond the legal deadlines could constitute a powerful legal weapon for a popular state against the entrepreneurial bourgeoisie).

However, we must analyze who will benefit from many other state measures announced in Finance Minister Zorrilla's exposition. The minister says, "among the measures for state aid to industry one must single out the new financial credit agreement for business, especially small and medium-sized businesses." He also mentions "on the other hand, state support for small and medium-sized agricultural producers." In addition, with regard to his "policy of supply," "the government will use all its incentive and stimulatory capabilities for producers in those sectors with slower reaction or subject to constriction or shortages," apparently without limiting itself to small or medium-sized companies. In this sense he says "we call special attention to a new instrument of economic policy, the production contracts, which will have particular importance. These consist of agreements between the state and businessmen, by sectors and branches of production with a buying guarantee by the state, eliminating all risk for the producer." The minister announces the state's use of this "new instrument" in industry and agriculture for the supply of the national market and for export. "Just as we pointed out in the introduction, private industry will play an important part in the future economic development of Chile," for which the finance minister expects "new private investments," notwithstanding that according to documents prepared by CORFO and ODEPLAN (the state planning office) during the Christian-Democratic government, already 80% of all investment in Chile is paid for by the state and the major portion of "private investment" is also financed by the state.

With regard to foreign investment, documents prepared in CORFO under the Christian Democratic government show that the "contribution" to the country is derived almost entirely from locally received credits and not from any foreign contribution of capital and still less of foreign exchange. Finance Minister Zorrilla himself recognizes that this so-called foreign investment amounts to a pillage of our economy, and yet—just like the aforementioned Christian Democratic documents—he proposes only to "modify some parts of the foreign exchange law and of the rules governing foreign investment" and to accept foreign capital "with preference in each case for mixed investment with state capital, which controls the majority of shares." It should be remembered that this formula is precisely the essence of the "Chilenization" of the Christian Democratic government and that in Chile, as in other underdeveloped countries, this formula has so far led to growing submission to and dependence on the so-called multinational enterprises and their imperialist governments not only for private firms but also for the state itself.

In regards to foreign trade, it is proposed that the "state slowly take over import business which will be passed over to state businesses . . . affiliates of CORFO and other state organisms," also increasing state participation in export business in some branches. With this intent it is mentioned that "ALALC and the subregion ANDINA will be given a decided boost insofar as our country's participation is concerned," as was also done by the Christian Democratic government even knowing that both treaties were only instruments for imperialist penetration into Latin American industry. "Toward the international financial organizations that have been the principal financial and political tools of the 'public sector' of imperialism in support of its large private monopolies, Chile will maintain its participation in such organisms and will fulfill the obligations that it contracts freely and independently," and "in regards to the foreign debt, the government reiterates its decision to fulfill obligations contracted" by the Frei and Alessandri governments in its eagerness to allow "the state to be taken advantage of by the big monopolies" where the interests of the big national bourgeoisie is allied with and depends on imperialist monopolies, especially in the North American ones."

"We will not return to the policy of periodic devaluations, all the more so because the outlook for foreign trade and the balance of payments [are] favorable," but he does not offer assurances that there will be no more devaluations when these circumstances become unfavorable (which they subsequently did, as we may add with hindsight).

"Yet the government will take measures to compensate for possible negative effects of this decision on those companies which export a substantial portion of their production or those that substitute imports as we have explained previously, assuring beforehand that they will be able to program their volume of production without seeing profitability affected by foreign exchange policies." Also "import policy will always be made with its effect on national producers in mind."

In conclusion, the "economic policy of the Popular Unity government in its fundamental plans has as a central objective the replacement of the present economic structure . . . in order to begin the construction of socialism. In order to accomplish these objectives the government will initiate the development of three large areas of property: state, mixed, and private. The state area will be the dominant and will be formed by the current state companies, plus those which are created in the future, those which are expropriated especially in the sector of our natural resources, the large national and foreign monopolies, the banks, foreign commerce, and all those activities that are strategic for national development."

"In this field the government proposes to begin the process with the great textile and cement monopolies." The development of three areas of property is nothing new in itself, since it has existed in Chile for some time. The state area experienced a big development under the

Popular Front government from 1938 to 1945 and a certain setback under later governments, which as Minister Zorrilla observed, transferred many businesses back to private hands in order to boost the mixed and private areas. Whether the announced nationalizations will have, as Luis Corvalan hopes, "a profound revolutionary meaning" will depend not so much on the transfer of these businesses to the state area per se but how and when and if "all the State apparatus passes to the hands of the people" as Corvalan stated in another part of his report, or in other words, on the extent to which mobilization and popular democracy succeeds in the Popular Unity government. In the meantime, the Christian Democrat senator, Renan Fuentealba, asserts that "the announcement of nationalization and structural reforms do not frighten us. Naturally we will support them as long as they are carried out as expressed in Tomic's presidential plan, on the basis of the legal structure." Notwithstanding this, one must observe, as the *Mercurio* (the main opposition newspaper) did, that the level of indefiniteness and the very slowness of the process until now could feed the anxiety of business circles, which is not very propitious for the increase of private investment which the government hopes for.

On the other hand, these structural changes cannot bring a direct benefit to the popular masses that they can immediately perceive: the masses of people do not eat copper, nor do they have bank accounts, and the economism of comrade Minister Zorrilla's language does not allow him to give any explanation of how these nationalizations could indirectly lead to direct economic benefits which the people expect for themselves immediately.

However, the wage policy of the U.P. government which directly and immediately affects the economic well-being of the people, and which could form the basis for the immediate mobilization of the people in the class struggle that comrade Corvalan announces, makes it extremely difficult to see how it is that the U.P. government is not just another government. When Minister Zorrilla says that the "minimum wage will increase at a rate equal to the consumer price index plus five additional percentage points, and the compensation for a sum that fluctuates between one and two minimum wages will be adjusted at a rate equal to the rise in the cost of living plus three percentage points," the minister speaks as if the consumer price index were really equal to the rise in the cost of living. However, as the Chilean housewife knows perfectly well and as it has been calculated in a study on "The Effective Rate of Inflation in Chile" (the preface of which was edited by the current minister of economics when he was director of the Economic and Planning Institute of the University of Chile), the real rise in the cost of living during this year has been at least 10 points higher than the consumer price index (of 29.5% until October 30), which was calculated or rather manipulated by the Christian Democratic government and which the minister of economics now cites and uses. How then can one see that this is not just one more government—but instead the popular revolutionary government that the nation needs—if in the three fundamental directives that guide the wage policy for 1971 the new government bases its wage adjustment on the intentionally falsified index of the previous government; if the present government suggests that a wage increase equal to the rise of this price index (but not of real prices) can restore workers purchasing power to the level of January 1, 1970; and if the government of the U.P. claims only to increase by a few more points the compensation of the one and two minimum wages knowing, as the minister of economics reports, that 30% of Chilean families receive *less* than one minimum wage and 60% less than two minimum wages, and leaving the private sector to "readjust its wages in the percentages or amounts that may be bargained and agreed upon" and that the wage readjustments will not even be received until January 1971? How then will one be able to see that we do not have just one more government, if this wage policy is just like the policy of former governments including the policy of Jorge Alessandri—"the rich man's candidate"—who at the beginning of his presidential term also tried to raise the wages of the very poorest a little more than that of those who are less poor? In order that in the U.P. government "such a policy corresponds entirely to the interest of the workers" and in order that one can see immediately that "this is not just one government more" and in order to permit an immediate mobilization of the popular masses, the immediate policy directly perceived by the people will have to be something different, which could begin with measures concerning prices and wages.

In this sense one could immediately begin to question the validity of the consumer price index prepared by the Christian Democratic government and inherited by the Popular Unity government. And while the new government questions the validity of the old index (although its composition was changed only a year ago) the people—who through their own suffering know very well that the rise has been greater than that indicated by the index—would be able to participate actively in establishing what the true rise in the cost of living has been during 1970. If, as the U.P.'s program points out, "the rise in the cost of living is hell in the homes of the people and especially for the housewife," who better than she would be able to measure the heat of this hell in its true intensity? Thanks to the Christian Democratic government there already exist mothers' centers. Could not the mothers of the people participate actively through these centers and collaborate with

DIRINCO (the state consumers bureau) to establish the true rise in the cost of living—the true decline in the standard of living—that the people must have suffered during 1970? And should not the readjustment of wage rise of "100 percent of the price rise" (plus the additional points that the minister proposed) be based on the true price rise and really restore for the people their buying power of January 1, 1970?

But even so, since—as the program of the U.P. points out—"Every day a little part of his wages or of his salary is robbed from the Chilean who lives by his work" the restoration of the buying power of January 1, 1970 would not mean the regaining of what has already been stolen each day for the past 365 days. And although the people will never be able to regain all of its patrimony, the Popular Unity government could initiate a small partial restitution by proclaiming an immediate Christmas bonus for the public sector (for salaries up to one or two minimum wages) and recommending it to the private sector.

Based on the Popular Unity program, the "Popular government will immediately begin a real administrative decentralization according to a democratic and efficient plan that eliminates bureaucratic centralism and replaces it with the coordination of all the state organisms" and "from the very day that it assumes power, the Popular government will open channels so that the influence of the workers and the people will be expressed, through the intervention of social agencies, in the adoption of decisions, and in the fiscalization of the function of the state administration." If this democratic plan also includes state enterprises and if they take into account the influence of the workers in the adoption of decisions of the state administration, could they not extend this democratic participation immediately to the decision about which private firms are to be integrated into the state administration—favoring the discussion of the same point within the unions of various large enterprises? And could they not do the same on the large estates, where the peasants would be able to express their influence on decisions about the future—private, cooperative, or state—of the properties or businesses where they work?

CLASS STRUGGLE

Comrade Luis Corvalan pointed out in his report that the "great battles are only now beginning. New class confrontations will come"—and he warned that it was wrong to minimize the strength of the enemy and his possibilities for maneuvering. He also warned that the enemy is again lifting his head and organizing strong resistance. In these circumstances, as comrade Corvalan explains in his report, "The total fulfillment of the program demands an incessant battle by the people, by the government, and by the popular classes walking in the same direction, always hitting the same target; in relation to each problem, to each task of the Popular government, the combative presence of the masses is indispensible . . . above all we trust the mobilization of the people."

However, in the program explained by comrade Finance Minister Zorrilla, who should—according to Corvalan—abandon economicist and apolitical thinking, the class struggle (and as we will see in the next section the mobilization of the masses as well) is conspicuous by its absence, even if the class struggle merits some isolated references set apart from the economic policy.

Minister Zorrilla does point out that the interests of the big bourgeoisie and imperialism are the same and says that his program "represents the beginning of the destruction of the material base that supports the most reactionary sectors of the country"—and in another part of his speech he says that "it will be necessary definitively to overthrow the ruling class." Nonetheless, the economic policy of the U.P. government set forth by Minister Zorrilla in fact completely ignores the class struggle and covers it up by his economicist and apolitical language.

After one of his allusions to big imperialist capital and dependence, the comrade finance minister reminds us that "recent experience shows that it is impossible to overcome an economic and social situation of this type by a reformist policy, which only tries to attack effects and not causes and whose final result is an even worse economic situation, since reformism definitely is directly favorable to the privileged sectors of the system, that is the ruling class." We will have to ask ourselves, then, in what way does the economic policy of this government set it apart from that of just another government? The comrade finance minister himself replies in various parts of the exposition of his economic policy: after September 4 (the date of Allende's election), "popular vigilance and the responsible action of many businessmen prevented damage to the productive structure, and the knowledge of the true policy of the U.P. restored tranquility." The comrade minister promises "to assure the normality of internal production" and to take measures that "guarantee the normal supply of imports." The public sector will be tending to rationalize the use of available material and human resources and in agriculture "it will be possible to rationalize the use of financial and human resources" in order to permit a "harmonious functioning of the economy." In that case, what new class confrontation, what incessant battle by the people, will assure this reasonableness, normality, and harmony in order to return tranquility to whom?

Minister Zorrila alleges that the "planned development that will have as its guiding thread the transformation of the social relationships of production prevalent today will assure a rapid and decentralized economic growth, a framework within which it is possible, for the first time in a real way, to resolve the immediate problems of the great majority," but in the reality of this world in both the developed as well as in the undeveloped countries it is precisely the capitalist social relationships of production that make planned development impossible, and which makes it an absolute necessity for the people to transform these relationships. If in reality planning of development could precede the transformation of the social relationships of production or would permit such a transformation, capitalist reformism would be viable, and socialism—not to mention the socialist revolution —would not be historically necessary. But the reality of the present day world shows that the true historical process marches in the opposite direction of what Minister Zorrilla says. The transformation of the capitalist social relationships of production has to precede planned development in order to permit it, and not the reverse as the comrade finance minister claims. In other words, the class struggle to transform social relationships cannot be replaced either by planned development or by the harmonious functioning of the economy or the normality of capitalist production.

We have already observed in the previous section that the U.P. government's wage policy scarcely contemplates the class struggle in the matter of prices, readjustments, and collective agreements in wage determination or that to the extent to which it implicitly recognizes that the class struggle also operates through the distribution of income, the U.P. government seems to put itself more on the side of business than on that of the worker whose interests it claims to serve by such a policy.

In the same diagnosis by the finance minister, inflation and government monetary policy do not appear as the instruments of the bourgeoisie in its class struggle against the people that they are. In pointing to the large producers and wholesalers as the source of the price rises, which is undeniable, the minister's report seems to deny the class struggle over the popularly immediately perceived exploitation at the level of retail merchants, which is an equally undeniable fact.

The intervention of the class struggle and the U.P. government's intervention in the same appear moderated when it offers almost unlimited facilities to the small and medium-sized industrial and agricultural firms, which are in competition with the big producers, and therefore often exploit the workers even more than the latter. Moreover, it also remains unclear how the possible incorporation of some of these large industrial and agricultural firms in the public sector might reduce instead of increase this competition with the medium-sized and small producers, which would lead the latter to exploit their workers even more.

With regard to the class struggle, the urbanization of peasants and the urban renovation program announced by comrade finance minister is also remarkable, since this program does not seem to contemplate any redistribution of already existing housing but only the financing of new construction through the "greater use of private savings," an effort to generate more internal savings and more credit from international organizations, which seems to avoid any contribution to this financing by the bourgeoisie and the monied middle class.

The rental ceiling of 10% of the renter's income, which was announced in the U.P. electoral program, receives no mention in the report by the finance minister. There is not even any reference to the already existing law that limits the annual rent to 11% of the assessed value of buildings, whose unprecedented enforcement by the U.P. government would drastically reduce the scandalous profits from urban construction, which results in luxurious housing for the few and none for the many.

The people are hardly able to see how the economic program outlined in the Congress by the finance minister is "designed to satisfy the people's interests" or how "it represents the real interests of the immense majority of Chileans." It is understandable how "behind this program stand the immense majority of all those Chileans whose objectives are basically the product of their struggle and whose hopes and wishes constitute a powerful instrument for their fulfillment," as the comrade minister claims in the last words of his report. If, as we believe, the objective interests of Chileans are the outcome of their struggle, then they really precede rather than follow this program. It becomes impossible to understand or to accept the choice that the finance minister poses when he claims that "for our future development there are two alternatives: either to activate dependent capitalist development by opening up and delivering our economy to foreign capital, which means politically complete submission to imperialism and indiscriminate reliance on internal repression; or alternatively to begin immediately with structural changes that lay out a new framework for the economic, political, and social development of Chile in the perspective of socialism. Obviously, we have chosen this latter option." It is not understandable how it might be possible to "activate" capitalist development through total submission to imperialism and internal repression at a political cost for a supposed economic gain. But it is also impossible to understand how it might be possible to "begin immediately with structural changes" without there being the fruit of a policy of class struggle in which the working masses mobilize themselves to defend themselves and win against their class enemies.

This class struggle could immediately express itself in democratic planning and in the influence of the workers and the people on the same, which means the initiation—or the acceleration—of processes such as those mentioned above: questioning the Christian Democratic government's price index and the construction of a popular index of the rise in the cost of living; denunciations—also through the mothers' centers— of illegal price rises; union pressure in the private sector for a bonus similar to that in the public sector; and wage adjustments that really restore lost purchasing power without excluding that they could and should raise real wages and salaries of workers; redress for workers against the exploitation and mistreatment by the bosses, which takes the form of pressure to expropriate or nationalize industrial, commercial, and agricultural firms, etc. In that case, what are we to make of the promised state guarantee to medium-sized and small industrial, agricultural (and also trading?) firms against expropriation and state support to them through credit and other help? Does that also imply a state guarantee of protection against the class struggle and in favor of these businessmen at the cost of the workers? The right of medium-sized and small firms to exist within the law as long as they abide by it, and the benefit of credit and other facilities that they need to operate, cannot make the bourgeois—nor the petit bourgeois—entrepreneur safe from the class struggle, which may express itself in worker redress against exploitation (which is often more severe in small than in large firms) or in the complaint by housewives against retailers that sell lower quality goods at higher prices in small towns and working class districts than they do in the elegant residential areas of the big and petit bourgeoisie. It is only thus, in the words of the U.P. electoral program, that the "present structures can be broken up, and progress in the task of liberation is only possible through the unified action and combativeness of the immense majority of Chileans."

MASS MOBILIZATION

Luis Corvalan said in his report that "this period is wholly favorable to the formative and revolutionary action of the popular government," but that this action "could only be the fruit of the struggle of all of the people, the mobilization of millions of Chileans" within which "a new responsibility lies with the working class." The secretary general of the Communist Party "emphasizes above all the importance of the U.P. base committees" (organized before and for the election), which he says "are and will be the real motor forces of the organization of the program." Thus, "they will permit the widest expression of the urgencies, concerns, and sensibilities of the people in the heart of the state apparatus, which will overcome inertia and bureaucratism." Nonetheless, the report of the comrade finance minister ignores such mass mobilization in practice, and insofar as the program is carried out as it was set out by the minister in the Congress, it would foreclose any mass mobilization, which is the only force that is really able to promote this program.

It is true that in his words Minister Zorrilla recognizes that mass mobilization is the decisive lever behind the implementation of the U.P. program and that the latter cannot be a gift but only the fruit of the people's struggle. It is true that the minister recognizes that under the U.P. government the economy should be guided with the participation of the workers and that it should be administered in close contact with mass organizations. But in that case we must ask why this report by the minister was itself prepared in great secrecy behind closed doors, which left the people waiting anxiously outside. Is that an example of worker participation and mass mobilization as the decisive lever for the implementation of the announced program? Does the economicist and sometimes unintelligible language of the minister's report to Congress serve as a fighting flag for the mobilization of millions of Chileans?

The comrade minister says that it will be necessary to defeat the Chilean ruling class definitively, which is "a task not only for a government but for an entire people. There the guarantee for the fulfillment of these objectives lies in the people's control of economic and political power expressed through the state sector of the economy and through general planning of the same." How, we may ask, can the people defeat the ruling class if in this stage of the struggle political power is to be expressed through the bureaucratized state sector?

The minister announces that "we will implement a series of mobilization programs, among which we may emphasize those of housing, public works, investment by state firms, revival of industrial demand, deepening of land reform, and promotion of exports." If these are the "mobilizing programs" that the government wants to emphasize, but which, with the partial exception of land reform, are those of the state bourgeoisie, then, we may ask, what place remains in the U.P. program for the mobilization of millions of Chileans?

The finance minister observes that "these objectives are accompanied by changes in the traditional forms of operation, among which we may mention: (a) organize the state-owned machinery and equipment to rationalize its use and avoid its deterioration; (b) coordinate all the state organisms for the production and distribution of financial resources...; (d) use all kinds of contracts...." Are these the changes in traditional forms of operation proposed by a minister who shows us that we are not dealing with just one more government?

Moreover, with regard to his "new instrument of economic policy" through production contracts, the finance minister proposes price, quality, and variety controls that are based exclusively on bureaucrats. With regard to land reform, the finance minister does not offer many details, but he announces the need for new legislation by the Congress. With regard to the formation of a new wage and social security policy, the finance minister mentions the direct participation of workers and proposes the recognition of CUT (the trade union federation). It remains to be seen what kind of mobilization this means of the working class, and especially of its still not unionized but most exploited part.

The finance minister says that "the discussions about price rises will be public, and any citizen will be able to have access to the pertinent authorities." It remains unclear if this public discussion will take place in the working and residential areas of the people affected by the price rises or not. There is no mention of any organized forum for the discussion of these price rises by the people; and there is no indication of how, in the absence of any people's committee to serve his interests in the matter, any citizen could have access to the pertinent authorites if he lives in a slum or indeed a world without telephones or has no knowledge of DIRINCO (the state price control agency). On the other hand, the finance minister makes quite clear that "we have initiated the strictest control of prices ... in the attempt, above all, to centralize the control over the big producers and wholesalers and to prosecute drastically anyone who violates the law." That is to say, he intends to centralize control in the state bureaucracy rather than to diffuse it through the people and to penalize the big producers and wholesalers with whom the people have no direct contact of any kind. So herein as well there seems to be no prospect of, and much less a place for, public but people's mass discussion of price rises by people's committees and still less for any intervention on their part before the "pertinent authorities."

In summary, all the proposed measures are based on "public" but not on "people's" or mass action. "The 1971 budget, which reflects the beginning of a process of change in the structure and function of the public sector tending to rationalize the use of human and material resources at its disposal . . . principal emphasis is put on planning . . . seeking the most effective integration of each public organism and institution into government policy." This clarifies what is public but not what is people oriented. Where in this program is the decisive lever of the people's mobilization of millions of Chileans?

CONCLUSION

In his report to the full session of the Central Committee of the Communist Party, Luis Corvalan proposes the "very important question of priorities and rhythm in the implementation of the program, in making important decisions," adding that this should be the "fruit of the realistic analysis at every moment." He also added that the "very mission of the committees of the U.P. is also the vigilance against manoeuvers and seditious plans of the reactionaries and imperialism." It is most urgent, therefore, to ask ourselves if the report and the program of comrade Finance Minister Americo Zorrilla is the fruit of the "realistic analysis" at this moment and if "in the very important questions of priority and rhythm" this program permits us to say it stimulates "the vigilance against the manoeuvers and seditious plans of reactionaries and imperialism" by millions of Chileans. It appears obvious, merely by posing the question, that the answer is clearly negative. With regard to priority and rhythm, the "government of the U.P. has decided to modify the budgetary exercise of November and December" to finance public works and pensions for the armed forces. Where then is the realistic analysis of priorities and the rhythm in the implementation of a program which lets us see that this is not a matter of just one more government but of a people's and revolutionary government that by immediately lowering prices and raising wages of the working masses could permit vigilance by millions of Chileans against the manoeuvers and seditious plans of the reactionaries and imperialism, which—as Luis Corvalan cautioned about, one day before Minister Zorrilla spoke—is again raising its head and organizing strong resistance?

Against the maneuvers and seditious plans of the reactionaries and imperialism, the working people will immediately have to make the realistic analysis, to establish the priorities and rhythm of the realization, and to organize and mobilize toward these goals. The Popular Unity program stated: "The committees of Popular Unity will not only be electoral organisms. They will be interpreters and combatants for the immediate vindication of the masses, and above all they will prepare themselves to exercise popular power. Thus, this new power *that Chile needs* must begin to form right now wherever the people organize to fight for their specific problems and wherever the consciousness of the necessity of exercising it develops." The U.P. electoral program also stated that "it would transform the municipalities into local organs of the new political organization . . . so that in conjunction with the neighborhood councils and coordinated among themselves, they can take care of problems of local interest to their communes and to their inhabitants" and that "an extensive network of Local Centers of Popular Culture would encourage the organization of the masses to exercise their right to culture." These organizations and others yet to be created—especially unions for the most exploited workers of small and medium-sized businesses, which according to the U.P. program will have the right to unionize and who while waiting for and in support of the necessary legislation will in the meantime be able to form committees—all have a role to perform in the class struggle and popular mobilization. And this mobilization would immediately be able to include specific problems such as "The cooperation of Neighborhood Councils to hear of and resolve special cases such as fights, acts of killing, abandonment of the home, and violation of the peace of the community" (No. 38 of the first 40 measures announced by the U.P. government), the fight against alcoholism, and the eradication of bootlegging (No. 18), and other measures. If the people themselves organize and mobilize in order to fight these social vices, supporting themselves and even developing their own moral force, why would transit and other police in the working class neighborhoods need to go around with firearms, which are a symbol and tool of the repression of the people? Instead—economically benefited and socially and politically mobilized—the people would be able to complete the task that ultimately depends on the masses "developing consciousness of the necessity of exercising it": "vigilance against the manoeuvers and seditious plans of the reactionaries and imperialism."

Everything depends ultimately on the immediate creation and activiation of an organized instrument in the social, political, and economic plan that truly "will permit the widest expression of the urgencies and concerns and the sensibilities" of the masses as the secretary general of the Communist Party stated in his report to the Central Committee.

It is necessary and urgent that the people themselves express the urgencies, concerns, and sensibilities of theirs; that these be translated into another 40 measures for the Popular government while the first 40 are being implemented with the massive participation of the people themselves. Could not the comrade president of the Republic himself, now that he is elected by the people, take the initiative of proposing and offering to the people an organizational instrument that permits them to catalyze and focus their concerns while at the same time expressing their urgency?

16

The Political Economy of the Economic Policy of the Communist Party of Chile

"The Political Economy of the Economic Policy of the Communist Party of Chile" is the title of an essay written in Chile in mid-1973, all copies of which were lost in the September 1973 coup. That essay made extensive quotations from the major speeches or writings of three successive Communist Party finance or economics ministers in Allende's Popular Unity Government and criticized the same, arguing that their non-, indeed anti-, revolutionary reformist theory, policy, and practice violated the Popular Unity's own announced program of political mobilization and that the Communist Party's constant demobilization of the masses—reflected and executed also through the Communist Party economic ministers' policies—would necessarily lead Chile into political disaster. The essay began with a summary and critique of the Communist Minister Américo Zorrilla's Programmatic Report to the Congress in November 1970, which outlined the official economic policy only three weeks after Allende assumed office on November 4, 1970. This critique, written in November/December 1970, argued that the economic policy was starting off on the wrong—the right instead of the left—foot. Since this critique is presented in Chapter 15, there is no need to repeat it here. The essay went on to quote and criticize the subsequently most widely discussed document,

---

Santiago, Chile, 1973 (Manuscript), quotations translated from the Spanish original.

"The Working Class in the Conditions of the Popular Government," delivered as a major speech by the leader of the right wing of the Communist Party, Orlando Millas, just before he assumed the finance ministry in mid-1972. The essay ended with quotations from and critiques of the article "Revolutionary Perspectives and Tasks on the Economic Front" (*Revista Universidad Tecnica del Estado*, Nov/Dec 1972-Jan/Feb 1973) published by the Communist Party's chief professional economist, José Cademartori, shortly before he in turn would become minister of economics. The critiques of these two documents are no longer available, and it would be difficult if not impossible to reconstruct them now. But since both Orlando Millas and José Cademartori were so crystal clear in certain parts of their speeches and writings, it may suffice to let them speak for themselves here and to add only the briefest commentary of my own.

About half way through Allende's 1,000 days, the more radical, independent Pedro Vuscovich was dumped as minister of economics (as distinct from finance), and the helm of the economic ship of state was confided to the Ministers Edmundo Flores (MAPU) and Orlando Millas (Communist Party). The latter, particularly, immediately cut the economic engines back to half speed, and on some parts of the zig-zag route—for instance nationalization of monopolies—he even sought to put the engines in reverse. It was the stewardship of Millas that launched the inflation—previously under control—to the runaway stage, while he instituted a wage and salary (*reajustes*) policy that cut the real income of the population and reduced the income of the poorest most of all. These measures and others designed politically to demobilize the masses had been foreshadowed if not announced by Millas' above-mentioned "NEP" speech.

This speech proceeded in the manner that was characteristic of all three and other such documents: first make a polite bow to Marxist orthodoxy and the need for working class struggle (reflected in Millas' title), and then proceed to do the opposite, which is the real purpose of the whole exercise. Thus, Millas began by repeating slogans about the importance of worker mobilization (which he more than anyone with a similar power did most to prevent or sabotage) and went on to mention in passing that there are important differences between Chile then and the Soviet Union at the time Lenin initiated the New Economic Policy. But Millas did not bother to say *what* any of these differences were, and he studiously avoided any reference to the crucial political difference: that in Lenin's Soviet Union the working class had already assumed state power and destroyed bourgeois—especially armed—power, and that in Allende/Millas' Chile it had not! Notwithstanding, Millas said that we can always learn something from Lenin. And the lesson that

Lenin supposedly offered for that moment in the Chilean process was, according to Orlando Millas, the following:

> The characteristic of today's juncture in our experience is that the correlation of forces has been effected against the working class and the popular government by political and economic errors that we can summarize by saying that we have gone too far beyond [transgressions of] the Popular Unity program. Therefore, it is time to place the accent on the defense of the popular government, on maintaining it and on continuing its work. It would be improper to continue to increase the number of its enemies. On the contrary, we should make concessions; and at least some sectors of certain social groups should be neutralized by correcting our tactical errors.

The "certain" social groups were, as always in Communist Party strategy and tactic, the middle classes and the "national bourgeoisie." Henceforth, instead of seeking to consolidate power by *advancing*, the new watchword became to advance by *consolidating*.

José Cademartori carried the same argument still farther and made it still more unmistakably clear in his article on the "Revolutionary Perspectives and Tasks." The principal general topic of debate in Chile at that time was whether, under the Government of Popular Unity, Chile had entered a stage or period of "transition to socialism" or not. The left said no, because that transition cannot begin until the working class has taken state power, which it had not done and showed no immediate sign of doing in Chile. The electoral program had avoided immediate claims about socialism, and even President Allende repeatedly emphasized that his was not only not a socialist government but not even one of transition to socialism. It was only intended to lead to socialism in the unforseeable future, a sort of transition to the transition to socialism. It was principally the Communist Party that increasingly insisted on making claims about a supposed transition to socialism here and now. In the following quotation, Cademartori observes that the transition to socialism only begins with the assumption of power by the proletariat and that in the Soviet Union, according to him, the transition lasted for 20 years *after* that. But then by a series of plays on words, *non sequitors*, and now-you-see-it-now-you-don't sleight of hands, Cademartori pulls the transition to socialism in Chile out of his hat here and now:

The Transition Period

From the economic point of view, what we are experiencing today in Chile is a transition period in which three types of economies exist simultaneously.

The first type is the non-monopolistic bourgeois economy represented by the haciendas, factories and commercial and service businesses that employ laborers.

The second type is made up of the petit bourgeoisie, formed by small farmers, craftsmen and self-employed workers in commerce and services (small businesses, fixed and ambulatory, taxi drivers, truck drivers, etc.) all of which are run without salaried employees.

The third type of economy is the social area in which we find State enterprises or those run by the Popular Government and the workers, the peasant economies in the reformed area, including cooperatives, agricultural reform centers, or peasant committees.

The transition period refers to the period between the assumption of power by the proletariat and the complete triumph of the establishment of socialism. In the Soviet Union, the transition period lasted close to 20 years (1917–1937). In the countries of Eastern Europe, it has lasted more than 25 years (1945–).

In our country, the transition period can already be divided into two stages: the first stage, since the victory of the Popular Government in 1970 which will last until the acquisition of complete power by the working class in alliance with the peasants and the middle classes; the second stage will begin with the acquisition of complete power and will last until the definitive triumph of the new means of production, socialism.

What characterizes our revolutionary process is that, despite not having won "complete" power for the proletariat and its popular coalition, we can speak of already having "initiated" a first phase, or a stage prior to the period of transition from capitalism to socialism. This affirmation is valid inasmuch as, although not all the power is in the hands of the working class and its allies, it is not less true that the popular forces have a "substantial" or "decisive" portion of power, the executive power.

On the other hand, the transition period begins with the socialization of the fundamental means of production and their conversion into social property. In Chile, the establishment of an ample and powerful area of social property, in addition to the mixed area and the reformed area of agriculture, gives a basis for maintaining that in our country the period of transition from capitalism to socialism has been initiated.

The Principal Contradiction:
The Struggle between Imperialism and Oligarchy

In the prior stage or the first stage of the transition period in which we find ourselves, the principal contradiction continues to arise, on the one hand between the popular and patriotic forces, headed by the working class, and on the other hand by imperialism, the monopolies, and the landholders. These sectors have been removed from executive power; however, they rely on strong positions in the judicial power in Parliament and in the "fourth power" (the means of mass communication). [The armed forces are not mentioned! AGF.] They still conserve positions in some important sectors in the economy although they have been removed from the control of the basic productive forces.

The struggle, the clash between these two forces, is the principal, the determinant which the following course of events must resolve. Either a step back, the counter-revolution, or the advance of the process, the affirmation, the triumph of all power for the popular and patriotic forces.

In this picture, it is necessary to situate the social classes which determine the other two types of economy: the bourgeois and the petit bourgeois economies.

The struggle between the forces that antagonize the principal contradiction largely depends on how the dilemma is resolved of who will will over these two intermediary classes; of who will put these two economies in its service: either in the service of the counter-revolution, incorporating them into sabotage or resistance or into the service of the revolutionary process by means of cooperation.

After performing this act of black magic and returning to the two political social groups or classes, the bourgeoisie and the petit bourgeoisie, whose support so vitally concerns the Communist Party in all these documentary declarations and even more so in their political practice, José Cademartori, just before becoming minister of economics in Allende's Popular Unity government in early 1973, gets to the real issue behind all these theoretical gobbledegook and expresses the real political premises, program, and policy of the Communist Party of Chile (and others like it elsewhere) as clearly as possible:

In the phase in which we find ourselves, we need the collaboration of all the productive forces, including those that are under the control of capitalist enterprises. It is not possible to win the battle of production without their participation. The capitalist enterprises need equipment, parts, access to foreign currency for their necessities, credits and payments in order to reinvest their earnings, adequate prices, and assured profitability. The conflicts between capital and labor can and must be resolved without takeovers, strikes, without interruption of production, on the basis of the maturity of the very workers and with them, the certainty that the

Popular Government possesses the means to look out for their rights and triumphs and does not permit the violation of the social laws as has happened in the past. In this way, all the conflicts of the class struggle can be resolved by means of persuasion and corresponding conciliatory mechanisms.

Out of respect for the 30,000 victims assassinated by the military junta and out of consideration of the (when written) still imprisoned José Cademartori, *no comment!*

17

An Answer to the Communist Party of Chile Which Went Unpublished in Its Newspaper

One of the unfortunate aspects of politics on the Left is the tendency to interpret independent and critical analysis of radical parties and governments as counter-revolutionary acts. In view of the way such an attack on Andre Gunder Frank, a frequent and respected MR contributor, has been blown up in Chile, we consider it desirable to give Frank space in MR to state his case. In addition, one of us, Harry Magdoff, was present at all the sessions of the New Delhi imperialism seminar referred to below, and confirms the correctness of Frank's version of events there.—The Editors

Monthly Review
116 West 14 Street
New York, N.Y. 10011

Dear Editors,

The participation of José Rodriguez Elizondo of the Communist Party of Chile and myself in the International Seminar on Imperialism, Independence, and Social Transformation in the Contemporary World,

---

Punto Final, Santiago, 1972. *Monthly Review*, New York, January 1973, *Economic and Political Weekly* (Bombay), March 31, pp. 621–22. Letter to *El Siglo* translated from the Spanish original by the author.

held in New Delhi in March 1972 with the attendance among many others of Harry Magdoff, has given rise to an ideological (non) debate in Chile. Rodriguez Elizondo published in *El Siglo*, the official newspaper of his party, an article taking exception to my participation in the New Delhi seminar. The essential parts thereof are quoted or summarized in my answering letter to *El Siglo*, which, after the latter declined to publish it, appeared in the Chilean bi-weekly *Punto Final*. Thereupon, Rodriguez Elizondo rebutted with another insertion in *El Siglo* and subsequently extended his critique in a two-page article in *Plan* and a twenty-page article in his party's theoretical journal, *Principios*. *El Siglo* also refrained from publishing an open letter addressed to it and other Santiago newspapers, signed by 36 people who took exception to the terms of Rodriguez Elizondo's insertions in *El Siglo*. By virtue of the origins and implications of the issues involved, which reach beyond the confines of Chile, may I ask you—and simultaneously the *Economic and Political Weekly* of India—to open the pages of your correspondence section for the reproduction of the following item of this debate.

Sincerely yours,

André Gunder Frank
Santiago, Chile

El Siglo
Santiago, Chile

Dear Editor,

Beyond disagreeing with the version presented by comrade José Rodriguez Elizondo about the seminar on Imperialism, Independence, and Social Transformation, held in New Delhi, which you published during my absence from Chile in your edition of April 18, 1972, I am sorry to say that I find myself obliged to deny categorically the affirmations made therein, concerning my alleged role in the above-mentioned seminar. Rather than invoking the protection of the bourgeois press law, which is still in effect in Chile, I urge you to publish my letter of refutation out of respect for the revolutionary truth that must guide us, and out of consideration for the revolutionary comradeship to which we aspire.

Comrade Rodriguez's claim that I made a diversionist motion allegedly for the purpose of excluding Chile from a resolution expressing solidarity with Vietnam and other countries is totally false. On the contrary—as the records of the final session of the seminar show—my motion expressly *included* Chile, together with the Palestinian and black North American liberation movements, all of which I proposed to add to the Vietnamese and others. In fact, one of the participants had proposed the addition of Chile to the original motion of solidarity with the peoples of Indochina, but the author of the original motion refused to accept this amendment, claiming it to be irrelevant. My motion, on the other hand, included Chile and, far from being diversionary as comrade Rodriguez alleges, it was passed by the assembly as a whole, including, I assume, Rodriguez himself. Thus, it is strange to find on my return to Chile that I supposedly tried to avoid or minimize expressions of international solidarity with the Chilean people at the time of the revelations concerning the ITT conspiracy.

It is totally false that "Gunder Frank attacked" the Communist party of Chile and that I termed the victory of the Unidad Popular coalition "ridiculous." In my statement—which was mimeographed and is available to any interested persons—I maintain that the drop in wages together with political mobilization generated progressive electorate movements in Chile, Uruguay, Venezuela, and Argentina, which systematically tried to give nationalism a class, and even an anti-bourgeois, character, and that in the case of Chile the Unidad Popular government had already suffered four attempted coups—and, at the time I drew up my statement, a fifth was being prepared. My statement maintains, furthermore, that the fascist menace grows to the extent that the Left puts its trust in constitutional guarantees and fails to prepare the masses to defend themselves. I did not violate the sense of the seminar in referring to the French and Italian Communist parties. Representatives of these and various other Communist parties had already intervened, in order to challenge the statement of an Indian who said, among other things, that the Communist parties were not always to be found in the political vanguard. Because of circumstances which made it impossible for the author of this statement to attend the seminar, and because half a dozen speakers rose to criticize him on this point alone, I considered it correct to express my solidarity (and that is the word I used), when I spoke during his absence. My intention was not, either in the aforementioned report or in my commentary, to attack the Communist party of Chile.

Inasmuch as the secretary of the seminar asked each speaker to present a written summary of his remarks on the reports, it may be opportune to reproduce my remarks here:

> The principal question is the winning of state political power by the working class and the peasants. This has to be done by stages, but the alliances and changes and economic benefits of a period must be used in such a way as to broaden political support and

strengthen political organizations among the masses, thus facilitating the advance to the next stage. Lacking this essential political mass line, the "noncapitalist" way leads to the possibility of neocolonialist and neofascist reverses. In Chile the short-term economic program of redistribution of income, employment, and popular consumption has been very successful in itself, but it is approaching its inherent limits. The statements and documents of the parties and leaders of the Unidad Popular coalition all express concern over the fact that the first fifteen months of the regime were not used profitably by the people's parties, which were organizing mass support to facilitate the transition from the economic short-term program to the structural transformation of the Chilean economy, society, and politics as envisioned in the program of the Unidad Popular.

The reader can see that this statement, which is the only summary of my intervention as delivered to the secretary of the seminar for eventual publication as part of the proceedings, has a tone and content very different from that attributed to it and employed by comrade Rodriguez.

Challenging comrade Rodriguez in a closed session, in which he attempted to borrow Fidel's authority in qualifying the Chilean process as revolutionary, I said that to the extent that it lacked sufficient people's mobilization—as Fidel himself had observed in his speech at the National Stadium—it was not revolutionary.

The version of my intervention as presented by comrade Rodriguez contains other distortions. For example, as far as Ceylon is concerned, I suggested—in the context of a discussion of the international political situation—that the possibility exists (as can be deduced from the summary above) that the political process in Ceylon is *arriving* at neofascism. A formulation very different from that which comrade Rodriguez attributes to me, i.e., that Ceylon is fascist. (I might add that two weeks later the General Secretary of the Communist party of Ceylon explained to me, as we dined in his home, why he had just voted in Parliament against the new repressive law passed by a majority which included the party of Prime Minister Bandanaraike and the Trotskyist party, and why the imminent resignation of the Communist party from the government coalition seemed to him to be a good thing, inasmuch as the party could then give leadership to the growing opposition to the government.)

Finally, and even more serious, comrade Rodriguez's claim that I "spoke in the name of a [Chilean] political group" is absolutely untrue. I never made such a claim, nor even hinted at it anywhere, because it is not the case. Very much to the contrary, when in India I stressed the fact that I spoke for myself alone. It is clear that anyone who claims that he or someone else speaks in the name of a political group or "represents" such a group would be lacking in respect for his listeners or readers were he not to *identify* the group in question—something which comrade Rodriguez does not dare to do.

I invite comrade Rodriguez's collaboration in the future in our common task, in a spirit of greater fraternalism and revolutionary truth.

Cordially,

Andre Gunder Frank

COMMENT BY LAJPAT RAI:
IMPERIALISM AND SOCIAL TRANSFORMATION

I am surprised at the defensive, even apologetic, tone of Gunder Frank's letter to *El Siglo* (not published) printed in the *Economic and Political Weekly* of March 31 (pp 621-2) — explaining his participation in and contribution to the so-called Seminar on Imperialism, Independence and Social Transformation — in response to Rodriguez Elizondo's attacks on him, published in the official Chilean Communist Party press. As an old acquaintance of Gunder Frank and as one who met him in Delhi a number of times when he, along with Harry Magdoff, strayed into this official 'anti-imperialist' jamboree, I have the following observations to make on his letter to *El Siglo*:

While in Delhi Gunder Frank insisted on not making any comment on the policies and actions of the Unidad Popular Government and refused to be involved in any discussion regarding it. We invited him along with Harry Magdoff to address a meeting of Delhi University Marxists, where despite our repeated requests he refused to speak on the current situation in Chile. He stuck to this position even in private talks he had with some of his friends in Delhi and at no time did he give the impression that he represented a 'group' or party in Chile. On the contrary, he told us he had come to participate in the Seminar in his individual capacity and had no representative position.

Frank made a significant contribution to the Seminar by raising a number of points concerning the political situation in Chile. He pointed out that the principal question in Chile was the winning of political power by the working class and the peasantry. The Unidad Popular no doubt controls the government, but political power is still in the hands of the bourgeoisie. He further pointed out that in the absence of a mass policital line, the non-capitalist path leads to the possibility of neo-colonial and neo-fascist reverses and that the "fascist menace grows to the extent the left puts its trust in constitutional guarantees and fails to prepare the masses to defend themselves". The recent elections in Chile are an indication of the fact that the constitutional course adopted by the Unidad Popular has reached a dead-end and a stage has been reached where if Allende does not move further to the left (which in the present context also means moving out of the constitutional shell), there is a serious danger of violence from the Right, not excluding intervention by the military. It is rather amusing to see Rodriguez Elizondo invoking Fidel Castro's authority in qualifying the Chilean political process as "revolutionary", and at the same time resenting Frank's expression of solidarity with the view that the traditional communist parties are not always to be found in the political vanguard, a view held and propagated by Castro till 1968.

I and Frank were present in the Chaplin Theatre in Havana in 1968, when in his closing speech to the Cultural Congress, Castro told his audience what he thought of Latin American communists. It would be advisable for Moscow-lining communists not to invoke Castro's authority in support of their political positions, lest it boomerang. Castro might regard the Chilean process as "revolutionary", but he is also on record for having stated: "Let no one dream we can achieve power peacefully . . . those who believe they are going to win against imperialist henchmen in elections are naive and those who believe they will take over power peacefully through elections are more than naive".

But Castro's own authority is now being questioned in revolutionary circles in Latin America and elsewhere, particularly since his declaration that "we have utmost faith in the foreign policy of the Soviet Union" and his entry into the conformist socialist club. Castro apart, Chilean communists would do well to heed the warning given by Frank and some others, that if mass mobilisation is not strengthened and the movement pushed to a higher stage, the situation in Chile could take a turn towards neo-colonialist and neo-fascist reverses, as happened in Brazil, though under different conditions and alignment of forces. How the non-capitalist path can lead to neo-fascism can be illustrated from political developments in Ceylon, Indonesia and Burma. Similar straws in the wind can be seen in India too. It is not surprising that the Chilean communists should be angry with Gunder Frank, an eminent Latin Americanist and non-conformist Marxist. What is surprising is that Frank should invoke "revolutionary truth" and "revolutionary solidarity" in relation to the traditional communists, for whom these phrases have lost all meaning.

Lajpat Rai
Delhi

18

The Lessons of Chile

One year ago, in a meeting in which many of those present took part, I said: "Dependence is dead, long live dependence and the class struggle." Dead, because that theory does not offer us an adequate context for dealing with the problems that our Chilean comrade has spoken to us about. Long life, because it is not a question of abandoning it but of expanding and deepening it.

It is not necessary to turn back to the belief, as some have done, that foreign investments do not have negative effects or that feudal structures exist in Latin America. Nor should we say, like Berlinguer, the secretary of the Italian Communist Party, on the basis of an old analysis dating from almost 20 years ago, that it was imperialism that overthrew Allende, or like Marshais, the secretary of the French Communist Party, that the real problem with Chile was that Allende had not received 51% of the vote.

The case of Chile will be examined in a context that is not purely Chilean but global, analyzing the situation and the prospects of the accumulation of capital on a worldwide scale. In Latin America there are

John Gittings, ed. *The Lessons of Chile*, Spokesman Books 1975 (part) and *Terzo Mondo*, Milano, No. 23, March 1974 (part), the latter translated from the Italian original and based on transcripts from a conference held in Amsterdam in January 1974.

relatively advanced countries such as Brazil, Mexico, and Argentina and particularly backward countries such as Haiti and some Central American states. In the middle are countries such as Chile, Uruguay, Colombia, Venezuela, and Peru, different among themselves but alike from the standpoint of the exhaustion of the easy phase of import substitution, which had been brought into being on the political plane by efforts to cope with economic problems with a social-democratic administration (of the type proposed, for example, by the "broad front" in Uruguay). Argentina has also sought, under Peronism, to pursue this path.

The Frei government in Chile had sought, in part with success and in part without, to cope with this crisis. The Popular Unity Party has tried to meet this same crisis that the Christian Democratic government had made acute, given that in the 1960s there was no economic growth but only a redistribution of income, with a falling off of production for the poor classes.

The Popular Unity (U.P.) administration has not been autonomous and that has not, as our Chilean comrade who spoke first said, caused the development of popular consciousness but is rather its result. The government was an attempt at arbitration between the bourgeosie, the petit bourgeoisie, and the labor and popular movement. But U.P. was not capable of raising income and of meeting the crisis in these terms. By the March elections (1973) the bourgeoisie (Freism included) saw that the only way to defend their interests was through a coup.

The U.P. government did not succeed in solving the problems either on the economic level or on the political one, and thereby to pave the way for further progress through initiatives in the social sector and by preparing the military for their administrative and political role. It has already been said that in the 1980s the military seems destined to assume the preponderant role in all the underdeveloped countries: in Asia, Africa, and Latin America.

The attempt to get out of the crisis through the social-democratic path of the U.P. was impossible. One could not do better or worse or differently. It was necessary that other forces come to power. For a certain time, a solution like the Peruvian one was considered with or without Allende, with a later turn towards the Brazilian model. There was conflict within the armed forces itself in this sense, but the Fascist wing won. This latter faction had to cope with the crisis using an economic policy that can be summarized in these points: (1) Installation of an economic liberalism almost forgotten in the world. Since 1945 Chile had had price control maintained by Presidents Alessandri, Frei, and Allende. The current government has made the country turn back

30 years, leaving the path open for inflation: (2) Destruction of the unions and outlawing of strikes. I do not know how they will restructure prices, but I suppose that those for mass consumption items will rise out of the reach of most of the public, who had been able to consume them at the time of Allende: (3) Extreme yielding to imperialism, with offers to pay for the nationalized mining enterprises and invitations to foreign investment in industry (elsewhere, even Allende, who was anti-Yankee, repeatedly solicited European and Japanese investors): (4) Attempts at a corporate restructuring of the state. This effort is on the agenda not only in Chile but in many other countries.

One may suppose that if the Chilean model of socialism has had a lot of influence, the military government of Chile will also be a model for many countries, not only in Latin America but also in other areas of the Third World such as the Philippines and Sri Lanka. Every social-democratic effort in Latin America, however, seems to be destined for failure: the attempts in Uruguay and Ecuador are already failing; even the effort in Peru, if you can call it that, seems to be on the path to liquidation; in Venezuela and Colombia they are talking about coups; in Mexico, Echevarria, after the coup d'état in Chile, has given in to the great pressure from the right; in Argentina, Peronism has declared a holy war against Marxism. The same thing is happening in other countries: in India, the government of Indira Ghandi, unable to cope with the growing necessities of the country, has been turning to the right; and the Arab countries, after the war, have also been leaning to the right, particularly Egypt.

In a new world crisis—of the kind that occurred in the 1930s—the underdeveloped countries appear to be destined to play a new role in the international division of labor. But not all countries can become subimperialist powers. This role seems reserved for Brazil, South Africa, India, and perhaps one or two others, among which is Indonesia. Others will be reduced to the role of client countries, like Taiwan, South Korea, and perhaps an increasing number of South American countries. These will try to imitate the Brazilian model, but they do not have the strength to achieve it and will have to content themselves with the Taiwanese model—which will hopefully resolve some of the immediate problems but will not be able to resolve the deeper problems. In Chile, through the irony of history, it will perhaps be the military government itself that will transform the petit bourgeoisie into allies of the popular forces, realizing the goal attempted without success by the U.P.

19

Is A Left Eurocommunism Possible?

Fernando Claudin was a leader of the Spanish Communist Party until his expulsion in 1964, and is the author of the already classic *The Communist Movement from Comintern to Cominform*.[1] The analysis of Eurocommunism and its relation to socialism put forward in his new book is very timely[2] — both because Claudin produced it after his return to post-Franco Spain, when the debate about Eurocommunism in that country and the problems faced by it in France and Italy as well had become highly topical, and also because its appearance followed closely upon publication of the much-discussed *Eurocommunism and the State* by Santiago Carillo, general secretary of the PCE.[3] Claudin's book can thus be taken as a kind of reply, by the most authoritative 'left Eurocommunist', to what was generally seen as a right-Communist book.

Claudin analyses brilliantly the conditions in which Eurocommunism arose and developed in Italy, France and Spain; the economic and

Published under the title "Eurocommunism: Left and Right Variants" in *New Left Review* (London) No. 108, March-April 1978.

[1]The book first appeared in Paris in 1970; English translation, London 1975.
[2]*Eurocommunism and Socialism*, Madrid 1977; English expanded edition, NLB 1978 (all page references in the present text are to this edition).
[3]Madrid 1976; English translation, London 1977.

political problems which, predictably, it is now confronting; and its party organization, political line/lines and inherent limitations. However, he then 'derives' political conclusions arguing for a democratic and socialist Eurocommunism which, as we shall see, unfortunately do not accord with his own very accurate analysis of Eurocommunism and its limitations, in whose light they do not seem realistically admissible.

Because of his judicious reflection upon historical and present reality alike, and because of the objective plausibility of his projections for the future, we can agree fully with Claudin on (among others) each of the following analytic theses. 1. World capitalism has since the mid-sixties entered a new deep structural crisis of accumulation, analogous to that of the inter-war period. This crisis engenders a host of political problems and responses: notably those of Eurocommunism, and the bourgeois austerity policies which are imposed with or without the agreement of the Communists.[4] 2. In the present stage of capitalism, monopoly is an integral aspect which is only reinforced by the crisis, and which—contrary to the Eurocommunist thesis—can be combated only through a successful anti-capitalist policy, without which an 'anti-monopoly' policy is impossible. (pp. 101-2) 3. However, there seems to be a kind of 'imperial historic compromise' between the United States and the Soviet Union in opposition to socialist revolution in Europe—including, it may be added, in opposition to a Euro-communist democracy. (pp. 136–7) Thus, more than ever, the problem of political and military power is the key question. (p. 117)

Drawing on his exceptional theoretical knowledge and his practical experience (already reflected in his earlier book on the Communist movement), Claudin analyzes with equal sureness the limitations—sometimes inherent, sometimes apparently circumstantial—of the Eurocommunist parties and their policies, which are not even remotely adequate to the difficult economic and political problems they face. 1. The Eurocommunist parties, whether separately or collectively, almost entirely lack any international policy matching the international character of the economic and political problems confronting them. (pp. 143–6) 2. The Eurocommunists advocate an anti-monopoly policy that is, however, not anti-capitalist as such. But such a policy is impossible to carry through (pp. 101-2): for it is based on the false assumption that monopolies are like some benign tumour which can be cut out of the economic system, thus rendering the patient more

---

[4]See all of chapter 1, except the two final pages. An almost identical analysis can be found in the present writer's *Reflections on the World Economic Crisis*, New York, Monthly Review Press, and London, Hutchinsons, 1981.

competitive and healthy (a further misconception!) than ever. 3. The reformist policy of the Eurocommunist parties in this and other respects—such as their support for austerity plans like those of the Andreotti government in Italy or those provided for in the Moncloa pact in Spain—seeks, and what is more threatens in fact, to consolidate the bourgeois régimes, saving from bankruptcy even their politically most representative parties such as the Christian Democrats in Italy or Suarez's Union of the Democratic Centre in Spain, as the 'lesser evil in face of the fascist danger' (recalling the identical formula used within the Popular Fronts during the last crisis), and thus aiding capitalism to overcome its period of economic and political crisis. (pp. 109-110 and 118) 4. Placing their hopes in the lengthy duration of a stage of democratic stability (p. 107), the Eurocommunists argue for a kind of 'transition to the transition' to socialism (pp. 101-2), as the Communist Party of Chile put it during the Popular Unity government. This represents a highly dangerous policy, in that it permits the mobilization and organization of counter-revolution (p. 107); it is also doomed to failure by its reformism in dealing with the most burning economic problems, leading to a popular backlash in favour of the Right (see Chile). Meanwhile, the Communist parties brake the trade-union and mass struggle and even oppose it, as we have already seen in France, Italy and Spain. (pp. 108-9) Moreover, the Communist parties place excessive confidence in the repressive bodies (police and military) of the bourgeois order (p. 112)—even on occasion to the point where they call for their use, as in Chile yesterday and Italy today. They disarm instead of mobilizing and organizing the working class and other popular forces, to confront the key question of power when this arises at the moment of truth.

Beyond this accurate analysis of the present issues and policies of Eurocommunism, Claudin returns again and again to what he views as the Achilles heel of Eurocommunism today: the problem of democracy, particularly its absence—indeed negation, to date—in the internal organization of these parties. He devotes many pages of his book to arguing that, because of their lack of democracy, the Soviet Union and other countries of East Europe are not genuinely socialist societies, since for him socialism without democracy is a total contradiction in terms. He apparently feels that, in his view, he is interpreting a widespread popular sentiment in the West, in that many workers (and others) will not be willing to sacrifice democratic freedoms in order to install socialism. Hence, the Eurocommunists will not be able to lead, or perhaps even accompany, the Western peoples to socialism, without first cutting once and for all the political umbilical cord which still binds them to the Soviet Union, and crossing the ideological Rubicon by stating that the latter and the other countries of the East are *not* socialist.[5] This fatal but liberatory step, taken with difficulty by Santiago Carillo, the most independent (but not therefore the most socialist) of the Eurocommunists, wetting one toe on this side of the Rubicon, is seen by Claudin as a necessary—though not sufficient—condition for a Eurocommunist transition to socialism.

In honour of this powerful democratic compromise, Claudin finds himself perhaps a little blinded by its brightness as he passed on from his analysis of objective and organizational reality to pose two separate sets of alternatives, and to the political conclusions which he derives from each of these. Seeking to draw out the political conclusions of his analysis, Claudin formulates the first set of alternatives on page 26: 'the global crisis of the system poses the concrete question: is the crisis to be solved by an "austerity policy" which imposes the main burden of sacrifice on working people, while repairing the mechanisms of capitalism to equip them for a further prolonged period of existence—a solution which it would be difficult to conceive without a turn to more authoritarian policies?'— an eventuality which Claudin goes on to analyse subsequently, on the already cited pages 109-10 and 118, where he comments on the Eurocommunist collaboration in such policies—'Or will the solution of the crisis introduce profound changes of economic and social structure which, even if they still involve sacrifices on the part of the masses, allow some sense of what a transition to socialism might be? The second option would necessarily involve the extension and deepening of democratic involvement in the political arena as well as in production . . .' Of course, Claudin himself comes out in favour of the second of these options—but in the name of a perspective which has little relationship with his own analysis of reality.

In the first place, the second option (as, in principle, the first also) contains a manifest contradiction, difficult if not possible to resolve, between the Eurocommunist support for 'policies which involve sacrifices on the part of the masses' and the 'extension and deepening' of democracy. In the second place, especially in the light of this same contradiction, neither objective conditions and Claudin's analysis of them, nor the latter's subjective wishes, offer a

---

[5]The terminology is Claudin's own, although he used it not in this particular book, but at a subsequent conference.

guarantee that these two options are in fact the only and exclusive ones. On the contrary, precisely Claudin's own analysis implies that this set of alternatives is incomplete, if not false, and that the most probable outcome will in fact be a third alternative: the extension of today's austerity policies to ultra-austerity measures designed to 'repair the mechanisms of capitalism to equip them for a further prolonged period of existence', by means precisely of 'profound changes of economic and social structure', which will not become the basis for a transition to socialism (and far less to a democratic socialism) but, on the contrary, for a transition towards an authoritarian society like that which Claudin himself glimpses on page 107 (and which in my little book cited in note 4 above I term, following George Orwell, '1984').

Claudin sets out the second set of alternatives/options, in terms of the political line and organisation implicit in the democratic resolution of the first, on page 119: 'The crucial need today on which any successful [read 'democratic'] solution to the crisis depends, is . . . [that] between the adventure of extremism and the adventure of the "historic compromise" (understood as collaboration with the forces that constitute the most fundamental block to the kind of change the present situation demands), space must be found for a realistic policy of advance towards the democratic socialist transformation of Italian society. The tempo of the crisis does not allow for a very long delay.' Apart from wondering what this 'adventure of extremism' is which Claudin rejects without further explanation, objective reality itself and the very analysis which Claudin makes of it pose the question for us: why *must* there be space for a realistic intermediate policy, especially if the crisis does not allow for much time to discover it and put it in train? No objective reason ordains this. If we can go along with Claudin in his subjective desire to find such space and such a policy, we must also insist on following him in his analysis of the way in which the authoritarian—i.e. anti-democratic and reformist, i.e. anti-socialist—organization of the Eurocommunist parties prevents any such positive outcome, thereby vitiating not the objective analysis but rather the subjective desire. Once again, Claudin's democratic compromise obscures his historical analysis.

The question remains: by what political path does Claudin— albeit in visionary guise—visualize this positive (in other words democratic-socialist) outcome being achieved? Answer: through a left Eurocommunism. Although Claudin does not leave this outcome entirely clear in the book itself, he has done so in other public and private statements.[6] Claudin (like the present writer and many others) predicts an intensification of the economic and political crisis of capitalism, and assumes that this general crisis will act in such a way upon the Eurocommunist parties themselves and upon their allies (for example, through a sharpening of the contradiction between austerity policies and internal democracy) that there will be space—though very little time—for the internal crisis of the Eurocommunist parties to be resolved through their conversion (or through the conversion of hegemonic segments of them in alliance with kindred organizations) into democratic-socialist parties: but still Eurocommunist ones, albeit of a left-wing variety. However, previous historical experience, and the magisterial analysis of it made by Claudin himself, not to speak of the 'not very long delay' which the crisis allows, all combine to make this democratic-socialist vision of Claudin's nothing more than a highly unrealistic hope, one might say an illusory utopia, an act of faith . . . in Eurocommunism.

Thus Claudin, after his far-ranging trajectory, as loyalist and as critic, inside and outside the Communist party and movement, when all is said and done remains with the Communist parties, self-regenerated into democratic-socialist organizations, which are themselves to lead us to a left Eurocommunism. But it is hard to see where this Eurocommunism, however far to the left it may be, poses 'the key question of the problem of power', nor when or how it will come to do so—let alone resolve it positively. Even Carillo, the most independent (though perhaps not the most democratic) of the Eurocommunists, does not so much as contemplate a socialist revolution, and would be the last to attempt one—even when the 'not very long delay' which History allows has already passed by.

---

[6] For example, at the conference organized in London by the journal *Critique*, on the occasion of the sixtieth anniversary of the October Revolution.

20

Kampuchea, Vietnam, China: Observations and Reflections

The events of 1979 in and between Kampuchea, Vietnam, and China oblige socialists to undertake an agonizing reappraisal.[1] This reappraisal must follow those previously associated with the Soviet Union and occasioned by the events of the 1920s before and after the death of Lenin, Stalin's purges and his pact with Hitler in the 1930s and 1940s as well as the subsequent revelations by Krushchev's secret speech, and the Soviet invasion of Hungary in 1956 and of Czechoslovakia in 1968.[2] Indeed, though these reappraisals have been made by previous generations of socialists, there may be occasion now to make them again for the present one — and perhaps also to extend them further back to the theory and praxis of revolutionaries and reformists in the first two decades of the century and maybe even to go back to re-examine the theory of Marx himself. In the present essay, however, we limit ourselves to some observations and reflections about the most recent challenges to the ideals of socialists and to the future socialism, which have been posed in — and between — precisely those countries in which there had been a deliberate and concerted attempt to avoid the errors of the past and to transcend the shortcomings of the previous roads to socialism in the Soviet Union and Europe.

AMPO, Tokyo, Vol. 13, No. 1, Spring 1981; *Social Praxis*, Amsterdam, Vol. 7, No. 3–4, March 1980; *Alternatives*, New York, Delhi, Vol. VII, No. 2, Fall 1981.

The obligation of committed socialists to submit the theory and praxis of socialism to an agonizing reappraisal in the light of the experience in and between Kampuchea, Vietnam and China is all the more necessary and perhaps all the more painful precisely because much of this experience had been offered and received as a more hopeful new beginning. Moreover, socialists are now faced with the difficult task of charting a course between the Scylla of another failure to draw any lessons from experience and the Charybdis of following in the footsteps to reactionary anti-communism of those who drew the wrong lessons during the last Cold War — especially now that the threat of another Cold War is upon us. To elude our responsibility as responsible socialists in this reappraisal and to permit the new cold warriors to make it for us would be to do the cause of socialism yet another disservice.

In this spirit, the following lines are an attempt to set out some substantially (and unfortunately) incontrovertible observations about recent events in Kampuchea, Vietnam and China and to reflect on some of their major immediate implications for socialist theory and praxis. Although all these events, observations and reflections are connected to each other, for the sake of simplicity and clarity we shall try to take them ad seriatim beginning with Kampuchea, going on to Vietnam and ending with China. Our purpose is in no wise to say any final word on anything but rather to incite to further reflection. For this purpose, perhaps the more provocative the following reflections are the better.

KAMPUCHEAN OBSERVATIONS

A number of factual observations may be made over and above the acrimonious debate about the merits and demerits of the Pol Pot regime in Kampuchea. The country suffered the highest concentration of physically destructive bombing and socially destructive dislocation — including particularly that of the rural population to the capital city, Phnom Penh — during the war from 1970 to 1975. The new Kampuchean Communist Party later headed by Pol Pot had been founded or redirected as recently as 1960 and was built in an extremely nationalistic and culturally self-conscious milieu of Kampuchean society. Until the Lon Nol coup in 1970, the Kampuchean Communist Party combatted an indigenous and nationalistic regime, which under the leadership of Prince Sihanouk subjected the Party to severe oppression and terror. Accordingly, the Kampuchean Communist party, unlike the Vietnamese one which collaborated with Sihanouk, adopted a strongly anti-ruling class line. For this and other reasons, the Kampuchean party was independent from, and in many respects even in opposition to, other communist parties and especially those of the Soviet Union, China and particularly Vietnam, all of which had already sacrificed the Kampuchean party's interests to their own before 1975. Kampuchean national and socialist interests had been particularly sacrificed by the Vietnamese Communist Party in the Paris Agreement of 1954-5 and in connection with the 1968 Tet offensive. Upon achieving victory substantially through its own efforts and sacrifices (although of course in the context of the war elsewhere in Indochina) the young party faced unprecedented tasks of assuring the economic survival of the population in the face of imminent starvation and the political survival of the revolution in the face of hostility from its internal and external enemies and to some extent even from its external allies. The evacuation of Phnom Penh, the dispersal of politically unreliable elements into the countryside and the reorganization of an agricultural society were attempts to face and solve all these economic, political, social and cultural problems in one fell swoop in 1975, although according to Heder this move was already planned in 1971 or 1973 and foreshadowed in the areas liberated before 1975.

Socialists and increasingly others as well have called for self-reliance and independence particularly in agrarian Third World societies. The Kampucheans practiced what others preached to a degree hitherto unknown — going so far as to abolish money — in an attempt to build a new self-reliant society that went beyond anything tried in Tanzania, North Korea or China. A radically independent social program of popular mobilization seemed appropriate in a poor and sparsely settled but fertile country in which foreign entanglements had brought little local advantage in the past and promised less for the future.

Moreover, the attempt seemed at first to succeed: the population was fed against all odds, and the circumstantially perhaps inevitable initial political repression soon subsided after the evacuation of the capital city in 1975. (The hostile anti-Cambodian propaganda about mass exterminations in 1975-76 was based on hand-me-down false eyewitness accounts and was soon shown to be mostly that for all those who honestly wished to see. However, Stephen Heder has documented some then-still selective liquidation of cadres by the Pol Pot group). In a word, Kampuchea seemed to have taken a giant radical step towards the construction of a juster socialist, and one day communist, society for a poor but proud people.

Subsequent developments and revelations have, however, destroyed and disqualified this Kampuchean experiment in the road to socialism and communism. This most independent grass roots Communist Party of Kampuchea turned out in 1977 and 1978 to have constructed an extremely stratified society with high degrees of privilege for "good" Kampucheans and extreme forms of sacrifice for "bad" ones. Apparently to make this distinction and division possible there was a *resurgence* or renewal of repression in 1977-78 far in excess of the previous one in 1975 and the *new* repression was an expression of intra-party and inter-regional political conflicts, which the Pol Pot group resolved through the physical elimination of its rivals and their followers. Moreover, the Kampuchean regime launched increasingly aggressive attacks against the Vietnamese, in part to recover the Parrot's Beak and other territory, which the Vietnamese had refused to dislodge since they occupied it along the Ho Chi Minh Trail. In part these attacks also emerged from domestic policies in Kampuchea, which also required a nationalist cover or at least credential. Additionally, Kampuchea became a cat's paw for China's anti-Vietnam policy (which we shall examine below). After the Vietnamese ousted the Pol Pot regime, its spokesmen such as Ieng Sary offered to ally themselves with any Kampuchean and foreign political forces, no matter how reactionary or imperialist, so long as they are anti-Vietnamese. In the meantime this apparently most determined socialist and supposedly most sanguinary repressive Kampuchean government has suddenly gained the diplomatic support of the United States, Western Europe and Thailand for its anti-Vietnamese — and by extension anti-Soviet — credentials.

REFLECTIONS ON KAMPUCHEA

Why did the dream of small-can-be-beautiful socialism in an agrarian society turn rapidly into the nightmare of the abuse of power especially during the Pol Pot regime's last year? Why did an apparently or supposedly grass roots peasant Communist Party desire or have to resort to the physical liquidation of its dissidents in intra-party disputes or power struggles and why did the dominant and domineering Party group resort to mass extermination of the population in the regions where Party and other opponents had some strength? Why did an independent and nationalist party exaggerate these qualities to the point of refusing all consultation with its neighbours and then turning on one of them through armed action? Why did the defense of supposedly national and popular Kampuchean interests require the negation of and the combat against all proposals of regional economic, social and political cooperation? In short, what are the implications of the Kampuchean experience for widely espoused small is beautiful self-reliance and for (or combined with) militant socialist mass mobilization against class enemies and for economic and social reconstruction?

VIETNAM OBSERVATIONS

The Vietnamese fought a long and heroic war of liberation that was widely regarded as a battle of David against Goliath. The embattled Vietnamese aroused world-wide sympathy and often active support for Vietnam, national liberation and socialism (in that order of popularity). Indeed, much of the wave of "third worldism" and of a whole new generation's sympathy for socialism and interest in Marxism both in developed and in underdeveloped capitalist countries around the world may be attributed to the force of Vietnamese example. The Vietnamese overcame the most incredible odds in combatting the most powerful enemy on earth; they resisted repreated pressures from both of their principal allies and arms suppliers to compromise with their enemies on terms other than their own. Yet at the same time the Vietnamese demanded several times that the Kampuchean Communists compromise with their own government. The Vietnamese sought good relations especially with Prince Sihanouk to further their own struggle by using what the Americans called the Ho Chi Minh trail and Cambodian sanctuary for the Tet offensive in 1968 but have refused to dislodge some of this territory since then. After their victory in 1975, the Vietnamese proceeded to reunify their country as they had promised.

As soon as the Vietnamese had driven the Americans out militarily in April 1975, they pleaded with the Americans to return diplomatically and economically with aid and trade as well as investment in off-shore oil. As quid pro quo to the Americans and also for their own regional purposes, the Vietnamese assiduously toured Southeast Asia to assure their neighbours' governments of Vietnam's friendly intentions for peace and trade. Accordingly, the same Vietnamese who had benefited from so many foreign arms in their own liberation struggle, now denied any of their huge stock of arms to other liberation movements, whom the Vietnamese effectively abandoned to their fate. On the other hand, the Vietnamese have been intent on creating an "Indochinese Federation" under their own tutelage; and they have interpreted their own and others' economic interests to be served by a regional collaboration and division of labour, including eventually an international Mekong River basin scheme, which would impose economic sacrifices on the Khmer and others that these peoples apparently do not regard equally beneficial to themselves. Only after — and probably because of — the steadfast refusal of the Americans to respond to Vietnamese overtures and to support these plans did the Vietnamese turn in desperation to the Soviet Union in search of help for economic reconstruction and political protection against China. Also, only then did the Vietnamese throw further fuel on their long burning disputes with their now Chinese-supported neighbors in Kampuchea.

Domestically in the meantime, the Vietnamese first proceeded to reunify their country as they had promised. Despite the inheritance of countless active collaborators from the Thieu regime in the south of the country, the new government proved to be extremely lenient and generous in treating even their most implacable internal enemies. The worst fate anybody met was a re-education camp, which never gave Vietnam's enemies any occasion for serious complaint or denunciation. After three years of severe shortages, due in part to two successive years of the worst climatological conditions in a long time, the Vietnamese went on to nationalize the network of food wholesalers in Ho Chi Minh City who had been using their monopoly power to speculate with food prices. The measure was a logical and necessary step in the socialization of the economy and the society, but its negative effects were concentrated in the Cholon area of the city among the middlemen of predominantly Chinese origin. These people reacted and made up some 80 per cent of the "boat people" many of whom had amassed the wherewithal to pay the equivalent of US$3,000 in gold to pay for their passage. Simultaneously, however, ethnic Chinese peasants and fishermen from the North began a mass exodus across the border into China. The Vietnamese Communist Party and the Army also purged their militants of ethnic Chinese origin from the base through the middle ranks and all the way up into the Central Committee of the Party and the senior officers of the Army. A member of the central committee of the Communist Party of Vietnam defected to China and denounced the Vietnamese for racial discrimination and persecution. In the south of the country, the NLF cadres who had fought against the Americans and Thieu to reunite their country with the north seem to have been systematically removed from almost all place and authority in the new civil and political administration and have been replaced by party functionaries who were brought from the north, wherever they may have been born.

The growing dispute with Kampuchea and the latter's incursions in territories belonging to or claimed by Vietnam threatened this process of economic, social and political transformation in the South. In part for this reason, the Vietnamese availed themselves of Kampucheans who had been in Vietnam since the days of the Indochinese Communist Party (before the organization of the Khmer Rouge in Cambodia itself) and invaded Kampuchea in order to force a change in its government. The Vietnamese army and these Kampuchean contingents were able in a lightening campaign to drive the Pol Pot government out of Phnom Penh and to replace it with a client government of their own. The Vietnamese and their Kampuchean allies have, however, been unable to eliminate the Khmer Rouge forces from Kampuchea despite more than a year's efforts by 100,000 to 200,000 Vietnamese occupation troops, and the Heng Samrin government in Phnom Penh is still regarded as completely unviable without the Vietnamese presence and support.

REFLECTIONS ON VIETNAM

What kind of international socialism or socialist internationalism in Vietnam, which received widespread international support for its avowedly socialist programme, is it that pursues its national interests under the guise of constructing an Indochinese Federation at the economic and political cost of the Kampucheans and even of non-ethnic Vietnamese in Vietnam and in the Vietnamese Communist Party itself? Why should socialist expansion in the south and socialist construction throughout Vietnam require discriminatory if not arbitrary measures against non-ethnic Vietnamese and especially Hoa people at home? How does the construction of socialism also permit or require attempts to reconstitute the most far-reaching economic ties with international capitalism in general and albeit unsuccessfully with the United States in particular? Why should these ties include the World Bank and IMF membership, 100 percent foreign equity foreign investment codes, and the low wage labor intensive manufacturing and agribusiness export drives that are usually associated with the most dependent capitalist underdevelopment? In short, what is the long run socialist programme and perspective now offered by Vietnam's national liberation, or is the long armed struggle for national liberation in Vietnam no more than the national liberation from political imperialism to pursue nationalism in a capitalist world?

CHINA OBSERVATIONS

The Chinese socialist revolution appeared as a world-shaking event of the greatest historical significance if only because it occurred in the oldest millennial civilization among the world's most populous people. Moreover, the Chinese revolution was carried through, in, and by a predominantly peasant people by methods that differed in significant respects from those taught by Marx and Marxists and in direct contravention to the desires and counsels of the world's first socialist state in the Soviet Union. Indeed, the Chinese revolutionary leadership deliberately and explicitly sought to avoid and overcome the mistakes and shortcomings of the first socialist revolution in the Soviet Union which therefore soon abandoned China to its own designs. Organized oppression and terror by a privileged party and or a bureaucratic state were to be avoided, while the mass line and self-reliance were enshrined as the guiding mottoes of the society. The cultural revolution was supposed to safeguard the gains of the revolution and the new generation and to prevent China from deviating back onto the capitalist road.

However, the cultural revolution — and therewith the continued advance to higher forms of socialism — was roundly defeated (or called off by the People's Liberation Army with the possible approval of Chairman Mao himself) at the latest by September 1971, when Lin Biao went to his death on his flight to Mongolia. Since then, the direction of domestic and foreign policy has become increasingly reactionary, the survival of Mao and the supposed continuation of the Maoist line by the "Gang of Four" until 1976 notwithstanding. Zou Enlai's and Mao's invitation to President Nixon and his friendly reception in Peking in 1972 while the United States was escalating its bombing offensive against Vietnam set the tone for a uniformly reactionary Chinese foreign policy. This policy went from unswerving support for Pakistan also in the war against Bangladesh and India and opposition to the JVP rebellion in Ceylon in 1971 through continuing support for Mobutu in Zaire, Holden Roberto in Angola, Pinochet in Chile, etc. Chinese policy involved ostentatious wellwishing to the most reactionary dictators and statesmen around the world from President Ferdinand Marcos and his wife Imelda in the Phillippines to Tory Prime Ministers Edward Heath and Margaret Thatcher in Britain and the anti-Soviet hawks Franz Joseph Strauss in Germany and James Schlesinger in the U.S.A. Everywhere the Chinese policy has been that the enemy of my (Soviet) enemy is my friend or at least, as a Chinese friend readily admitted, my ally and associate. China began doing all it could to keep the United

States to maintain a political and military presence in the Pacific Asian area, and China ended up de facto with an outright alliance with Washington and Tokyo. This same foreign policy line has remained unaltered except for its reenforcement all the way through the 1970s irrespective of the apparent zig-zags in domestic policy and independently of Mao's or anybody else's presence or absence at the helm.

A significant Chinese effort has been to isolate Vietnam. China pressed territorial claims to offshore islands against Vietnam. China presented the United States with the choice of a rapprochement with itself or a settlement with Vietnam. China supported and encouraged Kampuchea, not because it liked Khmer Rouge domestic policies (which China did not), but only because China wanted to use Kampuchea for the pursuit of its policy against Vietnam and the Soviet Union. China suddenly cut off its aid to Vietnam as the Soviet Union had to China twenty years before. China engaged in anti-Vietnamese propaganda outside and inside Vietnam. China supported the ethnic Chinese in Vietnam in the name of nationalism and against all principles of socialism. Finally, China invaded Vietnam "to teach it a lesson."

At first sight this invariability of Chinese foreign policy seemed to be at variance with the frequent changes in the direction of domestic policy. Upon further inspection however, all the changes in direction have invariably had a major characteristic in common: they have all been decided at the top, from the beginning and end of the Great Leap and the Hundred Flowers in 1956, through the beginning and end of the cultural revolution, to the displacement of Deng Xiaoping by the Gang of Four and the elimination in turn of the latter by Hua Guofeng and the second return of Deng. However widespread mass participation may be in day to day decision making at the base of Chinese society, the mass line has never been implemented to and at — as distinct from by — the top of the Chinese political system. None of the major decisions about and changes in political line seem ever to have been made with, let alone through, mass participation. To the extent that the masses have been mobilized in recent years in support of major political options, this mobilization in Peking's Tien An Minh Square or in Shanghai seem to have occurred as readily for Deng Xiaoping and his policies as against them, as quickly for the Gang of Four as against them. The Gang of Four may have been the inheritors and executors of Mao and his revolutionary left line or they may now be unduly maligned as objective capitalist roaders along with Lin Biao, but none of these seems to have been any more the incarnation of a more democratically socialist force than any other. Deng Xiaoping's dictum that the ideological colour of a cat does not matter so long as it can catch mice seems in retrospect to have been the ideological praxis of Chinese domestic and foreign policy no matter who has given it direction. If it is possible that Mao Zedong was a partial exception, it is certain that this praxis was carried to a refined art by Premier Zou Enlai who was a past master of diplomatically skinning cats.

China is now implementing under the stewardship of Deng Xiaoping the plan for the modernization, which was originally devised under the authority of Zou Enlai, supposedly with the blessings of Mao Zedong. According to Chairman Hua Guofeng, the four modernizations of industry, agriculture, technology and the military are designed to make China the world's third industrial power by the year 2000. The means to do so are supposed to be in part the import of foreign, and especially American and Japanese, technology with the encouragement of foreign investment with 100 per cent foreign equity in anything from Coca Cola to military jets. As an exporter in turn to pay for these imports, China threatens to swamp the world market with labour intensive cheap wage goods produced in export factories and zones designed to out-compete the modern sweatshops in Southeast Asia and other parts of the Third World. The political counterpart of these Chinese economic ties with the West seems to be the attempt to establish sufficient American and Japanese vested interests in China to assure their political and perhaps military support in any further conflict with the Soviet Union. The modernization programme of the domestic economy involves the accelerated increase of private incentives and social differentiation in agriculture, factories and education (where the exam system has been reintroduced) etc. Politically, the "capitalist roader" Liu Shaugi has been posthumously rehabilitated and insofar as possible all cadres who had been marginalized since the Great Leap Forward in 1957 have been reinstated in positions of influence and authority. In a word, modernization in socialist China now means wiping two decades of Maoism off the slate and starting all over again with 1957 when China still pursued the Soviet growth model that Mao then tried to replace — except that now the Soviet Union has replaced the United States as the principal enemy of the construction of socialism in China and the Americans have become the principal allies!

REFLECTIONS ON CHINA

What has happened to the world's biggest, most important and (perhaps excepting Kampuchea and North Korea) the most advanced model of socialist development based on the self reliant mass line — if

China itself never practiced the mass line in its major decision making at the top and has now decided to abandon self-reliance as well? Why has socialist egalitarianism been reversed to pursue modernization through increasing stratification and bureaucratization?

If Mao was right that transition to socialism, let alone communism, requires continuous or repeated cultural revolutions, what are the implications of the failure and reversal of the first such cultural revolution?

If Mao sought to avoid the errors and transcend the shortcomings of socialism in the Soviet Union, and if China appeared to many at home and abroad to offer a new alternative and farther reaching departure to socialism and communism, how must we revise our expectations now that — in the words of Charles Bettelheim as he resigned his chairmanship of the Sino-French Friendship Association — China has made a great leap backward? Indeed, what is left of our model — or even of our conception for those who reject models and the idea of models — of progressive transition to egalitarian non-authoritarian, participant non-alienating, self-reliant, non-dependent "socialist" society? Is there something wrong with the Chinese or with our conceptions, or both; or is there something wrong with us?

What are we to make of the idea — advanced especially by Mao and China — of putting politics in command and having ideology supersede economicism to alter if not break the bounds of economic determinism after China demonstrated the pragmatic equality of ideologically white and black cats to chase mice around the economic maze in pursuit of the national interest?

Does the pursuit of the Chinese national interest against the Soviet Union and Vietnam but in a marriage of convenience with bourgeois national interest in the United States promote the transition to *socialism* (let along to communism) and to *what kind of socialism*?

POSSIBLE IMPLICATIONS FOR MARXISM AND SOCIALISM

Whatever the disagreements and disputes among socialists and Marxists about the above and other questions, until recently there was agreement among them on at least one proposition: that war between socialist states is "impossible." This "self-evident" proposition was derived from the very core of Marxism and from the very essence of socialism as the negation of capitalism. (It is true that war had existed for a long time but since the rise of capitalism and imperialism war was supposed to be part of the political economy of capitalism.) War between two socialist states (allies only a few years before) eliminates the credibility of this perhaps last remaining agreed upon truth among Marxists and revolutionary socialists. Moreover, some of the apparent attitudes about these wars and some troop behavior in them seem to have been tinged with racist chauvinism. Where ethnicity, nation and race coincide, do nationalism and racism become indistinguishable, all socialism notwithstanding?

What went wrong? Was the Marxist thesis about war between socialist states (and the prior but related thesis about the withering away of the state) wrong from the beginning? Or is it that these states are not socialist (and there is no reason to expect them to wither away in the foreseeable future)? The answer is perhaps implicit in or to be derived from some further reflections about all three of these (as well as other) socialist countries.

What are the implications of this entire experience for socialism and socialists? One country fought for its liberation under the banner of socialism for a generation and then treats the collaborators of the previous genocidal regime with kid gloves, seeks the maximum reinte-gration in world capitalism but fails to achieve it only because of capitalist recalcitrance (and the opposition of its socialist neighbor to the north), but then invades its socialist neighbor and expels cadres of long standing from its own Communist Party and Liberation Army in the name of nationalism in the guise of socialism. The Communist Party of another socialist country initiates the most far-reaching self-reliant mass based social transformation in an agrarian society but then stratifies the same to an extreme degree and has recourse to the most brutal repression before being displaced by neighboring socialists, after which the former offer to make pacts with the devil — any devil — to oppose the invading socialists. The world's most populous country and most self-conscious socialist society pursues a steady course of policy zig-zags which violate all tenents of its supposed mass line and pursues the haughtiest nationalist foreign policy and even military adventures against a socialist neighbor in the supposed defense of socialism.

Should all these observations of the evidence not lead us to suspect that the banner of "socialism" is little more than a fig leaf for naked nationalism perhaps confined with racism? And should we not regard this national assertion to be the attempt by a ruling class to promote its own interests where possible and to accommodate them to the limitations of reality in a capitalist world system where necessry? Is it possible that often the emphasis on and utilization of socialist ideology are really non-ideological attempts by pragmatically striped nationalist cats in socialist disguise to gain access to the super or at least relatively privileged core positions and benefits in this world capitalist and capitalist world system and its still continuing development? Are appeals to socialism sometimes more effective to this non-socialist end in the Third World than appeal to outright reactionary ideology or to a supposedly technocratic end of ideology would be? If so, or even if any of the above is partially so, how many further reflections and how far backwards a rethinking of socialism and Marxism are now necessary by those of us who still wish to profess one or the other or both as a real alternative to de-humanizing capitalist reality?

NOTES

1. These observations and reflections were sparked by the debate launched by our Japanese socialist friends in AMPO (Vol. 11, No. 1, 1979) and their invitation to continue the discussion. One occasion to pursue the discussion was an evening in March 1980 in New Delhi among a dozen participants and the following day between one of them, my friend Kitazawa Yoko from AMPO and myself. These observations and reflections draw on these discussions to extend them, but the sole responsibility for the present formulations and especially for any errors, rests with the present writer.

2. The present reappraisal may be more difficult for several reasons, however. The events of the 1920s then and now have been rationalized as the unique exigencies of the unique first break with capitalism in a hostile world. The purges and the denunciation of Stalin were often attributed to his partly defensive actions and have also been hopefully regarded as dead and buried with their author. The urgency of the reappraisal of the Hitler-Stalin Pact was removed by the Nazi invasion of the Soviet Union. The recent events in and mutual invasions by socialist states in Asia not only pose a renewed and additional challenge, but they seem to foreclose further easy rationalizations or escapes from the agony of a real appraisal — perhaps also of the earlier events.

21

After Reaganomics and Thatcherism, What? From Keynesian Demand Management via Supply-Side Economics to Corporate State Planning and 1984

Keynesian demand management by Western governments has been replaced by the monetarist policies and supply-side economics of the Reagan, Thatcher and other governments. Why has there been this change in economic theory and policy, what are the chances of success or failure for the new policies, and what is likely to happen in the future — about election time, 1984?

KEYNESIANISM – ITS RISE AND DECLINE

The Keynesian revolution was generated by a major world capitalist crisis of inadequate effective demand in the 1930's, following the political defeat of the working classes in the major capitalist countries during the 1920's. It was also associated with the beginning of expansionary demand management by governments in Britain, the United States, Germany and elsewhere. With the partial exception of German rearmament, Keynesian demand management failed to elimi-

Contemporary Marxism (San Francisco) No. 4, Winter 1981–82.

nate the economic crisis which stubbornly persisted — 10 million unemployed in the United States — until World War II generated supply scarcities along with public supply management analogous to that of the socialist (and in part the fascist) command economies.

Keynesianism became the new orthodoxy in economic theory and political policy after World War II, in close association with the generalization of social democracy and the welfare state which were political economic components of the postwar economic expansion in the West. The Keynesian revolution in economic theory and policy abandoned the classical supply-side approach in which, according to the nineteenth-century economist Say's law, supply creates its own demand in the free market. In its place, Keynesianism launched a public policy of government demand management and expansion, based on a theory of otherwise insufficient market demand and the thesis that an increased in demand will call forth a corresponding increase in supply. The Keynesian gurus such as Paul Samuelson, Nobel economics laureate and presidential adviser, made so bold as to attribute the postwar expansion itself to their Keynesian theory and policy. They argued that the automatic demand stabilizers they had built into the economy guaranteed its continued prosperity, so that the monstrous dinosaur of prewar business cycle stagnation had been converted into a postwar lizard.

The renewed economic crisis of the 1970's obliged Paul Samuelson and other Keynesians to swallow their own words like reptiles. These developments made it increasingly plausible to argue that the postwar success of Keynesianism was much less the cause than it was simply the effect of postwar economic expansion and political democracy. This expansion had followed the previous stagnation in the normal course of the uneven waves of capital accumulation, and it was in due course followed by yet another long period of stagnation and apparently a renewed turn to political conservatism.

The renewed stagnation crisis of capital accumulation began in the mid-1960's and became universally visible in the recession of 1973–75. Economists suffering from theoretical lag finally acknowledged the crisis during the unsuccessful 1975–79 recovery and the current post-1979 recession. The economic crisis has manifested itself in the stagnation of investment and growth, consequent unemployment and inflation combined into stagflation in an increasingly monopolistic economy, and the wholesale bankruptcy of industrial firms and some finanancial institutions. The development of this new world economic crisis also engendered a crisis in Keynesianism, followed by its bankruptcy and its replacement by classical monetarism and neoclassical supply-side economics as the new orthodoxy. This neoconservative shift in economic theory and policy has been the most important component of the general rightward shift under the banners of Reaganism or Reaganomics in the United States and Thatcherism in Britain.

Ironically, the recent attack on Keynesianism and its replacement by monetarism and supply-side economics are not based on the major theoretical shortcomings of Keynesianism, which its conservative rivals also share. The shortcomings of Keynesianism that are the most important in theory, but the least popular among theorists, include the following:

The original, crude Keynesianism rather turned Say's law on its head and supposed that demand creates its own supply (for economists: the aggregate demand curve shifts rightward on a horizontal aggregate supply curve of unemployed resources). The theoretical limitations of this analysis are really the same as those of its classical Say's law and the monetarist obverse (in which, for economists, the rightward shift of the aggregate demand curve is matched by higher prices on a vertical aggregate supply curve at full employment). Both the classical/neoclassical theory of the market economy and the Keynesian theory that replaced it assumed that the market is competitive and therefore fully responsive. In reality, the market is substantially monopolistic — technically oligopolistic or characterized by monopolistic competition — and increasingly so, especially during periods of stagnation when capital becomes even more concentrated and centralized.

The assumption of perfect competition (which is also shared by neoclassical microtheory) is the first Achilles' heel of Keynesianism and renders it lame in its contest with an increasingly monopolistic economy. For it is precisely the monopolistic structure of the economy that (contrary to both classical/neoclassical and Keynesian theory) simultaneously generates unemployment or stagnation and inflation, that is, so-called stagflation. Keynesian theory, in which supply is responsive to changes in demand, cannot account for this existence of simultaneous unemployment *and* inflation. Keynesian demand management policies are unable to combat stagflation in a monopolistic economy, since increasing demand would stimulate inflation and decreasing demand would promote unemployment.

This monopolistic basis of stagflation also suggests that inflation is caused neither by monetary demand-pull, nor by commodity-push (oil!) or labor cost-push, but fundamentally by monopolistic profit-push in the high-concentration industries (including oil) of a highly monopolistic economy. The theoretical and empirical substantiation of this monopoly profit-push theory of inflation is beyond the scope of this article (it is examined further in Frank 1980 and 1981, as well as in studies cited in those works). However, the monopolistic profit-push theory of inflation should have some intuitive appeal by virtue of the obvious acceleration of inflation, and specifically of price increases by private and public monopolized industries, precisely during times of slow or negative growth and profit stagnation or slumps — hence "stagflation" or "slumpflation."

Another theoretical Achilles' heel of Keynesianism is its reliance on a strong state to implement expansive or contractive "stabilization" policy, as in either the substantially closed national economies of the 1930's and 1940's, or an imperialist world-economy with substantial hegemony by Pax Britannica in the mid-nineteenth century or Pax Americana in the mid-twentieth century. This nationalist or imperialist Achilles' heel of Keynesianism becomes apparent only in the 1970's with the decline of American hegemony (and perhaps — again following British experience — with the decline of American imperial abilities to finance domestic Keynesian expansion partly out of foreign imperialist earnings). The 1970's witnessed increasingly open national economies (unlike the 1930's but perhaps like the 1920's), that is, the so-called internationalization of capital and the economy. But now this internationalization was accompanied by the decreasing ability of any one national economy or state to impose its monetary and fiscal policies on other national economies or on the world-economy as a whole. The United States had this ability in the 1950's (Marshall Plan) and the 1960's (foreign investment through dollars freely printed to finance the Vietnam War), but lost it first to France, Germany and Japan (as symbolized by the delinking and devaluation of the dollar with respect to gold by President Nixon on August 15, 1971), and then with regard to the OPEC Third World (as a response to U.S. weakening and ultimate defeat in the Vietnam War).

During the 1970's and also the 1980's — until and unless the world-economy suffers another crash and breakdown which is a distinct possibility — we find absent a state that is able to impose its policy on a national economy without significant spillover of expansive/contractive effects or isolation of the national economy from economic developments and policies elsewhere. Also absent is a hegemonic economy able to impose its own Keynesian policies on the world-economy. Given those absences, national Keynesian theory and policy have become inapplicable to world international political economic reality.

The proof of the Keynesian theoretical pudding is in the eating: the Keynesian "locomotive" theory of pulling the world-economy by state-regulated fits (literally speaking, unfortunately) and starts and stops has not worked, either for the United States as it was accustomed to having it work, or for Germany and Japan (to whom the Americans applied this new denomination, which was rejected by Chancellor Helmut Schmidt from the start). The Keynesian locomotive is certainly not applicable in formerly Great Britain, where domestic economic policy has inevitably spurred international capital flight from British industry, whose (mis)fortunes in turn are substantially affected by the rise and fall of the petropound in response to the demand for and supply of oil on the world market. Keynesian macrotheory has no relevance to this international reality, because theoretical Keynesianism (perhaps as distinct from practical policy) does not even recognize this international reality to be relevant.

Yet these two Achilles' heels of Keynesianism — the competition/monopoly one and the national/international one, which in turn reflect the Keynesian failure to recognize, let alone come to terms with, the class nature of the state and the imperialist structure of the international economy and state system — are *not* the most used targets or reasons for the currently popular attack on Keynesianism, if only because most of the critics of Keynesianism themselves suffer even more from these same weaknesses. The attack on Keynesianism comes from the right, and for other economic and political reasons.

The fundamental economic and political reason for the bankruptcy of Keynesianism, and its replacement by monetarism and supply-side economics as the new orthodoxy, lies in the present stage of the world capitalist economic crisis and the economic exigencies of capital and the political interests of its representatives in the state and elsewhere, including the universities. The advent and development of another (long wave) crisis of overaccumulation of capital and reduced rates of profit have rendered Keynesian expansive effective demand management irrelevant to the present needs of capital and have placed cost reductions in the forefront of the economic and political interests of capitalists and their representatives. Hence this shift in economic interest is manifested in a consequent political shift to the right. Hence the recourse to monetarist policies and to cost-reducing supply-side economics, which are obligingly supplied by ideologues in the universities for appropriate reward.

With profit rates low since the late 1960's, and with excessive installed productive capacity as well as excessive finance capital for profitable investment, the prime objective of capital is to raise the rate of profit again. The first and foremost policy mechanisms for achieving this goal are to cut the private and social costs of production and, through bankruptcy or consolidation, to eliminate competing capital that is insufficiently able to do the same. Expansionary Keynesian demand management will not be in the general interest of capital again unless and *until* these cost reductions have become effective in raising the rate of profit and generating a new period of major investment and expansion.

The major mechanisms to cut costs (or increase supply, as those on the side of capital would have it) are to reduce direct real wage costs; to cut social wage costs of "unproductive" health, education and other welfare expenditures (hence welfare: farewell); to lower the taxes that finance these expenditures and are regarded as costs to business; and to eliminate costly regulations that protect consumers and the public generally from business abuse in production, packaging, advertising, etc., from environmental pollution and from monopoly practices.

Another major mechanism to cut costs is the introduction of certain technological innovations, such as microchips and some robots, that immediately cut labor costs of production without requiring huge new investments that the profit outlook does not yet justify. A further mechanism is to shift production from older, high-cost industrial regions in Western Europe, and especially in Great Britain and the Northeast of the United States, to sites in the non-unionized Southwest of the United States and in the Third World, especially East Asia, and to the socialist countries where the costs of labor and/or raw materials or infrastructure and pollution control as well as taxes are lower.

To relocate production in these areas through the runaway shop, and to convert them into export platforms for the world market under the banner of "export led growth," involves the imposition in those areas of often even greater measures of economic austerity than in the older industrial areas. It also involves enforcing such austerity measures by political repression, as in South Korea and the Phillipines, Israel and Egypt, Morocco and Tunisia, Chile and Argentina, and increasingly against popular resistance in Poland and China. But the trade competition for production and employment from these lower-cost industrial areas, and the resulting credibility of the threat to relocate still more industrial plants, also serves to enforce greater labor discipline and lower wage costs in the older areas and therefore in the capitalist world-economy as a whole. In the meantime, the old Keynesian welfare state in the industrial North and the neo-Keynesian import substitution policies in the Third World South, as well as autonomous planning and social welfare (also Keynesian?) in the socialist East are universally sacrificed to the new or, more precisely, old but newly labeled economic orthodoxies: monetarism, supply-side economics and free world market incentives.

MONETARISM AND SUPPLY-SIDE ECONOMICS — THE NEW ORTHODOXY, QUO VADIS?

The new orthodoxy, a sort of "reverse Keynesianism," is composed of an uneasy alliance (perhaps more accurately, a mixed bag) of monetarists, supply-siders and military Keynesians. The monetarists are led by Milton Friedman, the Nobel Prize theoretical economist turned best-seller with his *Free to Choose* book and television series, and they have several centers of power, including the U.S. Federal Reserve (chaired successively by Arthur Burns and Paul Volcker) and the British Treasury. They argue that the quantity of money alone determines the level of prices — so that too much money chasing too few goods produces inflation — and that too much government (deficit spending) means too much money. Therefore they want to reduce both substantially, in order to combat inflation (which they regard as the main evil), even if doing so increases unemployment.

The new gurus of supple-side economics include Arthur Laffer, who drew his ")" shaped Laffer curve on a napkin in a Washington restaurant to argue that increasing the tax rate only increases government revenue until high taxes discourage economic activity so much as to begin reducing the government tax take again, and George Gilder. In his best-selling, populist and ideologically charged book, *Wealth and Poverty*, Gilder explains, "capitalism begins with giving. . . . Egalitarianism in the economy tends to promote greed over giving. . . . To lift the incomes of the poor, it will be necessary . . . to enlarge the wealth, if not the consumption, of the rich" (pp. 21, 30, 67). Gilder also writes that "the essential thesis of Say's Law remains true: supply creates demand. There can be no such thing as a general glut of goods. There can be a glut of 'bads' . . . " which are "equality, bureaucratic rationality, predictability, sexual liberation, political 'populism' and the pursuit of pleasure — all . . . simply inconsistent with . . . economic and technical advance." Therefore, "when wives earn more, the men feel a decline of urgency in their work and a loss of male nerve and drive . . . [women's] benefit levels destroy the father's key role and authority. He can no longer feel manly in his own home" (pp. 39, 114, 151, 259). Another leading supply-sider, Jude Wanniski, explains *The Way the World Works* in the past (including the causes of the 1929 Wall Street crash and the Great Depression), present and future exclusively through changes in tax rates.

These and other supply-siders found their first major political expression in U.S. Congressman Jack Kemp, who introduced the Kemp-Roth bill to cut federal taxes by 30%. Kemp offered to cut the Gordian knot of Keynesianism and stagflation by promising a simultaneous decrease of both unemployment and inflation through the supply-side increase of incentives and production in response to lower taxes. This new gospel was then taken up by Ronald Reagan, as it had been by Margaret Thatcher in Britain before him (although before George Bush joined the team as the U.S. vice-presidential candidate, he aptly called it all "voo-doo economics"). Indeed, hardly any other economists — including the monetarists — or businessmen believe that a 10% tax cut will significantly increase either saving or investment, or that it can effect any more than a 1% reduction in inflation. On the other hand, cutting the taxes of the rich can help effect a massive redistribution of income so that the redistribution economic means becomes the political end.

This political reason for the tax cut was dramatically confirmed by the other high-flying supply-sider, Reagan's Budget Director David Stockman, in an interview with *The Atlantic Monthly* (December 1981).[1] This interview, as exemplified in the following quotes, was a serious embarrassment to the Reagan Administration, which felt that its rug of political credibility had been pulled out from under it. According to the *Atlantic* reporter:

> Stockman . . . was conceding what the liberal Keynesian critics had argued from the outset — the supply-side theory was not a new economic theory at all but only new language and argument to conceal a hoary old Republican doctrine: give the tax cuts to the top brackets, the wealthiest individuals and largest enterprises, and let the good effects "trickle down" through the economy to reach everyone else.

Or from foot-in-horse's mouth Stockman himself:

> The hard part of the supply-side tax cut is dropping the top rate
> from 70 to 50 percent. . . . In order to make this palatable as a
> political matter, you had to bring down all the brackets. But, I mean,
> Kemp-Roth was always a Trojan horse to bring down the top rate. . . .
> It's kind of hard to sell "trickle down," . . . so the supply-side formula
> was the only way to get a tax policy that was really "trickle down."
> Supply-side is "trickle-down" theory.

Stockman confirms what others had long suspected:

> None of us really understands what's going on with all these
> numbers. . . . The tax program . . . and the defense program [were]
> just a bunch of numbers written on a piece of paper. And it didn't
> quite mesh. That's what happened. But, you see, for about a month
> and a half we got away with that because of the novelty of all these
> budget reductions.[2]

This "reverse Keynesianism" of the monetarists and supply-siders is backed up by a more traditional Keynesian remnant among the supporters of government spending for the military. Mrs. Thatcher, Mr. Reagan and Mr. Carter before him, as well as most other Western governments, have substantially increased military expenditures for military hardware and a military-related high-technology industry at a time when the demand for civilian investment is sluggish, exports have to be fought for competitively, and consumer demand is unstably supported by instalment credit finance, which in turn is regarded as inflationary. Thus, public military and high-technology spending is demanded and welcomed by newer industries and regions, especially in the Southwestern United States, where the most right-wing economic and political interests prevail.

To justify these increases in military expenditures in the face of budget cuts everywhere else (except for the police), it appears appropriate to heat up a new cold war hysteria against the Soviet "militarism and terrorism." Such is the justification, despite the fact that the Soviet Union has repeatedly demonstrated by word and deed its urgent concern for arms control and disengagement in Europe, which it needs in order to face a severe economic crisis at home, and while the Chinese Communists have become the most fervent supporters of U.S. and NATO militarism. However, the renewed militarist policy of the United States — which has overcome its "Vietnam syndrome" — also represents an effort to reimpose U.S. hegemony and again to expand U.S. control over markets and raw material supplies in the Third World. This reason for increased U.S. military expenditures is revealed by the fact that so far they are primarily for weapons and a Rapid Deployment Force designed to be used in the Third World, rather than in preparation for direct confrontation with the Soviet Union.

However, serious dissension and therefore internal obstacles to implementing economic policy emerged in the Reagan and Thatcher ranks almost as soon as they took office and have been growing ever since. In Britain this conflict has manifested itself in the governing Conservative Party, where the wing led by former Prime Minister Edward Heath and representing important industrial interests has offered increasing resistance to the dismantling of industry that is promoted by strong pound, high interest rate, and reluctant industry subsidy policies. Those are the policies pursued by the Thatcher government in alliance with, and at the behest of, British financial capital in "The City" (London's Wall Street), which has been decapitalizing British industry while sending investments abroad. Also, after an initial euphoria, it proved impossible to continue with the tax cuts first promised by Mrs. Thatcher (and then Mr. Reagan). Even within Mrs. Thatcher's government itself there has been further conflict between the hard-liners, including her, and those whom she has called the "wets," such as Labor Secretary James Prior, who have sought to mitigate open conflict with labor and industry.

In the Reagan government, as observers have pointed out,[3] economists and policymakers have been divided between monetarists and supply-siders, and among the latter between those who are openly on the side of capital and the more populist supply-siders. The Reagan monetarists support high interest rates that detract from the supply-siders' tax investment incentives, and reject the supply-siders' tax cut proposals as inflationary. This conflict between monetarists and supply-siders emerged in a curious fashion at the very beginning of the Reagan Administration when the former rejected the latter's new-fangled, Claremont College expectations-based forecasting techniques as an unrealistic method of projecting higher government revenues in the federal budget proposal then under discussion. They won the battle for lower projections and hence tighter fiscal discipline, and also the battle for high interest rates.

The supply-siders, on the other hand, won the first battle for tax cuts and accelerated "10-5-3" depreciation/amortization allowances (which permit firms to write off their books for tax purposes different types of capital assets in the number of years specified by that formula). But they had to compromise by accepting lower and slower tax cuts than the 10% in each of the first three years that Reagan and the Kemp-Roth bill originally promised. For their part, the more populist supply-siders, led by Congressman Jack Kemp, have complained loudly — "I wasn't elected to cut spending, I was elected to cut taxes" — and even threatened noncooperation because of the success of the monetarists and the visibly great bias of the tax cuts. These cuts and other allowances too obviously benefit the major corporations rather than small businesses and individual income earners, many of whom receive no benefit at all from the Reagan expenditure and revenue budgets. Low-income people, of course, will be hard-hit by expenditure cuts that reduce welfare and increase unemployment without reducing inflation, and they will be penalized by increased social security taxes more than they can benefit from lower income taxes. At the same time, Reagan has proposed and seems likely to implement the highest and fastest increase in military expenditures in over 30 years. Efforts to check this increase have been made by those conscious of the budget deficit that threatens as a result of the impending failure of other Reaganomic policies, like tax cuts, to deliver the goods. But such attempts seem to bear only meager fruits.

In short, and in accord with the experience of the Thatcher government, the initial battles within the Reagan Administration have been won by the monetarist representatives of finance capital against the supply-side representatives of industrial capital, and by the agents of big capital against those of small capital. Domestically, the *economic* concerns of business have received almost exclusive attention during the first period of the Reagan (like the Thatcher) Administration, to the virtual exclusion of the *social* concerns of the petty bourgeois, far-right "moral majority," "right to life" movement, which has accused Reagan of betraying its support for his election. Similarly, foreign policy and particularly far-right belligerency have had to take a back seat and Reagan has been obliged to retreat from the weak limb on which he had gone out too far, the El Salvador issue. But the time for more focus and stronger stances on domestic social and foreign policy issues may still come, after the economic basket in which Reagan put all his initial eggs falls apart and he fails to deliver the political goods before the 1984 election.

The question arises as to whether the political-economic policies of Reaganomics and Thatcherism will serve to deliver their proponents' promises to reduce inflation and unemployment, to increase investment and productivity, and to restore national power and dignity — and if they fail to do so, then what? The prospects are dim indeed that Reaganomics and Thatcherism (and similar policies pursued by the conservative governments of Fraser in Australia, Muldoon in New Zealand and others) can and will really deliver on their economic promises. Disbelief is widespread even among parties and political supporters of Reagan and Thatcher, as well as in business, the financial press and perhaps most significantly the stockmarkets of Wall Street, London and elsewhere, which have indicated their negative evaluation of the prospects by turning sharply downward. In Britain, Australia and New Zealand, where these policies have already been implemented for several years, economic failure and political disillusion have proceeded apace. Under the Thatcher government in Britain, unemployment has risen from one million to three million without any lasting reduction in inflation.

Initially, the proponents of these theories found no difficulty in persuading business to accept the corresponding tax reductions, along the Laffer curve of the supply-siders; the elimination of obligations to bear some of the external social costs of their pursuit of private profit through deregulation; or reduced government welfare expenditures, a sacrifice to the new monetarist and supply-side sacred cows. However, business has completely failed to give even the slightest indication either in word or deed that it will respond by increasing investment or nonmilitary technological progress as a consequence of the implementation of these theories. Nor is there any theoretical or practical reason why it should. With overcapacity in major industries and excess capital funds to their own account and in the banking system, as well as the diversion of technological research and development towards military uses, there is no reason why tax reductions for business or high income earners, or exemption from environmental and consumer protection regulations, or monetarist high interest rates should induce business to increase investment at this time. Nor do these policies give business an inducement to promote high technology for the civilian economy, except insofar as business already has incentives to reduce labor costs, through microchips, for example.

To illustrate what is at issue, the supply-side vision of the economy has been compared to a coiled spring *on* which the weight of government taxes and regulation contain the pent-up entrepreneurial energy. The argument is about the degree of tension in the spring: it is explosive, according to the supply-siders who have faith in capitalism as "individual creativity and courage, leadership and morality, intuition and faith. . . . faith, love, openness, conflict. . . . faith, altruism, investment competition and bureaucracy" (Gilder, pp. 27, 265). It is a rather feeble tension, more as in a piece of string, for those who recognise the weight of the bureaucracy and monopoly power resting with the Fortune 500 list of the largest corporations, and some less noble morals *within* — not just weighing on — capitalism. To grant tax relief to these corporations, and especially to the major oil companies that are already awash with windfall profits and surplus capital, may be less like uncoiling a spring than like pushing on a string.

Thus, there is not much theoretical or practical evidence that this supply-side and monetarist transfer of income from poor to rich will result in the promised increases in output, investment or productivity. Therefore, the promised anti-inflationary effects of this supply-side program are also without foundation. For the same reason, the promised increase in tax revenues and decrease in the budget deficit, at lower tax rates but supposedly higher output, are illusionary. In reality, the inflationary business fires are kept burning by the increase in military expenditures through cost-plus contracts financed via continued budget deficits, and the inability or unwillingness of the monetary authorities to put a real lid on the money supply — a lid that business needs to support its monopolistic price increases.

It need occasion no surprise, then, to hear the conservative former head of the American Federal Reserve Board, Arthur Burns, observe that "this theory underlying the Reagan economic program has not yet won as much support as the program itself. . . . Skepticism concerning the underpinnings of the Reagan program is not confined to traditional liberals. It is also felt to some degree by economists, businessmen, and others who are entirely sympathetic to the President's philosophy" (American Enterprise Institute Reprint No. 122, April 1981). Thus, the resounding failure of Thatcherism and Reaganomics to produce the promised supply-side and monetarist results will not surprise most economists, who never accepted this promise in theory, or businessmen who never accepted the corresponding obligations in practice, even in each national economy taken separately.

WHAT FUTURE THEN — 1984?

If and when Reaganomics and Thatcherism fail, then what? Some argue for a return to Keynesian neo-orthodoxy. But this theory and policy have been abandoned as unworkable or at least unsuited to the present circumstances by more and more economic theorists, business practitioners and national politicians.

In Britain and the United States, Keynesianism was already abandoned by James Callaghan (with Denis Healey as Chancellor of the Exchequer) and James Carter respectively (it was Carter who called Ronald Reagan insufficiently pro-business) several years before Margaret Thatcher and Ronald Reagan extended the monetarist and supply-side orthodoxy to its logical conclusion. Even the American

Enterprise Institute, a conservative Reagan think tank, observes that "most of the elements in the Reagan economy can be found in the last year and a half of the Carter administration: the slowdown in the growth of nondefense spending, the proposal of a tax cut oriented toward increasing productivity (what is now called a supply-side tax cut), the reduction of government regulations, and an effort to achieve steadier and slower growth in the money supply" (AEI *Economist*, April 1981, p. 2). In Australia, New Zealand, Germany, France, and even Scandinavia and elsewhere, Keynesianism was similarly abandoned in the mid-1970's.

The only partial exceptions among major politicians have been Edward Kennedy, whose bid for the U.S. presidential nomination was defeated tactically by the Iranian and Afghan foreign crises, but strategically because of his domestic national Keynesian program and Pierre Trudeau, who is still proposing a modified national Keynesian program for Canada on the basis of a nationalist energy and raw materials program financed by Canada's privileged resource position in the world-economy today. Now François Mitterrand has won an electoral mandate for a Keynesian program for France, and the Labour left is seeking one in Britain. However Mitterrand began to face reality as soon as he tried to implement his first major economic promise to increase the salaries of public employees; in round one, he was obliged to do only half of what he had promised. The prospects for the successful implementation of such national Keynesian programs in the world-economy today are dim in view of the domestic obstacles examined above and the international ones to be reviewed below.

In the absence of viable Keynesian alternatives to fall back upon after the impending failure of Reaganomic and Thatcherist supply-side monetarism, obviously the next economic policy on the agenda is the imposition of controls on wages, prices, *investment*, and perhaps imports. This new attempt to rescue the economy might be presented as corporate supply-side planning with state controls. In the United States, controls including specifically a new Reconstruction Finance Corporation (recalling the RFC of New Deal fame) have already been proposed across a broad political economic spectrum. That spectrum includes, at one end, the explicit proposals of Wall Street financier Felix Rohatyn (who already saved New York City from fiscal crisis by implementing, on a municipal level, the kind of corporate-public planning at the expense of the poor which he now proposes on a national level) and *Business Week* (in its special issues on "re-industrializing America" and on "America's Restructured Economy").

At the other end, there is the Bar Harbor statement of the AFL-CIO unions, which also pleads for a new social contract, and — less clearly — Nobel Prize economist Wassily Leontieff (writing in the *New York Times*); the Center for Economic Alternatives of Gar Alperovitz; Democratic Socialist (DSOC) spokesman Michael Harrington; David Gordon, a leading member of the Union for Radical Political Economics (URPE) and the Institute for Labor Education and Research (ILER), and others. Thus sectors of the U.S. left run the danger of becoming the social democratic and even democratic socialist tail wagged by the corporate dog.

Even the pro-Reagan American Enterprise Institute, after observing that the present evidence does not augur well for the success of the Reagan program especially with regard to productivity, asks "what if it doesn't work?" and answers in part: "a second option in these circumstances would be some form of price and wage control." This of course, seems utterly alien to Reagan's philosophy. But, we must remember it also seemed alien to Nixon's philosophy right after his first inauguration. We cannot rule it out, even though it now seems extremely unlikely" (AIE *Economist*, April 1981, pp. 7-8). For the time being, of course, such controls are ideological anathema to Reaganites and Thatcherites and remain cries into the political wind. But Nixon was able to impose his New Economic Policy wage and price controls on August 15, 1971, in the face of much less pressing economic problems. Why then should a significant part of the Republican Party and perhaps even Ronald Reagan himself not be able to opt for such controls — for want of any better economic alternative — to fight the 1984 election? And whether or not the Republicans are able to rise to the challenge, the Democratic Party, which cannot return to the orthodox Keynesianism of its past and has nothing better to offer, would seem to be an ideal candidate to fight coming elections, and if successful to administer future governments, under the banner of such planning controls.

In Britain, investment planning and import controls are so far central only to the Labour left program of Tony Benn, who advocates the national abandonment of the Common Market and of British and American nuclear arms. But the Labour Party as a whole, which cannot return to the economic program that led to its defeat by Mrs. Thatcher, is unable to offer any other plausible Alternative Economic Strategy. Similarly, the new Social Democratic-Liberal alliance, which began with no economic or other program at all, would seem to risk remaining without any unless it also contemplates the economic exigencies and political attractions of extensive planning controls. Of course, Pierre Trudeau's national energy, resource and industrial investment program in Canada and François Mitterrand's new economic program in France also rest heavily on corporate state planning and controls of investment, if not wages, prices and perhaps some foreign trade as well.

All this raises the obvious political question: control of, by and for what part of the people? Little political economic science is required to suggest that in a bourgeois state the contention for political coalition, to say nothing of competition, between the representatives of big capital and big labor is more than likely to end up with political economic state controls of, by and for capital or some sectors thereof. With this goes the necessary political repression of those who oppose such controls because they don't benefit from them.

It should not be surprising then if the exercise of such controls, like Reaganomics and Thatcherism, fails to satisfy economic and social needs or to still the political demands of the underprivileged sectors of the population — and indeed is implemented increasingly at their expense. These sectors include unorganized labor, public employees facing cuts, the minorities, and even some disadvantaged sectors of business; the political consequence is likely to be that some of them rebel, and that the more they do so, the more will they be repressed. In the United States, electoral politics can increasingly abandon the industrially declining Northeast snowbelt to its fate, as shifts of population to the Southwest sunbelt can increasingly swing presidential elections. At the same time, minority rebelliousness will increasingly be met by political repression from the ultra-right, led by senators such as the ex-Dixiecrat Strom Thurmond at the head of the Senate Judiciary Committee (where he has already proposed to reimpose the death penalty against the poor, to ban abortions for women, to eliminate affirmative action for minorities and to strengthen the FBI against the rebellious) and the ultra-right-wing Jesse Helms in Foreign Relations. The forces of political repression also include organizations like the "Moral Majority," the ideological "right to life" and "defense of the family" movements and others that seek to put women "back where they belong" in the home, and to roll back progressive education and affirmative action precisely when the unemployment and rationalization of labor use generated by economic crisis render these social advances of the 1960's useless and literally counterproductive for capital. All these ultra-right political forces, which have so far felt defrauded by President Reagan's economic priorities, may yet receive their political due. So they will, if they are put in charge of state-orchestrated political repression when their reactionary social programs are moved to the Administration's front burner in order economically to complement and politically to compensate for the increasing failure of the initial Reaganomic program and the incipient corporate state planning.

Another option, which is to be regarded not so much as an alternative but more as a further political complement to the reorientation of domestic economic and social policy, is a still more nationalist stance and belligerent foreign policy. This policy would count on the support of Jesse Helms in the Chair of the Senate Foreign Relations Committee; it makes another foreign war in the Third World a more realistic prospect, in the attempt to foster national political unity and impose domestic political repression. Thus, in the United States and elsewhere, 1984 is not far off and may soon become politically more meaningful than a mere calendar or electoral year.

The real prospect of greater national chauvinism and a more belligerent foreign policy are only some of the possible consequences of the second Achilles' heel that Keynesianism, Reaganomic and That-cherist monetarist and supply-side policies, and corporate state plan-ning controls share equally, namely the limitations of their confinement to the sphere of national power in a time of *world* economic crisis. In an open international economy, *national* monetarist supply-side policies are just as subject to spillover effects abroad, and backwash effects from abroad, as Keynesian ones. Monetarist high interest rates and strong currencies generate investment problems abroad and export problems at home. Even if supply-side tax reductions were to increase investment incentives, there is no guarantee that such investment would be made at home. The effective disinvestment in industry and capital flight from Britain in response to Thatcherism have been higher than ever. There is no good reason why Reaganomics should offer a quick fix for the decline of productivity in the United States *relative* to Europe and Japan. Indeed, his military program may again aggravate the productivity problem in other sectors of the American economy, except insofar as military high-technology development has immediate applicability elsewhere.

The effects of *national* economic controls or planning are also limited by, and in, an international economy. Of course, the possible effectiveness of controls is greater in the American economy, although even there foreign trade doubled in its share of GNP from 5% to 10% over the 1970's. In the foreign trade dependent, open economy of Britain, a neo-Keynesian planning program with import controls outside the Common Market (and NATO?) such as that proposed by Tony Benn would require the wholesale reorganization of society. Even then, it would offer scant promise of success unless the entire capitalist world-economy breaks down simultaneously. Mitterrand's short-run Keynesian program for France and the proposals to redirect industrial investment do not mention any abandonment or breakdown of the European Common Market. But it is difficult to see how this program could be implemented by France within the Common Market, unless France could persuade its partners to follow similar policies; Mitterrand seems inclined to attempt this, but with what appears even less likelihood of success. Even then, it would still be necessary to reckon with competitive opposition and obstacles from the remainder of the capitalist and indeed socialist world. West Germany and France, which depend heavily on trade with the Soviet Union and Eastern Europe, resisted joining the embargoes against the Soviet Union by President Carter in the United States, which is much less engaged in such East-West trade. There is growing West European disenchantment with Carter's and Reagan's belligerent anti-Soviet nuclear strategy, which is setting up Europe as the "theater" of a possible nuclear war that the United States might thus seek to escape. Such responses are further manifestations of growing nationalist rivalries and dissension.

In the absence of a hegemonic global economic, political and military power, it is difficult to see how any capitalist Keynesian demand, monetarist-supply-side, or corporate-state social contract-control programs can effectively stem or reverse the economic crisis during the 1980's as their proponents promise, so long as the world capitalist economy continues to function at all. Paradoxically, therefore, the very failure of these national economic policies and the exacerbation of nationalist competition in an international economy in crisis may lead to a substantial breakdown of international trade or at least to the formation of rival political economic blocs (United States-Americas, Japan-East Asia, and Western Europe-Africa and perhaps Middle East, or indeed a European bloc including Western and Eastern Europe along a Paris-Bonn-Moscow axis with Africa and the Middle East as its hinterland, opposing a Washington-Tokyo-Peking axis). Both the multipolar breakdown of the world-economy and any such new bloc formation would threaten renewed global warfare on a scale that would render all of the above-mentioned economic policies and claimants to new orthodoxy, as well as other human endeavors, quite obsolete. That is why the development of another anti-war movement, even more massive than the one of the Vietnam years and allied to the emerging anti-nuclear arms and power movement in Western Europe, is an essential component of any progressive, political-economic alternative to Reaganomics in the United States.

NOTES

1.   This article was written long before Stockman's revelations were published. I have added the following comments because they so accurately confirm and illustrate my analysis.

2.   William Greider, "The Education of David Stockman," in *The Atlantic Monthly* (December 1981), pp. 27, 40, 46, 47.
3.   James Campen and Arthur MacEwan in an unpublished paper and Pat Clawson in discussion at conferences and in private have been particularly helpful to me in making these distinctions.

REFERENCES

Frank, Andre Gunder

1981   *Reflections on the World Economic Crisis* (London: Hutchinson); New York: Monthly Review Press.

1981   *Crisis In the Third World* (London: Heinemann); New York: Holmes and Meier.

1980   *Crisis In the World Economy* (London: Heinemann); New York: Holmes and Meier.

Global Crisis and Transformation

The world economic system is undergoing another of its historically recurrent crises, which like previous ones is generating far-reaching and deep-going economic, social, and political transformation through technological change and modifications in the division of labor and power. We briefly review here some of the manifestations of the contemporary crisis and then examine two of the attempted alternative transformation responses: further integration in the world economy by adapting to the changing division of labor through export promotion from the Third World and the socialist economies, or resistance and rebellion against this integration by attempts to *de*-link from the world economy through national liberation and the promotion of self-reliance and socialism. We will examine some of the economic possibilities and limitations, social consequences, and political implications of these apparently alternative responses to crisis and approaches to transformation in the recent past and foreseeable future.

Development and Change (The Hague), Vol. 14, No. 3, July 1983. This chapter is based on and is an extension of the author's recent books, *Crisis: In the World Economy* and *Crisis In the Third World* (Heinemann, London and Holmes & Meier, New York 1980/81), *Reflections on the World Economic Crisis* (Monthly Review Press, New York and Hutchinson, London, 1981), and with Samir Amin, Giovanni Arrighi and Immanuel Wallerstein, *Dynamics of Global Crisis* (Monthly Review Press, New York, Macmillan Press, London 1982).

The world system has experienced periodic crises throughout its history. A crisis is a period in which the previous expansion cannot continue on the same basis. In order to survive at all during a crisis, it is necessary for the system to undergo vast economic, social, political, and cultural transformations, including technological change. During these periods of crisis there is a need for the reduction of costs of production by lowering wages, by moving production to places where production is cheaper, and—of great importance in the long run—through technological change that lowers costs of production. In the periods of crisis, there are new inventions which require vast investments in order to transform them into a new basis for production during the subsequent expansion. The world system is once again in such a crisis today. The question is whether the world capitalist system will be able to make the necessary readjustment. If it cannot, then of course the system will destroy itself. But if it can make these readjustments, then there is reason to believe that it may have another period of expansion similar to that of the post-war years which would begin after these readjustments have been made, which may be 10 or 15 years from now or perhaps longer. During this period of readjustment, there will again be vast economic, social, political, and cultural convulsions in the world. These readjustments appear as a significant transformation of economy and society in the various parts of the world, North and South, East and West. From a worldwide and longer historical perspective, however, the question remains open whether these apparently often revolutionary changes really represent a fundamental transformation of the unequal regional, sectoral, and class structure and the uneven temporal or even cyclical development of this world economic system. Perhaps these local, sectoral, and national transformations represent changes of position in a global game of musical chairs to the tune of economic crisis, in which the fundamental structure of polarity, exploitation, and oppression and the long rhythm of uneven world development remain fundamentally unaltered.

The present world economic crisis is another general crisis of capital accumulation in the world capitalist system analogous to those of a half century (1914–1940/45) and a century (1873–96) ago. There have been such crises in capitalist development for several hundred years, and they are a natural part of the historical process of world capitalist development. After the last major crisis during the inter-war years, there was a renewed expansion during the post-war period. This expansion apparently lasted until 1973, but in reality it had already begun to slow down in 1967 and to turn into a renewed period of relative stagnation and crisis. Initially, this crisis took the form of reduced rates of profit and a renewed increase in recessions. There was a recession in

1967, which excluded the United States and Japan, the former (and in part the latter) because of the U.S. expenditures to finance its war against Vietnam. In this recession, official unemployment in the industrial capitalist countries (of North America, Western Europe, Japan, Australia, and New Zealand) rose to 5 million. Unemployment declined again during the 1968–69 recovery. Then came the 1969–70 recession, in which the United States and Japan were also included, and unemployment in the industrialized countries grew to 10 million.

This recession already had very serious consequences. Before the recession, the world had been flooded with dollars issued by the United States to finance the Vietnam war. There had been important changes in relative productivity among industrial producers during the 1960s. Productivity in Europe had grown twice as fast as in the United States, and in Japan twice as fast again as in Western Europe or nearly four times as fast as in the United States. This change in the relative competitive abilities on the world market and the flood of dollars were exacerbated when growth rates declined during the 1969–70 recession and led on August 15, 1971 to what President Nixon called a New Economic Policy and what the Japanese called Nixon Shokku: Nixon imposed wage and price controls in the United States, took the dollar off its fixed relation to gold, permitting it to be devalued, and imposed a special discriminatory surtax of 10% on imports from Japan. Thereby, he effectively destroyed the basis of the international monetary system that had been established at Bretton Woods after the Second World War with fixed exchange rates, and he opened the way to widespread currency fluctuations and further devaluation of the dollar. This decision was an attempt to increase U.S. competitiveness in world markets again and led to the rapid increase of U.S. exports, especially of armaments and agricultural products. Then followed the recovery from 1971 to 1973 which was, however, short-lived and led to the major 1973–75 recession, which was worldwide, and in which official unemployment grew to 15 million, including nearly 9 million in the United States alone.

The world recession of 1973–75 also led to an end of the fast Japanese growth rates and to a decline in output in 1974 in Japan as well as in the other industrial countries. After that time there was another recovery—from 1975 to 1979—in which unemployment decreased again in the United States but continued to increase in Canada, Western Europe, Japan, Australia, and New Zealand. Total unemployment in the industrialized world during the so-called recovery rose from 15 million to 17 million. In 1979–80 there began a renewed recession and, of course, unemployment increased again very substantially, to about 23 million in 1980; the OECD predicted an increase to

30 million by 1982. This is equivalent to nearly the entire labor force of a major industrial country. Moreover, these unemployment figures are the officially recorded ones. Real unemployment is much higher than what governments say. This seems to be particularly the case for Japan. In 1974, for instance, registered unemployment in Japan was 730,000; but according to an Employment Status Survey, real unemployment was 3,276,000 and male unemployment was twice as high and female unemployment *ten times* as high as officially registered unemployment. These figures for Japan still do not include the 4 million other people who either worked part time but wanted to work more or those who were discouraged from looking for work. This problem is now exacerbated by the enforced earlier retirement age. Real unemployment in the industrialized world is very much higher than what governments say.

Investment has also declined. The rate of profit began to decline in 1967. The major consequence for economic policy everywhere has been that expansionist demand-maintaining Keynesian policy has been abandoned on the argument that it would be inflationary. Everywhere Keynesian expansionism has been replaced by deflationary policies, the decline of the welfare state, and the attempt to reduce real wages, which has been more successful in some countries than others. Real wages have certainly declined in the United States and Great Britain, and during part of the 1970s they also declined in Japan as inflation grew more than money wages. The drive to reduce costs of production has also led to changes in the nature of investment in order to reduce labor and its costs in the industrial process.

In an attempt to justify and legitimize these measures it has become common to appeal to the return to traditional values, to national unity, and to economic and political nationalism. In a word, there has been a very marked political shift to the right in the industrialized world. This shift is visible in the election and policies of Ronald Reagan in the United States and Margaret Thatcher in Britain. But it also extends to the Frazer and Muldoon governments in Australia and New Zealand, respectively, and to the pronounced rightward shift in the municipal and parliamentary elections and the government of Japan. Even the labor and social democratic parties have experienced very significant shifts to the right and are pursuing more conservative economic policies in Germany, Scandinavia, and elsewhere. Indeed, it was the Labour government of James Callaghan in Britain and the Democratic President Jimmy Carter in the United States who first abandoned Keynesian economic measures and imposed the new austerity policies in their countries. That is the reason why they lost their electoral support to the Conservatives and Republican parties, who, however, only continued and further extended these same monetarist austerity policies. Among the industrial countries only France has moved somewhat to the left, but with severe limitations to the economic policy of the Mitterand government.

Another very significant way to reduce costs of production has been to move parts of the productive process from areas where labor costs are high to areas where labor costs are lower. The policy applies particularly to those industrial processes that use much labor, such as in the textile, clothing, shoe, toy, and electronic-components industries. More recently, capital-intensive crisis-ridden industries (and those that are polluting or incur high antipollution costs), such as automobiles, shipbuilding, steel, and petrochemicals, are also being moved increasingly to Third World and socialist countries. The northern border of Mexico south of the Rio Grande river began to see the establishment of factories for production for export to the U.S. market in the 1960s. Then, South Korea, Hong Kong, Taiwan, and Singapore began their so-called export-led growth in the late 1960s based on the production of labor-intensive commodities for export to the world market. Particularly in South Korea and in Southeast Asia (but not in Hong Kong), much of this investment was by foreign capital, especially Japanese.

Under the impact of the growing economic crisis of the 1970s, this process of industrial relocation has spread to Malaysia and the Philippines (it is no accident that Mr. Marcos imposed martial law in 1972 when this policy began), Thailand, Sri Lanka, and to India, Pakistan, Egypt, Tunisia, Morocco, various countries in sub-Saharan Africa, everywhere in the Caribbean (except Cuba), and throughout most of Latin America. In this rapid change in the international division of labor under the impact of this world economic crisis, the Third World is also becoming a place for increased production of agricultural commodities for export by agri-business. New mining methods on land and on the sea bottom are also being introduced. What the Third World countries have to offer in this new international division of labor is, first and foremost, cheap labor. Additionally, their governments offer all kinds of concessions to international capital, including tax-free holidays to the corporation for several years. Third World states provide the infrastructure of ports, airports, railways, cheap electricity, cheap water, free land, and so forth; and often they even build the factory buildings and lend international capital the money or at least guarantee private loans to them in order to set up production in their countries to export to the world market—in competition with other countries that bid to do the same.

The worldwide political economic mechanism to promote a new international division of labor by relocating these manufacturing, agricultural, and mining and even some financial processes in the Third

World and the socialist countries is fuelled and oiled by the international financial system. The recessions and inflation (so-called stagflation) in the industrial capitalist countries in the first instance and secondarily the increases in the price of oil (part of the cost of which to the First World has also been shifted to the Third World) have sharply aggravated the balance of payments deficits of the non–oil-exporting countries in the Third World (and some socialist countries such as Poland). To cover these growing deficits, these countries have increasingly turned to the private international capital markets, which have recycled some of the OPEC surplus funds to them and have additionally lent them other funds at high rates of interest that found no borrowers in the industrial countries where investment has been low. The extension of these loans and particularly their roll-over rescheduling to finance the growing debt service when the borrowers are unable to pay have become the basis of stringent economic and political conditions that the private banks and/or the International Monetary Fund (IMF) acting as their intermediary have imposed on Third World (and some socialist and developed) countries. The standard "conditionality" to the IMF package that governments are obliged to accept in their "letter of intent" before being certified to receive further loans always includes devaluation of the currency, reduction of government expenditures especially on consumer subsidies and popular welfare, the reduction of the wage rate through various devices, and more favorable treatment for private and especially foreign capital. These conditions have sometimes led to "IMF riots" as the people sought to resist the enforced curtailment of their standards of living. It has been said that the IMF has overthrown more governments than Marx and Lenin put together. An important political economic consequence, if not rationale, of these IMF-promoted government policies in the Third World is to promote "export-led growth" by cheapening Third World labor and its fruits for international capital and foreign importers (by lowering the price of Third World wages and currencies) and to lend support to the domestic forces in these Third World countries that have an economic interest in export promotion. Thus, the international financial system and the financing of the Third World debt serves to fuel and oil the mechanism of the emerging international division of labor based on Third World export promotion. The political consequences of all these economic policies are that it is necessary to repress the labor force in order to keep wages low or to reduce wages. In the case of Brazil, which after Mexico has been the principal example of this process in Latin America since the military coup in 1964, wages were reduced by over 40%. In Argentina, since the military coup in 1976, wages were reduced by over 50%. But already before the coup real wages were going down as a result of the economic policy of the right wing of the Peronist government in 1974–75. In Chile, real wages since the coup were reduced by two-thirds, that is to say, from an index of 100 almost to an index of 30, and unemployment increased from 4% to 20%, fell to 12% and rose to 30%. To be able to do this it was necessary first to destroy or to control the unions, to eliminate—often physically—the leadership, to repress all political opposition, and to throw people in jail, torture them, murder them, exile them, and so forth. Second, it was necessary to reorganize the economy for producing for the internal market through so-called import substitution to producing for exports.

During the last major crisis of the 1930s and early 1940s when the Third World had a balance of payments crisis and was unable to earn foreign exchange to buy imports, some countries like Mexico, Brazil, Argentina, India, and South Africa started to produce manufactures internally for the internal market, substituting these for imports. To be able to do that, however, they had to import capital goods. They had to import machinery and later technology with which to produce these, and they had to pay for these capital imports through exports. In order to earn these exports they had to invite in the multinational corporation that they thought would bring capital equipment and capital into the country, and they had to borrow and increase their debt. Then in the 1950s and 1960s this movement spread through other parts of the Third World and most particularly through many countries of Latin America. This process of import-substitution for the internal market required people with incomes with which to purchase these commodities. Therefore, there were political alliances between the labor movement and the sector of the bourgeoisies that worked for the internal market to support populist more-or-less democratic nationalist governments. When these economies switch from this import substitution model of economic growth to that of "export-led growth" by promoting exports for the world market, they no longer require this effective demand on the internal market to purchase the industrial or agricultural commodities that they produce. Because manufactured and agricultural commodities are exported, they now require a world market. They also require the lowest costs of production possible. Therefore, the main thing they now want to do is to reduce the wage cost of production, and they do not care if that also reduces internal demand because they do not want to sell internally; they want to sell externally.

However, this requires a significant reorganization of the economic and political structure of Brazil, Argentina, Chile, and elsewhere in the Third World as well, from producing for the internal market to producing for the external market. This means that the sector of industry as well as labor that had been producing for the internal market, or that wants to produce for the internal market, also has to be repressed politically. And this leads to the political measures of these authoritarian and military regimes and the imposition of martial law and of emergency rule that we have seen nearly everywhere in the Third World in the 1970s. The repression is used first and foremost against labor and second against a sector of the bourgeoisie itself in order to restructure the economy and reorient it toward export production. This political economic process is behind the political repression of Kim in South Korea and Aquino in the Philippines, both of whom are bourgeois leaders who do not propose a revolutionary alternative but simply a more democratic alternative. They are the political representatives in these countries of bourgeois capitalist interests that are dependent on the development of the internal market. These economic interests and their political representatives have to be at least politically eliminated. The whole political regime is based on an alliance between the sector of the bourgeoisie in these countries that is allied to international capital and particularly to the multinationals of the United States, West Germany, and Japan. Internally this alliance rests politically on the military as the force that cements these relationships. This is the political economic basis of the events we have observed in South Korea, the Philippines, Chile, Argentina, and so forth. This crisis-generated political economic exigency is what really explains the wave of political repression throughout the Third World.

We may distinguish two major kinds of alternative responses and transformation in the Third World and the socialist countries with regard to these crisis developments: acceptance and rejection. Recent experience offers examples of both approaches, each of which is proposed as a "model" of development policy for others to follow until supposedly the whole world is transformed in their image. The acceptance policy of integration in the emerging division of labor is particularly associated with the so-called newly industrializing countries (NICs) of the Asian Gang of Four—South Korea, Taiwan, Hong Kong, and Singapore—plus Brazil and Mexico in Latin America, whose development "miracles" supposedly offer a "model" of "export led growth" and socioeconomic transformation or development strategy to be pursued by the remainder of the Third World and even parts of the socialist (Second) and industrial (First) world. The alternative rejection policy of de-linking from the world economy and promoting self-reliance as much as possible is associated with the struggle for national liberation from colonialism and neocolonialism or imperialism and the transition to/promotion of socialism from the

Soviet Union and Eastern Europe to China, North Korea, Vietnam, and Cuba as well as more recently Nicaragua and Grenada, Angola and Mozambique, Zimbabwe and Ethiopia, and so forth. Both approaches may be and often are regarded as major sociopolitical transformations in response to economic crisis, the former so to say accepting and promoting the transformations generated from the center or demanded from above, and the latter rejecting the same and initiating and participating in a transformation at the periphery and from below. We may examine some of the economic limitations, social consequences, and political implications of these transformation responses in the recent past and foreseeable future.

The thesis and policy that the miraculous success of the Asian Gang of Four and Latin American NICs offer a model of development and transformation for the Third World and elsewhere is, to begin with, internally inconsistent and contradictory. If the experience of South Korea, Taiwan, Hong Kong, Singapore (and sometimes Mexico's border region with the United States and São Paulo in Brazil) are really miraculous—that is, extraordinary and almost inexplicable in normal terms—then they can hardly serve as a model for the remainder of the Third World, which would be hard put to duplicate the same circumstances and experience. This limitation is at least two-fold, general and particular.

The general limitation is that export-led growth by a few small countries and the absorption of their exports as imports by the rest of the world is one thing; and the generalization of the same export-led growth to that same rest of the world (who would export to/be imported from by whom?) is another matter. Consider the prospects and problems of Hong Kong and Taiwan style exports on a Chinese or Indian, let alone Third World scale! The sheer impossibility of such a "model" is intuitively clear. World system analysis can offer the "scientific" reasons: particular growth experiences, such as those of the NICs, that of post-war Europe and Japan, or indeed of the industrial revolution itself, can and could not be generalized to the rest of the world, precisely because they took place where and when they did and thereby exclude(d) and prevent(ed) the rest of the world from doing the same. Eric Hobsbawm has already pointed out, without the benefit of "world-system analysis," that in 1800 there was room in the world for no more than the industrial revolution in Britain. He had in mind, apparently, demand-side limitations to British, let alone other, export-led growth. Similar demand-side limitations obtain with regard to the NICs, and today we can see that there are resource supply-side limitations as well (in brief, one-fourth of the world's population uses three-fourths of the world resources). But as the analysis of imperialism, dependence, and the world system has emphasized, the very growth pattern of the "leaders" has been based on, indeed has generated, the *inability* of much of the world to follow. The underlying reason, as world system analysis would have it, is that this development or ascent has been misperceived as taking place in particular countries, when it has really been one of the processes *of* the world system itself. The recent export-led growth of the NICs also is part and parcel of the process of capital accumulation on a world scale (to cite the appropriate title of Samir Amin): to reduce costs of production and to make room for more technologically advanced development elsewhere, a part of the labor- (and some capital-) intensive production is relocated in the NICs and the "socialist" countries. However, this process is far from trouble free, as it generates protectionist pressures in the "traditional" producing countries, exacerbates trade and financial imbalances, and is threatened by the possible breakdown of the world trade and financial system, to whose instability this process itself contributes. More NICs would only do more of the same.

But there are also many particular limitations to the generalization of NIC export-led growth on the "gang of four" NICs model that are particular to these countries and to others that may seek to follow in their footsteps. All four of the Asian NICs are fundamentally characterized by very particular *political* reasons for their establishment and survival, and two of them additionally are city-states for the same reason. South Korea and Taiwan clearly were created as "independent" entities as a result of the Cold War against China and the Soviet Union and have been politically supported and economically subsidized as strategic pawns against them. Hong Kong emerged from history to a similarly peculiar position, and Singapore became a state because of the preponderance of overseas Chinese population on the Malay Peninsula (and behind them also the perceived threat of China). These world political circumstances, let alone the advantages of city-states that draw on their respective hinterlands without economic and political responsibility for them, may be politically miraculous—and go some way toward accounting for their economic miracles—but hardly offer a model to be duplicated *ad infinitum* elsewhere in the Third World (except with modifications in Israel). It would be tedious and should be unnecessary to review particularities elsewhere all around the Third World to establish that they do not and cannot match those of the Asian NICs. Suffice it to point out the obvious: that India, or even Pakistan or Bangladesh, are in no position to duplicate the *relatively* socially incorporative on nonmarginalizing growth patterns of gang-of-four NIC export-led growth, and that the larger Brazil and Mexico have completely failed to do so—witness the 50% unemployment rate in Mexico *after* exporting several million workers to the United States. Indeed, even tiny Hong Kong excludes a large proportion of its population from the benefits—if not from the costs—of export-led growth, if its world's most unequal distribution of income is any measure.

Beyond the impossibility of following the gang of four NICs as a model, the desirability of their "miracles" as models of development is also questionable, to say the least. The supposed merits of export-led growth are that it generates foreign exchange to improve the balance of payments, that it provides employment to eliminate or reduce unemployment, that it imports technology and improves skills to advance technological development, and that it furthers integral national development generally. But export-led growth scores very badly in the test of experience on each of these four counts of its supposed merits, and for very good reasons.

Far from improving the balance of payments, export-led growth deteriorates it to the point of generating serious balance of payments crises, as the three largest NIC exporters—South Korea, Brazil, and Mexico—have found to their and the banking community's alarm. To export, the NICs have to import raw materials, components, technology, and high-priced businessmen, which are frequently overpriced through transfer pricing within the multinationals who in turn underprice the resulting exports, thus reducing or eliminating the foreign exchange earning and taxpaying value added in the NIC. But since the principal attraction of the NICs is their low wages, and secondarily the state subsidies that often involve imported components for local infrastructure as well, the national valued-added and export-minus-import foreign exchange earning was low to begin with and is only lowered through transfer pricing and other tricks. The result is that the NICs have to borrow increasingly to pay for their import requirements, which grow additionally as export production interferes with domestic production and therefore increases import requirements especially for agricultural products, and then the NICs have to finance and roll over their debts at increasingly onerous interest costs and other conditions.

Export-led growth undoubtedly generates employment, but apart from being unsteady due to ups and downs in the world market and/or the market penetration of the particular NIC industry, this employment itself generates unemployment as it interferes with domestically oriented industry and agriculture and draws more labor into the cities than the jobs that it creates. In Hong Kong and Singapore this process is invisible within the "country," but in Mexico and Brazil—as well as Malaysia, the Philippines, and elsewhere, and now China itself—this structurally generated unemployment is increasingly evident. The technological development is also uncertain. To the extent that NIC export production is of a component or process that is produced through labor-intensive routine operations on an assembly line that is no more than a part of a worldwide industrial process, in which other places specialize in the more advanced technological processes and in advancing the technological development itself, the NIC and its labor force experience only questionable technological development and skilling of the labor force. Even where the NICs produce entire end-products such as shirts, radios, or even automobiles they are simply increasing their dependent integration into a worldwide division of labor and technological development in which they are allocated the least remunerative and technologically obsolete contributions and the corresponding meager benefits. Far from contributing to or even laying the basis for relatively autonomous and self-propelling technological development based on national resources and capacities as North Korea has pioneered, dependent export-led growth on the South Korean model renders integrated national development increasingly impossible. At the same time it still maintains the economy low on the totem pole of world technological development.

It should not be forgotten that "export-led growth" is nothing new in the history of world development. Beyond British growth on its own terms and U.S., Canadian, and Australian export-led growth in exceptionally favorable times and circumstances within the process of world capital accumulation, much of the Third World went in for or was pushed or pulled into raw materials export-led growth on unfavorable terms dictated by the requirements of accumulation on a world scale, but elsewhere in the world, without themselves becoming developed beneficiaries of this process. The new dependent export-led growth of manufacturing and agri-business production for the world market are in no way significantly different from the old raw materials export-led growth that underdeveloped the Third World in the first place. And if it does turn out to be different, the recent experiences of South Korea, Brazil, and Mexico, with their respective resultant export-led growth-generated economic, social, and political crises of recent years certainly do not augur well for this difference.

Finally, we should consider the political costs of export-led growth, which have found echoes even in the halls of the U.S. Congress. Testimony there established how

> At the heart of South Korea's human rights problems is the economic growth strategy of the country, a strategy which requires the repression and manipulation of labor . . . and the tight control of free political expression. . . . The absence of full human rights is neither arbitrary nor coincidental; it is the product of the choice to have an export-oriented economy which leaves internal needs unmet. (Congressional Record, 5, April 1978: H 2517).

The U.S. Senate itself prepared a document in which

> As we have shown, in many countries there seems to be a direct correlation between economic difficulties and political repression. ... The problem with these measures [to create a favorable climate for foreign investment and for the private sector in general] is that... they can also lead to greater unemployment, to the reduction of social welfare, and to a lower standard of living for the people. ... Creditor demands to implant drastic economic austerity programs ... could only be imposed at the expense of civil liberties in the countries that adopt them. (U.S. Senate Foreign Relations Committee, "Foreign Debts, the Banks and U.S. Foreign Policy." August 1977)

These unpalatable truths, which have been recognized even by the unimpeachable authorities quoted above, have in turn led to right and left political responses, which however different, seem nevertheless to have in common that they both appear as "lesser evil" policies. The right-wing response is to justify and support these authoritarian tendencies and regimes as lesser evils than and as necessary and useful allied bulwarks against "totalitarian" world communism and socialism led by the Soviet Union. (This response is typified by the U.S. representative to the United Nations, Jeane Kirkpatrick, and the Reagan Administration generally.) Short of the rejectionist answer, the left responses are to limit some of the economic excesses of export-led growth through some measure of return to import substitution and economic nationalism and to curb the political excesses through the return to some form of democracy under the title of "viable democracy," "popular government," or some other variation on that theme, that would be a lesser evil than military or other authoritarian rule. Thus since 1977/78 there has been an apparent redemocratization and the installation of what U.S. President Carter called Viable Democracy. Elections have been held as in India, in Sri Lanka, even in Bangladesh. There has been the replacement of military regimes by civilian ones in Ghana and Nigeria. There have been elections or the proposals for elections in a number of countries in Latin America: Bolivia, Peru, Ecuador, and so forth. Is this a new wave of democratization that represents a return to the period of import substitution and the kinds of political alliances between labor and peasantry and the bourgeoisie of the period of import substitution?

A number of people believe or at least hope that. I also hope so, but I do not believe it. On the contrary, my impression is that this move to what President Carter called viable democracy is rather the institutionalization of the same model of export-led economic growth that had already been imposed earlier in the 1970s through the use of force. Once this model is operating, it is possible to use a bit less force in some places to keep it going and therefore it is possible to have some democratization. In other places not even this relative democratization is possible and it is necessary to use force, particularly if and when there is a renewed recession, such as there has been since 1978, and the economic problems increase again. As President Marcos said, he cannot afford to abandon martial law or to democratize now. (The subsequent replacement of martial by another law has everywhere been condemned as a farce and the "elections" as largely meaningless.) Thus, this apparent democratization is really making this model of export-led growth viable for the 1980s.

This viability takes the following political expression, among others. In Chile former Christian Democratic President Eduardo Frei was leading (until his recent death) the opposition to General Pinochet. In the recent election in Peru, Belaunde, the same man who was president until 1968 prior to the military coup, became president again. In this election Belaunde was supported by many sectors of the left. In Bolivia, Siles Suazo and Paz Estensoro, both previous presidents before the military government, were candidates for president. Siles Suazo was elected but prevented from taking office by the military. Since then a compromise candidate was deposed by another coup. In Brazil Magalhaes Pinto and Brizola, both important political figures from the 1960s, have been active again politically. In Nigeria Azikwe and Awolowo, politicians from the 1960s, were candidates again in the recent elections. In Ghana, of course, N'Krumah is dead; but the people from his movement were candidates. In India Mrs. Ghandi was reelected. In the Philippines Mr. Aquino was again the main opposition leader, and so forth. Two things are remarkable about these old political leaders from the 1960s who reappeared in the 1980s after this period of military rule. The first is that today they all have political and economic programs that are much further to the right than those that they had in the 1960s. And the second is that the progressive and revolutionary forces of the left, who in the 1960s opposed these political leaders as too conservative, today support these same old political leaders although now they have a much more conservative right-wing program than they did in the 1960s, when the left opposed them. This is a political measure of how much there has been an effective shift to the right even among the progressive and in many cases revolutionary forces in the Third World, who in pursuit of a lesser evil policy find themselves obliged to support old politicians who have programs that are much more to the right than the ones they had years ago when they still opposed them. In a sense this means that General Pinochet is in part realistic when he says that there is no real alternative to him in Chile. Maybe there is another political formula that might replace Pinochet. The supposed alternative was Frei, who also proposed a much more right-wing program than he did when he was president until 1970.

The economic program that all these politicians are proposing and that the new civilian governments in Peru, Ghana, and Nigeria are promoting is the very same export-led growth model that the military regime before them put into place. In Peru, already before the election there was reason to believe and events now bear out that the civilian government of Belaunde would be even more to the right than the military government that he replaced. Moreover, the deeper the world economic crisis manifests itself in any new cyclical economic recession/depression in such countries as Peru, Brazil, Nigeria, South Korea, and so forth in the early and mid-1980s, the greater is the realpolitik regression to the already latent authoritarianism likely to be.

Thus it appears that the economic crisis transformation of the world economic system as it is implemented through the positive acceptance response and transformation of the Third World and some other (including socialist, to be examined below) export promotion is beset by quite a number of very serious economic, social, and political limitations and costs.

The apparently opposite and supposedly alternative response to crisis and approach to transformation is to reject the imperialist world economy and to seek self-reliance through de-linking, national liberation, and socialism.

The widely felt negative consequences of imperialism, colonialism, neo-colonialism, and dependent capitalism generally and now the pressures and economic, political, and social costs of export promotion have led to numerous movements in the Third World for national liberation, socialist revolution, African socialism, de-linking, collective and national self-reliance, and so forth. But, as many revolutionaries have observed, if taking political power is difficult, its subsequent use in the pursuit of popular liberation is even more problematical. A review of some recent experience can provide a guide to some of the limitations and perhaps, through their better understanding, to the means to overcome them.

Take the case, for instance, of President Mugabe of Zimbabwe. He came to power after a long guerilla struggle, followed by negotiations with the British and the Rhodesian right leading to an election, and after having the support for a long time of Samora Machel in neighboring Mozambique and other Front Line states and leaders in Africa. But Samora Machel already told Mugabe before the election that he should become very moderate in order to be elected at all and that, if he did not, Mozambique would not be able to continue to support him, because it was costing Mozambique too much economically and politically to do so. So, since Mugabe has become president of Zimbabwe, he has completely failed to pursue the policies that he had promised. First of all, he has not instituted the land reform that he had promised as his first priority. President Mugabe recently gave an interview in which he said, "I am not only a practicing Marxist but also a practical Marxist." Therefore, he said, he now recognizes a need for foreign capital, for the multinationals, for good relations with South Africa and so forth. Thus, the "terrorist" Mugabe has now become a supermoderate.

The newly independent ex-Portuguese territories in Guinea-Bissau, Angola, and Mozambique also reached independence through prolonged revolutionary guerilla struggle (as well as the thereby induced 1974 revolution in Portugal). Yet none of them have sought to de-link significantly from the world capitalist economy. Angola was enjoined by the Soviet Union not to become another Cuba, and the Cubans in Angola are guarding the Gulf oil installations that provide Angola's principal source of foreign exchange, the remainder of which comes from coffee and minerals that are also sold primarily to the West. Mozambique still depends on South Africa (and the decline in its supply of labor to the South African mines is due less to Mozambican policy than to changes in the price and production of gold), and the FRELIMO regime has recently backtracked on its earlier policies and is again renewing Mozambican reliance on Western aid and trade and private enterprise at home.

In Nicaragua the Sandinistas have had a very spectacular and important success. Nonetheless, they have agreed to assume the foreign debt of about U.S. $1.2 billion (a big sum for small Nicaragua) that Somoza had accumulated under his dictatorial regime. In order to pay this debt, the Sandinistas have had to borrow more money from international banks, the International Monetary Fund, and even $70 million from the United States to roll over the previous debt and finance current imports, which they have to curtail as well to finance the debt. Thus they have to accept important economic and political conditions imposed by these leaders, which make it extremely difficult for the Sandinistas to pursue a progressive, let alone revolutionary, economic policy at home and a supportive foreign policy toward the revolutionary movements in El Salvador and elsewhere in Central America. That is, of course, the express objective at least of the United States. Thus, the Sandinistas are caught in a dilemma. Either they say no to international capital by renouncing the Somoza debt, in which case they would receive no further loans or export credits and would be subject to an economic blockade even more severe than that which Chile suffered under President Allende and which contributed to his downfall. Or the Sandinistas accept to pay the Somoza debt and play along with international capital; but thereby they also accept the conditions that international capital imposes on them and which very much limit their ability to act. In the conditions of the current world economic crisis and the already very serious domestic economic crisis in Nicaragua itself, these conditions imposed on the Sandinista government will cost the Nicaraguan people dearly in terms of their well-being. Therefore, these conditions may also reduce the popular political support for the Sandinistas and thus help the bourgeois forces in Nicaragua undermine and challenge Sandinista political power. That is, of course, precisely what the U.S. government is trying to achieve through its own policy. This poses a very serious danger.

In Jamaica, the intervention of the International Monetary Fund and the conditions that it imposed on the progressive government of Prime Minister Michael Manley served to undermine his economic and political base and finally defeated him in the recent election. He was replaced by the avowedly right-wing pro-U.S. government of Edward Seaga, who immediately received ample U.S. and international economic, financial, and political support. Recently, there has also been a significant shift to the conservative right in progressive Tanzania, which is also doing valiant battle with the IMF. President Nyerere still commands substantial respect while he is trying to hold out against the conditions the IMF seeks to impose, but at the same time there has been a significant shift to the right in the last elections and in administrative policy. President Nyerere is under pressure increasingly to abandon the policy of self-reliance, for which Tanzania had become a model in the Third World, as the economic crisis deepens.

The political exigencies of deepening economic crisis are having similar effects elsewhere in the Third World. Angola, Mozambique, and Guinea-Bissau have renounced any substantial de-linking of their economies from the world capitalist system and are moving back to greater reliance on market incentives and private enterprise in their domestic economies. Vietnam and China, not to mention Poland, have been facing serious economic crises by attempts increasingly to re-link their economies to the still capitalist world economy and to place renewed reliance on market organization and private initiative and reward in their domestic economies and especially in agricultural production and distribution. The recognition of these realities in no way belittles the major progressive popular achievements in these countries and offers a realistic basis to safeguard and advance their progress.

The real economic limitations, social costs, and political short-comings of both the integrationist and rejectionist options—and the failure of Marxist theory and socialist models in the Soviet Union, China, and elsewhere still to offer sufficiently persuasive alternatives—are also bringing novel populist movements and policy options to the fore in which a combination of nationalist and religious values mobilize millions of people against the status quo, and apparently more massively and effectively so than the more secular alternatives. The Ayatolla Khomeini's revolution in Iran—perhaps the vanguard of a Muslim revival around half the globe—and Lech Walesa's Solidarity movement in Poland are the most noteable recent expressions of this new (or renewed) motive force. We cannot exclude that the near future will witness the development of analogous movements and the spread of their force possibly also incorporating appeals to race or racism, in such regions as Southeast Asia (with special reference to China and overseas Chinese), South Asia (through the spread of communalist forces), the Middle East (as a response to the complex economic–political–military–social–cultural–religious conflicts), Southern Africa (as a legacy of colonialism and apartheid), Latin America (as a repercussion in part of the realignments generated by the Falklands/Malvinas war), and last but not least within and between the capitalist West and the socialist East. It is too early to foretell the prospects and possible consequences of such social movements and their politico-economic consequences.

However, the observation and comparison of past experience with other recent projects at de-linking and transition to socialism suggest the following theoretical or at least classificatory reflections on trans-formation and development policy in the foreseeable future of the present world crisis. The break with capitalism and the transition to socialism require a revolutionary process, an internal transfer of power and popular participation, and the achievement of a greater degree of external independence. Attempts at transitions in the Third World have attempted either neither, or one, or the other, or both. In some cases there has been no real attempt either at de-linking or at a redistribution of power and popular participation. I am thinking for instance of Indonesia under Sukarno, India, much of the so-called African socialism, and Brazil in the time of Goulart from 1961 to 1964. All these attempts have failed miserably. In some places, there have been attempts at external *de-linking*, so to say external isolation from the world capitalist system, but without concomitant, simultaneous, far-reaching internal social and political changes. I am thinking particularly of Nasser's Egypt and of Burma until recently. These regimes have lasted a bit longer but in the medium run have been very substantial failures. The policies of subservient re-linking undertaken by Sadat are in part attributable to the important failures of the Nasser regime. Burma is now also re-linking at a very rapid rate. In other attempts there has been little external de-linking but attempts of some kind of internal reorganization without the external de-linking. I am thinking, for instance, of the Ghana of N'Krumah and in a certain sense of Allende's Chile. These have also been disastrous failures.

One of the lessons of this experience is that to try neither de-linking nor popular participation gets you nowhere. To try only external de-linking without internal participation also gets you nowhere and leads back to rapid re-linking. To try only internal participation without external de-linking is extremely dangerous, very difficult to do, and also is likely to lead to a disaster. External de-linking and internal participation, and social and political mobilization, reinforce each other and are necessary to be able to pursue rapid structural change to a threshold from which one would not immediately slide backward. The only countries where this has been possible are those that we today call socialist. That is to say that external de-linking and internal political change have been carried so far as to be called socialist. None of the other ways—the noncapitalist path, the popular-democracy path of African socialism, and so forth—have produced results.

One of the paradoxes of these experiences and attempts at de-linking, with or without internal political change, is that de-linking is in essence voluntary; but it is immediately complemented, supplemented by involuntary de-linking or "destabilization," the term Kissinger applied to this policy toward the Allende regime in Chile. That is to say, there are attempts, both intentionally and through the normal operation of the market system, to undermine this process of de-linking and internal political change from the outside and through the Quisling fifth column on the inside of the country to de-link the country even faster or farther than it would like to go, or at least to de-link it under the control of the opposition to this process (externally and internally) rather than to de-link it voluntarily under the control of the political forces that are carrying the process ahead. That in itself gives cause to ponder on the real possibilities of de-linking. The very fact that de-linking is not only a policy that is attempted by progressive governments but is also an arm that is used against the progressive governments gives cause for reflection about the rational utility of de-linking in the world today.

The socialist East is also caught up in this world capitalist crisis and provides another cause for concern. There is a process of increasing rapid reintegration or "re-linking" into the capitalist international division of labor, not only through trade but also through production.

There is also an increasing productive crisis throughout the COMECON countries in general; each of them separately, and all of them put together, have achieved only half or less than half their growth targets for the 1976–80 five-year plan.

In Poland, production declined and "growth" was negative by 2% in 1979, by 4% in 1980, and by 14% in 1981. Poland is perhaps the most extreme crisis case in this regard, being caught between, on the one hand, the increased oil prices that the Soviet Union charges to its partners in Eastern Europe and, on the other hand, the export difficulties that they face in the West because of recession. So they are caught in a "scissor's crisis" on an international level, reminiscent of the scissor's crisis during and after NEP in the Soviet Union on an internal plane. Inflation is increasing: as the papers say, inflation goes East. They have been unable to isolate themselves from the effects of this crisis. This is not unrelated to the workers' revolt and deepening economic crisis of 1980 and 1981 and the subsequent repression.

During the previous crisis from the 1920s to the 1940s, socialists and socialism welcomed capitalist crisis; they were in favor of the crisis and against capitalism. In the present crisis, it seems very evident that the socialist world does not welcome the capitalist crisis at all; in fact it is anticrisis and it is procapitalist. That is to say, it is doing all it can to contribute to the recovery of capitalism and even to eliminate the effects of the crisis. The prime minister of Bulgaria, Theodore Zivkoff, put this very clearly, in saying that "the crisis in the West affects us immediately and very deeply, because of our trade and other ties with the West. We hope that this crisis will pass as soon as possible." Socialism could then get back to business as usual. Deng Xiaoping in China speaks very eloquently for himself and, at least for the time being, for many millions of Chinese, in his alliance with U.S. imperialism and in the attempt to reintegrate China into the world capitalist economy as quickly as possible, with the proclaimed end of making China a world industrial power by the year 2000.

The economic and then political crisis in Poland and the growing economic crisis in Czechoslovakia and Rumania, as well as the general economic difficulties in Eastern Europe and the Soviet Union, are clarifying that fundamental economic reorganization and concomitant political adjustment are becoming (in Poland, has already become) imperative. A major source of this impasse has been the attempt to graft extensive integration in the world capitalist economy (itself in crisis) on to inflexibility in economic and political organization in COMECON and at home, except in Hungary. One possibility out of the impasse might be a retreat and involution to de-link again, but even if that is still possible, which is doubtful, it might require unacceptable economic and political readjustments at home. The other option is a forward flight to remedy the capitalist integration/socialist inflexibility impasse by, paradoxically, even further re-linking with the capitalist world economy and greater, but politically perhaps ultimately less costly, complementary flexibility at home. That has been the option so far followed in China and Vietnam (not to mention Kampuchea whose ousted Khmer Rouge now renounces communism and socialism for the rest of the century), and it is the policy of those in North Korea who seek to avoid the son of Kim II Sung as his successor and maintainer of past policies.

All this is not to say that the attempts at socialism were mistaken or useless. The socialist countries have all made significant advances of considerable benefit to the population in the countries in which they have happened; they have very much increased social services. What the World Bank now calls "basic needs" are met in the socialist countries; they have increased production, but they have not been very successful in increasing productivity. They have managed to produce an important expansion in production by mobilizing all inputs and therefore increasing outputs. Compare China with India, for instance, or Rumania, Bulgaria, and so forth with Turkey or Greece, or take the most obvious case of the Soviet Union: by having made a socialist revolution, they are now able to rejoin the world capitalist division of labor, but with an entirely different productive basis internally (in one word, industrialization) and an entirely different bargaining power externally.

This expansive growth approaches limits, however, which seemed to have been reached in many socialist economies around 1970, unless and until they reorganize production to increase it intensively be raising productivity. Here the socialist economies have been much less able to show successes. The need for increased productivity is the major reason why they are now recurring to technology from the West and are trying to reorganize their economies internally. But—very significantly —productivity comes at the cost of the relative equality that has been achieved during the earlier period, as experience in Eastern Europe and now China suggests.

Thus these socialist experiences have been very important and very useful, but they have not produced precisely what was expected of them, either internally or externally. Just as the French Revolution did not bring the peasants to power, so the Soviet Revolution certainly did not bring the Russian proletariat to power, and internationally they have not brought what we previously understood by socialism. Originally socialism was understood to be a process of transition to communism. It seems extremely difficult, if not impossible, still today to sustain the thesis that the "really existing socialist societies" in Eastern Europe are in any sense in a transition to communism. On the contrary, if they are in transition to anything today, they are more likely in a transition to capitalism.

But capitalism itself is undergoing another crisis-generated transition or transformation, of which the re-linking of the socialist economies and the analogous reorganization of the Third World to participate in a new international division of labor through so-called export-led growth, are integral elements. Both contribute to the necessary lowering of production costs and to capital's ability to reorganize the world economy during this period of crisis and to lay the basis for a possible subsequent period of renewed capitalist expansion. Whether these and other developments will fundamentally alter the structure and operation of the world capitalist system remains to be seen, but it seems unlikely for the foreseeable future.

23

Policy Ad Hockery:
Unemployment and World Crisis
of Economic Policy Formation

Policy has in the recent past degenerated to what might best be described as "systematic ad hockery!"

GATT Press Release 1333,
4 March 1983

The present 1979–83 recession is the fourth in a world economic crisis that may be said to have begun in 1967. The succession of recessions, the advance of inflation, and the doubling of unemployment in the West between the 1967 and the 1973–75 recessions and its doubling again from the latter recession to the present one, as well as economic restructuring in the world economy including the differential decline in productivity and the consequent shifts in the political economic balance of power in the West, have so far posed insurmountable and still growing obstacles to the effectiveness of both international and national formation and implementation of political economic policy.

In the 1967 recession, from which some industrial countries were exempt (particularly the United States, which avoided it through the

Economic and Political Weekly, Bombay, May 28, 1983.

Vietnam war) unemployment in the OECD industrial countries of North America, Western Europe, Japan, Australia, New Zealand, rose to 5 million. It then declined again until the recession of 1969–70, when unemployment rose to 10 million. Unemployment then declined again, but only to 8 million in the recovery of 1971–73. During the 1973–75 recession—the biggest post-war recession prior to the present one— unemployment rose to 15 million. In the then long recovery from mid-1975 to mid-1979 unemployment declined in the United States, but it rose so much elsewhere in the industrialized countries that total unemployment during the so-called recovery rose from 15 million to 17 million. This is where it stood at the beginning of the present recession which began in mid-1972 and continues today and has again doubled the level of unemployment to over 32 million at the end of 1982.* Every responsible economist, business analyst, and government spokesman today certainly anticipates that unemployment will continue to rise. The OECD predicted for 1984 an unemployment level of 35 million, but the Trade Union adjunct to the OECD immediately criticized that figure as unrealistic and said unemployment would be certainly nearer to 40 million, and I have seen Labour Union estimates of 70 million for later on in this world economic crisis.

The rate of profit began to decline in 1967, and in the 1969–70 and 1973–75 recessions there came to be substantial unutilized productive capacity particularly in industry. The combination of idle resources plus low rates of profit meant that the rate of investment declined substantially in 1973 and did not receover until 1978, and then only for a year, since with the present recession that began in 1979 the rate of investment declined again. Furthermore, the nature of investment changed from investment to produce more productive capacity in order to expand output—which is what is had been in the long post-war expansion—to so-called rationalizing investment essentially to produce the same kind of output or the same amount with a lower cost and most particularly with lower labour cost. This had various policy implications that we will examine below, but first we should mention the most popular of the supposed explanations for the crisis—namely, the price of oil.

Since 1973 everybody has put the blame on the price of oil—first the increase in the price of oil for the crisis, and now in the last few months the decline in the price of oil for the same deleterious consequences. In point of fact, the 1973–75 recession began in the United States in the second quarter, that is to say May/June of 1973,

---

* The development of this crisis is examined up to 1980 in the author's *Crisis: In the World Economy,* New York, Holmes & Meier, and London, Heinemann, 1980.

whereas the so-called first oil-shock did not come until October of 1973, about five months later. So, strictly speaking, it is hardly possible to blame the recession on something that began later than the recession itself did. The same goes for inflation, which people tend to blame on the oil price increase. In point of fact, the rate of inflation had increased dramatically from 1972 on and *declined* after the first oil-shock. Essentially the same thing happened with the second oil-shock at the end of 1979, which has also been blamed for the present recession, but the present recession began approximately in June of 1979 and the second oil-shock did not come until the end of 1979. At the time the second oil-shock also brought a reduction rather than an increase in the rate of inflation. So, the evidence shows that oil has not been the cause of even the sparks of these events. This is dramatically illustrated by the newest complaints, now that the price of oil has fallen and threatens to continue to fall. Everybody now feels threatened by the *decline* of the oil price and is blaming all kinds of present and prospective serious economic consequences in the world on this fact: this decline will make the oil-producing countries unable to import as much as before from the industrial countries; it will make the oil-exporting countries and the oil- or energy-producing industries unable to finance the debts that they incurred on the basis of prospective earnings based on high oil prices. Therefore, both the companies and the Third World countries are now threatening to initiate a financial crash and possibly to slow down or even to interrupt world trade and to destroy the present international trade system as a whole.

These problems in the world economy—be there a crash and breakdown or not—are some of the manifestations and mechanisms of a far-reaching process of restructuring engendered by the economic crisis, which should be viewed in greater historical perspective. We are in a long structural crisis of overproduction or overcumulation that started in 1967 with the beginnings of the decline in rate of profit and the increase in the number and depth of recessions. This crisis, now of 15 years duration, is likely to continue for another decade or even 15 years more. In analogy to the last crisis, I believe we are still in the 1920s and have not yet even got into the 1930s, with which an analogy is often made. The previous crisis, in fact, began in 1914 and lasted to 1940–45; it included the great depression, two World Wars, the rise of Fascism, two major Socialist Revolutions—in other words, vast economic, political, social, cultural changes in the world as integral parts of the readjustment process. The crisis before that started in 1873, after the long expansion from 1848 to 1873 which was characterized by Pax Britannica in which Britannia ruled the waves and free trade reigned in Britain's interest. This period was followed by a major crisis from 1873 to 1896, which brought the rise of monopoly capitalism, the rise of classical imperialism, the renewed rise of colonialism, and also vast changes in the international division of labour. The evidence in the present crisis so far shows that we are in a similar situation again and the recovery that is often being talked about by President Reagan and others is not from that crisis, but only from the present recession within the crisis.

This proposition seems to hold not only with regard to economic growth and employment, and so forth, but also with regard to the declining power of the United States, which President Reagan promised to make Number One again. The crisis of 1873–95 of a century ago was the beginning of the decline of Great Britain as the dominant economic and political power in the world. In the interwar crisis of half a century ago, Britain lost absolutely to the two rivals, the United States and Germany, which had literally been battling for the mantle of Britain's supremacy in two World Wars. Of course, the United States won. We enter the period of so-called Pax Americana in the American century which, however, also lasted even less than a quarter of a century. The United States began to lose out relatively in this crisis, as Britain did in that of a century ago, beginning in the late 1960s with the war in Vietnam in international political terms but I think really based on important shifts in economic competitiveness that are in turn based on changes in productivity.

In the 1960s Western Europe (excluding Great Britain) was increasing its rate of productivity, that is to say its output per input of labour, at twice the rate of the United States, and Japan did so at nearly twice the rate of Western Europe or nearly four times as fast as the United States. This differential growth in productivity and export competitiveness is essentially behind the relative decline of U.S. hegemony in the 1970s. Beginning with the recession of 1973, the rate of productivity growth in all these economies slowed down markedly from 3% a year to 1% a year average, except that in the United States since 1979 productivity has in fact gone down absolutely while it has continued to grow but at much lower rates in Western Europe and Japan. This is what is essentially behind the increasing break-up of the Atlantic Alliance between the United States and Western Europe that became so manifested as the tip of an iceberg in the pipeline controversy and is behind all the talk about a new, greater East-Asian coprosperity sphere that would be under the sovereignty of Japan and/or the Pacific Rim or Pacific Basin strategy. Jacques Attali, the economic advisor of President Mitterand in France, suggests that there is a shift in the center of gravity of the world economy from the Atlantic in the past to the Pacific now.

So, in each of these three crises, as in many centuries past, there has been a radical shift in the international division of labor and the intersectoral and intranational division of labor, in which some lose out in a sort of world game of musical chairs. Particularly the leaders lose out and others come to occupy their respective positions, and much of the battle is about the sharing out of the costs and the benefits of this major process of readjustment in the world economy. I submit that this process is largely beyond the capability of policy to either affect or even to stem the tide. We will return to this theme in the discussion below on the effects of Reagonomics and Mitterand's economic policies.

In the past also, there really were these international economic forces that were not national and were not subject to the control of national policy—if they had been, Great Britain would have taken care not to decline, but there was apparently nothing that Great Britain was able to do about that.*

Today, transnational corporations and their ability to plan are often given more credit than they deserve. The evidence is that, if the transnational corporations were able to do as they wish, they surely would not have lead us into this world economic crisis. So, there must be something very substantial that is beyond even their capacity to plan. Some corporations used their internal planning and transfer pricing throughout the world to place the principal cost of this crisis on others and to remain relatively unscathed. But it is also true that corporate profits have declined and a number of multinational corporations have been very seriously affected by the crisis. AEG Telefunken in Germany nearly went bankrupt. Chrysler nearly went bankrupt and had to be bailed out by the U.S. Congress. In fact, Chrysler, General Motors, and Ford between them lost about 5 billion dollars last year, of which Chrysler alone lost about 3 billion.

Moreover, everyone has been looking at the transnational corporations. Some claimed that they are the savior of mankind and are going to produce a new technological revolution that will make everybody sit at home and simply watch TV or play around with his computer while the machine is doing the work. Others charged that they are the villains of the piece, that essentially they are working against the interest of the people and in favor of profit and so forth and so on. While there has been all this attention to the TNCs, lo and behold in the 1970s it was not

---

*The decline of hegemonic powers and shifting balances of power are further examined in Samir Amin, Giovanni Arrighi, Andre Gunder Frank, and Immanuel Wallerstein, *Dynamics of Global Crisis*, New York, Monthly Review Press, and London, Macmillan Press, 1982.

primarily the TNCs that were reorganizing the world economy, but other primarily bank-financed forces which promoted the restructuring of the world economy by the so-called recycling of the OPEC surplus and other sources of loans, both to the corporations and significantly to the Third World and to the so-called socialist countries such as Poland. This has now lead to the debt-crisis, which began with Poland's inability to service its 27 billion dollars of debts, followed by the similar inability of Argentina during the Falkland's War, Mexico in August 1982, and Brazil in October/November 1982. This is also evidence that what is going on is quite beyond the control of the multinationals and, in fact, that they are not even the major actors any more as they were in the 1960s.

Hand in hand with these international financial flows, world productive activity has also been subject to international restructuring through some selective de-industrialization in the major capitalist powers such as the United States, Britain, and Australia and the growth of manufacturing production in the Third World countries and particularly in free trade zones. Seen from the "supply side," this restructuring is driven by the need to reduce costs of production during the crisis, and seen from the "demand side" it appears as a drive for markets. One way of reducing cost of production is through belt tightening, austerity policies, and a decline in real wages at home. Another way of reducing costs is to relocate production from high-cost producing areas to low-cost producing areas, first in the highly labour intensive industries such as textile, clothing, shoes, and so forth and then increasingly also in the capital intensive industries like steel, automobiles, ship building, and petrochemicals, which are the four major crisis industries in the West, and to move them to the South or the Third World and to the East, to the socialist economies, where wages are lower and worker discipline, until recently in Poland, has been higher. That is one of the reasons for and mechanisms of the change in the international division of labor, leading to the development of the so-called newly industrializing countries or NICs, like the gang of the four: South-Korea, Taiwan, Hong Kong, and Singapore. This relocation then spread to Malaysia, to the Philippines, and to South Asia (Sri Lanka now wants to do the same), and through North Africa and all around the Caribbean and into South America. The so-to-say "supply side" aspect thereof is that they now supply these manufactured commodities, in part competing with manufacturing in the "traditional" industrial areas and contributing to, but not causing, the decline in employment and the rise in unemployment in the industrial ones.

The other aspect is from the "demand side." Since there is low investment demand in the industrial economies, particularly in the manufacturing sector, it is necessary to have demand from somewhere. Now, one source is military demand, which is very clear in Reaganomics but was already so in the Carter administration. A second source of demand has come from the socialist countries, which were very important in the 1973–75 recession. A third source of demand is from the OPEC countries with new oil earnings, and that is why the construction industry has had a field-day in the Middle East. And fourthly, there has been demand for capital goods by the so-called NICs that are producing electronic components, automobiles, steel, and textiles, etc. for export. But this latter demand is in fact credit financed. With the rise of the OPEC surplus after the 1973 oil price increase and the rise of the Euro-currency market—the liquidity in which the banks were unable to loan to Western industries that were not investing—and the simultaneous increase in balance of payments deficit of the Third World and of the socialist countries, both the OPEC surplus and this other money was swashing around the world financial system and was loaned out to the Third World and to the socialist countries. The socialist countries' debt increased from U.S. $8 billion in 1971 to $80 billion in 1981; the debt of the Third World increased from $100 billion in 1971 to $500 billion in 1981 and probably $700 billion today; nobody really knows exactly how much.

There is a very close connection between the real relocation of industry and this financial flow. This finance has, so-to-say, "oiled the machinery" of the transfer of production from the West to the South and to the East of the world. This combination of financial flows and real restructuring has become increasingly important to the health of the Western world to prevent industry from deteriorating still further, particularly in the capital goods sector that cannot sell capital goods to Western industry that is not investing. Instead, these capital goods have been sold to the OPEC countries and to Brazil and Korea and Mexico and so forth. The share of the Third World in Western exports has increased very substantially during the 1970s. The United States, for instance, sells more goods to the Third World than it does to Europe or Japan. Western Europe sells more to the Third World than it does to either the United States or Japan. And Japan, despite the propaganda, sells over 50% of its exports in the Third World, which has become absolutely crucial as an importer.

The financial crunch of the last year and prospectively of next year—if there is not a crash, that would be even worse—has cramped the style of this whole strategy. It now turns out that the NICs have become heavily overindebted: Brazil $80 billion, Mexico $85 billion, Argentina and South Korea about $40 billion each, and Poland has a debt of $27 billion. These debts make it increasingly difficult to continue this debt-financed process of relocation. The banks have become scared and have started to restrict their short-term loans. But these countries now have to borrow and incur new debts from Peter in order to pay off their old debts to Paul, and the banks have to loan them this new money to prevent defaults but are now frightened of this dangerously overextended position. The ten largest U.S. banks, for instance, have loaned out more than 150% of their equity—and the Chase Manhattan Bank and Citicorporation each more than double the value of their equity—to Third World countries. By now restricting their short-term loans the banks are making these countries even less able to finance their debt and help push them into a debt crisis such as that which has already befallen, in chronological order, Poland, Argentina, Mexico, and Brazil. But, since then, also Chile, Costa Rica, Cuba, Yugoslavia, Nicaragua, Romania, Turkey, Zaire, Zambia, and more and more countries one after another declare themselves unable to keep up repayments of their borrowed capital. The best thing they can do—if they can do even that, and some of them cannot—for the time being is to continue to pay the interest on the money they owe, which is already 50% of their export earnings. They are no longer able to import, as they had been, from Western industry. This has clearly been the case of Poland and now of Mexico and Brazil.

This Third World and socialist demand bailed out the industrial economies to some extent in the 1973–75 recession. But this is no longer possible in the present recession. Therefore, the 1979–83 recession has been more serious than the previous one, and this accounts for the fact that Germany and Japan, which weathered the 1973–75 recession quite successfully, have been hit much more severely by the present recession. Unemployment has increased even in these countries very substantially, because the export markets, on which they have been very much dependent, are no longer so available. The world financial system is no longer able to provide the export credit to permit this system to continue working, and the situation has become so bad that many people—particularly in financial circles and in government circles—are talking about a possible world financial crash that would make the 1929 Wall Street crash seem like a storm in a teacup. This experience offers several more interesting lessons. One is that while everybody was watching the supposedly epoch-making multinationals (as saviors or devils), in the 1970s the real action took place elsewhere—through the financial system. The other lesson is that tight monetary policy, which became the gospel preached and practiced by each national monetary authority and government, completely failed to control the supply of money at the world level, which on the contrary exploded completely out of control in the Euro-currency and other markets. It has been estimated that in the decade of the 1970s the amount of bank reserves alone multiplied by eleven or twelve times— the amount of money created in the world since its invention! It is also interesting to note that the very "link" between money creation and its transfer to the Third World as purchasing power, which the Group of 77 Developing Countries demanded at UNCTAD III in 1972 (and which has again been proposed by the Brandt Commission more recently) but which has been steadfastly rejected by the industrial countries as a matter of policy, has as a matter of praxis been established—through the loans of this new money to the NICs—without the intentional intervention of any policy-making body. Ironically, moreover, despite the very "tight monetary policy," Western governments are now urging their private banks to keep this financial flow going and growing, lest failure to do so might lead to failure of the entire banking and international trade system!

These crisis developments suggest that the world economy is not very much subject to political or economic policy control. This limitation to the effectiveness of economic policy is particularly evident at the national level. In the United States, Jimmy Carter came to power on a program of fighting unemployment first and inflation second. One year after he came into office, Carter felt obliged by circumstances to make inflation public enemy number one instead and to pursue a restrictive policy, which was then carried to its logical conclusion by Ronald Reagan with his monetarism and supply-side economics. The same happened in Britain. In 1976, James Callaghan switched from Keynesianism to monetarism. The same thing happened in France under Raymond Barre and Giscard d'Estaing, and in Germany under Schmidt, and so forth throughout the industrialized countries. Essentially, Keynesianism was abandoned and monetarism and supply-side policies were enshrined in the drive to cut costs of production (instead of managing demand) and to promote productivity, which declined despite all efforts to the contrary.*

After Jimmy Carter had tried, but failed, to rebuild the confidence of the United States, Ronald Reagan promised to make the United States Number One again. His supply-side tax cuts were going to revive the economy so much as to reduce the budget deficit to zero by 1984. All these well-laid plans of mice and men have gone down the drain: the U.S. budget deficit is likely to be $150–160 billion this year, and they are talking about $200 and $300 billion next year, because none of these policies has worked.

---

*These reasons are further examined in Chapter 21.

Mrs. Thatcher came into office like Mr. Reagan to get the government off our backs. Far from having decreased, government expenditures as a proportion of income have increased. In fact, it was the Labour government of Jim Callaghan that reduced government expenditures as a proportion of gross national product from about 48% to 43%, and it was Mrs. Thatcher who has brought them back up to 48%, despite her supposed antigovernment policies. In the meantime, she has completely scuttled British industry. The depression in British industry under her government has been greater than at any time in recorded history including 1930 to 1933 and including the time after 1873 and in the 1880s.

But it is not strictly correct to blame Ronald Reagan or Margaret Thatcher for these failures. They simply make policy ripples on a major long wave of the world economy that do not respond to these policies and that certainly are not caused one way or the other by these policies. The wholesale failure of monetarist policy among Friedman's disciples in Chile, Argentina, Israel, and the like in the Third World, which have been struck by near total economic disaster during the past year, are spectacles to behold—and traumas to suffer by their victims.

Social democratic policy makers in Canada and France and socialist ones in China, the Soviet Union, and Eastern Europe have not fared any better. After abandoning Maoism, China began its "four modernizations" drive in 1976 with increased investments and technology imports from the West, but domestic and world economic circumstances—and their connection!—has obliged China to retrench on this program again since 1979. In the Soviet Union the growth rate has declined each year since 1979, and according to some estimates has been zero. Because of nonfulfillment each previous year, planned output and growth targets had to be revised downward each year but nonetheless still remained unfulfilled. The 1983 growth target is the lowest since before Stalin and is likely to go unfulfilled again. The decline in the world price of oil and gold, as well as of other commodities for which the Soviet Union depends on export earnings, poses further threats to the Soviet economy. After embarking in 1971 on a major drive to import Western technology—like other socialist economies in Europe and Asia—and after an apparently successful growth program in the mid-1970s, Poland found that in 1979 production went down by 2%, in 1980 by 4%, in 1981 by 14%, and last year, 1982, probably by 10% or 12%; they have a long way to plan until they can even get back to square one. Romania, Czechoslovakia, and even the reformed economy of Hungary have suffered balance of payments and debt crises and negative growth rates. Yugoslavia suffers from a major economic crisis. Planning has now failed in all these countries.

Elsewhere, Trudeau was reelected in Canada and proposed a modified Keynesian policy to take advantage of Canada's position as a producer of oil to try to parlay the resource oil boom money into Canadian industry. This strategy failed and is now completely unrealistic because the price of oil has gone down. Australia's resource boom bubble also burst in 1982.

Similarly, Mitterand was elected in France on a national Keynesian program and wanted the French market for the French by reflating. This policy also failed. In fact, what Mitterand did was to expand the French market for the Germans. The balance of payments went completely to hell; he had to devalue twice and is likely to have to devalue a third time. At the beginning of July 1982 he had to completely turn about his Keynesian policy and impose a wage and price freeze, abandon all his reflationary policies, and go back to the same kind of policies that everybody else is pursuing.

The other thing that Mitterand has done is a preview of what I think is the coming thing everywhere: a sort of state planning, state investment policy, macroindustrial policy. In the United States the financier Felix Rohatyn is proposing a revival of the Roosevelt New Deal Reconstructing Finance Corporation (RFC) in which the state would guide investment into high-tech areas and in some cases abandon the low-tech areas or low-tech industries, such as steel, textiles, and so forth, and let the Brazilians and the Koreans produce steel and textiles. In the case of France, Minister Chevènement proposes to save these industries by switching them from low-tech to modern high-tech.

The question comes whether it is possible to do this on a national basis. It may not be possible to do so in a country as small as France and as dependent on the Common Market and on the world economy, and I have my doubts about whether perhaps even the United States economy with all of its power may be able to do so or to pursue the so-called reindustrialization alone through this kind of policy. But it is probable that in 1984 the Democratic party in the United States will inscribe on its electoral banner some kind of motto about the state investment guidance. They may not use the word planning because it is a dirty word in the United States, but the Democrats are likely to propose a sort of RFC. But even the Republicans, with or without Reagan, may do so beforehand, to forestall the Democrats.

Everywhere in the industrialized world, not withstanding all the ideology about getting the government off our backs and letting free enterprise do its work in the market and all that, macroindustrial policy is the coming thing in the 1980s. It will be promoted through tripartite cooperation between the state, labor, and industry. Labor unions or trade unions will be asked to cooperate and the trade unions will say: we want some industrial democracy in return; that is to say, we want to have some kind of say in what goes on, particularly in the distribution of the costs of this investment program, so that the rich do not get off scot-free while we bear all the costs. Much of the political battles in the 1980s may be around that kind of issue.

But the question still will come whether it will be strictly on a national level or on a regional block level, such as a West European block or an East-West European block, a Japanese led Greater East Asian Coprosperity sphere or a Pacific Rim in which Australia and other countries will have to try to find some kind of privileged niche from which to draw some benefits rather than being made to bear all the costs.

It seems that the international economic system is on a roller-coaster that is out of control. It seems that we cannot get off the roller-coaster but are stuck on it, and we are just going to go through to wherever it is going or finally stops. If that is the case, are we going to have to accept that we are not in any way the masters or even have much of a voice now in political economic destiny? Another analogy for the roller-coaster is: "Stop the world, I want to get off." It is not clear that in this day and age this is a really realistic prospect, or indeed whether it has even been. The socialist economies to some extent did this— incidentally, not so much of their own volition as because the United States embargoed them into doing it—and they made some important progress in being relatively isolated. But they now find, particularly with regard to technological change, that they are now coming back, whether they want to or not, whether they have to or not, into the world capitalist economy. Ironically, they are coming back into the inter-national capitalist international division of labor under the banner of socialism, while governments lead by the likes of Ronald Reagan are going to go into planning under the banner of free enterprise.

This illustrates, among other things, that we suffer from some ideological confusion or at least irrelevancy of some of our traditional ideologies. Industry and government, and probably labor as the other part of the tripartite arrangement as well, will be pursuing policies that respond to circumstances and that have precious little to do with their stated ideologies or their stated preferences, and they are not likely to be very much in a position to dictate terms to anybody or to formulate policy in the usual sense of the word. Many will essentially pursue practices that are governed by the apparent needs of the moment, and these needs of the moment are determined by forces completely beyond their control and often beyond their understanding and sometimes beyond their recognition. If we recall what happened with the present world crisis, we were a long way into the world crisis before any of these leaders—West, East, and South—even recognised where they were, let alone were formulating any kind of policy to get us out of it.

Nonetheless, not all is in vain. It is better to light a candle than to curse the darkness—or to claim illumination where there is none. Honest observation of reality and critical analysis of our pathways through it can still illuminate our way. Realistic policy formation guided by the stream of events—instead of swimming against it or going off the deep end—still offers programmatic alternatives for political choice. In Europe, for instance, new options are posed by the simultaneous decline of the Atlantic Alliance and the impossibility of the Soviet bloc to continue without substantial change. Some realistic options for Europe (and some unrealistic policies) are examined—and a preference is stated and defended—by the author in a book entitled *The European Challenge: From Atlantic Alliance to Pan-European Entente for Peace and Jobs* (Nottingham Spokesman Books, April 1983).

ANTI-CRITIQUE

24

An Answer to Critics*

The philosophers have only interpreted the world in various ways;
the point, however, is to change it.

Karl Marx, *Theses on Feuerbach.*

The mark of an important contribution, whether in the hard or the
social sciences, is not that it reveals some eternal truth. It is, rather,
that existing knowledge and analysis are put together in new ways,
raising questions and offering conclusions which allow and force
friends and enemies alike to push their own research and analysis
into different areas.

Doug Dowd, referring to C. Wright Mills.

For social scientists it is a sobering and useful exercise in self-
understanding to attempt to see clearly how the direction of our
scientific exertions, particularly in economics, is conditioned by the
society in which we live, and most directly by the political climate
(which, in turn, is related to all other changes in society). Rarely if
ever, has the development of economics by its own force blazed the

World Development, Oxford, Vol. 5, No. 4, 1977.

*This essay was written in Chile in August 1972 and revised in February 1974. The
revisions incorporate answers also to critiques that appeared between these dates, and
they eliminate some passages referring to political events in Chile before August 1972.

way to new perspectives. The cue to the continual reorientation of
our work has normally come from the sphere of politics. Responding
to that cue, students turn to research on issues that have attained
political importance... So it has always been. The major recastings
of economic thought . . . were all responses to changing political
conditions and opportunities.

Gunnar Myrdal, in Asian Drama.

The development in Latin America of the 'dependence theory' of
underdevelopment in the post-war era was a response to the changing
political conditions and opportunities that had been wrought, for
historical reasons particularly in this area of the world or certain parts of
it, by the crisis of world capitalism during the 1930s and 1940s.
Analogous to the rise of the Popular Fronts (including the New Deal)
and Keynesianism in the imperialist metropolis, certain Latin American
countries witnessed the rise of populist bourgeois nationalist regimes
dedicated to the economic reality of import-substituting industrialization, the political policy of developmentism, and the ideological
legitimation through 'structuralism' and 'dependence'. Ultimately, the
latter found its most important and influential expression in the work of
the United Nations Economic Commission for Latin America (ECLA)
under the directorship of the former finance minister of Argentina, Raul
Prebisch, who subsequently went on to inspire the formation and guide
the fortunes of the United Nations Conference on Trade and Development (UNCTAD).

Apparently, born of — and borne by — progressive nationalist
aspirations, the new developmentist ideology/dependence theory
immediately encountered strong 'scientific' opposition and rejection at
home and abroad from the orthodox 'monetarists' in their long-winded
debate with the 'structuralists'. Moreover, in the course of two decades
and in response to the accumulating difficulties with 'easy' import
substitution at home, as well as the expansion of the multinational
corporation, the promotion of 'planned structural reform' abetted by
'foreign aid' and indebtedness by the Alliance for Progress and then the
turn to 'economic integration' through the Latin American Free Trade
Association (LAFTA/ALALC) and its Central American and Andean
regional derivatives — which were duly and dutifully rubber-stamped
by the Latin American (excepting Cuban) governments at successive
conferences at Punta del Este — the ECLA/CEPAL doctrine penetrated ever wider circles and enjoyed — or suffered — various
modifications. Whatever the subjective intentions and self-perceptions
of such prominent cepalista/desarrollistas economists/ideologues as
Raul Prebisch, Aldo Ferrer (Argentina), Celso Furtado, Antonio
Barrios de Castro, Maria Conceicão Tavares (Brasil), Jose Mayobre

(Venezuela), Horacio Flores de la Peña (Mexico), Anibal Pinto, Osvaldo Sunkel (Chile), and many others, two important developments transpired since the mid-1960s. On the one hand, quite evidently, developmentism was running into ever acuter economic and political crises in one Latin American country after another (as reflected in ECLA/CEPAL's own analysis reviewed in the author's *Lumpenburgeoisie*), while the Cuban Revolution pointed to a radically different alternative strategy (also reflected in some of the author's other writings, particularly in the essays collected in *Latin America*). On the other hand, though less perceptibly particularly to the cepalistas and their camp followers, their apparently progressive nationalism in its economic, political and ideological manifestations, had in fact been co-responsible for the development of the development(ism) crisis; a growing younger group of social scientists and an especially youthful audience in Latin America (and elsewhere) became increasingly dissatisfied with the ever more conservative appearing developmentism/dependence of ECLA/CEPAL inspiration with the result that they sought and claimed to offer a critically alternative 'dependence theory' and revolutionary strategy inspired by the Cuban revolution and the Sino–Soviet debate.

It is noteworthy that this new critical departure did not come from the old left and especially not from the communist parties, either in Latin America or in Europe. On the contrary, with the notable exception of Mariátegui in Peru, in the half century since the death of Lenin these parties have only produced the Comintern and Browderism of the Stalin era and the peaceful 'non-capitalist' existence of the Khruschev years (their relations to the later trends under examination here is discussed by Alberto Filippi in his Foreword to the Italian edition of *Lumpenburgeoisie*). In all this time up through the 1960s, the Latin American communist parties and their ideologues (always excepting the present Cuban party) have made no contribution to Marxist or any other theory that anyone has been able to discover (before or since the Organization of Latin American Solidarity — (OLAS) — in 1967 Fidel Castro ridiculed their archival models 12, 13, 14). Programmatically they have been scarcely as advanced as the bourgeois developmentists from whom they differed at most in their largely Soviet-inspired and propagandist opposition to American imperialism; politically they have been little more than a tail wagged by the national bourgeois dog who used the Communist parties — temporarily excepting in Guatemala, Venezuela and Colombia — to keep a leash on the labour movements. In the face of the challenge from the new dependence theorists, the Communist parties at home and abroad loyally joined the opposition.

The numerous publicizers, summarizers and classifiers of the dependence theory (Olmedo, Graziani, Filippi, Sechi, Martinelli,

Valenzuela, Bodenheimer, Murgo, Acevado, Guzman, etc.)* are mutual-ly in almost entire agreement in distinguishing between the 'old right' group of developmentist dependence theorists referred to above and a 'new left' group whom they predominantly name as Dos Santos, Quijano, Cardoso and Faletto, Marini and Frank among others. The latter group supposedly distinguished itself from the former by rejecting the former's 'dualism' both internationally and nationally, and replacing it by an insistent analysis of the total imperialist relations and the domestic economic/national politically active, conscious and volun-tary participation of Latin America in the neo-imperialist system under bourgeois — including progressive national — leadership as manifested in the 'new dependence' of the 1960s. *Capitalism and Underdevelop-ment in Latin America*, written by the author between 1963 and 1965, and some of the author's other early essays collected in his *Latin America: Underdevelopment or Revolution* are frequently mentioned as the opening gun in this 'new departure'. The author now regards his *Lumpenburgeoisie: Lumpendevelopment*, written in 1969, as a (though perhaps not the) swan song of this concert, although some new stars in Latin America are still singing new variations on the theme (and reflections thereof have only recently begun to be recorded or played back in other parts of the world).

Within limits, and within its own limitations, the importance of the dependence theory of underdevelopment is undeniable in terms of the criteria of Myrdal, Dowd, and Marx cited above. It certainly represen-ted an important reorientation in response to changing political conditions and opportunities and it allowed and forced friends and enemies alike to raise different questions and other other solutions. It has even been co-instrumental in changing the world, though it did not revolutionize it as some of its proponents had hoped and its opponents had feared. The same may probably be said of the new dependence theory as well, both with respect to its liberal positivist grandfather and relative to its reformist developmental father before it. But implicit in the rise of 'dependence' in response to changing political conditions (and these in relation to changing economic ones) is the possibility, or probability, nay necessity, of a renewed fall of the same to make way for new scientific explanations and ideological orientations as economic and political conditions change again. The more important a theory has been in view of its relation to concrete reality, the less it will be eternally true, which is a condition at best reserved for empty tautologies.

---

* See References at end of this chapter.

The evidence is accumulating that 'dependence' — both old and new — has ended or is completing the cycle of its natural life, at least in the Latin America that gave it birth. The reason is the newly changing world economic and political reality that in a word may be summarized as the crisis of the 1970s. Whatever its cause and its nature, as well as its outcome or resolution — questions and answers, precisely, that are to be co-determined by the necessary alternative to 'dependence' and 'Keynesianism' — the reality of the new crisis is increasingly evident in the world. Declining rates of growth and, more importantly, of profits and investment in the industrialized capitalist countries, and the intensified struggle among them for markets at home and abroad are evidence of a renewed impasse in the historical process of capitalist capital accumulation. Recent domestic and foreign policy developments in some socialist countries indicate that in them also the process of capital accumulation is changing pace or direction and that they are intent on placing their participation in the newly emerging international division of labour on a modified wider basis. The concomitant negotiations and the passage from the 'bi-polarity' of the Cold War to the re-emerging 'multi-polarity' is accompanied by a new detente and 'dialogue' (to borrow a term from the previously unthinkable relations between South Africa and increasing number of new African states), making itself heard around the world both between and within many of its regions. Neo-social democratic movements and neo-fascist threats in case they should fail (to borrow and preface terms from the last major crisis of the past until contemporary analysis affords us a more adequate or perhaps false-conscious ideological new terminology) are spreading in the industrialized capitalist countries in response to their crisis-generated mass mobilization. Then there is the development of social imperialism (to use the Chinese terminology) and its economic and diplomatic offensive in important underdeveloped regions. An important modification of the earlier division of labour also is the sub-imperialist development of Brazil, South Africa, Iran, India, and perhaps other contenders along paths both similar and different from those of Japan and Israel before them. A further new or renewed dimension is the outbreak or threat of war between or among Third World states who turn their 'nationalism' not only against the imperialist countries, but, with imperialist backing in times of crisis, against each other. And elsewhere in the underdeveloped world (again temporarily to borrow terms from the past) neo-fascist corporative trends also vie with neo-populist attempts to pave the way towards socialism from Bangladesh and Ceylon to Tanzania and Zambia to Peru and Chile.

Since writing this essay in August 1972, there have been numerous developments that are immediately relevant to — and in my opinion supportive of — the argument: among these are the deepening of the — in 1974 now universally evident — world economic and political crisis of capitalist accumulation (over which the 'Watergate scandal', 'petroleum crisis', etc. have thrown temporary smokescreens); the still extended 'dialogue' and 'detente' between East and West; the corresponding rightward shifts in the foreign policies of the socialist countries and the related tactical moves to the right of the Communist parties in the West; the military coup and emerging fascistoid regime in Chile (not unrelated to these developments), which accompany similar trends in parts of Asia (Philippines, Ceylon, Bangladesh, Indonesia) and Latin America (Uruguay, Peru, ever more threateningly in Argentina), while the Chilean events themselves reinforce the foregoing rightward tendencies (vide for instance the reaction of the reactionaries and of the Communist parties elsewhere); and — also not unrelated to these developments albeit admittedly of a different order of importance — the appearance of still more and deeper critiques of 'dependence' and also of Andre Gunder Frank.

In the face of this world crisis and the attendant critical problems in Latin America and elsewhere, the developmentist old dependence theory, and indeed ideology, appears to be entirely bankrupt. It may be hazarded that the once revolutionary new dependence theory as well, if not bankrupt, is at least short of ready cash to meet the immediate economic, political and ideological demands of revolutionaries faced with the formulation of strategy and tactics in these present circumstances. So it would seem in the varying circumstances of Brazil, Uruguay, Argentina, Chile, Peru, Venezuela and Mexico among others and perhaps of Cuba as well. (This raises some doubt about the advisability of the belated export of 'dependence' to Asia and Africa after 'third worldism' had reached the peak of its influence in the metropolitan student revolts of 1968-69.) Furthermore, the apparent simultaneity of the impasse of both the old and the new dependence theories raises the question of how radically different they really were or are. Perhaps less so than some of us would like to have had it. We may observe with a reviewer of the commemorative Nr. 150 of *Trimestre Económico* that the erstwhile radical desarrollistas, who have taken over much of the still more radical new dependence analysis, now commemorate dependence in the pages of the most established journal of the continent while many of the writers themselves occupy ministerial posts in their respective countries. So much has *part* of the new dependence analysis been accepted by the establishment, that — as quoted in *Lumpenbourgeoisie* — the assembled foreign ministers of Latin America were able to have one of them make a representation to President Nixon in the White House that foreign aid was flowing from

Latin America to the United States. Much of the critiquer of foreign investment proposed by the analysts of new dependence has found its way into the restrictions on foreign investment enshrined in the code of the Andean Pact and recommended to others by the UNCTAD Secretariat. And at UNCTAD III new dependence, the development of underdevelopment, and even subimperialism had gained currency in the official declarations of various delegates. This perhaps constitutes grounds for considerably more concern than pride for these terms' inventors. Further reflections on the relations and differences between the old and new dependence theories made by critics will be discussed below.

The new dependence theory has, of course, been the subject of various critiques. Here we may examine, classify and review — if not exhaustively answer — the principal tendencies reflected by those that have made special reference to the work or person of Andre Gunder Frank. Before proceeding, however, we may observe that though this work has been no more than the socially determined part of a wider current as reviewed above, many critics have singled out AGF or his work for special and often exclusive treatment as supposedly representative of the remainder, sometimes going so far as to claim explicitly or implicitly that a (successful) critique of this one example will do and hold for all. Perhaps this (inverse) preference may be traced to the critics' supposition that AGF offers a more vulnerable or destructible target, or a more visible one, or an earlier encountered one, or a supposedly more extreme one, or some combination of these. One thing is sure, and it has been frankly clarified by the author and universally appreciated by friend and foe alike: the work has been intentionally and consciously political and substantially inspired by the Cuban Revolution. Be all that as it may, there is evident reason for these critiques, especially of the 'frankian thesis', to be reviewed by the present author.

The critiques, and especially the critics (see list of references), seem to fall into three major tendencies: (1) the backward-looking right-wing, (2) the traditional marxist left and (3) the forward-looking new left. Each of these may be subdivided into two sub-groups (A and B). The belated (relative to its writing) publication of the complete book *Capitalism and Underdevelopment* in 1967 and 1969 in English and French and in 1970 in Spanish was at first greeted by a favourable, if uncritical, reception in various leftist circles, some of which still continues (Amin, Palloix). But the same also stimulated the critical reaction, which was not long in coming, beginning especially with (1) (A) on the reactionary and liberal right (The John Birch Society's *American opinion*, King) and then (B) the left liberals and social democrats of various stripes (Halperin, de Kadt, Sauvy, Morner, Sauvy, Dedjer,

Dalton, Alba, *Aportes*, Pinto, and in general various contributors to the *Current Anthropology* symposium on 'responsibility' and various reviewers in American academic journals).

(1) These critics from the right lack either the perspective, the competence, or the interest, or all three, to examine the argument on its own ground and still less, of course, to carry it forward onto higher ground. Their academic and political interest is to disqualify the argument — and through their reviews to forewarn the unwary against it — by recourse to the 'disqualifiers' that positivism has enshrined in the minds of its victims, empirical 'error' and lack of 'objectivity'. With few exceptions, the critics from the conservative, liberal and social democratic right limit their reviews and critiques of the argument to highlighting minor empirical disagreements that are beside the point or steering the discussion all the way off the point and invectively charging that the political commitment of AGF — but not so their own — precludes objectivity and therefore credibility or validity. According to them — and in their own terms — the work amounts to repetitive refurbishing of the imperialist thesis (which they thought dead with the dodo). It is ideological rather than empirical, prophetic in tone rather than analytic in content — indeed, a particularly rigid brand of Leninism (notwithstanding that the last cited author also claims that the work is directed against the Communists). 'As an objective indictment (whoever sought to indict?) the book is plainly inadequate, since the case for the defense (of capitalism) is not examined, let alone demolished' — writes Timothy King of Queens' College, Cambridge in his *Economic Journal* book review and continues — 'Only those who already know in their hearts that the capitalist system contains only exploiters and exploited are likely to be convinced of the truth of the general thesis of this book on the basis of the evidence put forward'. And in his 'reply' to the present author's critique of George Dalton and others' work on economic anthropology, the latter writes:

> Frank hates social science that does not serve to justify revolution
> ... His comment is not on economic anthropology. It is bombastic
> denonciation of almost everyone who does not share his revolu-
> tionary rage. There is no point in responding further to writing so full
> of anger and ideology (*Current Anthropology*, Vol. 11, No. 1, p. 70).

Amen! A reader wrote to the 'discussion and criticism' section of the journal to observe that one who needs recourse to this sort of reply only demonstrates that he lacks the means to meet the argument. So much for these critics from the right. [See Chapter 6 above.]

More recently, the latterday 'reading of AGF' by Alec Nove (sometime 'sovietologist' who claims not to criticize socialism or nationalizations) goes to far as to throw out not only the baby with the bathwater, but the very bathtub and the bathroom as well and apparently seeks to uproot the whole plumbing system! Though he only cites his reading of AGF, Nove argues that in fact the whole dependence thesis, right through CEPAL/ECLA and the early Prebisch — and apparently even back to Friedrich List in the 1840s — is patently absurd and without the slightest foundation in fact, and that foreign investment and capitalism offer the best of all worlds to everyone. With this argument Nove aggressively seeks to take us back at least several decades if not more in one giant reactionary step. He is joined by the University of Miami based *Journal of Inter-American Studies and World Affairs*, which devotes an issue especially to the anti-critique of 'foreign investment and dependence' by writers who profess disclaimers and advance arguments similar to those of Alec Nove to challenge the 'fallacies . . . that dependency is caused by the economics of capitalism . . . that private foreign investment is invariably exploitative and invariably detrimental . . . that dependency/non-dependency is a dichotomous variable' (p.7). Then — writing in *New Left* (sic!) *Review* — Bill Warren builds on these same writers to contruct a more documented version of the Nove thesis that dependence is absurd and that under the aegis of imperialism the industrialization and development of the so-called Third World is in full swing. *NLR* editorializes: 'however controversial its explanatory theses, Warren's pioneering study provides a fresh starting-point for discussion of socialist strategy in the ex-colonial periphery of the capitalist world'. It is difficult to see how. Though these critiques — probably written, as Houtienne suggests, under the influence of the 'Brazilian miracle' — correctly recognize and underline that much of the 'dependent underdevelopment' thesis was accompanied by the corollary of a mythical opposite 'independent development' possibility, these critiques limit their and our purview to the application of orthodox or self-invented, more or less reactionary criteria or indices of dependence and development, which far from contributing to, intentionally or unintentionally detract from the advance of historical materialist analysis of the process of world and local capital accumulation and class formation. Even the latest auto-critical reflections on dependence of Fernando Henrique Cardoso (who himself contributed much to dependence theory and who does not belong in this first and reactionary category) whatever the merits of his critique of the 'development of underdevelopment' in Brazil today, are partial, unwarrantedly extending his conclusions to Latin America from his analysis of Brazil; and his analysis is inconsistent, taking account of the cycle of capital when it suits his conclusions and not when it does not. The political conclusions he would have us derive seem to be a step to the right in the direction of those of the Communist Party second tendency.

(2) A second major tendency of critics and critiques stems from the major Marxist parties and their official or unofficial spokesmen. Among these, we may distinguish particularly the (A) Soviet and Moscow or aligned Communists and (B) the Maoists and Trotskyists.

(A) Among the former, the work and thesis — or often rather the person — of AGF has come under the criticism of, for example, Victor Volski, Director of the Latin American Institute at the Academy of Sciences of the USSR; B.N. Brodovich, writing in *Latinskaya America* (Moscow); L. Becerra in *Problems of Peace and Socialism* (Prague); N. Ram in India; Renato Sandri, Latin American specialist of the Central Committee of the Communist Party of Italy; Ruggiero Romano in half a dozen places in Europe and Latin America; the supposedly major Marxist historian, Eugene Genovese, in the United States; and in Latin America, Mauricio Lebedinsky of Argentina, Jose Rodriquez Elizondo in Chile, and conceptually though not politically allied, Armando Cordova of Venezuela. Speaking at two scholarly congresses in Latin America in 1974, Augustin Cueva of Ecuador has further aggravated the conceptual and political charges against the new dependence theory in general and against AGF in particular; and at the second of these congresses, he was in part joined conceptually by Enrique Semo, Roger Bartra and Sergio de la Peña from Mexico, Cirio Cardoso of Brazil, as well as Manfred Kossok from the DDR, and others.

These Communist Party and related criticisms in a way fall between the right-wing ones of the first tendency and the third tendency new left critiques, sharing some characteristics of one and some of the other. With the third tendency, the communist criticisms share the recurrent critique that AGF is not Marxist because he emphasizes circulation to the total or virtual exclusion of production or that he confuses the two in constructing the argument about the development of capitalism. The merits of this critique, which is much more seriously constructed by the new left, may more suitably be reserved for comment in the review of the third tendency below, leaving for inquiry here the communist *reasons* for this line of attack. These, in turn, would seem to be related to a second characteristic that the communist critics share with the new left: the timing of their counter-offensive. It is noteworthy that although these AGF articles have circulated and have been the object of some isolated communist sniper fire since 1963, they did not begin to turn their big guns on it until 1969 and especially since 1970.

Far from being a coincidence or even the 'natural' time lag between publication and review, it may be suggested that this timing of the criticism is a consequence and reflection of the crisis referred to above and that it is designed, in its small way, to help affect its resolution one way or another. Why and how the new left responds to the crisis through its constructive critique may be examined below. Here we may inquire in what way or which direction the communist parties wish to lead us. During much of the 1960s, the advance of the Cuban Revolution and its increasing attraction and prestige in Latin America and elsewhere, obliged the traditional communist parties — who were simultaneously battling on another ideological front with the Chinese — to adopt a relatively conciliatory attitude toward the Cuban policy and related positions in Latin America. In some cases they temporarily accepted armed struggle and in many they changed their tactical line or at least language. The by then classical formula of the 'democratic' struggle against 'external' imperialism and internal 'feudalism' began to disappear from the communist party programmes — witness, for instance, the change as well in the electoral programme in Chile from that of the Frente de Accion Popular (FRAP) in 1964 and that of the Unidad Popular in 1970. Some Latin American communist parties sent representatives to OLAS in 1967, and others — including those of Brazil, Argentina and Chile — sent their General Secretaries to Moscow to make oblique but sufficiently transparent references to it to the effect that:

> Petit bourgeois nationalists who deny the significance of international Marxism–Leninism have created a conception of local or continental exceptionalism . . . while accusing those parties that have remained loyal to the principles of Marxism–Leninism of being traditionalist, orthodox and moderate (Ghioldi).

It was not until the end of the decade, and perhaps not accidentally until some time after the death of Ché Guevara, that the Latin American communist parties were again able to achieve substantial unity in 'international Marxism–Leninism' and to launch a general counter-offensive on a broad front, including targets as diminutive as AGF.

In what direction, we may ask, is this communist counter-offensive pointed? Politically, it is marked by the increasing economic and political rapprochement between the USSR and imperialism, marred only by the obstacle of the nasty war in Vietnam and the stand-off in the Middle East. The French Communist Party — the Secretary General of the Chilean CP once said that it was the one that most resembles his own — declared, and what is more demonstrated, itself to be 'the party of order' during the 1968 revolt that, beyond students, mobilized 10 million workers in France. In Italy, the year-long 'May' of 1969–70 in

Torino, Milano and elsewhere obliged the Communist Party to follow, rather than to lead, the massive worker mobilization. Between 1970 and 1973, as observed above, both parties became admirers — and for their own purposes major propagandists — of 'the Chilean Way'. In Latin America, the Venezuelan Communist Party returned to 'Democratic Peace' before splitting in two. Elsewhere, in the face of the crisis-generated increase in mass mobilization, the communist parties have increasingly joined, promoted, and where possible led old or new, popular, united, broad fronts. Are these communist initiatives, or more accurately responses, to mobilize workers and peasants onto the road of socialist revolution; or are they attempts to steer this objectively generated mobilization into reformism? The evidence of Communist Party policy and practice in Chile and elsewhere (cited in the 1972 version but now omitted) confirms the second hypothesis.

These political circumstances and policies also underly and determine the Communist Party counter-offensive on the ideological front, including that against AGF and neo-dependence. Vitally important enough in its own right, the course of the 'Chilean Way' has assumed far-reaching implications for the fate of the united front movements in several other countries of Latin America — however different they may be from the Chilean one. At a historical juncture when 'third-worldism' is widely regarded to have receded to a backseat of the centre of world political gravity, Chile is evidently still regarded as a vital piece for the communist parties who are engaged in an earnest contest in which king and queen, or at least rook and bishop, are in France and Italy. The comradely interest in Chile and even in otherwise insignificant ideological 'aberrations' centred in Chile is no accident.

These circumstances perhaps explain, more than they justify, the principal tactic that some of these 'comrades' — one of them has written that he is no comrade of AGF — employ to combat the 'contentions' — another suggests that they are not truly theses — of AGF who is an

> eminent paper-wise man [all in quotation marks] with a talent and passion worthy of a better cause; conspicuous theorist of an anarchic left, provocateur, diversionist, confusionist, divisionist; this marxist [sic] researcher [sic, again], under pseudo-marxist pretext carries his agility to extremes: in the deliberate attempt to create confusion his intellectual lightness, triviality and superficiality and his scientific superficiality and triviality end up in political inconsistency (or would it be better to say dishonesty?) which is their natural product of the work of a petit bourgeois with revolutionary marxist pretensions (Romano).

> No, there is no possible illusion. Gunder Frank concludes his work proposing as the only and correct strategy of development, armed

revolution and the construction of socialism. The truth is that in Chile, Peru and Bolivia liberation can only be the result of an articulated, worked out anti-oligarchic and anti-imperialist battle. ... Marxism–Leninism emphasizes, given the structure, the key alliance of the proletariat and the peasantry in a front with the petite bourgeoisie, the middle classes and the progressive sectors of the national bourgeoisie to resolve the agrarian problem as the axis of the necessary revolution. In the socialist revolution proclaimed by Frank and those that accept this point of view, the working class would march alone. Therefore, it would be unnecessary to work in the heart of the peasantry. Neither would it be necessary to try to have the participation in the struggle of the petite and middle bourgeoisie, of the more advanced sectors of the national bourgeoisie, there would be no immediate tasks to be completed before proposing oneself the socialist revolution. It is not a matter, therefore, of a little 'detail', it is a matter of no less than the kind of revolution, the problem of alliances (Lebedinsky, p. 79).

The CIA and the cat's paw. Naturally, it is not Gunder Frank, but what he represents that is at the centre of the debate. He represents, basically, the existence of a widely promoted ultra-left thinking in international politics. A thinking that, the more diffusion it has, the more it facilitates the work of imperialism with respect to the revolutionary processes ... the very presence of this kind of theorist signifies . . . the tendency to divide anti-imperialists in two blocs, that of the Marxists and revolutionary intellectuals on the one side and that of the Communists on the other . . . the handful of amorphous, anarchic and hypercritical intellectuals ... defend the positions of imperialism by joining the trenches of anti-imperialism (Rodriguez Elizondo, pp. 79-81).

It is not a matter of agreeing or disagreeing; that even reduces the possibility of discussion. Because, let us say it to conclude, discussing would make one into an accomplice of Andre Gunder Frank who, objectively — and on a political level — is no more than a veritable provocateur. One might ask, if all these writings are so useless, why speak of them? Because to unmask his aspect of provocateur strikes me as an obligation, an obligation of scientific morality, of intellectual hygiene, of political prophilaxis. . . . Faced with an excess of incapacity-in-the-presumption of capacity, one is obliged to react and indicate that, behind all this cheap conceptual glitter there exists nothing other than the most total emptyness (Romano).

Under these circumstances, we may ask, what indeed remains to be discussed with or in relation to these comrades? The reader will have observed for himself one of the critical features that this second tendency of critics has in common with the first one reviewed earlier.

The other similarity with them refers to the direction of their argument, to the limited degree (though perhaps not extent) to which they offer one: backward-looking. The contemporary Communist Party resurrection of the ghost of their 'anti-imperialist', 'anti-oligarchical' political programme, which some had thought dead and buried with the Comintern, is matched — and, as they would have it, supported — by no more than the refurbishing of the self-same scientific and ideological arguments of old. However well taken their charge of scientific inadequacy of AGF may be for his failure to adequately analyze the productive relations or mode of production (of which more below), it must be observed that these Communist Party comrades do no better. They do not try, let alone succeed, to carry the analysis beyond that achieved during the 1960s, profiting by the — even if limited — Latin American and world renaissance in Marxist studies of the past decade, to reorient their work raising new questions and offering new answers that are appropriate to the changing political conditions and opportunities (as do some of the new left critics reviewed below). No, instead our Communist Party spokesmen simply call for a retreat to the same old schematic substitutes for the real analysis of the transformation of the mode of production in the process of capital accumulation that they already offered us a generation ago. But these were to all intents and purposes (except perhaps some of their own) inadequate then, and are all the more so now. Evidence can be found in the very fact that the renaissance of Marxist studies was necessary and that it occurred with no recent contribution from any such Marxist intellectual who remained loyal to the Moscow line of his Communist Party that anyone, anywhere has been able to discover. Comrade Lebedinsky (pp. 82–93) complains that the 'apologists of the new dependence theory nearly arrive at a Marxist thesis, but the first effort is to differentiate themselves from the Communists'. But who, today, is prepared to follow or able to join the comrade in his implication that these 'apologists' differentiate themselves in that they stop short of the Communist Party theory and praxis, rather than advance beyond it? Whatever the objective answer, one personal note may be in order. I have *never* had the temerity myself to *claim to be* a Marxist nor the desire to deny it; and nowhere in my published — or unpublished — writings can or will anyone find such a personal claim. Who then makes false or pseudo claims?

(B) Some, but much less, criticism has also emanated from other Marxist parties and writers: Trotskyist (Novack, Becard and Bailly, Alberti and Horowicz) and Maoist (Arrighi, Circolo Lenin, Fernandez and O'Campo).

Among Trotskyists, Ernest Mandel, in the Postscript to the Spanish language edition of his *Marxist Economic Theory*, expressed a certain affinity with our arguments. But then his fellow leader of the IV International, George Novack, repeated the same critiques about the relations of production, etc. and summarized as follows:

> Frank's approach to the socio-economic development of Latin America is highly over-simplified. It leaves no room for complex historical situations, class relations, and contradictory socio-economic formations . . . That is also why Frank's attempt to divide Marxism from Trotskyism and contrapose one to the other does not hold water (pp. 981, 983).

Over-simple, yes; no room . . . no. As for Marxism and Trotskyism, I have never claimed to be or to represent one or the other nor to divide them, counterpose them or otherwise.

Among other Trotskyists, Becard and Bailly, who formulate their critique within a broader re-examination of dependence theory undertaken in *Critiques de l'Economie politique* should perhaps be classified with the new left critics. More difficult to classify anywhere or to respond to are the self-proclaimed Trotskyists of Jorge Aberlardo Ramos' inspiration, Alberti and Horowicz, who claim to 'demonstrate' that AGF and Theotonio dos Santos are 'bourgeois stalinists'.

Arrighi identified with the argument of AGF in the Preface to his own quite independently written book on Africa. Upon returning to Italy to become a Maoist militant, he published a self-criticism of this earlier acceptance. Reiterating and reinforcing his earlier reservation about the insufficient analysis of the relations of production, he now added the charge that the analysis is not Marxist and still less Maoist insofar as it erroneously supposes that 'external' rather than truly 'internal' contradictions determine the historical course of events in Latin America and elsewhere. In his famous example, Mao observed that with the same 'external' temperature applied to an egg and a stone, 'internal' conditions determine the birth of a chicken from one and not the other. Despite his reliance on this Marxist authority, Arrighi has not succeeded — even with the additional kind recourse to personal correspondence and conversation — in sufficiently clarifying to the present author just how one is to distinguish between the 'external' and the 'internal' contradictions in the process as it unfolds in any particular part of the imperialist system. No doubt, the limitation to this success resides in the 'internal' limitation of AGF. But along with the efforts of others, he is trying to overcome it in future work. The political conclusions to be derived from the critique in Italy are not so immediately clear. In Latin America, however, some Maoists have taken partial exception to the argument insofar as it does not support the applicability at all times and places of the Maoist strategy with respect to the 'four groups'.

Special attention is perhaps merited — albeit not for the substance or construction of their argument — by a self-styled 'Maoist' attack dated the 1st of May 1973 at the Center for Democratic Institutions in Santa Barbara, California by Fernandez and Ocampo: 'The ideas of AGF will be our favorite target' to bombard with 'sophistry', 'utterly absurd', 'truly preposterous', 'nonsense', 'a period abstraction', etc. Apart from recourse to this style, they attribute to 'dependentistas' in general, and to AGF in particular, straw-man intentions, positions and arguments — eg. focus against the Marxist conception of historical materialism, artificial separation between capitalism and imperialism, negation of classes, ignoring the role of the bourgeoisie in history, arbitrary attribution of backwardness to external causes, saying next to nothing about the contemporary nature of imperialism, etc. — which we have never sustained and have in fact, as the written record shows, been intent to rebut and combat. And along the way they rely on long references to and citations of Marx on ground rent, Lenin on imperialism and Mao on New Democracy, and quite untenably purport to derive the following 'scientific' conclusions: 'Latin American backwardness cannot be attributed to the capitalist character of their economies and their integration within the world capitalist system, but rather the opposite' (p. 13) (a thesis identical to that of Nove and all imperialist diffusionists); and 'we can easily conclude that in Latin America not only is the agricultural sector characteristically semi-feudal, but that this may also be true of the total economy in some instances'; 'surplus value in . . . industrial profit . . . may be true in very *few* countries, if any, and that in the vast majority we are dealing with strongly feudal or semi-feudal countries' (pp. 36–37); 'for all these reasons, the adequate marxist category used to describe the backwardness of Latin America is not underdevelopment, but feudalism, semi-feudalism, or strong remnants of feudalism depending on the individual case. To generalize further: *Latin American backwardness has a pre-capitalist nature*' (p. 46, all emphasis in the original).

If, after the development of the whole discussion in and about Latin America during the 1960s, we were to regard these arguments on their own merit, they would merit no regard at all. But our purpose is and must be to go beyond the merits and demerits of all these arguments and inquire into their *raison d'être*. Fernandez and Ocampo write: 'The belief in the predominance of industrial capital permits the 'dependentistas' to regard the struggle against imperialism as secondary to the class struggle and the battle against capitalism' (p. 45).

(More correctly, 'dependent on' rather than 'secondary to'.) Their belief in (or reinvention of) the predominance of feudalism permits Fernandez and Ocampo to comment that 'the Latin American revolution has as its object not the dictatorship of the proletariat but liberation from imperialist domination' (p. 60), which history in Latin America and the AGF 'dependentistas' have so far shown to be inseparable; and that 'the other fundamental aspect of the revolution in Latin America . . . means generating a *limited* capitalist development . . . [which] has a democratic character since it protects private property in the land and the development of a *new capitalism* . . . a new democracy' (pp. 60–61). This quaint agrarianism — it would not be correct to dignify it with 'Maoism' — hardly even merits confrontation with the sub-imperialist development of Brazil, the industrial proletarian class struggle in Argentina, the imperialist-bourgeois-petit bourgeois military reaction in Chile, in the absence even of traces of the Fernandez–Ocampo 'mode of production', or other Latin American industrial capitalist reality in the imperialist world. What Fernandez and Ocampo merit is the question why, cloaking themselves in the mantle of Maoism (and specifically of the 'New Democracy' which was launched after 1937 and particularly 1940 under conditions of Japanese imperialist occupation of China), they seek to set us at least a decade back precisely at this time while imperialism is on a counter-offensive and not incidentally, while Chinese internal politics and foreign policy is undergoing a delayed reaction to the Cultural Revolution.

Indeed, all these backward-looking, downright retrograde and reactionary critiques — and they have become even more so since the first draft of this review was written in 1972 as critics in each group seem to have taken a further step towards those on their right — more than inviting an 'answer', pose the question of why this counter-offensive is in swing at all, why it is growing so fast, and why its self-(and sometimes other-) appointed mouthpieces dare to go so far backwards. It would be a mistake — and un-Marxist to boot — to suppose, as some of these protagonists suggest, that their latter-day reversion to the conventional wisdom of decades past is the product of divine inspiration or superior intelligence or even of plain down-to-earth realism, lacking among ordinary mortal students of 'dependence.' No, it is part and parcel of a reactionary political counter-offensive, not only from the right but unfortunately — albeit understandably — also on the part of much of the left, which is itself the reflection of the political–economic developments already alluded to, and which now permits these ideological apprentices their daring in trying to turn the social scientific clock from one to several decades backward.

Of course, the same political–economic crisis and this same reactionary counter-offensive themselves also sharpen the class struggle and generate political and ideological manifestations — including new left critiques and forward-looking reformulations, analyses and resolutions of the processes once discussed under the title of 'dependence' — which offer positive contributions to man's knowledge and liberation. The X Latin American Congress of Sociology celebrated in August 1972 (after the main body of this essay was written), witnessed a flowering of several such critical contributions (eg. Olmedo), many of which are now no longer available at least in an organized collection.

(3) Therefore, it is possible to distinguish a third major tendency among critics and critiques, which may unsatisfactorily be labelled the independent new left, although many of its authors also related their intellectual work to militant, and party, political praxis. What distinguishes them in the present context is that their critiques are not backward but forward-looking. These critics and critiques may, perhaps still less satisfactorily to them and the present author, in turn be sub-divided into two groups: (A) mostly relatively early ones who, albeit forward-looking, do not yet advance their critical work very far into different areas; and (B) the more recent — and surely future — ones whose important contribution is — in the words of our epigraphs from Dowd and Mills — that 'existing knowledge and analysis are put together with new ways, raising questions and offering conclusions which allow and force friends and enemies alike to push their own research and analysis into different areas 'resulting in' major recastings of economic thought . . . that are responses to changing political conditions and opportunities'. The more successful they are in so doing, the more welcome are such critics and critiques.

(A) The early critiques of Cabral *et al* and Dos Santos were already cited and commented on in the 'Mea Culpa' that prefaces *Lumpenburgeoisie*; and, insofar as was then possible, their forward-looking critiques were incorporated into the extension and reorientation of the earlier argument in the text of that book, which emphasized the active 'internal' class participation in the determination of the historical process — and some of its variations as between countries — through the various stages. On the other hand, it did not and does not seem necessary to face the (I believe) false charges of 'geographical schematicism' and 'structure-functionalism' or the internal contradictions in their own arguments. In any case, Dos Santos has drawn on his own critique to advance still more in his and his co-workers' analysis of the new dependence. Both this progress and its limitations — confined as it has been to substantially the same political moments and theoretical conceptions — has been noted by other critics, friendly and not.

The critique of Weffort, directed simultaneously at Cardoso & Faletto and AGF, that our argument supposes an unfounded existence of a *national* basis of class power and policy, is itself unfounded and has already been disposed of by Cardoso in an answer that itself suggests questions and conclusions that are more interesting and far-reaching than those of Weffort. Rodriguez and Sechi limit themselves to charges of over-simplified schematicism, which though they may be accurate, are not very helpful as long as they do not interpret and evaluate the schema in the economic, political, ideological and scientific context in response to which they were originally proposed and unless they contribute to recasting our questions and answers in response to the context that is newly emerging. Sempat divides his critiques into essentially two parts. As historian he claims that the historical record is not that which appears in the AGF essay based on Chile. But, as Torres (see below) has observed, such an empirical critique *per se* necessarily remains within the theoretical confines of what it criticizes and does not suffice to recast the theoretical problem. This is all the less so insofar as in the original essay AGF had explicitly denied any attempt to write a *history* of Chile while expressing only the hope to reformulate theory. In that part of Sempat's essay which *is* devoted to a theoretical critique, on the other hand, he attributes to AGF relations between metropolis/satellite and development/underdevelopment, which are the precise *inverse* of those sustained by AGF in the essay based on Chile as well as others. These critiques, although — as any reader may see — they are forward-looking in intent, 'tone' and some non-central suggestions, do not yet succeed in carrying the critique forward to any substantial theoretical recasting of questions and answers.

(B) We finally arrive at a new critical departure. The last year (since 1971) has not only witnessed the extension and deepening of the economic, political and ideological crisis as reviewed above; it has also brought forth new work by politically committed scholars who, on the one hand, were schooled in the advances of the previous decade but, increasingly aware also of the limitations of the same, on the other hand are now able to help meet this crisis by offering critical departures that promise to recast economic thinking — and political praxis — on newer and higher ground. Particularly important and meritorious of our consideration in these critiques is not so much the old ground that they cover, however *very* critical they may be of those that have trodden on it before them, but rather the new ground onto which these critiques take us, employing the old essentially to construct the new. Such is the case, for instance, of the spate of recent fundamental critiques of the theses of A. Emmanuel — as it is also for those of AGF and others associated with the new dependence. Outstanding among the recent critiques of the latter are those of Laclau; Hinkelammert and Glauser (then both at CEREN of the Universidad Católica de Chile); and Marini and Torres (then both at CESO of the Universidad de Chile, where the present author was as well). But it is not so much these writers' critiques of AGF's arguments on the questions of colonial and capitalist under-development that need detain us, as it is their progressive reformula-tion of the questions — and *thereby* the answers — themselves.

The importance of Laclau's effort, therefore, resides less in his critique of any insufficiencies in Frank's analysis of feudalism and capitalism in Latin America (as his title reads) and not at all (in my opinion) of his proof that AGF cannot rightly claim to be a Marxist (which AGF never claimed), but in the possible substantiation of his belief that 'it is possible within this theoretical framework to situate the problem of dependence at the level of relations of production' (p. 34) — which the Communist Party theoreticians, for instance, have never even sought to do. Laclau, for his part, himself only begins to do so through an incipient analysis of the changing rates of organic composition of capital and surplus-value in the process of capital accumulation.

Glauser passes over the inadequate earlier efforts to analyze the colonial regimes of production in Chile and other parts of Latin America, only to design an elaborate analytical breakdown of the relations of production at successive times and various places, and to conclude that his analysis suggests that

> the necessity of differences in the degree of development of the productive forces between one zone called center and another called periphery seems to be an indispensable condition to the existence of capitalist production. . . . Structurally the center is in the interior of each region of the periphery and, at the same time, all of the periphery is immanent to the center (pp. 142, 149),

implicitly rising therein to the problem posed by Arrighi above. Hinkelammert, for his part, also finds the AGF analysis of the transition to industrial capitalism unsatisfactory; but he does so only to carry his own analysis of the dialectics of unequal development through from capitalist to socialist accumulation.

Finally, Marini expresses similar well-taken reservations about the theoretical foundation of AGF and other analyses of the 19th century transformations and 20th century dependence, old and new, only to proceed to analyze the entire historical experience of Latin America from the conquest to today (and tomorrow) in terms of the world and local process of capital accumulation. In the meantime, Torres embarked on a thorough meta-theoretical critique of the entire dependence theory, also old and new, to clear the way for his own (and hopefully others!) reconstruction of the entire process of capital accumulation in the world as it has been visited on Latin America. For all these critical and original efforts we can all only be thankful. And AGF, for his part, is seeking to express his thanks through his own attempt to rewrite if not to reanalyze the process of capital accumulation in the world — with special reference to the participation of Asia, the Middle East, Africa, and Latin America — from 1500 to the present, and hoping thereby to make whatever small contribution he may to the ideological renovation, and political revolution, and socialist accumulation of the future.*

Finally, perhaps it should not be surprising that social scientific attention is (re)turning to the problems of capital accumulation — launching another new departure in its analysis — precisely now that the process of the accumulation of capital again appears problematical. Like the study of one of its principal aspects or manifestations, the business cycle (which is popularly identified rather only with the crisis and downswing phase of the cycle), the cyclical process of capital accumulation tends to be analyzed as such only during times of crisis and their aftermath eg. Boehm-Bawerk and Robinson, for instance, during each of the preceding 'great' depressions. In times of long cyclical upswing, the capitalist process of capital accumulation tends to appear rather more as a long-term naturally autonomous trend, as viewed from the accumulating metropolis, and as a 'dependent' one perhaps, as viewed from the underdeveloped countries. But having come full circle, in our argument as well as in the cycle, the *problem* of cyclical capital accumulation again appears as the order of the day, be it to respond to its changing political conditions or to its political opportunities. These conditions and opportunities also manifest themselves through the renewed intensification of the class struggle and the concomitant renewal of efforts to analyze, and — in one direction or another — to co-determine the contemporary transformation of the underlying class structure and the mode of production.

---

*In the books *World Accumulation 1492–1789* and *Accumulation, Dependence, and Underdevelopment* and in the book in preparation on *The Contemporary World Crisis*.

REFERENCES

[Available up to the mid-1970s. Selected later critiques are added at the end.]

I. *Books on A.G. Frank's writings*

Cordova, Armando, *El 'Capitalismo Subdesarrollado' de Andre Gunder Frank* (Caracas: Editorial Nueva Izquierda, 1972), 72 pp.

Ingrosso, Marco, *Modelos Socioeconómicos de la Interpretación de la Realidad Latinoamericana: de Mariátegui a Gunder Frank* (Barcelona: Anagrama, 1973), 88 pp.

Oxall, Ivar, Tony Barnett and David Booth (eds.), *Beyond the Sociology of Development: Economy and Society in Latin America and Africa* (London and Boston: Routledge & Kegan Paul, 1975), 295 pp.

Sempat Assadourian, Carlos, C.F.S. Cardoso, H. Ciafardini, J.C. Garavaglia, E. Laclau, *Modos de Producción en América Latina* (Cuadernos de Pasado y Presente 40; Buenos Aires: Siglo XXI Argentina Editores, 1973), 242 pp.

II. *Essays devoted entirely or substantially to A.G. Frank*

Ago, Kenji, 'Underdevelopment and capitalism: Frank theorems revised by Laclau and Muto', *Seinan Economic Review* (Japan), Vol. 9, Nos. 2-3 (January 1975), pp. 179-198 (in Japanese).

Alberti, Blas M. and Alejandro J. Horowicz, 'La penetración imperialista en las ciencias sociales en América Latina: A propósito de Andre Gunder Frank y Theotonio dos Santos', presented at X Latin American Congress of Sociology (Santiago, Chile: September 1972).

Arrighi, Giovanni, 'The relationship between the colonial and the class structures: A critique of A.G. Frank's theory of the development of underdevelopment', UN African Institute for Economic Development and Planning, Dakar (October 1971), mimeo. Italian translation in *Problemi del Socialismo* (Rome), No. 10 (December 1972).

Arrighi, Giovanni 'Struttura di classe e struttura coloniale nell'analisi del sottosviluppo', *Giovane Critica* (Milan), No. 22-23 (1970).

Bartet, Leyla, 'Sobre el origén histórico del subdesarrollo', *Economia y Desarrollo* (Havana), No. 17 (May–June 1973).

Booth, David 'Andre Gunder Frank: An introduction and appreciation', in I. Oxaal, T. Barnet and D. Booth (eds.), *Beyond the Sociology of Development* (London: Routledge & Kegan Paul, 1974), Chapter 4.

Brodovich, B.N. 'Capitalism and under-development', *Latinskaja Amerika* (Moscow), No. 6 (1970), pp. 181-189 (in Russian).

Cabral, B., Roberto *et al.*, 'Importancia y evaluación del trabajo de A.G. Frank sobre el subdesarrollo latinoamericano', México, Escuela Nacional de Economia, Universidad Nacional Autónoma de México (1969), mimeo, 40 pp.

Cardoso, Fernando Henrique, 'As contradicoes do desenvolvimento associado', presented at Seminar of the German Foundation for International Development (Berlin: November 1973).

Cueva, Augustin, 'El uso del concepto de modo de producción en América Latina: algunos problemas teóricos', Centro de Estudios Latinoamericanos, Facultad de Ciencias Politicas y Sociales, Universidad Nacional Autónoma de México (1974), mimeo. Presented at XI Latin American Congress of Sociology (San Jose, Costa Rica: June 1974).

Cueva, Augustin, 'Problemas y perspectivas de la teoria de la dependencia', Centro de Estudios Latinoamericanos, Facultad de Ciencias Politicas y Sociales, Universidad Nacional Autónoma de México (1974), mimeo. Presented in the Symposium on Modes of Production at the 42nd International Congress of Americanists (Mexico: September 1974).

Dos Santos, Theotonio, 'El capitalismo colonial según A.G. Frank', *Monthly Review, Selecciones en Castellano,* Vol. 5, No. 52, (November 1968). Reprinted in T. Dos Santos, *Dependencia y Cambio Social* (Santiago, Chile: CESO, 1971), pp. 139-50.

Fernandez, Raul A. and José F. Ocampo, 'The Latin American revolution: a theory of imperialism, not a theory of dependence', Program in Comparative Culture, University of California — Irvine (1 August 1973), mimeo. Subsequently published in revised form as 'The Latin American revolution: a theory of imperialism, not dependence', *Latin American Perspectives* (Riverside), Vol. 1, No. 1 (1974).

Filippi, Alberto, 'Un modello storico-strutturale del sottosviluppo', *Problemi del Socialismo* (Rome), No. 42, (September–October), pp. 945-959.

Foster-Carter, Aidan, 'From Rostow to Gunder Frank: conflicting paradigms in the analysis of underdevelopment', *World Development,* Vol. 4, No. 3 (March 1976).

Hopkins, A.G., 'On importing Andre Gunder Frank into Africa', *African Economic History Review* (Wisconsin), Vol. 2, No. 1 (Spring 1975).

Ingrosso, Marco, 'Modelli socio-economici di interpretazione della realtà latinoamerica: de Mariátegui ad Andre Gunder Frank', *Terzo Mondo* (Milan), No. 19-20 (March–June 1973), pp. 38-76.

'Introduzione' a A.G. Frank, *Sociologia dello Sviluppo e Sottosviluppo della Sociologia* (Milan: Lampugnani Nigri Ed., 1970), pp. vi-xxvi.

Kula, Marcin, 'Capitalismo y atraso de América Latina según A.G. Frank', *Estudios Latinoamericanos* (Ossalineum, Poland), (1972).

Laclau, H., Ernesto, 'Feudalism and capitalism in Latin America', *New Left Review* (London), No. 67 (May–June 1971), pp. 19-38; and *Problemas del Socialismo* (Rome), Nos. 5/6 (September–December 1971). *Sociedad y Desarrollo* (Santiago), No. 1 (January–March 1972), pp. 178-192.

Levero, Renato, 'L'ineguale sviluppo del capitalismo', followed by 'Lacuni interrogativi sul modelo e la concezione di A.G. Frank su raporto sviluppo–sottosviluppo', *Vita Sociale* (Milan), No. 147 (July–October 1971).

Muto, Ichiyo, 'Gunder Frank: capitalism and underdevelopment in Latin America', in *Solidarity, New Debate on Imperialism* (Tokyo: Aki Shobo, 1973), pp. 79-123 (in Japanese).

Novack, George, 'Permanent revolution in Latin America', *Intercontintal Press* (New York), Vol. 8, No. 38 (1 November 1970), pp. 978-983. Reprinted in George Novack, *Understanding History: Marxist Essays* (New York: Pathfinder Press, 1972).

Nove, Alec, 'Capitalismo y subdesarrollo. Leyendo a Andre Gunder Frank', *Panorama Económico* (Santiago, Chile), No. 276 (March–April 1973).

Nove, Alec, 'On reading Andre Gunder Frank', *The Journal of Development Studies*, Vol. 10, Nos. 3 & 4 (April–July 1974).

Ocampo, José, 'What's new and old in the theory of imperialism', *Latin American Perspectives, No. 4 (Spring 1975)*.

Paso, Leonardo, 'Feudalismo o capitalismo en América Latina?', *Desarrollo Indoamericano* (Baranquilla), No. 23 (1973).

Pinto, Anibal (Lautaro, pseodónim), 'Diagnóstico y catastrofismo en el continente', *Panorama Económico* (Santiago), No. 252 (February–March 1970), pp. 15-19; reprinted in A. Pinto, *Tres Ensayos sobre Chile y América Latina* (Buenos Aires: Ed. Solar, 1971), pp. 19-20.

Rodriguez Elizondo, José, 'El cerco contra Chile', *Principios* (Santiago, Chile), No. 145 (May–June 1972), pp. 68-76.

Romano, Ruggiero, 'Sobre las "tesis" de A.G. Frank', *Marcha* (Montevideo), (12 and 19 March 1971); *Migajas* (Lima: Fed. Universal de Mov. Estudiantiles Cristianos (FEMUC), 1971), 16 pp.; *Desarrollo Económico* (Buenos Aires), No. 37; *Cahiers Wilfredo Pareto* (Geneva), No. 24 (April 1971), pp. 271-297.

Sandri, Renato, 'Capitalismo e sottosviluppo nell' America Latina. A proposito dell'opera di Andre Gunder Frank', *Politica ed Economia* (Rome), No. 2 (September 1970), pp. 150-157.

Sandri, Renato 'Stravaganze e aberrazioni di A. Gunder Frank', *Politica ed Economia* (Rome), Vol. 3, No. 5 (October 1972).

Sau, Ranjit K., 'The dialectics of underdevelopment', *Economic and Political Weekly* (Bombay), (5 July 1975).

Sempat Assadourian, Carlos, 'Modes de producción capitalismo y subdesarrollo en América Latina', *Cuadernos de la Realidad Nacional* (Santiago), No. 7 (March 1971), pp. 116-142.

Silva Michelena, Hector, 'Liminar' in A.G. Frank, *Lumpenburguesia: Lumpendesarrollo* (Caracas: Editorial Nueva Izquierda, 1970), pp. 7-10.

Sternberg, Marvin, 'Dependency, imperialism, and the relations of production', *Latin American Perspectives* (Riverside, Calif.), Vol. 1, No. 1 (Spring 1974).

Taylor, John, 'Neo-Marxism and underdevelopment — a sociological fantasy', *Journal of Contemporary Asia* (Stockholm & London), Vol. 4, No. 1 (1974).

Tenenbaum, Barbara H., 'Straightening out some of the lumpen in development. An examination of Andre Gunder Frank's explanation of Latin American history in terms of Mexico, 1821-1856', *Latin American Perspectives*, Issue 5 (Summer 1975).

Valenzuela Feijoo, José, 'Andre Gunder Frank: una teoria del subdesarrollo', *Pensamiento Crítico* (Havana), No. 28 (May 1969), pp. 101-120.

Vascos, Fidel, 'Gunder Frank: teoria del subdesarrollo', *Verde Olivo* (Havana), Vol. 9, No. 48 (29 November 1970), pp. 26-28.

Weffort, Francisco, 'Notos sobre la teoria de la dependencia: teoria de clase e ideologia?', *Revista Latinoamericana de Ciencia Politica* (Santiago, Chile), Vol. 1, No. 3 (December 1970), pp. 389-401. *Comercio Exterior México*, Vol. 22, No. 4 (April 1972), pp. 355-365.

Yoshida, Hideho, 'A.G. Frank's Latin American studies and their theoretical formation', *Ajia Keizai* (Tokyo), Vol. 12, No. 11 (November 1971), pp. 90-103 (in Japanese).

III. *Works devoted to dependence theory and partially to A.G. Frank*
(References to A.G.F. in parentheses.)

Aguirre Beltran, Gonzalo, 'El indigenismo y la antropologia comprometida', in *Obra Polémica* (Mexico: Instituto Nacional de Antropologia e Historia, Colleccion Sep/Inah, 1976), pp. 177-186.

Alavi, Hamza, 'India and the colonial mode of production', *Economic and Political Weekly* (Bombay), Vol. 10, Special Number (August 1975), pp. 1235-1262.

Amin, Samir, *L'Accumulation à l'Echelle Mondiale* (Paris: Anthropos, 1970), 589 pp. (9-47).

Aportes (Paris), No. 21 (1971), 'Capitalismo y subdesarrollo en América Latina'.

Arrighi, Giovanni, 'Prefazione' a *Sviluppo Económico e Sovrastructture in Africa* (Torino: Einaudi Editore, 1969), 358 pp. (9-11).

Barrat-Browne, Michael, *Economic Imperialism* (London: Penguin Books, 1974), Ch. 11 on 'Neocolonialism'.

Becerra, Longino, 'Carácter y contenido del proceso revolucionario latino-americano', *Revista Internacional — Problemas de la Paz y del Socialismo* (Prague), No. 12 (1969), pp. 81-87.

Bodenheimer, Susanne, 'Dependency and imperialism: the roots of Latin American underdevelopment', in K.T. Fann and D.C. Hodges (eds), *Readings in US Imperialism* (Boston: Porter Sargent Publisher, 1971), pp. 155-282 (165-169).

Brett, E.A. *Colonialism and Underdevelopment in East Africa* (New York: NOK Publishers, 1973), (1-35, 305-312).

Cardoso, Fernando Henrique and Enzo Faletto, *Dependencia y Desarrollo en América* (Mexico: Siglo XXI, 1969).

Chase-Dunn, Chris, 'The effects of international economic dependence on development and inequality: a cross-national study', Department of Sociology, Stanford University (1974), mimeo; presented to the Annual Meeting of the American Sociological Association (Montreal: August 1974).

Chilcote, Ronald H., 'A critical synthesis of dependency literature', *Latin American Perspectives* (Riverside, Calif.), Vol. 1, No. 1 (Spring 1974).

Chilcote, Ronald H. and Joel Edelstein, *Latin America: The Struggle with Dependency* (Boston: Schenkman, in press).

Circolo Lenin di Milano, *Teoria, Prassi e Realtà Sociale del Movimiento Operaio* (Milan: Sapere Edizioni, 1971), 270 pp. (26-38).

de la Peña, Sergio, 'Acumulación originaria y modos de producción en América Latina', Instituto de Investigaciones Sociales, Universidad Nacional Autónoma de México (1974), mimeo; presented at 42nd International Congress of Americanists (Mexico: September 1974).

Deward, Jeanne and Jean Bailly, 'Note sur la formation du sous-développement en Amérique Latine', *Critiques de l'Economie Politique* (Paris), No. 3, (April–June 1971), pp. 17-27 (18 ff).

Emmanuel, Arghiri, *Unequal Exchange* (New York: Monthly Review Press, 1972); translation of *L'Echange Inegal* (Paris: Maspero, 1969).

Evers, Tilman T. and Peter von Wogau, 'Lateinamerikanische theorien zur unterentwicklung', *Das Argument* (Berlin), No. 79 (July 1973).

Foster-Carter, Aidan, 'Neo-Marxist approaches to development and under-development', *Journal of Contemporary Asia*, Vol. 3 No. 1 (1973).

Friedmann, Harriet and Jack Wayne, 'Functionalism and dependency: replacing old orthodoxies with new'; paper presented at the VIIIth World Congress of Sociology (Toronto: August 1974).

Genovese, Eugene D., *The World the Slaveholders Made*, (New York: Random House Vintage Books, 1971), pp. 60-64.

Genovese, Eugene D., *In Red and Black*, (New York: Random House, Pantheon Books, 1968), pp. 384-388.

Glauser, Kalki, 'Origenes del régimen de producción vigente en Chile', *Cuadernos de la Realidad Nacional* (Santiago de Chile), No. 8 (June 1971), pp. 78-152 (78-79, 132-152).

Godzik, Wolfgan, Gerd Laga and Kurt-Peter Schütt, 'Zur kritik der dependenz-theorie: methodologische anmerkungen zu einem neo-marxistischen ansatz in der entwicklungsländerfroschung', *Kölner Zeitschrift für Soziologie und Sozialpsychologie*, Vol. 28, No. 3 (September 1976), pp. 543-551.

Graciani, Giovanni, 'Imperialismo e sottosviluppo, il caso de América Latina', *Classe e Stato* (Bologna), No. 5 (December 1968), pp. 22-58. Spanish translation: *América Latina, Imperialismo y Subdesarrollo* (Mexico: Editorial Diógenes, 1971), 70 pp.

Guzman, Gabriel, *et al.*, 'Economia Latinoamericana', *Información Comercial Española* (Madrid), No. 460 (December 1970), pp. 33-136 (54-57, 65-73, 77-80, 91).

Halperin, Ernst, *Terrorism in Latin America*, The Washington Papers, No. 33 (Beverly Hills/London: Sage Publications, 1976), pp. 58-79.

Hinkelammert, Franz, *El Subdesarrollo Latinoamericano. Un Caso de Desarrollo Capitalista* (Santiago: Universidad Católica de Chile, 1970), 134 pp. (78-79).

Hurtienne, Thomas, 'Zur ideologiekritik der Lateinamerikanischen theorien der Unterentwicklung und Abhängigkeit', thesis presented to the Department of Sociology, Freie Universität Berlin (1973).

Journal of Inter-American Studies and World Affairs. Issue devoted to Foreign Investment and Dependence in Latin America, with articles by David Ray, Russell Martin Moore, and William G. Tyler and J. Peter Wogart (Coral Gables, Florida), Vol. 15, No. 1 (February 1973).

Kossok, Manfred, 'Feudalismo y capitalismo en la historia colonial de América Latina', *Comunidad* (Mexico), No. 46, (December 1973). German version in *Asien, Afrika, Lateinamerika* (Berlin: 1974). Presented at 42nd International Congress of Americanists (Mexico: 1974).

Kowaleski, Marcin, *Antropologia de la Guerrilla* (Caracas: Ediciones Barbara, 1971).

Laclau, H. Ernesto, 'Modos de producción, sistemas económicos y población excedente, aproximación histórica a los casos argentinos y chilenos', *Revista Latinoamericana de Sociologia*, Vol. 5, No. 2 (July 1969), pp. 276-316 (279 ff.).

Lebedinsky, Mauricio, *América Latina en la Encrucijada de la Década 70* (Buenos Aires: Ed. Centro de Estudios, 1971), 198 pp. (pp. 76-79, 92-93).

Mandel, Ernest, 'Postfacio', *Tratado de Economia Marxista* (Mexico: Ediciones Era, 1970), especially Vol. 1 (336-337).

Mandle, Jay R., 'The plantation economy: an essay in definition', *Science and Society* (New York), Vol. 36, No. 1 (Spring 1972), (49-52).

Marini, Ruy Mauro, 'Dialéctica de la dependencia: la economia exportadora', *Sociedad y Desarrollo* (Santiago, Chile), No. 1 (January–March 1972), pp. 35-51 (37-39).

Martinez Alier, Juan, '¿Un edificio capitalista con fachada feudal? El latifundio en Andalucia y en América Latina', *Cuadernos de Ruedo Ibérivo* (Paris), No. 15 (October– November 1967), pp. 3-54 (43-52).

Murga, Antonio, 'Dependency: A Latin American view', *NACLA Newsletter* (New York), Vol. 4, No. 10 (February 1971), pp. 1-13 (5-8).

O'Brien, Philip J., 'A critique of Latin American theories of dependence', in Ivar Oxaal, Tony Barnett and David Booth (eds), *Beyond the Sociology of Development* (London: Routledge & Kegan Paul, 1975), Chapter 2.

Olmedo, Raúl, 'El mito del capitalismo post-ciclico y sus efectos ideológicos en la interpretación de la realidad latinoamericana'; paper presented to X Latin American Congress of Sociology (Santiago, Chile: 1972), mimeo, 11 pp.

Olmedo, Raúl, 'Introducción a las teorias sobre el subdesarrollo', *Pensamiento Critico* (Havana), No. 36 (January 1970), pp. 3-21 (16-20).

Palloix, Christian, 'Connaître l'impérialisme; de Karl Marx à A.G. Frank' in *L'Impérialisme. Colloque d'Alger* (Université d'Alger, SNED, 1970). 'Echange inégal et polarisation dans la thése d'Andre Gunder Frank' in *L'Economie Mondiale Capitaliste* (Paris: Maspero, 1971), Vol. II, pp. 200-205, 228-236; 89-94, Vol. I, pp. 215-222.

Pinto, S.C., Anibal, 'Notas sobre desarrollo, subdesarrollo y dependencia', *El Trimestre Económico* (Mexico), Vol. 39 (2), No. 154 (April–June 1972), pp. 243-264.

Rodriquez, Octavio, *Informe sobre las Criticas a la Concepción de la CEPAL* (Santiago: ILPES, July 1971), (CDP/27), 154 pp. (122-152).

Sandri, Renato, 'Nazione e lotta di classe nel'America Andina', *Rinascita* (Rome), No. 32 (6 August 1971), pp. 12-13.

Shah, S.A., 'What is development — an introduction' (Dakar: UN African Institute for Economic Development and Planning, July 1973), mimeo.

Stein, Stanley and Shane J. Hunt, 'Principal currents in the economic historiography of Latin America', *Journal of Economic History* (New York), Vol. 31, No. 1 (March 1971), pp. 222-253 (241-253).

Torres, Jaime, 'Para un concepto de formación social colonial', (CESO, Universidad de Chile, 1972), mimeo. 135 pp. (86-101).

Turner, Barry A., *Industrialism* (London: Longman, 1975), 125 pp. (86-101).

Volski, Victor, *Social Science* (Moscow), No. 2 (1971).

Vyasulu, Vinod, 'On the Latin American view of underdevelopment', *Economic and Political Weekly* (Bombay: 13 April 1974).

Warren, Bill, 'Imperialism and capitalist industrialization', *New Left Review* (London), No. 81 (September–October 1973).

Zahar, Renate, *Kolonialismus und Entfremdung — Zur Politischen Theorie Franz Fanons* (Frankfurt: Europäische Verlag, 1969; and Mexico: Siglo XXI, 1970), 132 pp. Spanish ed.: *Colonialismo y Enajenacion Contribucion a la Teoria Politica de Frantz Fanon* (Mexico: Siglo XXI, 1970).

IV. *Debates*

Dalton, George and A.G. Frank, 'Theoretical issues in economic anthropology', *Current Anthropology* (Chicago), Vol. 10, No. 1 (February 1969), pp. 63-102; Vol. 11, No. a (February 1970), pp. 67-71; Vol. 12, No. 2 (April 1971), pp. 237-241.

Dedijer, Stefan and A.G. Frank, 'Scientific research and political power', Lars Dencik (ed.), *Scientific Research and Politics* (Lund, Sweden: Studentlitteratur, 1969), pp. 84-90, 152-160, 166-173, 187-190, 196-200.

Ghioldi, Rodolfo (Secretary General of the Communist Party of Argentina), in *Pravda* (Moscow: 25 October 1967), and Luis Corvalan (Secretary General of the Communist Party of Chile), in *Pravda* (Moscow: 27 October 1967); cited in Andre Gunder Frank, 'Chile: el desarrollo del subdesarrollo', *Monthly Review, Selecciones en Castellano* (Santiago: 1968; Second Edition), p. 3.

Morner, Magnus and Anders-Stefan de Velder, 'Debate', *Dagens Nyhetter* (Stockholm: 18 January and 4 February 1970).

Puiggros, Rodolfo and A.G. Frank, 'Los modos de producción en Iberoamérica', *El Gallo Illustrado, Suplemento Dominical de El Dia* (Mexico), Nos. 173, 175, 177, 179, 181 (17 October–12 December 1965). Reprinted in *Izquierda Nacional* (Buenos Aires), No. 3 (October 1966). *América Latina ¿Capitalismo o Feudalismo?* (Medellin: Oveja Negra, 1972).

Symposium on 'Social responsibility in anthropology' *Current Anthropology* (Chicago), Vol. 9, No. 5 (December 1968), pp. 391-435; Vol. 10, also in *Temps Modernes* (Paris: December 1970).

V. *Principal reviews (other than short ones, book notes, etc.)*

American Anthropologist (Menosha), by David Enstein, Vol. 70, No. 6 (1968), p.1243.

American Anthropologist (Menosha), by Richard N. Adams, Vol. 74, Nos. 1-2 (February–April 1972), pp. 76-77.

Annals of the American Academy of Political Science, by Jay Mandle, Vol. 395 (May 1971).

Asahi Journal (Tokyo: 2 November 1973).

Canadian Dimension (Winnipeg), by George Lermer, (1967).

Comercio Exterior (Mexico), by Renward Garcia Medrano, Vol. 17, No. 4 (April 1967).

Cultures et Développement (Louvain), by Andre Cortin, Vol. 1, No. 2 (1969).

Dagens Nyheter (Stockholm), by Gunnar Persson (February 1968).

The Economic Journal (Cambridge), by Timothy King (June 1968), pp. 452-454; by Geoffrey Maynard (June 1971), pp. 432-434.

Hispanic American Historical Review (Durham), by Warren Dean (August 1968); by Roland Ebel (November 1970).

Hispanic American Historical Review (USA), by John M. Hunter (May 1973), pp. 305-306.

Historisk Tidskrift (Stockholm), by Magnus Morner (1970), pp. 116-122.

International Affairs (London), by Emmanuel de Kadt (April 1969).

International Socialist Journal (Rome) by James Petras, No. 22, 2967 (August).

The Journal of Development Studies (England), by Phillip O'Brien, Vol. 10, Nos. 3 & 4 (April–July 1974).

Journal of Economic History (Austin), by Murdo MacLeod, Vol. 31, No. 2 (June 1971), pp. 477-479.

Journal of Economic Literature (USA), by Bertram Silverman (June 1974), pp. 498-499.

Latin American Review of Books (London and Leeds), by Richard Gott, 'The pelican view of Latin America', No. 1 (Spring 1973), pp. 209-218.

Le Monde (Paris), by Alfred Sauvy (3 January 1970).

L'Unità (Rome), by Mario Spinella (18 December 1970).

Marcha (Montevideo), by Hiber Conteris (19 February 1965); by James Petras (16 June 1967).

New York Review of Books, by Ernest Halperin (13 July 1967), pp. 36-37.

Pensamiento Crítico (Havana), by Sebastian Elizondo, No. 11 (December 1967), pp. 182-185.

Il Popolo (Rome), by Manilo Lucaresi (1 December 1969).

Problems of Communism (Washington), by Victor Alba (July–August 1970).

Revista Española de Opinion Publica (Madrid), No. 20 (April–June 1970), p. 390.

Science & Society (New York), by Kit Sims Taylor, Vol. 34, No. 1 (1970) and Vol. 35, No. 3 (1971).

Social Scientist (India), by N. Ram (February 1973), pp. 73-80.

The Spectator Review of Books (London), by Raymond Carr (1 January 1972).

Storia Contemporanea (Rome), by Salvatore Secchi, I. (1970), pp. 641-649.

Author's Additional Note 1983:

Since the compilation of the above list in the mid-1970s, numerous other critiques (of which the author does not have a complete record) have been published. Some of the major ones, which in turn include further references to other critiques, are listed below.

Selected Recent Critiques of Dependence and A. G. Frank Writings
(books listed contain one or more chapters thereon)

Seers, Dudley, ed. *Dependency Theory. A Critical Reassessment*, London, Frances Pinter Publishers 1981.

Limqueco, Peter and McFarlane, Brude, eds. *Neo-Marxist Theories of Development*, London, Croom Helm, New York, St. Martins Press 1983.

Taylor, John G., *From Modernization to Modes of Production*, London, Macmillan 1979.

Brewer, Anthony, *Marxist Theories of Imperialism. A Critical Survey*, London, Routledge & Keagan Paul 1980.

Brookfield, Harold, *Interdependent Development*, London, Methuen & Co. 1975.

Roxborough, Ian, *Theories of Underdevelopment*, London, Macmillan 1979.

Warren Bill, *Imperialism, Pioneer of Capitalism*, London, New Left Verso Books 1980.

Hoogvelt, Ankie M.M., *The Third World in Global Development*, London, Macmillan 1982.

Chilcote, Ronald H., and Edelstein, Joel C. *Latin America: The Struggle with Dependency and Beyond*, New York. Halstead Press/Schenkman Publishers 1974.

Bernstein, Henry, O'Brien, D. C., and Nafziger, W., *Development Theory: Three Critical Essays*, London, Frank Cass Publishers 1978.

De Kadt, Emmanuel, and Williams, Gavin, eds., *Sociology and Development*, London, Tavistock 1974.

Mack, A., Doyle, U., and Plant, D., eds., *Imperialism, Intervention and Development*, London, Croom Helm 1979.

Chilcote, Ronald H., and Johnson, Dale L., *Theories of Development: Mode of Production or Dependency?* Beverly Hills, Sage Publications 1983.

Weisskopf, Thomas E., *Dependence as an Explanation of Underdevelopment: A Critique*, Ann Arbor, Center for Research on Economic Development, February 1977.

Cardoso, Fernando Henrique, "The Consumption of Dependency Theory in the United States," *Latin American Research Review*, vol. XII, No. 3, 1977.

Brenner, Robert, "The Origins of Capitalist Development: A Critique of Neo-Marxism," *New Left Review*, No. 14, July–August 1977.

Palma, Gabriel, "Dependency: A Formal Theory of Underdevelopment, or a Methodology for the Analysis of Concrete Situations of Underdevelopment?" Vol. 6, No. 7/8, 1978.

Browett, John, "Into the Cul-de-sac of the Dependency Paradigm with A.G. Frank," *Australia and New Zealand Journal of Sociology*, 1981.

Browett, John, "Out of the Dependency Perspectives," *Journal of Contemporary Asia*, Vol. 12, No. 2, 1982.

Higgott, Richard, "Beyond the Sociology of Underdevelopment: A Historiographical Analysis of Dependencia and Marxist Theories of Underdevelopment," *Social Analysis*, Vol. 7, 1981.

25

Real Marxism Is Marxist Realism

*Man makes his own history,
but not as he pleases.*

Karl Marx

Freedom means to understand necessity.

Friedrich Engels

In commemoration of the 100th anniversary of the death of Karl Marx, I would like to examine the continued relevance of Marx and Marxism today by concentrating on the principal end, means, and resulting problems of the same.

The principal objective of Marx and Marxists has been to change the world for the better: "Heretofore philosophers have only interpreted the world; our objective is to change it," especially to eliminate the exploitation, oppression, and alienation of man (and woman) by

Socialism in the World (Belgrad), Special Issue on Marx in Our Time, 1983; *Vierteljahres-berichte* (Bonn), No. 93, September 1983; *St. Mark's Review* (Australia), No. 13, March 1983; *Shiso* (Tokyo), No. 705, March 1983; *Nueva Sociedad* (Caracas), No. 66, May/June 1983.

man. The fundamental method of Marx, adhered to in name if not always in practice by Marxists, has been that of historical materialism: "it is not consciousness of men that determines their existence, but on the contrary it is their social existence which determines their consciousness." The practice of historical materialism requires scientific "concrete analysis of concrete reality" (Lenin) and not ideological adherence to sacred texts or political allegiance to received doctrine. The combination of this method and objective, especially of the means of historical materialist analysis with a view to liberating man and his spirit—or the other way around, that man makes his own history but subject to material limitations—poses a long list of as yet unresolved and perhaps insuperable dialectical contradictions and interpenetration of opposites. We may examine some of them.

MARXIST OBJECTIVES

The objectives of Marx and Marxists pose the contradiction 100 years after his death and 135 years after the publication of the *Communist Manifesto* that now one-third of mankind is ruled (more than it rules itself) in the name of Marx, his objective, and his method. However, this numerical success is less than Marx had predicted on the basis of his historical materialist analysis and hoped for in terms of his objective. Moreover, this change has occurred not in the materially advanced parts of the world where his historical materialist analysis led him to expect it but rather where, at least until just before his death, he least expected it: in Russia, China, and parts of the so-called Third World. The Marxist objective is nonetheless still a beacon of hope in much of the world, but more so in the South than the North and arguably more so in the West where it is not established than in the East where it is. This Marxist hope is now weaker in the North and East because of the failure so far in the name of Marx to eliminate exploitation, oppression, and alienation in the East; despite these shortcomings, the hope of attaining Marxist objectives remains stronger in parts of the South and some sectors of the West. These shortcomings in the achievement of Marxist objectives may be attributed to the continued limitations of material development of the productive forces and of Marxist consciousness and materialist analysis, and to the contradictions between them, which we may also analyze with the aid of Marxist historical materialist analysis.

MARXIST METHOD OF HISTORICAL MATERIALISM

MARXIST METHOD IN THE WEST AND WORLD

Marx and his followers up to Lenin developed the method of historical materialist analysis on the basis of capitalist development in particular countries, especially England, and in the capitalist West for use in the study (interpretation) and change (transformation) of the same. This derivation and use of Marxist historical materialism contradicts (or is contradicted by) the development of capitalism on a world scale, which was recognized and commented by Marx and Lenin but hardly incorporated in their own analytical models (Marx's vol. I of *Capital* and Lenin's *Development of Capitalism in Russia* and even his *Imperialism, Highest Stage of Capitalism*– in the West but not the South). Since their writing, the integration and interdependence of all parts of the world in a single historical process of world capitalist development has become so strong and immediately determinant—of the limitations under which men make their own history—that historical materialist analysis now *must* take much greater account of them than the early Marxists did and many late Marxists still do. The latter have not yet been able to resolve the contradiction between what, counter to the method and objectives of Marx and Lenin themselves, has become a Marxist doctrine supported by quotations from the sacred texts to which some would-be Marxists adhere in disregard of the Marxist method of historical materialist analysis, and which is contradicted by historical developments and material experience.

Thus, the present world economic crisis developed out of deepening structural disadjustments within and between the West, East, and South; the crisis affects all countries—albeit differentially so—in each of these parts of the world; and the resolution if any of the current crisis will involve far-reaching economic, social, cultural, ideological, and political change in most parts of the world. Some of this change is already manifest in an emerging new international division of labor, new technological developments, and the renewed decline of a hegemonic power, now the United States, relative to challengers elsewhere—but primarily other capitalist powers, such as Japan, and not from the socialist world. This historical development is contrary to what many on both the left and the right like to claim in erroneous references to the supposedly greater military might, political power, and ideological superiority or offensive of the Soviet Union. Change will also be promoted by heightened social, cultural, and political consciousness and earthshaking mass movements under banners of nation, religion, race, and class—and some of these also in the name of Marx. All of this momentous transformation of the world and popular consciousness is properly the object of Marxist historical materialist analysis of the world as a whole and of its increasingly differentiated parts, but recognizing that the whole is greater than the sum of its parts. Notwithstanding the often parochial limitations of Marxist historical materialism, which was not developed in this worldwide context or for such world-embracing purposes, its method still seems to offer more analytic capacity than rival economic, political, and socio-cultural approaches and analyses.

For instance, relying on historical materialist analysis Marxists were the first to predict, announce, and analyze the current world economic crisis, while bourgeois economists and publicists still remained unaware of it, or denied that there was one. Ironically, Marxists and especially the regimes governing in the name of Marx in the socialist countries also failed to see the coming of this world economic crisis and still less its likely effects on them: they were literally banking on the continued prosperity of the West when they embarked on their major drives to import technology from the West in the early 1970s hoping to pay for it with exports to the West since then. The consequence was the socialist countries' balance of payments and debt crises since 1980 and the resulting political events in Poland (so far, and others to come).

MARXIST METHOD IN THE EAST

The so-called socialist countries and those there and elsewhere who speak for them in the name of Marx are often exempt from the above-named contradictions by their own declarations, but ironically world historical development and its historical materialist analysis contradicts them perhaps most strongly of all. The recently accelerated reintegration of the socialist economies in the capitalist international division of labor—not only through trade relations of exchange but equally through labor process relations of production—and the far-reaching effects of the present crisis in the capitalist West on the economies, societies, politics, yes and ideological consciousness in the socialist East completely contradict Stalin's thesis of two world markets and social systems, one capitalist and another socialist. On the contrary, the so-called socialist world has not escaped from the historical process of world capitalist development or even from the operation deep within the socialist economies of the capitalist world's law of value or the use and exchange of labor power as a commodity, which is the historical material basis of the continued exploitation, oppression, and alienation of man (and woman) by man in the supposedly socialist world, which according to those who speak for it in the name of Marx has achieved or at least is in the transition to these Marxist objectives. None of these claims are true to fact; all of them are contradicted daily by the material experience or social relations of the masses and especially the proletariat and peasantry there; and all of this development is subject to Marxist analysis of historical materialism. Ironically, those who speak in the name of Marx in these supposedly socialist countries are least given to undertaking such historical materialist analysis of their own societies and least of all the material basis of the consciousness of the proletariat as in Poland. It has been availing itself of nationalism and religion to promote the class struggle of and for itself in a supposedly post-revolutionary socialist country, which Marx had prophesized and expected—so far largely in vain—only in capitalist countries!

A century after Marx's death then, there is a crying need for more real(istic) Marxist historical materialist analysis of the socialist countries within the world capitalist economy, all the more so as Marx and Lenin did not trouble to develop Marxism for this purpose and as long as those who speak in his name in these countries and do not seek to overcome these limitations of classical Marxism fail to apply historical materialist analysis to their own societies and least of all to the material and social class basis of their own false consciousness.

MARXIST METHOD IN THE SOUTH

The Marxist historical materialist method and its use to analyze both their own societies and the development of world capitalism as a whole is arguably more developed in the underdeveloped South than in the developed West and the Marxist East. This is another contradiction in the development of Marxism, especially in recent decades; and it deserves a historical materialist analysis of the material basis of this consciousness itself. Perhaps, indeed probably, it was the exaggeratedly higher degree of exploitation, oppression, and alienation to which the Third World has been subject in the course of world capitalist development that has led to the development also of this higher degree of Marxist consciousness, theory, and analysis among the intellectuals and to a not insignificant degree among some of the masses in much of the Third World.

They have contributed or inspired most major recent advances in political economic theory and analysis of modes of production, dependence, imperialism, the world system, capital accumulation, structural economic change, the authoritarian state, populist movements, and revolutionary strategy, some of which have been imported by the supposedly Marxist East and anti-Marxist West. However, this development of Marxist historical materialist analysis—a form or consciousness—in the South, has not been matched by an equal development of anti-capitalist and socialist revolutionary progress in the Third World, and much less elsewhere. The reason must be sought, through historical materialist analysis, in the fundamental contradiction between the Marxist method and its objectives, and especially the material, including social, limitations on man's ability to make his own history as he pleases.

CONTRADICTIONS BETWEEN MARXIST ENDS AND MEANS

Beyond the contradiction between Marxist objectives and accomplishments and the contradictions in the use of Marxist method, most major contradictions during the past century have been between Marxist means and ends themselves and promise to remain so for the foreseeable future. Of course, Marx and Marxists never suggested that the world would change toward the achievement of their objectives simply by interpreting it through the method of historical materialism. For Marx and Marxists since his death "class struggle is the motor of history." But Marxist historical materialism was to reveal both how this class struggle develops out of the contradiction between the development of the forces and the relations of production *and* how men and women—with their consciousness heightened precisely through historical materialism itself—could learn where, when, and how consciously to intervene in the history of class struggle to guide and lead it to the achievement of Marxist objectives. The failure of Marxists during the century since the death of Marx to do so satisfactorily according to the ends and means he himself set out is their major shortcoming so far, and the promise that they will soon overcome it in the future is not bright or credible. Perhaps the reason is to be found in some fundamental contradictions between Marxist means and ends themselves.

CONTRADICTIONS IN THE WEST

In the West, for which Marxist means and ends were set out first and foremost, the method of historical materialism has not been able to lead the class struggle to a successful conclusion or scarcely even to advance it anywhere. The first major disappointment was the First World War and the failure of the revolution in Germany and elsewhere outside of Russia afterward. Thereafter came Nazism—which had been faultily diagnosed by the Communist International—the Second World War, and the failure of Marxist parties since then. With the advance of the welfare state and bourgeois democracy, even if both are now again under threat by the economic crisis, the Marxist dream for the capitalist West has receded further and further, and Marxist parties from social democrats to Eurocommunists and others have been integrated in the capitalist system and coopted to help maintain and run it. Contemporary historical materialism analysis can reveal why: essentially because the proletariat has little reason to play the role originally ascribed to it by Marx's historical materialism.

CONTRADICTIONS IN THE EAST

In the so-called socialist East, especially of Europe, for which Marx and Marxists had ill prepared their historical materialist method and analysis, Marxism has become the official religion, temporarily replacing Christianity—and often science. Historical materialist analysis, especially of socialism itself, shines by its absence there. Otherwise historical materialism could have revealed why Leninist "socialism = Soviets + electricity" plus his Taylorist/Fordist time-and-motion studies/labor processes minus Soviets after all. In other words the continued commodification and alienation of labor, as well as the also Leninist integration in the world capitalist market, not to mention Leninist democratic centralism (more centralist than democratic), despite the progress of extensive growth and considering the planned obstacles to intensive growth and technological progress, have all barred these socialist societies from the Marxist objectives of socialist transition to communism—if they have not guided them altogether to a new nonsocialist society or arguably even back to capitalism. "Socialist realism" has given way to "real(ly existing) socialism." Significantly also, Marxists in the socialist world no longer see the current crisis of capitalism as the vehicle within which the motor of class struggle might drive the world on the road from capitalism to socialism, let alone communism: First, as observed above, they did not see the crisis coming at all; then they expressed the sincere hope that the capitalist crisis, which damages their own real interests as well, would go away as soon as possible—so that they could get back to business as usual. Only for the Third World do these official, especially Soviet Marxists, express much more hope for socialism; but their supposedly historical materialist analysis and political guidance has been mostly wrong before, from China and Vietnam to Cuba and Chile, to India and Egypt, to Ethiopia and Somalia, Angola and Mozambique, and the many Third World countries that can remain unnamed as long as the goals of Marxist socialism still remain so distant.

CONTRADICTIONS IN THE SOUTH EAST

These Third World countries—including China, which likes to be known as one—reveal the contradiction between Marxist methods and objectives most sharply. First of all as already observed above, according to classical Marxist historical materialist analysis of particular countries and the West, the transition to socialism was not even supposed to begin outside the West at all. But it did. Perhaps this surprise should and could have been obviated by historical materialist analysis of the process of capitalist development and polarization on a world scale as a whole, which would reveal where and when the weak links really are. However, if Mao Dse Dung did so for China, Ho Chi Minh and Giap for Vietnam, and Fidel Castro for Cuba, they did so against the orthodox analysis and institutional pressure from Moscow: otherwise their revolutions would not have happened at all, for according to Marxist orthodoxy the development of the productive forces and their contradiction with the relations of production in these countries were not yet ripe for revolution. But these revolutionary leaders and most especially Mao's "politics in command" argued and persuaded many that the development of consciousness itself could help change the material determinants of social existence. With scarcely a proletariat and on the long march over the Yenan way, Mao worked for the proletarian socialist revolution in a peasant society. When this progress faltered and was threatened by reaction in the mid-1960s, Mao launched the "cultural revolution" in a last vain attempt to save the day and develop the forces of production further by changing the relations of production through further heightened consciousness. But the cultural revolution failed, and Mao's death opened the way for a "great leap backward" (Bettelheim) to 1957 and before to pursue Zou En Lai's "four modernizations" under the stewardship of Deng Xiao Ping. Mao's politics has been bereft of command and historical materialism is back in charge—and not only in China.

In Vietnam and Cuba as well as in China—after all their heroic achievements against the military, political, ideological, and economic opposition of imperialism—realist "socialism" has again replaced socialist "realism" in the face of their inability to introduce sufficiently rapid and deep-going modifications in the relations of production and exchange—including those with the capitalist world—and development of the forces of production, especially through technological change and economic restructuring. Privatization of land management and market-ization of more production and trade, foreign investment and export promotion, elitization of education, and other concession to historical material reality are all the order of the day in these Third World socialist countries as they are in those of Eastern Europe. Realist historical materialism there seems to have abandoned advancing further on the road to socialism so as to "consolidate" it and has turned instead, at least for the time being, to consolidate socialism there in order to "advance" it. In other words, this socialist historical materialism has become more conservative than revolutionary.

CONTRADICTIONS IN THE SOUTH

Elsewhere in the Third World the contradiction between Marxist means and ends is essentially similar, the appearance of recent and prospective revolutionary advances notwithstanding. Since the 1960s, the "noncapitalist path" to socialism in Indonesia, India, Egypt, Ghana, Guinea, Mali, and arguably Algeria, Iraq, and elsewhere led straight back to capitalism, as any honestly realistic historical materialist analysis could have shown or did show. Since the mid-1970s develop-ments in Angola, Mozambique, Guinea Cabo Verde (ex), Zimbabwe, Somalia (temporarily and then replaced by) Ethiopia (despite its oppression of) Eritrea, South Yemen, Syria, Afghanistan, Grenada, Nicaragua, and prospectively in El Salvador and Guatemala and elsewhere have heightened the fears of Washington and its friends and the hopes of Moscow and its comrades—but in significant measure falsely so if past experience and present realistic historical materialist analysis are any guide. For the time being, there is little historical materialist reason to support the fears or hopes that these contem-porary historical processes will lead far beyond the "noncapitalist" ones of the 1960s. Indeed, in some cases, the attempts externally to de-link from world capitalism and to modify the domestic relations of pro-duction have not even gone as far as they did then and/or are already in reverse gear again. For instance, Angola never de-linked, Zimbabwe never proposed to do so, and Mozambique is already re-linking and re-privatizing its economy. The Sandinistas in Nicaragua are suffering from severe economic limitations and political obstacles derived from the legacy of the foreign debt, export dependence, and productive structure inherited from the Somoza administration and used by the Reagan administration to complement its military and political economic program to destabilize the Sandinista government. Even if Reagan, hopefully, fails to do so, any realistic historical materialist analysis does not hold out a very bright immediate future. And to the extent that it does anywhere in Latin America, much of the credit must go to two allies that historical materialism did not expect or until recently want: nationalism and religion.

CONTRADICTIONS OF MATERIALISM, NATIONALISM, AND RELIGION

A major and newly again deepening contradiction between and within Marxist means and ends turns on the unexpectedly significant role of nationalism and religion. According to classical historical materialism both of these forms of consciousness would soon disappear, especially as forces to mobilize the masses, as capitalist development proceeded and all the more so under socialism. Yet not only has the opposite happened—nationalism and religion have subsisted and are again growing in strength even within and between the socialist countries— but as consciousness and mobilizing forces they have become the necessary allies, yes and even the most important instruments, of those who speak in the name of Marx and seek to complement his historical materialist method to pursue his objectives 100 years after his death! What an ironical contradiction. No socialist party or movement now speaking in the name of Marx ever came to power without relying on the force of nationalism perhaps even more than on Marxism. Marxism as a historical materialist method of analysis was then subverted and converted into an official state religion, complete with holy scriptures, doctrine, dogma, inquisition, catechism, and ritual obedience to the Marxist method they deny in practice. Class, nationalism, chauvinism, yes and racism have been invoked to lend supposedly Marxist absolution to ones own sinful violation of the true gospel and to deny true legitimacy to the Marxist faith of others that must be combatted with fire and brimstone not excluding sacred crusades and holy wars against them if necessary.

On the other hand, where state power has not yet been achieved or consolidated in the name of Marx, the method of the historical materialist head must increasingly be joined to the anti-methodical madness of the religious heart, soul, and body. For as a Marxist Christian advocate of the theology of liberation has explained, without the historical materialist head the religious body is blind, and without the religious soul the head has no way to lead the body. In Latin America, where many would celebrate the centenary of Marx's death with a decade of revolution in his name, which was once regarded as the anti-Christ by himself and others, now the soldiers of Christ are in the forefront of the revolutionary march, and the generals of historical materialist analysis must follow them because they are their leaders! Arm in arm they are knocking on the doors of paradise, but not the secular one predicted by Marx or his historical materialism.

Nonetheless, while Christians may invoke the wrath of God and the love of his son, Jesus Christ, or the Holy Spirit to sanctify this marriage with Marxists, the latter can still avail themselves of the method of historical materialism to explain the renewed vigour of religion and their marriage of convenience with it. Indeed the religious revival, often fused with nationalism and even racism, as among Iranian and Arab Muslims, is sweeping the world again, long after a mistaken historical materialism had pronounced it dead and buried. However, in the wide crescent from North and West Africa through the Middle East and South Asia to Southeast Asia this religious revival and mobilization, not just of Islam but also of other faithful, is threatening to crucify the historical materialism of Marx and to bury any foreseeable prospects for socialism in his name, let alone in his image. Yet even there historical materialism may still be of use to those who now would honestly inquire how and why earlier historical materialist analysis, not to mention "Marxist" gospel, led us so far astray from the real material determination of consciousness. However, now Marxist historical materialism must be used not so much to deny the persistence of this consciousness or even to transform it to pursue the objectives of Marx, as to facilitate better accommodation to this historical material reality and to help guide man to make his own history within the limitations of changing historical material reality and consciousness.

APPENDIX

26

Introduction, Contents, and Requiem for a Reader on Underdevelopment

Andre Gunder Frank and Said Ahmad Shah

The following pages present the preface, introductory notes, and table
of contents of an Anthology or Reader on *Underdevelopment: Theory,
History, Policy, Politics* compiled and edited by Andre Gunder Frank
and Said Ahmad Shah in 1968–69. Drawing on then existing fragment-
ary analyses, the editors sought at that time to put together, as in a
jigsaw puzzle, a picture—or even to develop a theory—of "dependence" as *the* fundamental factor in the underdevelopment of Asia, the
Arab World, Africa, and Latin America, for each of which the Reader
pieced together the process of development of underdevelopment. This
conception and the table of contents of this undertaking are now made
available here for whatever they may still be worth, particularly to Asian
and African readers, because it has not yet been possible to publish the
actual anthology/reader.

Progressive, that is, small, publishers found the text, including 88
selections in English, French, and Spanish, running from 800 to 1,000
pages for Volume I alone, to be too expensive to produce, and they
would not have been able to distribute the book where it was meant to
be read and used, that is, in the misnamed "Third World." Commercial
publishers and university presses for their part also found the project a
bit expensive to publish—and much too progressive for their taste.
(Two major English publishers and their referees put their ideological

position in black and white in raising objections to the ideology of the editors and their selections.)

Indeed, the failure for so many years after its completion in 1969 to publish the first volume dedicated to the proposition that "theory is history" and devoted to the historical development of underdevelopment in Latin America, Africa, the Middle East, and Asia, respectively, discouraged the editors from proceeding and completing the second volume on contemporary problems of imperialism, class structure, ideology, and politics beyond the initial outline of the volume and the preselection of the then available material. Too much historical water has passed under the dam—and with it too much progress has been achieved in the analysis of contemporary problems of underdevelopment—for the work on Volume II, "Policy = Politics," still to be of value today.

However, despite the substantial progress in historical analysis and theoretical development since 1969 and notwithstanding renewed interest by publishers in two languages in now publishing Volume I, there may still be some value to readers and students, particularly in Asia and Africa, from now making available at least the conception, as reflected in the preface, the general argument in the introductions to the sections and areas, and particularly the selection and order of the selected readings, as indicated by the table of contents, including author, title, and pagination of the selection, title of the book or journal, name of the publisher, as well as place and date of publication, in English if possible and in the other original language if not. Making this information available here, even if the 800 or more pages of edited text of Volume I never see the light of day, may still at this late date offer interested readers some opportunity of pursuing and perhaps reconstructing part of the argument of this ill-fated Reader on Underdevelopment. (On a 1975 trip to parts of Asia and Africa, AGF found, for instance, that people in various countries were reading his and other works on Latin America in an attempt to apply a similar "dependence" approach to the analysis of their own societies—as AGF and SAS had sought to do in this Reader.)

The preface, introductions, and table of contents reproduced here speak for themselves even if the initially planned 25-page theoretical introduction is missing; because in the process of writing it became longer and longer and changed in scope and orientation along with the editors' own theoretical and political development, to emerge as several essays and books, including *World Accumulation 1492-1789* and *Dependent Accumulation and Underdevelopment*, which were written by AGF before 1973 but only published since 1978. It may be well, however, to stand back and to examine the intent and hope expressed in the first paragraph of the original 1969 preface: "Our purpose will be accomplished in the measure that others . . . develop the revolutionary theory and policy that they need and thereby make our book out of date." It may be said today that this purpose has been substantially advanced without the publication of this Reader, and that this book is now indeed out of date.

If one were to compile a similar book today, there would be much less need for the "critique of received theory," since this theory has substantially discredited itself alone by its failure. The section that argues that theory is the history of world capitalist development could today be substantially refined and at the same time shortened by drawing on the many excellent analyses of parts of this process that have been published since. The section on Latin America would use new studies incorporating significant advances in the analysis of capital accumulation, modes of production, and class structure that go far beyond the earlier formulation of "dependence." But especially the sections on Africa and the Middle East (a Eurocentric term) can now be presented in very much improved form because of the quantitative increase and the qualitative improvement in the analysis, especially by new students of their own societies as foreseen in the 1969 preface, of these areas since the editors laboriously sought to spin their argument out of the rather thin thread and cloth available to them in the late 1960s. The same advance is true for some parts of Asia, albeit apparently not for the areas in the neocolonial ASEAN Association of Southeast Asia, nor—at least among foreign scholars—apparently for the history of China, where progress is still very much wanting.

It would be useful to publish annotated bibliographies of these advances in this decade (though it should perhaps be emphasized in this context that the present table of contents is *not* a list of the perhaps 1,000 items examined for possible use in the Reader and does not pretend to be a bibliography of works on these areas).

If a "similar" book were attempted today, it would be done quite differently. Of course, the selection of material for Volume I, which cuts off in the early twentieth century, was premised on the assumption that it would be accompanied by a Volume II on contemporary affairs, which explains the now unfortunate absence of these in this Reader. If Volume II were to be done today, it would be even more different from its conception in 1968–69 than Volume I would be, essentially because world political circumstances have changed substantially. But today, neither of the two volumes (or the then anticipated third one on problems of transition to socialism) would be done as a book on "theory of underdevelopment" at all. Still less would each of the continents, regions, or countries be examined separately, one after the other. Instead, the attempt today—on the part of the editors as well as others— is to encompass the historical process of worldwide accumulation of capital as a whole, examining all parts simultaneously and in mutual relation to each other, and in relation to this global process to analyze the particular process of capital accumulation and the class structure and struggle in the particular part(s) of the world of immediate concern, as called for already in the preface and introductions and only incipiently attempted in the text of the Reader on *Underdevelopment.*

November 1975
August 1983

AUTHOR'S NOTE 1983

The following pages reproduce the general table of contents and preface of the Reader together with the original introductions of its various subject sections, each of which is followed by the corresponding list of selected readings (and their authors, titles, and sources) taken from the original detailed table of contents proposed for the Reader.

UNDERDEVELOPMENT

THEORY, HISTORY, POLICY, POLITICS

by

Andre Gunder Frank and Said Ahmad Shah

Volume I
UNDERDEVELOPMENT: THEORY = HISTORY

PREFACE

Past and present experience with underdevelopment in Asia, Africa, and Latin America urgently demands a *theory of underdevelopment*, as distinct from orthodox "development" theory. Our objective in preparing this book is to encourage the development of such a theory of underdevelopment in Asia, Africa, and Latin America. We hope that this theory will be scientifically more adequate and politically more capable of generating real development policy for these continents (and also for the underdeveloped areas of Europe and North America) than received orthodoxy. To do so, such theory and policy would have to be a radical departure from orthodoxy. Our purpose will be accomplished in the measure that others—who, we believe, must be primarily the people in the underdeveloped countries to whom this book is above all addressed—develop the revolutionary theory and policy that they need and thereby make our book out of date.

Underdevelopment in Asia, Africa, and Latin America was caused by capitalist development and can only be overcome through socialist development based on a successful outcome of victorious struggle for national liberation. This—the thesis of our book—is the clear lesson of all historical and contemporary experience, which is examined in these two volumes. Our first volume examines the historical record of how world capitalist development caused the development of underdevelopment in Latin America, Africa, the Middle East and North Africa, and Asia as the price for generating economic development in the dominant capitalist parts of the world. In the second volume, we go on to show why underdevelopment is still being deepened by capitalism today. We begin by analyzing the fundamental factors of contemporary capitalism in the underdeveloped world, which are imperialism, class structure, politics, and ideology. We conclude our study by comparing the economic and social performance of capitalism, as well as of the so-called "noncapitalist path" and "African socialism" in India, South Korea, South Vietnam, the Caribbean, Egypt, and other parts of Africa and Latin America with the performance of socialism in China, the Democratic Popular Republic of Korea, the Democratic Republic of Vietnam, and Cuba.

Thus, to study underdevelopment—the objective of our *single* book— both volumes are essential; contemporary underdevelopment is inexplicable without an examination of its historical development, and theoretical enquiry is sterile unless it is translated into policy and tested in political praxis. However, for those readers who may wish to concern themselves with only a part of the problem or its manifestation in only one area at a time, we have endeavored to make each of the volumes and even most of the sections (but not the individual selections) intelligibly meaningful in themselves. Nonetheless, since the full meaning of underdevelopment is only discernible from comparative analysis of its varieties and fundamental commonality in its global setting, we would encourage readers who are familiar with one aspect or geographical manifestation of underdevelopment not to yield to the temptation of just reading up more on that in this book, but to take advantage of the elsewhere inaccessible material brought together here to familiarize themselves with other problems and areas of underdevelopment—and to compare and draw their own conclusions.

Since existing theory is inadequate, the available analyses of historical and contemporary underdevelopment are also insufficient. Nevertheless, the best of this analytical material, which is often written by people from the underdeveloped countries themselves—and on which, we believe, we have drawn in choosing the selections included in this book—can be used to develop the elements of a theory of underdevelopment and a policy adequate to overcome it. Therefore, the criterion we have used in choosing and ordering the material selected and written for this book is exclusively the contribution such material can make to the development of more adequate theory and policy. For the same reason, and unlike most "readers" or anthologies, we do not intend or pretend to offer a balanced diet of all approaches to our subject, nor do we claim that our selections are the most representative ones of their authors—for these are neither our criteria nor our objectives in selecting the material presented here.

Any attempt to find the fundamental element of a more adequate theory of underdevelopment and a more effective policy of development must necessarily examine the really relevant experience of the major underdeveloped areas of the world, as we seek to do here. However, we do not pretend to write a book about Asia, Africa, Latin America, or any of their parts, or all of them put together, per se; that is a task we leave to our more qualified colleagues who are specialists in one or another of these areas. Therefore, we have also not sought to include material on all or even on all "important" countries in these three continents (and space limitations have obliged us to desist from our original intention of also including material from the underdeveloped areas in Europe and North America, such as the Mediterranean regions, parts of the British Isles and Ireland, regions in the Canadian Maritimes and Quebec, and Afro-America). Instead, always pressed for space in these already enormous volumes, we have pursued our central objective of making sense out of the most essential elements of a realistic theory and an effective policy to overcome under-development. Toward this task we have chosen some selections because of the importance of the problems, others for the exceptional quality of their analysis or theoretical contribution (though the geographical area dealt with may not be of the greatest interest). Yet, we have tried throughout to analyze all the most essential elements of each section of the book in the most logical order and the fewest words that the available material permits.

Our objectives also oblige us to refer to aspects of the reality and theory of underdevelopment about which we cannot supply any material, because nothing minimally adequate has yet been written (and we, even more than others, do not know enough to write it). However, since we are preparing this book precisely because the many important missing pieces in the jigsaw puzzle of theory and policy for the underdeveloped areas cannot be supplied by any one or a few people working individually, the gaps that we see are clearly identified in our introductions to each of the two volumes and to the various sections of this book. Finally, we wish to stress that even once these gaps are filled and/or a theory of underdevelopment is built, it must still be inadequate, just like "development" theory is now, because it will still be only partial. For what is really needed is a global theory to reflect and explain—and thereby to help change—the total reality we face: the until recently world-embracing capitalist system, in which the dominant developed metropolis and the exploited (neo)colonies are only the opposite sides of the same coin.

After an introduction, which represents our own attempt to distill a theory of underdevelopment from the material presented here, Volume I begins with a "Critique of Received Theory" to show why this book and an alternative theory are needed. The examination of the historical record and the simultaneous building of theory begins in the next section, entitled "Theory = History." This section reviews the history of world capitalist development between the transition from feudalism in the fifteenth century and the consolidation of a worldwide imperialist system in the nineteenth and twentieth centuries. The principal purpose of this section is to show that over the past five centuries the world has experienced the development of a single capitalist system that came to be world embracing and to derive a theory from this historical process that can explain how underdevelopment developed as an integral part thereof, no less than development did. This theory, as this section as well as the introduction will suggest, must be as historical as capitalist development and underdevelopment; it must be holistic enough to refer to the entire world system of which underdevelopment is a constituent part; it must be structural so as to explain how the structure of the whole system determines the underdevelopment of its major parts; and that is why it must be dialectic to account for the contradiction of capitalist development and underdevelopment.

Since the first major event in world history to initiate contemporary underdevelopment was the discovery of America, we begin our enquiry there and proceed to examine the principal processes in Latin America and the Caribbean that appear to have given rise to the underdevelopment its people suffer today. From there we pass on to Africa, where we begin the same enquiry again, starting with the conditions existing before the arrival of the white man and Africa's incorporation into the world capitalist system. The development of underdevelopment in the Middle East and North Africa is examined next. The last section of Volume I examines the historical experience of Asia after its incorporation into the world capitalist system. We begin with India, then examine China, pass on to Southeast Asia and especially Indonesia, and conclude with an analysis of the industrial development of Japan, which was the only major area of Asia, Africa, and Latin America that had not been incorporated into the world capitalist system as a colony. Thus in each of these major area studies the comparison with the situation before its incorporation into the capitalist system and world history and the comparison between areas that were relatively more colonized and others that were relatively less colonized—or not at all colonized such as Japan—reveals how political and especially economic colonization by the metropolis in the single world-embracing capitalist system has been *the* crucial cause of underdevelopment.

This still-existing cause must be understood and eliminated before under-development can be overcome. Therefore, we have given Volume I the subtitle "Theory = History."

That the defeat of capitalist colonialism, neocolonialism, and imperialism is absolutely essential, and that revolutionary change of the capitalist class structure is equally necessary because of the integral nature of world and national capitalism is shown by the evidence examined in the second volume. Since the main focus of both volumes remains the causes of and remedies for underdevelopment, the problems specific to socialist development cannot be examined here but could only be dealt with in a third volume that we hope to be able to prepare at a later date. Similarly, many of the sociocultural mechanisms and manifestations of dependence, exploitation, racism, repression, insecurity, mistrust, and other forms of alienation, which are integral and often most acutely perceived aspects of underdevelopment, have had to be denied the attention they deserve in preparing these two volumes in order to inquire into the elementary political economic causes of underdevelopment that have been denied virtually all attention by orthodox works on "development."

However, particularly since our—and we hope our readers'—interest is not history or theory for their own sake but for the sake of contemporary practice, we have sought scientifically to examine the political and ideological problems of overcoming underdevelopment in Volume II. Indeed, for this reasoning we have given it the subtitle "Policy = Politics."

We have had to call on the advice and often accept the generous help of many comrades and friends in our search for and evaluation of material on the parts of the underdeveloped world—especially Africa—or its problems that we do not adequately know. Though many more than these have helped and encouraged us, we would like especially to thank Anouar Abdel-Malek, Aurelio Alonso, Samir Amin, Sergio Aranda, Giovanni Arrighi, Giorgio Backhaus, Jose Bell Lara, Yves Benot, Charles Bettelheim, Feiling Blackburn, Wilfred Burchett, Catherine Coquery-Vidrovitch, Gerard Chaliand, Laura Gonzales, Rolf Gustafson, Eric Hobsbawm, Steve Hymer, Kewes S. Karol, Geoffrey Kaye, Lars Kronvall, Ernest Mandel, Sidney Mintz, Peter Meyns, Hiroji Okabe, Nicos Poulantzas, Ulf Renmark, Maurice Rue, Robert Sutcliffe, and Luis Vitale. We have also received material and editorial aid as well as further encouragement from François and Fanchita Maspero in Paris; Tony Malik, Estelle Dorais, and Marcel Nouvet in Montreal; Marta Fuentes in Santiago; and Frances Welch at Cambridge University Press. Without them and their generosity the preparation of this book would have been quite impossible.

August 6, Hiroshima Day, 1969

A.G.F.   Santiago, Chile
S.A.S.   Montreal, Quebec

I. CRITIQUE OF RECEIVED THEORY

INTRODUCTION

This prefatory section is supplementary to, rather than an integral part of, the main argument of this book on "underdevelopment." Nonetheless, this section is intended to supplement or preface the argument about underdevelopment in two important ways: (1) By pointing to the inadequacy of orthodox "development" theory, as it is received from both bourgeois and some Marxist sources, this critique is intended to establish a *prima facie* case for the need to develop more adequate theory and then policy for underdeveloped Asia, Africa, and Latin America. Indeed, precisely because orthodox *development* theory and policy are the product of the historical experience of the metropolitan developed countries—irrespective of whether it was examined by bourgeois or Marxist theorists—this theory and policy are quite inappropriate to the quite different historical experience and present needs of the underdeveloped countries. Hence, the need for a theory of *underdevelopment* and for policy that is necessary and sufficient to overcome it. (This is not to deny the additional need, recognized elsewhere in this book, for a theory that is able to encompass the entire historical process, past and present, that simultaneously generates development of underdevelopment.) (2) The other purpose of this section is to show that perception of the inadequacy of orthodox theory, particularly from bourgeois sources, is not new but rather as old as the theory itself. This perception—and critique of received theory and policy—is abundantly clear in the writings of Marx and Lenin. Less known and therefore in need of special emphasis is the acute perception of this inadequacy over a century ago in the nonmetropolitan countries. Therefore, this section begins with critiques of "orthodox" development theory and policy from representatives of two countries, the United States and Germany, which at the time of writing were *not* the principal metropolitan countries—but which were able to develop precisely because they accepted the critiques of received theory and policy and because they pursued development policies quite different from those that the then British and partly French new orthodoxy sought to impose on the rest of the world (but which were similar to the policies these countries had used in their own early stage of development). The critiques of Alexander Hamilton and Friedrich List, written in the 1820s and 1840s and which introduce this section, have since become famous and acceptable because, one may venture to suggest, their countries have successfully developed and not because their critiques and policies were any better than those of many of their contemporaries whose names are hardly recorded by world history—because their countries did not manage to develop.

The critique of received theory therefore proceeds with two selections from nineteenth century writers and statesmen in Mexico and India, whose critiques of the same received theory were equally or even more cogent *and correct* as those emanating from the United States and Germany. These selections, of course, are only representative of countless other contemporary similar critiques throughout Latin America and in Asia and Africa. (In the case of India, the recent analysis of *The Rise and Growth of Economic Nationalism in India*, which is excerpted in this section, provides a convenient selection of a whole range of views and quotations from that country.) If these critiques of received theory were not translated into an alternative policy—and thus have not become famous—as was the case in the United States and Germany, or in Japan, for that matter, it was because economic, social, and political—including military—circumstances in the world and Asia, Africa, and Latin America did not permit the pursuit of development policies but rather imposed policies that generated their present underdevelopment—as this book seeks to show in the case studies devoted to these areas. It is *essential* to understand, then—contrary to what is explicitly or implicitly so commonly claimed—that Asia, Africa, and Latin America are not now underdeveloped because their peoples were or still are ignorant of what is good for them, and that that is why they now need the gracious help of U.S. know-how. This "ignorance theory of history," no less than the remainder of orthodox theory criticized in this section, is false because it is empirically totally unfounded. But since the thesis about the "ignorance" of other peoples is even more insidious than most orthodox theory, it is especially important to negate it before going on to look for an alternative theory of underdevelopment, which is the principal purpose of this book.

The selection from Bettleheim suggests that orthodox contemporary theses about underdevelopment reflect bourgeois ideology and correspond to very particular political interests. Emmanuel challenges the classical theses about the international division of labor, and particularly of the theory of comparative advantage with which international trade, which has developed the metropolis at the expense of underdeveloping the colonies, has for a century and a half been justified as being according to—virtually—natural law. Though Emmanuel's critique is very recent and the orthodoxy of the "law" of comparative advantage has resisted other valid criticism, including that of Edgeworth, Grahm, and Williams between 70 and 50 years ago, the "law" had already been disproven by history before David Ricardo even invented it in 1817. The exchange of cloth and wine—to return to Ricardo's famous example—between England and Portugal, far from being of advantage to both as the "law" claimed, had already contributed to the industrial development of England and the deindustrialization and underdevelopment of Portugal for over 150 years, since several treaties between the mid-seventeenth century and that of Methuen in 1703 obliged Portugal, which sought political protection against Spain from Britain, to cede to the latter the trade rights at home and in the Portuguese colonies that Ricardo later enshrined in his natural law. In fact, each and every one of the about 30 assumptions on which the validity of the "law" explicitly or implicitly rests, have been totally out of keeping with the realities of domestic economic structure and international trade during both the century and a half preceding and that following the formulation of the "law." Yet, neither bourgeois nor Marxist economists have yet offered an alternative theory quite adequate to replace it. This book is intended to supply a few of the empirical and theoretical elements necessary to construct a realistic theory of the international division of labor and international trade.

Orthodox theory attributes development to the presence of particular "modern" characteristics—such as wealth, proper institutions, and values, as well as knowledge and know-how—and also claims to account for underdevelopment by noting the absence of these characteristics and/or claiming the presence of other characteristics such as improper socioeconomic organization, resourcelessness, laziness, stupidity, as well as ignorance and other marks of "traditionalism." The selections on stages of economic growth by Coatsworth and about dominant economic views by Aguilar argue that these orthodox theories, which attribute underdevelopment only to characteristics peculiar to this or that area, are quite unacceptable and cannot account for the real causes of underdevelopment (which the remainder of this book is intended to establish). The manifest inadequacy of this orthodox theory has recently led some self-styled liberal bourgeois "heretics" to propose revisions. Most notable among these is Gunnar Myrdal's *Asian Drama*; but Barrington Moore Jr.'s *Social Origins of Dictatorship and Democracy*, though written for somewhat different purposes, is perhaps more important. Since both books are as recent as they are important, sufficiently considered judgement has perhaps not yet been possible (and adequate critiques are not available for inclusion here). But the following observations are possible.

Myrdal devotes 10 years of study by himself and his assistants and the three volumes of his book to argue that "conditions that are peculiar to the South Asian countries . . . are responsible for their underdevelopment" (p. 20). In so doing, Myrdal amply confirms that what he says of others is especially true of himself: "Even heretics remain bound by traditional thought in formulating their heresies" (p. 17). For what Myrdal's 2,500 pages boil down to is simply the argument that India is underdeveloped because of the sacred cow which is peculiar to India. (Interestingly enough, another reformist, Kenneth Galbraith, recently argued that underdevelopment is due to poor physical resources in Asia, to poor human resources in Africa, and to poor institutions in Latin America, thus agreeing with Myrdal that underdevelopment in Asia is due to its peculiarity but disagreeing about what that peculiarity is.)

What is really sacred to all the revisionist heretics, however, is the orthodoxy that underdevelopment is due to the peculiarity of the under-developed. Thus, Barrington Moore Jr., who examines England, France, Germany, Russia, United States, China, Japan, and India to locate the origins of dictatorship in the long-time survival of landed aristocratic power and the origins of democracy in the early destruction of same, nonetheless examines each of these countries as though its history had been isolated from that of the others and the remainder of the world. Though Moore's argument (excepting his crude identification of China with a fascist-type dictatorship, which is belied by his own analysis of China) is far more sophisticated than that of the others—and therein lies the danger that he may mislead more than the others' quite obvious falsification of reality can—he remains equally bound by traditional thought in failing to analyze his particular cases as mutually determined within the historical development of the single capitalist and imperialist system of which they were only parts (so that Moore also fails to note how the late development within that imperialist system of Germany, Italy, and Japan determined the recourse to fascist dictatorship at home for imperialist expansion abroad by these countries).

Although orthodox development theory was combatted by successful or would-be policy makers in the nineteenth century, and although the alternative bourgeois capitalist development policies they proposed were successful where it was then possible to apply them, these same policies could not be effective after a century of changing circumstances in the world as a whole and in the underdeveloped countries in particular. The selections from Coatsworth and Aguilar are also intended to suggest why the theory and policy that might once have been adequate no longer are so now. Finally, the essay by Alonso—written in Cuba in the midst of a reevaluation of the "Manuals" through which the Soviet Union exports what purports to be the synthesis of Marxist orthodoxy— suggests that this or any "metropolitan" produced schema is also inappropriate to the reality of Asia, Africa, and Latin America and inadequate for their needs. Hence, there is the need for an alternative approach that is scientifically more realistic and politically more effective.

Readings on
I. CRITIQUE OF RECEIVED THEORY

1. REPORT ON MANUFACTURERS
   Alexander Hamilton, In Jacob E. Cooke, ed., *The Reports of Alexander Hamilton.*
   New York, Harper & Row, 1964, pp. 137–138.

2. NATIONAL SYSTEM OF POLITICAL ECONOMY
   Friedrich List, *National System of Political Economy.*
   Philadelphia, J.B. Lippincott and Co., 1856, pp. 61–80.

3. BRIEF IN FAVOR OF SPINNERS AND WEAVERS
   Matias Quintana in Miguel A. Quintana, *Estevan de Antuñano.*
   Mexico, Secretaria de Hacienda, 1967, pp. 42–48.

4. ECONOMIC NATIONALISM IN INDIA
   Bipan Chandra, *The Rise and Growth of Economic Nationalism in India.*
   New Delhi, Peoples Publishing House, 1966, pp. 56–66, 95–99, 106–107, 111–113, 653–670.

5. BOURGEOIS DESCRIPTION OF UNDERDEVELOPMENT AND ITS CRITIQUE
   Charles Bettleheim, *Planification et Croissance Accélérée.*
   Paris, Maspero, 1965, pp. 28–31.

6. INTERNATIONAL DIVISION OF LABOUR
   A. Emmanuel, "La Division Internationale du Travail et le Marché Socialiste."
   Paris, Centre d'Etudes de Planification Socialiste, *Problèmes de Planification*, No. 7, 1966, pp. 1–14.

7. THE STAGES OF ECONOMIC STAGNATION
   John Coatsworth, "The Stages of Economic Stagnation."
   Ann Arbor, Michigan. Radical Education Project, 1966, mimeo. pp. 2–14.

8. EVALUATION OF THE DOMINANT ECONOMIC VIEWS
   Alonso Aquilar, *Teoria y Politica del Desarrollo Latinamericano*.
   Mexico, Universidad Nacional Autonoma de Mexico, 1967, pp. 12–13, 45–79.

9. MANUAL OR NOT MANUAL. A NECESSARY DIALOGUE
   Aurelio Alonso, "Manual o no Manual. Dialogo Necesario."
   La Habana, mimeographed, 1967, pp. 1–9.

II. THEORY = HISTORY

INTRODUCTION

This section introduces and assembles some major elements of the alternative approach to the study of underdevelopment advanced in this book. The point of departure is the real *historical* process that comes to incorporate the whole world into a *single capitalist system*. The development and structure of this system so *integrates* most of the world into the system, and becomes so *integral* to Asia, Africa, Latin America, and some other regions of the world, as to result in what is today commonly called underdevelopment. The fundamental cause and condition of underdevelopment is the joint condition of dependence and exploitation. This relation of dependence is not one of simple interdependence—which is the relation that characterizes all parts of the above-named worldwide system—but of subjection or subordination. The peoples of Asia, Africa, and Latin America (and some others not considered here) have not been and are not masters of their own destiny; and that is why they suffer from underdevelopment.

This dependence, this determination of the destiny that is under-development, is not, however, an "external condition." On the contrary, the integration, albeit insubordination, of the now underdeveloped countries in the world capitalist system has rendered dependence fully integral or "internal" to these countries. Because of the development of capitalism through mercantilism, "free trade," colonialism, imperialism, and now neocolonialism or neoimperialism and its extension in the now underdeveloped areas through internal colonialism (within each country or area) and the class structure, this dependence manifests itself through manifold economic, political, social, cultural, ideological, and psychic relations of subordination *within* underdeveloped society. Not the least of these manifestations is the widespread propaganda and acceptance in Asia, Africa, and Latin America of the ideology and "theory" of development exported by the metropolis and criticized in Section I of this book. This ideology and theory with the accompanying inferiority complex, which are themselves products of this same dependence, is what this book is designed to help combat and supplant.

The approach to the understanding of underdevelopment as the product of the historical process of the development of capitalism as a worldwide system begins with an examination of the transition from feudalism to capitalism in Europe. The discussion between Dobb, Sweezy, and others conveniently summarizes the most important interpretations of this problem, including that of Marx. They are still in dispute. One of the editors of the present book inclines more toward the interpretation of Dobb, which focuses on domestic changes in productive relations leading from feudalism to capitalism in Europe. The other editor is in greater agreement with Sweezy who emphasizes the mediation of non-European commercial expansion, particularly overseas, in the transition. All possible disagreements about the dynamics of the transition notwithstanding, the historical record clearly shows that the rise of capitalism was associated with European mercantile expansion, and particularly with the discovery, colonization, and exploitation of the New World—which initiated the underdevelopment of Latin America and the Caribbean—as analyzed in the selection from Henri Sée's book on the origin and evolution of modern capitalism. The emergence of a world-embracing system as early as the sixteenth century is evidenced by European extraction of precious metals from the Western Hemisphere and their use to maintain and expand European trade with the Orient, where much of the silver came to rest, as Adam Smith observes in the selection included here.

The systematic character of these growing worldwide commercial and productive relations is exposed through the "intercontinental model" of these relations in selection 4. By the eighteenth century, large parts of Asia, Africa, and Latin America had been substantially integrated into a single system whose center was in Western Europe. Since circumstances in these various areas differed considerably before their incorporation into this system, these are omitted from this section dedicated to the common causes of underdevelopment; and these variations, which also help determine differences in the subsequent forms of underdevelopment, are taken account of in the subsequent sections dedicated to underdevelopment in Asia, Africa, and Latin America themselves. However, the crucial contribution of the triangular trade between Europe, Africa, and America to the development of the first of these areas—at the cost of generating underdevelopment in the others—is examined in the chapter from *Capitalism and Slavery* by Eric Williams. The expropriation of capital from Asia, Africa, and Latin America and its employment for primitive capital accumulation in Europe, which is associated particularly with the take-off into industrialization in England after 1760, is noted by Ernest Mandel. Paul Mantoux, in turn, shows in his classic study of the industrial revolution in the eighteenth century how the latter, far from being the simple growth of artisan shops into industrial factories, was first and foremost the result of the worldwide commercial relations that Europe, and particularly Britain after its victorious struggle for supremacy with Spain, France, and Holland, forged by the mercantile capitalist period. The selection by Crowder argues that, once this industrial supremacy was achieved and her West Indian slave colonies had become relatively high-cost producers, Britain's economic interest supported the abolition of the long-since-condemned slave trade.

Friedrich List, whose German nationalist critique of Britain's subsequent "liberal free trade" policy and theory was cited in Section I, confirms this observation from his vantage point in the first half of the nineteenth century; and he goes on to give an early explanation of why participation in the same mercantile capitalist development did not generate development but rather developed underdevelopment in Spain, Portugal, Asia, Africa, and Latin America. The fundamental reason was, to use the emerging modern terminology, that these peoples had come to have a subordinate exploitative dependence on the metropolitan center(s) in this single worldwide mercantile capitalist system. The transition from mercantile to industrial capitalism in the metropolis, as observed by Dobb, did not and could not engender the same in the economic colonies.

On the contrary, the industrialization of Europe, the imposition of free trade, and the rise of imperialism in the nineteenth century accelerated and deepened underdevelopment in Asia, Africa, and Latin America, as dramatically related by Rosa Luxemburg in her account of the struggle against natural and peasant economy in the Middle East. Paul Baran argues why this capitalist development, which generated economic development in the metropolis, necessarily led to the further development of underdevelopment elsewhere; and one of the present editors extends this argument to spell out a number of specific analytic hypotheses about this capitalist underdevelopment, which are subjected to empirical test in the parts of this book devoted to underdevelopment in the three continents.

Thus, the title of this section has been developed through the selections: the examination of concrete history has led to the elaboration or distillation of some major elements of a theory of underdevelopment, whose basis is the subordinate exploitative dependence of the now underdeveloped areas in the historical process of the development of capitalism as a single world-embracing system. For the generation of development and simultaneously of underdevelopment, and for the analysis of the latter which is the central concern in this volume, two factors emerge as crucial. One is the economic surplus beyond consumption which is necessary and potentially available for investment. This factor was most emphasized by Paul Baran, but for reasons of expository convenience is here analyzed by Bettleheim and elaborated by Novik and Farba. The generation, use, or misuse of this surplus appears as the single most important determinant of development and underdevelopment in the approach emerging from the historical analysis of this volume. The other crucial factor is the structured set of determinants, in turn, of the generation and utilization of this economic surplus. For the development of underdevelopment this factor may be summarized by dependence, which occasions the partial loss of investible surplus through capital drain to the metropolis, which in turn requires a national or regional economic, political, social, cultural, and psychic structure of underdevelopment in the economically colonial areas that sustain the capital drain and occasions the mischanneling of the remaining capital into limited development and general underdevelopment-generating directions.

The first selection of the next section can equally serve as the culmination of the argument that theory is history, since it analyzes—for Latin America, though the same is equally true of Asia and Africa—how in each historical stage of world capitalist development the nature and changes in exploitative economic dependence have formed and transformed the class structure, how this has given rise to the specific class interests of the dominant sector of the colonial and neocolonial bourgeoisie, and why the pursuit of these interests necessarily did and does generate the development of underdevelopment. The major historical manifestations of this process in Latin America, Africa, the Middle East and North Africa, and Asia are examined in the remainder of Volume I; the contemporary problems to which this process has given rise are analyzed in Volume II. The development of more adequate theory to analyze the historical process of the development of underdevelopment, and the use of this theory along with other weapons, by the people of Asia, Africa, and Latin America, to overcome underdevelopment and to develop a new society is the task ahead.

Readings on
II. THEORY = HISTORY

1. THE TRANSITION FROM FEUDALISM TO CAPITALISM
    Paul N. Sweezy, Maurice Dobb, and H.K. Takahashi, et al.
    New York, *Science and Society*, 1954, pp. 17–20, 27–29, 47–55, 63–64.

2. MODERN CAPITALISM, ITS ORIGIN AND EVOLUTION
    Henri See, *Modern Capitalism, Its Origin and Evolution.*
    New York, Adelphi Company, 1928, pp. 177–183 (and corresponding 40–43 Spanish ed.).

3. OF THE MOTIVES FOR ESTABLISHING NEW COLONIES
    Adam Smith, *An Inquiry into the Nature and Causes of the Wealth of Nations.*
    New York, Random House, 1937, pp. 528–529, 204–207.

Santiago, Facultad de Ciencias Economicas de la Universiad de Chile (thesis) 1963, pp. 14–24, 9–11.

III. A. CAPITALIST DEVELOPMENT OF UNDERDEVELOPMENT IN LATIN AMERICA

INTRODUCTION

This section is not an economic and social history of Latin America. Rather, it is an attempt to identify the principal cause of the development of underdevelopment by inquiring into the historical experience of Latin America and the Caribbean. The fundamental factors of world capitalist development and the resulting colonial and class structure in Latin America are analyzed in the historical overview.

The most important aspects of the colonial and class structure imposed by the Conquest are examined first in the Caribbean, where the aboriginal inhabitants were rapidly killed off and replaced by a new population stock and thus an entirely new society, and then in Mexico, where the colonial economy and society was built with indigenous labor. In both cases, historical analysis is here limited to establishing how, notably, the most fundamental underdevelopment-generating factors came to be common to the Mexican society as transformed by mercantile capitalism and the Caribbean society as newly formed by the same. The longer historical development of this essential colonial and class structure is reviewed in the case of Brazil from the time of its discovery to the late nineteenth century. The selections on Paraguay and Argentina examine the conscious attempt to avoid this colonial underdevelopment by people living in the interior, where they were initially protected from the economic colonization by the poverty of their resources and their distance from the colonial port cities. In this relative isolation, which also rendered a different class structure and interest possible, the interior provinces of Argentina and especially the Paraguayans adopted a Hamiltonian–Listian development policy until they were defeated by the force of arms of the colonial ports backed up by the latters' metropolitan allies. For this experience, and still less for similar experience in other isolated parts of the continent, adequate scientific analysis is not available precisely because the attempt was frustrated by the liberal neocolonial interests who have since then sought to misrepresent and belittle this experience in their own historical analysis, which their own political power has made dominant. Therefore, until students who have liberated themselves from liberal ideology return to the historical evidence to analyze it more scientifically, we must rely on the more journalistic account reproduced here. The full incorporation in the nineteenth century of these regions and most of Latin America into world capitalist development as primary-goods exporters has, however, been treated more scientifically, as in the selection on the development of the primary-exports system in Argentina. The most far-reaching nineteenth and twentieth century underdevelopment of a previously relatively more self-sustaining and coherent society is that of Cuba, which is therefore examined in the concluding selections on Latin America and the Caribbean.

Thus, although it is not a history, this section does reflect the historical development of underdevelopment in Latin America and contribute to the development of historical theory of underdevelopment in two ways: each of the major problem areas is treated historically, and these problem areas are examined not only in roughly chronological order but also in historical context. However, it would not have been possible to present an economic and social history of the continent as a whole even if desirable, because an even minimally adequate one has not yet been written. Indeed, even some of the major problems have not yet been adequately studied in the most important areas— for example, the economic basis of society in the colonial and national periods in what was the Inca Empire, then became the Viceroyalty of Peru, and today still is the half Indian populated Peru, Equador, Bolivia, and parts of Columbia. In the absence of virtually any scientific analysis of even the colonial period in this area, the similar problems are here examined by using the more available material on Mexico. Similarly, it is not yet possible to do much more than sketch in the history of the Caribbean plantation economy and society, as is done in these pages. We can only hope that others will soon do more.

Readings on
III. CAPITALIST DEVELOPMENT OF
UNDERDEVELOPMENT
A. IN LATIN AMERICA

1. ECONOMIC DEPENDENCE, CLASS STRUGGLE AND UNDER-
   DEVELOPMENT IN LATIN AMERICA
   Andre Gunder Frank, "Economic Dependence, Class Struggle and Underdevelopment in Latin America" (Ms.).

2. DEVELOPMENT OF UNDERDEVELOPMENT
   Andre Gunder Frank, "The Development of Underdevelopment."
   Monthly Review, Vol. 18, No. 4, pp. 23-28.

Caribbean

3. THE SEARCH FOR GOLD AND ACCELERATED DECLINE OF
   THE NATIVE POPULATION
   Carlo O. Sauer, The Early Spanish Main.
   Berkeley, University of California Press, 1966, pp. 23-24, 155-156.

4. THE LABOUR PROBLEM IN BARBADOS
   Vincent Harlow, *A History of Barbados, 1625–1685.*
   London, Clarendon Press, 1926, pp. 40–44, 306–310.

5. THE CARIBBEAN AS A SOCIO-CULTURAL AREA
   Sidney W. Mintz, "The Caribbean as a Socio-Cultural Area."
   Journal of World History, Vol. IX, No. 4, 1966, pp. 914-932.

Mexico

6. LAND TENURE PREVIOUS TO THE CONQUEST
   Helen Phipps, "Some Aspects of the Agrarian Question in Mexico. A Historical Study."
   University of Texas Bulletin, No. 2512, April 1925, pp. 11-20.

7. NEW LORDS OF THE LAND
   Eric Wolf, *Sons of the Shaking Earth.*
   Chicago, University of Chicago Press, 1959, pp. 149–51, 176–201.

8. CAPITALIST LABOR EXPLOITATION AND HACIENDA FORMATION IN COLONIAL MEXICO
   Andre Gunder Frank, "An Economic History of Mexican Agriculture."
   Manuscript 1968.

9. DIALECTICS OF THE MEXICAN ECONOMY
   Alonso Aguilar, M. *Dialectica de la Economia Mexicana.*
   Mexico, Nuestro Tiempo, 1968, pp. 90–93, 95–109.

Brazil

10. CAPITALIST DEVELOPMENT OF UNDERDEVELOPMENT IN BRAZIL
    Andre Gunder Frank, *Capitalism and Underdevelopment in Latin America*
    New York, Monthly Review Press, 1967, pp. 150–169.

Paraguay and Argentina

11. PARAGUAY AND HER NEIGHBORS
    Pelham H. Box, *The Origins of the Paraguayan War.*
    Urbana, University of Illinois Studies in the Social Sciences, Vol. XV, No. 3, 1927, pp. 11–13, 50–51.

12. PARAGUAY IS SELF-SUFFICIENT
    Efraim Cardozo, "Paraguay Independiente."
    In *Historia de America*, Vol. XXI, Barcelona, Salvat Editores 1949, pp. 65, 75–76, 144–147, 269, 286–287 and Efraim Cardozo, *Breve Historia del Paraguay,* Buenos Aires, Editorial Universitario de Buenos Aires, 1965, pp. 76–78.

13. UNITARISTS AND FEDERALISTS: THE SECOND WAR OF INDE-
    PENDENCE IN ARGENTINA
    Eduardo B. Astesano, *Rosas: Bases del Nacionalismo Popular.*
    Buenos Aires, A. Pena Lillo Editor, 1966, pp. 15–18, 49–55, 68–72.

14. DEFENSE AND LOSS OF OUR ECONOMIC INDEPENDENCE
    Jose Maria Rosa, *Defensa y Pérdida de Nuestra Independencia Econó-
    mica.*
    Buenos Aires, Libreria Huemul, Segunda edición 1954, pp. 133–139,
    161–62, 166–67.

15. DEVELOPMENT OF THE PRIMARY EXPORTS SYSTEM
    Aldo Ferrer, *The Argentinian Economy.*
    Berkeley, University of California Press 1967, pp. 103–125.

Cuba

16. THE DEVELOPMENT OF AN AGRARIAN SOCIETY IN CUBA
    Ramiro Guerra y Sanchez, *Sugar and Society in the Caribbean.*
    New Haven, Yale University Press 1964, pp. 35–36, 44–45.

17. ROAD TOWARDS THE PLANTATION
    Manuel Moreno Fraginals, *El Ingenio. El Complejo Económico Social
    Cubano del Azucar.*
    La Habana, Comisión Nacional Cubana de la UNESCO 1964, pp. 4–14,
    34–37.

18. THE INEXORABLE EVOLUTION OF THE LATIFUNDIUM:
    OVERPRODUCTION, ECONOMIC DEPENDENCE, AND GROW-
    ING POVERTY IN CUBA
    Ramiro Guerra y Sanchez, *Sugar and Society in the Caribbean.*
    New Haven, Yale University Press, 1964, pp. 62–81, 91–93, 116–120.

III.B. CAPITALIST DEVELOPMENT OF
UNDERDEVELOPMENT
IN AFRICA

INTRODUCTION

The cultural colonialism and neocolonialism that on all continents was and is
one of the bourgeoisie's major instruments in the development of underdevelopment has nowhere been so cruelly imposed as in Africa. In this
continent, which—as is summarized by the first selection below—was the
birthplace of man, of writing, and of the working of iron, and which was the home
of several high-civilization empires long before the coming of the white man and
capitalism, the process of liberation from the dark ages of colonialism and
neocolonialism, including cultural colonialism, has only begun. For this reason,

many of the causes and problems of underdevelopment, which everywhere have been falsely analyzed by bourgeois orthodoxy, are especially inadequately analyzed in Africa and by Africans. Therefore, although some of the African problems are discussed in the two volumes by Africans, many of them are not; and some problems are not analyzed at all, because no adequate analysis seems yet to have been written. For instance, there is no general political economy of the Central and South African mining regions, even though the exploitation of the latter has been the principal engine of African underdevelopment during the last century.

Nonetheless, the outlines of the development of underdevelopment in the experience of Africa emerges from the selections below. The slave trade not only deprived Africa of 100 million of its most able citizens, but it thoroughly transformed—that is, underdeveloped—the structure of the economy, polity, and society in vast areas of the coast and interior of Africa. As an integral part of the development of the world capitalist system, and not unlike Asia and Latin America, Africa was converted into an exporter of a single product—enslaved people. Like elsewhere also, the resulting export economy structure of underdevelopment remained largely intact after the cessation of the export boom. The third selection shows that, given the new structure of the world economy and of the local society, the abolition of the slave trade and its replacement, especially in West Africa, by the oil trade, did not and could not permit Africa to pass from underdevelopment to development. Beginning with the late nineteenth century, the particularities of imperialism and colonialism differed from one part of Africa—and the world—to another in accordance with the national styles and even more with the different local needs of the colonializing powers; but, as the selection about colonial contrasts and similarities suggests, these differences were outweighed by the underlying fundamental commonality of the structure and process of colonial under-development. Selections 5, 6, and 7 bring various perspectives to bear on the process of African land expropriation and labor recruitment and mobilization, particularly in British colonial Africa. Although they do not afford a global analysis of the colonial economy, they do demonstrate the development of structural underdevelopment in much of Africa and its fundamental similarities with the same process elsewhere. The selection from Suret-Canale marshalls the same evidence from French colonial Africa, which in its most essential respects is also representative of the areas colonized by the Belgians and the Portuguese, and earlier by the Germans. The last selection sums up the main results—underdevelopment—of the imperialist regime everywhere in Africa.

Readings on
III. CAPITALIST DEVELOPMENT OF UNDERDEVELOPMENT
B. IN AFRICA

1. AFRICAN EMPIRES
   John D. Hargreaves, *West Africa: The Former French States.*

Englewood Cliffs, New Jersey, Prentice Hall Spectrum Books, 1967, pp. 16–27.

2. AFRICAN SLAVE TRADE
Basil Davidson, *The African Slave Trade*.
Boston, Atlantic-Little Brown 1961, pp. 79–87, 153–162, 201–214, 224–229, 255–260, 278–290.

3. BLACK AFRICA IN THE PERIOD OF INDUSTRIAL CAPITALISM
Endre Sik, *The History of Black Africa*.
Budapest, Akademiai Kiado 1966, Vol. I, pp. 191–197.

4. COLONIAL CONTRASTS AND SIMILARITIES
Yves Benot, "Développement Accéléré et Révolution Sociale en Afrique Occidentale."
La Pensée, No. 126, April 1966, pp. 24–29.

5. IMPOVERISHMENT OF THE PEASANTRY—AN AIM
Jack Woddis, *Africa: The Roots of Revolt*.
New York, Citadel Press 1960, pp. 1, 7–30.

6. TYRANNY OF ECONOMIC PATERNALISM IN AFRICA
S. Herbert Frankel, "The Tyranny of Economic Paternalism in Africa."
Optima (supplement), December 1960, pp. 17–30, 39–42.

7. PROLETARIANIZATION OF THE AFRICAN PEASANTRY
Giovanni Arrighi, "Labour Supplies in Historical Perspective: A Study of the Proletarianization of the African Peasantry in Rhodesia."
Manuscript, pp. 7–8, 12–33.

8. BLACK AFRICA IN THE COLONIAL ERA
Jean Suret-Canale, *Afrique Noire. L'ère Coloniale 1900–1945*.
Paris, Editions Sociales 1964, pp. 39–52, 90–92, 369–378.

9. MAIN RESULTS OF THE IMPERIALIST REGIME
Endre Sik, *The History of Black Africa*.
Budapest, Akademiai Kiado 1966, Vol. II, pp. 19–24, 102–121.

III.C. CAPITALIST DEVELOPMENT OF UNDERDEVELOPMENT IN THE MIDDLE EAST AND NORTH AFRICA

INTRODUCTION

The Middle East and North Africa, far from simply suffering the weight of over a millenium of Islam and "traditionalism" as is so often claimed, have suffered from fundamentally the same experience under capitalism as other Afro-Asian and Latin American areas and exhibit at least two classic cases of development of underdevelopment. The first selection below shows that Islam has not been incompatible with capitalism and that in itself Islam would not have been an obstacle to economic development. The second and third selections review the destruction of the manufacturing base for industrial development in Turkey, which is not unlike similar experience elsewhere, notably in India. One of the classic cases of arrested autonomous development efforts and of the generation of underdevelopment through colonial conversion into a raw materials export economy is that of nineteenth-century Egypt, which is analyzed in three selections below, including the account of this process by Rosa Luxemburg, which is itself a classic. Algeria—another classic case reviewed below—became similarly underdeveloped through its incorporation into world capitalist development by the French colonial empire after 1830. That all of the Maghreb or North Africa suffered essentially the same fate for the same reason emerges from the last selection in this section, although its analysis is not as global or incisive as others.

Readings on
III. CAPITALIST DEVELOPMENT OF UNDERDEVELOPMENT
C. IN THE MIDDLE EAST AND NORTH AFRICA

1. ISLAM AND CAPITALISM
   Maxime Rodinson, *Islam et Capitalisme.*
   Paris, Editions du Seuil, 1966, pp. 131–148.

2. OTTOMAN INDUSTRY AND THE WEST
   Omer Celal Sarc, "Tansimat ve Sanayimis" ("The Tanzimat and Our Industry").
   Chicago, University of Chicago Press, 1964, pp. 48–52.
   Charles Issawi (ed.), The Economic History of the Middle East, 1800–1914.

3. ECONOMIC METABOLISM BETWEEN PEASANTS OF ASIA MINOR AND GERMAN CAPITAL
   Rosa Luxemburg, *The Accumulation of Capital.*
   New York, Monthly Review Press, 1964, pp. 444–445.

4. EGYPT SINCE 1800: A STUDY IN LOP-SIDED DEVELOPMENT
   Charles Issawi, "Egypt since 1800: A Study in Lop-sided Development."
   The Journal of Economic History, Vol. XXI, No. 1, March 1961, pp. 4–13.

5. ISMAIL'S CRAZY ECONOMY AND EUROPEAN CAPITAL
   Rosa Luxemburg, *The Accumulation of Capital.*
   New York, Monthly Review Press, 1964, pp. 434–438.

6. PENETRATION OF IMPERIALISM IN EGYPT
Anouar Abdel-Malek, *Egypt: Military Society.*
New York, Random House 1968, pp. 7–16.

7. DESTRUCTION OF THE ALGERIAN ECONOMY
Yves Lacoste, André Nonschi et André Prenant, *L'Algérie, Passé et Présent.*
Paris, Editions Sociales, n.d., pp. 315–326, 370–392, 429–443.

8. COLONIAL ECONOMY IN NORTH AFRICA
Pierre Marthelot, "Incidences de l'Economie Coloniale sur Certaines Donnés de Base de l'Agriculture en Afrique du Nord."
Jacques Berque and Jean-Paul Charnay (eds.), *De l'Impérialisme à la Décolonisation.*
Paris, Editions Minuit 1965, pp. 175–188.

III.D. CAPITALIST DEVELOPMENT OF UNDERDEVELOPMENT IN ASIA

INTRODUCTION

Nascent world capitalism extended its systematic invasion of the East with the help of the silver it had accumulated from the Indian labor of the Western Hemisphere in the sixteenth and seventeenth centuries. The already existing agro-industrial civilizations of Asia at first welcomed the European "newcomers"; but, later, because of the rapacious practices of the traders and adventurers, Asians attempted to exclude them. In some areas the latter policies (most notably in Japan) were successful; but, in most parts of Asia, the attempts at exclusion were too weak or too late.

The selections dealing with India demonstrate the ruination of an advanced agro-industrial civilization first through the policies and practices of the East India Company and later by direct British rule. The incursion of capitalist commercial practices and the flooding of the market with industrial goods aided by preferential tariffs, when coupled with wars of conquest and intrigue, directly caused the destruction of the rural productive system by reorganizing agricultural production and eliminating local manufacturing production. This capitalist economic, political, and military aggression produced famine, deindustrialization, and rural and urban pauperization and created a dependent stagnant socioeconomic system in India. The essential reason for this process was the transfer of a significant amount of economic surplus from India to England, where it was invested in metropolitan economic development. The concluding selection on India clearly shows that the inevitable effect of this colonial capitalist relationship between England and India was to generate development of underdevelopment in India.

The next two selections show that the process of capitalist expansion also led to the destruction of an advanced agro-industrial civilization in China. The spread of commerce on the heels of the British importation of opium into China led to growing indebtedness, increasing taxes, transfers and concentration of land, the emergence of new property owners, and the destruction of local manufactures as part of the integration of much of the Chinese economy into the imperialist one. The last two selections review this process of deindustrialization and ruination of the rural poor and middle classes in China. Thus, although these selections show that the same fundamental mechanisms of the development of underdevelopment were at work in China as well, the analysis is not such as to contribute much to the development of theory. It may be hoped that this limitation in the available literature will soon be remedied.

The Southeast Asian area, and particularly the regions now known as Vietnam and Indonesia, is another classical case of how the expansion of world capitalism has wrought the destruction of previously integral socioeconomic systems and cultures. The first selection reviews this process of the development of underdevelopment in Southeast Asia as a whole. The selection on Vietnam and the two on Indonesia analyze the mechanisms and consequences of growing colonial capitalist integration for these countries.

The first selection on Japan analyzes the internal class changes, associated particularly with the conflict and struggle over land use and agricultural production in the eighteenth and nineteenth centuries. The second selection shows how these changes laid the foundations for Japanese industrial development and how the latter was promoted. The next selection argues why this development—the only one in Asia and indeed in all three now underdeveloped continents—was possible only because Japan avoided direct colonial capitalist domination or neocolonial foreign investment during this period of its history. Not the supposed Japanese functional equivalent of the protestant ethic, but rather this exceptional circumstance (shared in a lesser degree in Asia only by Thailand, which therefore also avoided the ravage of underdevelopment until its virtual occupation by the United States in our days) is what crucially determined Japan's path from feudalism to capitalism, imperialism, and fascism; and it was the colonial and semicolonial fate, rather than any supposed "traditionalism," of the remainder of Asia—and of Africa and Latin America as well—that denied their people capitalist economic development and damned them with capitalist development of underdevelopment. This fundamental lesson of history—which must be the cornerstone of any real theory of underdevelopment—is underscored again in the final selection of this volume, which compares the isolated capitalist development of Japan with the dependent capitalist underdevelopment in Java.

Readings on
III.   CAPITALIST DEVELOPMENT OF
UNDERDEVELOPMENT
D.   IN ASIA

India

1.   THE MEDIEVAL SYSTEM
Bhowani Sen, *Evolution of Agrarian Relations in India.*
New Delhi, People's Publishing House, 1962, pp. 50–56.

2.   THE EAST INDIA COMPANY AS THE RULER
Ramkrishna Mukherjee, *The Rise and Fall of the East India Company.*
Berlin, VEB Deutscher Verlag der Wissenschaften, 1955, pp. 174, 180–
186, 189–193, 197–198, 203–206.

3.   EVOLUTION OF AGRARIAN RELATIONS IN INDIA
Bhowani Sen, *Evolution of Agrarian Relations in India.*
New Delhi, People's Publishing House, 1962, pp. 56–70, 76–79, 89–90,
103–104, 130–133, 138.

4.   FAMINE
R. Palme Dutt, *India Today.*
Bombay, People's Publishing House Limited, 1949, pp. 119–120.
B.M. Bhatia, *Famines in India.*
Bombay, Asia Publishing House, 1963, pp. 7–13.

5.   INDUSTRIAL DEVASTATION
R. Palme Dutt, *India Today.*
Bombay, People's Publishing House Limited, 1949, pp. 112–119.

6.   DE-INDUSTRIALIZATION IN INDIA, 1881–1931
Daniel and Alice Thorner, *Land and Labour in India.*
Bombay, Asia Publishing House, 1962, pp. 70–77.

7.   THE DRAIN
Bipan Chandra, *The Rise and Growth of Economic Nationalism in India.*
New Delhi, People's Publishing House, 1966, pp. 643–653.

8.   LONG-TERM TRENDS IN OUTPUT
Daniel and Alice Thorner, *Land and Labour in India.*
Bombay, Asia Publishing House, 1962, pp. 103–112.

China

9.   LAND AND LABOUR IN CHINA
R. H. Tawney, *Land and Labour in China.*
Boston, Beacon Press, 1966, pp. 11–22.

10. ECONOMIC CONDITIONS IN THE LATE CH'ING PERIOD
Albert Feurerweker, *Modern China.*
Englewood Cliffs, N.J., Prentice Hall, Inc., 1964, pp. 107–125.

11. THE INDUSTRIAL IMPACT ON CHINA, 1800–1950
Owen Lattimore, "The Industrial Impact on China, 1800–1950."
First International Conference of Economic History, Stockholm, 1960.
The Hague, Mouton and Company, 1960, pp. 103–113.

12. LANDLORD AND PEASANT IN CHINA
Han-Sheng Ch'en, *Landlord and Peasant in China: A Study of the Agrarian Crisis in South China.*
New York, International Publishers, 1936, pp. viii-xvii.

Southeast Asia

13. THE SOUTH EAST ASIAN WORLD
Keith Buchanon, *The South East Asian World.*
London, G. Bell 1967, pp. 74–82.

14. VIETNAM IN THE XIX CENTURY AND UNDER THE COLONIAL REGIME
Jean Chesneaux, *Contribution à l'Histoire de la Nation Vietnamienne.*
Paris, Editions Sociales, pp. 65–80, 183–206.

15. THE COLONIAL PERIOD IN INDONESIA
Clifford Ceertz, *Agricultural Involution. The Process of Ecological Change in Indonesia.*
Berkeley, University of California Press, 1966, pp. 47–52, 60–69, 82, 87–90, 95–97.

16. SOCIAL CHANGE IN JAVA, 1900–1930: THE "ETHICAL POLICY"
W. F. Wertheim, *East-West Parallels. Sociological Approaches to Modern Asia.*
The Hague, W. Van Hoeve Limited, 1964, pp. 211–223.

Japan

17. AGRARIAN CHANGE AND MODERN JAPAN
Thomas C. Smith, *The Agrarian Origins of Modern Japan.*
Stanford, Stanford University Press, 1959 (reprinted Atheneum, New York, 1966), pp. 201, 208–213.

18. RISE OF MODERN INDUSTRY AND TRADE
William W. Lockwood, *The Economic Development of Japan. Growth and Structural Change.*
Princeton, Princeton University Press, 1954, pp. 18–34.

19. EXCLUSION OF FOREIGN CAPITAL IN EARLY JAPANESE INDUSTRIALIZATION
E. Herbert Norman, *Japan's Emergence as a Modern State.*
New York, Institute of Pacific Relations, 1940, pp. 114–118, 123–132.

20. JAVA AND JAPAN COMPARISONS
Clifford Geertz, *Agricultural Involution. The Process of Ecological Change in Indonesia.*
Berkeley, University of California Press, 1966, pp. 130–143.

COMMENTS BY R.B. SUTCLIFFE ON THE READER ON UNDERDEVELOPMENT

Jesus College
Oxford

February 19, 1970

On two occasions I have been asked by the Cambridge University Press to comment on a book of readings, entitled *Underdevelopment: Theory, History, Policy and Politics,* edited by Andre Gunder Frank and S. A. Shah. The following are the essential paragraphs of my comments on these occasions (I have omitted very detailed notes about particular extracts included in the book). I am very happy for these comments to be seen by anyone who may be interested.

This is a volume of readings from a great diversity of sources, many of them not easily accessible to English readers; they are also of varying length and quality. The first group are all devoted to a critical analysis of most conventional theories of economic development for under-developed countries; the second group concerns the genesis of indus-trial capitalism and economic development in the developed capitalist countries and later the emergence of these countries into the world economy, stressing, particularly the effects of this on more backward countries; the third group takes examples of the economic, social and political history of particular underdeveloped areas and countries, linking this to their relations with the developed capitalist world. The readings are not (except within narrow limits) designed to present opposing viewpoints about the roots of underdevelopment. They all more or less support the same view; the whole volume is a contestation of what passes for orthodox theory in development economics. The readings are certainly not all from the same standpoint, however; some are anti-capitalist, some nationalist, etc. To be more specific the diverse readings are unified by two general themes; (a) underdeveloped countries now find it more difficult to develop than European countries in the 19th century because of the nature of their involvement with the world (capitalist) economies; (b) underdeveloped countries, again unlike 19th century Europe, are hampered by a social and political

system inimical to economic development. Very crudely, two requirements are suggested by this: (a) less involvement with the world
economy, (b) social revolution. These are the unifying themes very
broadly stated. All the readings, which may look impossibly diversified
at first sight, become relevant in the light of those themes. For example,
Hamilton and List justifying the protection of industry in the U.S. and in
Germany against English competition were in a position in some ways
analogous to underdeveloped countries today. This approach to the
analysis of economic development possibilities demands much concern
with the history of both advanced and backward countries—a concern
for the similarities and the differences. Frank himself has advanced a
theory (reprinted in this volume) that embraces both of these; it is a
controversial but certainly interesting thesis.

With the basic approach I agree emphatically and I think that an
increasing number of development economists also do. It is still,
however, a minority approach (in a way it is becoming left-wing
orthodoxy); this accounts for lack of really high quality literature on
these lines. But the tradition is an old and widespread one, as the variety
of these readings shows. In general I think the editors have chosen their
readings very well. . . .

I have now been pretty carefully through the Frank-Shah manuscript for Volume I. I must say first of all how impressive I think it is.
Although "only" a book of readings, it adds up to a massive and
intellectually very powerful challenge to orthodox theory in the subject
of economic development. No teacher could possibly continue with his
old methods once he had become acquainted with this volume. I can see
it being in considerable demand in any university at which economic
development courses of any form are given. Also, as a sort of source
book of left-wing thinking on all parts of the world I would imagine that
even the most remotely progressive student in the field would like to
have a copy. I can see it becoming a radical's Bible on the 3rd World. I
definitely think it is as important as this. In which case I really do not
think you should have many qualms about a market for it. Obviously I
appreciate that depends on the price—and it is massive in bulk. But in
my view you should make every possible effort *not* to have it shortened
any further. If you do have to shorten it you will weaken the case it
makes and you will reduce its market, which depends partly on the
geographical spread of the book.

On the contents. I am left now with no major disagreements with
the editors' very judicious choice, which is anyway based on much wider
reading than my own. The readings are still inevitably uneven in
quality—but less so than in the earlier version on which I commented.
They have omitted some that I was critical of then—and added some

more good ones—like the Arrighi which is excellent and Frank's own paper Section III No. 1, which is to my mind the very best thing he has yet written—and that makes it better than anything *anyone else* is writing on the 3rd World at the present time. In general there is no one extract that I would very much rather see which is now absent; nor is there any one included which would certainly be better left out. We could quibble for moons on this; I don't think it is worth it. From the point of view of length I suppose this is not quite what you wanted to hear. But I do strongly feel that to shorten it would be a mad mistake. One could have a small effect by ruthless pruning of footnotes—but that would not be desirable.

Now the *editorial material.* It is generally exactly on the lines I thought was necessary when I saw the thing first. All the comments I have are rather trivial, often stylistic points. In general the editors have pulled together the diverse material very cogently in the short editorial pieces. I think somewhere in the preface it should be stated that it is *very strongly recommended* for readers to read the editorial material before the extract. . . .

What would really be ideal for Section V is a series of case studies showing how reformist governments within the capitalist system have failed at some crucial point to pull a society towards full economic development. That they are bound to fail is the message of the first volume and earlier parts of this one. But very few such case studies which are any good actually exist. This is no accident; but it is not because the Frank/Shah analysis is wrong—but because economists have just simply ignored the political–social dimension in their writing. The absence of good case studies is a demonstration in fact of just how significant the Frank/Shah volumes will be. I think that the two books will have considerable influence on empirical work in particular countries. . . .

(signed)
R. B. Sutcliffe
(Fellow and Tutor in Economics)

Index

Buchanon, K., 321
Bulgaria, 80, 227, 228
Burma, 166, 225
Burns, A., 195, 201
Bush, G., 196

Cabral, P. A., 262, 267
Cademartori, J., 156, 157, 159, 160
Callaghan, J., 201, 211, 238, 239
Cambodia, 178, 180
Camelot, 22; Project, 19
Campen, J., 207
Canada, 65, 202, 203, 210, 239, 240, 299
capital: accumulation, 64–67 [crisis of, 209; problem of, 265]; flows, international, and Marxist theory, 82–86; internationalization of, 192; supply of, 68–69
capitalism, 17; consequences of, 59; expansion of, 45, 47; and feudal modes, 58–61; financial, 7; and freedom, 134; history of, in Mexico, 104–9; impact of, on China, 18; industrial, 7; mercantile, 7; and revolution, 92; role of in underdevelopment, 4; spread of, 7; world, 171; historical development of, 103
capitalist: crisis, effect of on socialist countries, 227; democracy and capitalist dictatorship, 26; development, 101, 281; reformism, 147; structure, 102; system [colonial structure of, 4; in crisis, 208; development of, 99; Marx's debate on, 122]
Cardoso, C., 254, 266
Cardoso, F. H., 45, 53, 248, 253, 263, 267, 270, 277
Cardozo, E., 313
Caribbean, 93-95, 101, 212, 235, 298, 300, 311
Carlos, S. A., 266
Carr, R., 276
Carrillo, S., x, 170, 173, 175
Carter, J., 197, 201, 202, 211, 221, 236, 238
Castro, F., 115, 164, 166, 247, 286
Ceertz, C., 321
Ceylon, 64, 71, 164, 183, 249
Chandra B., 305, 320
Chase-Dunn, C., 271
Chattopadhyay, P., 59
Chesneaux, J., 321
Chevènement, J. P., 240
Chilcote, R. H., 271, 277
Chile, vii, ix, 29, 91, 125, 137, 155, 156, 161, 162, 164, 167, 168, 172, 183, 194, 214, 215, 221, 222, 224, 226, 237, 239, 246, 247, 249, 250, 254-57, 261, 263, 264, 286; Milton Friedman's theories on, 125–36

Chilean Way, 256
China, x, xi, 7, 15, 16, 18, 26, 33, 37, 39, 45, 92, 98, 101, 114-17, 176-81, 184-86, 194 194, 215-18, 224, 225, 227, 228, 239, 255, 261, 280, 286, 295, 298-300
Ciafardini, H., 266
class power, national basis of, 263
class structure, 92
class struggle: in Chile, 145–49; the motor of history, 284
Claudin, F., x, 170-75
Cleaver, H. M., Jr., 62, 64, 65
Clower, R., 45, 54
Coatsworth, J., 305, 306
Cockcroft, J., 123
Colombia, 168, 169, 247, 312
colonial: relationship, weakening of, 101; structure of capitalist system, 4
colonialism: Dutch, 48; struggle for liberation from, 215
colonialization, internal, 100
colonies, control of by metropolitan bourgeoisie, 97
commercial imbalances in the Third World, 77-81
communist counter-offensive, direction of, 255
communist dictatorship and fascist dictatorship, 26
competition, perfect, assumption of, 191
competitive market model, 7
competitive model, 134
consumer price index, validity of, in Chile, 144
Conteris, H., 276
Cordova, A., 254, 266
corporate state planning, 189–206
Cortez, H., 91
Cortin, A., 275
Corvalan, L., ix, 137–39, 143, 144, 146, 149, 152, 274
cost-cutting mechanisms, of Keynesian demand management, 194
Costa Rica, 237
Council of Castille, 91
crisis: global, 208–29; world, and economic policy formation, 230–42
critiques, 245–77
Crowder, M., 308, 310
Cuba, vii, 7, 212, 215, 237, 247, 251, 255, 286, 298, 305, 312
Cueva, A., 254, 267
cultural structure of Latin America, 95
Czechoslovakia, 176, 227, 239

Dalton, G., viii, 22, 24, 42, 44–48, 53, 252, 274

Manchester Liberalism, 19
Manchuria, 33
Mandel, E., 99, 259, 273, 310
Mandle, J. R., 273, 275
Manley, M., 224
Mantoux, P., 307, 310
Mao Ze-Dung, 39, 115, 117, 183–86, 239, 258, 259, 286
Maria Rosa, J., 314
Marchais, G., 167
Marcos, F. E., 183, 212, 221
Marini, R. M., 67, 248, 264, 273
Marroquin, A., 45, 55
Marthelot, P., 317
Martinelli, A., 247
Martinez Alier, J., 273
Marx, K., 32, 52, 58, 59, 63, 83, 104, 114, 121–23, 176, 183, 213, 245, 248, 260, 279, 307
Marxism, 21, 32, 36, 83, 109, 118, 121, 169, 180, 186, 188, 255, 257, 259, 279–89; implications for, 186–88; relevance of, 279–89
Marxist ends and Marxist means, 284–88
mass consumption stage of economic development, 89
mass mobilization, in Chile, 149–52
materialism: historical, 280, 283; and nationalism, 288–89; and religion, 288–89
Mauro, F., 310
Maynard, G., 275
Mayobre, J., 246
McCoy, A., 72
McFarlane, B., 277
McGovern, G., 116
McNamara, R. S., 135
Mead, M., 36
Medrana, R. G., 275
Meeropol, R., 64
Menger, A., 8
mercantile capitalism, 45
metropolis, as cause of underdevelopment, 91–93
Mexican Communist Party, 104
Mexico, xi, 28, 49, 51, 63, 66, 67, 91, 93–95, 98, 101, 104, 107, 108, 115, 168, 169, 212–19, 235–37, 247, 250, 254, 302, 311, 312
Micronesia, 33
military government of Chile, 169
Millas, O., 156, 157
Mills, C. W., 245, 262
Mintz, S. W., 313
Mitterand, F., 202, 203, 205, 212, 233, 234, 240
mobilization: mass, in Chile, 149–52; worker, importance of, 156

Mobutu, J. D., 183
modernism, 88
modernization, growth of, 115
Moncloa pact, 172
monetarism, 189–206; link with banking, 130
monetarists, and supply-siders, conflict between, 198–99
monetary policy, government, instrument of bourgeoisie, 147
Mongolia, 33, 183
monopolies, nationalization of, in Chile, 156
monopolistic economy, 192
monopoly, 85, 130, 134, 140; capitalism, 45
Moore, B., viii, 25, 304
Moreno, M., 107
Morner, M., 251, 274, 275
Morocco, 194, 212
Morris, D., 44
Mozambique, xi, 48, 216, 222–24, 286, 287
Mugabe, R. G., 222
Mukherjee, R., 16, 45, 320
Muldoon, R. D., 199, 211
multinational corporations, 84, 102
Murga, A., 248, 273
Murphy, R., 35, 41
Muto, I., 268
Myrdal, G., vii, viii, 9, 44, 87, 90, 91, 95, 98, 102, 246, 248, 304

Nadel, S. F., 35, 41
Nafziger, W., 277
Nasser, G. A., 115, 225
National Defence Education Act, 9, 37
National Indian Institute, 49
nationalism: and materialism, 288–89; and religion, 288–89
nationalist movements against the status quo, 225
nationalization, in Chile, 143, 156
nations, new, political study of, 20–24
Nazi Germany, 129
Nehru, J., 16
neo-classical economic theory, 7
neo-classic economy, 8
neofascism, in Ceylon, 164
neo-isolationism, in United States, 116
neo-Marxism, 38, 85
Nepal, 71
Newton, I., 115
New Zealand, 126, 200, 202, 210, 211, 231
Nicaragua, xi, 216, 223, 224, 237, 287
Nigeria, 220, 221, 222
Nixon, R., 39, 114, 116, 123, 124, 192, 203, 210, 183, 250; Shokku, 210
Njamba, K., 45, 53
N'Krumah, K., 115, 221, 226
Nonschi, A., 318

sub-Saharan Africa, 212
substantivism, 42; and economic
  anthropology, 22
Sudan, 41
Suharto, 128
Sukarno, 115, 225
Sumanta Banerjee, 72
Sunkel, O., 247
supply-side economics, 189–206
supply-siders and monetarists, conflict
  between, 198–99
Suret-Canale, J., 44, 56, 316
Sutcliffe, R. B., 322
Sweden, 100
Sweezy, P. N., 85, 307, 310
Syria, 287
Szymanski, A., 82, 83, 85

Taiwan, xi, 33, 169, 212, 215–17, 235
Takahashi, H. K., 310
Tanzania, 178, 224, 249
Tavares, M. C., 246
Tawney, R. H., 320
Tax, S., 30
tax rates, effect of, 196
Taylor, J., 269, 276, 277
Taylorist/Fordist, 285
technology and science, 15
Tenenbaum, B. H., 269
Thailand, 22, 36, 179, 212, 319
Thatcher, M., x, 183, 189, 191, 196–98, 200–
  5, 211, 239
Thatcherism, 189–206
theory, Marxist, and international capital
  flows, 82, 86
theoretical issues, in economic anthropology,
  42–57
Thieu, N. V., 181
Third World, x, 6, 8, 37, 79–81, 84, 85, 87,
  169, 178, 185, 188, 194, 195, 198, 208,
  212, 214–17, 219, 221, 222, 224, 225,
  229, 232, 235–39, 249, 253, 280, 283,
  285–87, 293; commercial imbalances in,
  77–81; concept of, 87–88; meaning of
  term, 6–7
Third Worldism, 180, 250, 256
Thorner, A., 45, 56, 320
Thorner, D., 44, 45, 56, 320
Thurmond, S., 204
Tomic, R. R., 143
de la Torre, H., 118
Torres, J., vii, viii, 263, 264, 265, 274
trade, effect of, on India, 97
traditionalism, 8; first stage of economic
  development, 89; role of in underdevelopment, 3–5; of the Third World, 88

transnational corporations, inability of to
  prevent economic crisis, 234–35
Trinidad, 93
Trotsky, L., 107
Trotskyism, 164, 259
Trudeau, P., 202, 203, 240
Tunisia, 194, 212
Turin, 100
Turkey, 115, 228, 237, 316
Turner, B. A., 274

underdevelopment: capitalist criteria for, 18;
  causes of, 89–92, 95, 97, 102; in Latin
  America, dependence theory of, 246–49;
  reader on, 293–325; scientific value of
  study of, 3–5; study of, 88
unemployment: generated by export-led
  growth, 218; increase in, 210–11; and
  inflation, 132, 133, 199, 238; and
  Keynesianism, 191; as a result of
  recession, 210; and world crisis, 230–31
unions, destruction of, in Chile, 169
United Nations, 102, 220; Conference on
  Trade and Development, 246; Economic
  Commission for Latin America, 246;
  Economic Development Decade, 114;
  General Assembly, 135; International
  Labor Organization, 62
United Kingdom, 80
United States, 9, 11, 12, 26, 30, 36, 65, 93–
  95, 102, 108, 116, 122, 128, 134, 136,
  179, 180, 182, 183–86, 189, 190–95, 197,
  202–6, 210, 211, 215, 217, 219, 220,
  223, 231, 233, 235–38, 240, 241, 247,
  250, 254, 281, 302, 304, 319, 324;
  Department of Commerce, 84; House of
  Representatives Subcommittee on Defense
  Appropriations, 21; Social Science
  Research Council, 37
urbanization of peasants, in Chile, 148
urban renovation program, in Chile, 148
Uruguay, 163, 168, 169, 250

Valenzuela Feijoo, J., 248, 269
values, of South Asia, 90
Vascos, F., 269
Venezuela, 163, 168, 169, 246, 247, 250, 254
Vergas, G., 28
Verhagan, B., 45, 56
Versailles, 80
Velder, Anders-Stefan de, 274
Vietnam, Democratic Republic of, x, 7, 22,
  26, 114, 116, 162, 176, 177, 179, 180–
  84, 186–88, 192, 206, 210, 215, 224, 227,
  213, 233, 255, 286, 298, 319
Volcker, P., 195
Volski, V., 254, 274

About the Author

ANDRE GUNDER FRANK is Professor of Development Economics and Social Sciences at the University of Amsterdam and Director of its Institute for Socio-Economic Studies of Developing Regions (SMOG).

He was educated in the United States and has taught economics, history, sociology, and other social sciences and particularly Third World development at universities in North America, Europe, and Latin America, especially at the University of Chile between 1968 and September 1973. From 1974 on Professor Frank was Visiting Research Fellow at the Max-Plank Institut in Starnberg, Germany, and held the Chair in Development Studies (Social Change) at the University of East Anglia in England.

Professor Frank has written widely on the economics, social and political history, and contemporary development of the capitalist world system, the industrially developed countries, and especially the Third World and Latin America. His writings are associated particularly with the historical study of "development of under-development" and "dependence" and recently also with the analysis of the present world economic crisis. His writings have been published in 21 languages and include 20 books, among them *Capitalism and Underdevelopment in Latin America* (1967); *Sociology of Development and Underdevelopment of Sociology* (1969); *Lumpen-bourgeoisie: Lumpendevelopment* (1972); *World Accumulation 1492-1789* (1978); *Crisis: In the World Economy* (1980); *Crisis: In the Third World* (1981); *The European Challenge* (1983).